Christian Education:
Its History and Philosophy

Christian Education: Its History and Philosophy

by
KENNETH O. GANGEL
and
WARREN S. BENSON

MOODY PRESS

CHICAGO

Library of Congress Cataloging in Publication Data

Gangel, Kenneth O.
  Christian education.

  Bibliography: p. 371
  Includes index.
  1. Christian education—History. I. Benson,
Warren S. II. Title.
BV1465.G36   1983   207   82-8065
ISBN 0-8024-3561-0   AACR2

6 7 8 Printing/EB/Year 93 92 91 90 89

Printed in the United States of America

To Jeffrey Scott, Julie Lynn, Scott Warren, and Bruce Ellis
Young adults whose Christian commitment produces profound
gratefulness in their parents

Acknowledgments

The publisher and the authors wish to express appreciation for permission to quote from the following:

The Rise of Christian Education, by Lewis J. Sherrill, copyright © 1944 by Macmillan Publishing Co., Inc., renewed 1972 by Mrs. Lewis J. Sherrill, used by permission of the publisher.

Understanding Christian Education, by Wayne Rood, copyright © 1970 by Abingdon Press, used by permission of the publisher.

Eerdmans' Handbook to the History of Christianity, edited by Tim Dowley, copyright © 1977 by William B. Eerdmans Publishing Co., used by permission of the publisher.

A History of Educational Thought, by Frederick Mayer, copyright © 1960 by Charles E. Merrill Publishing Co., used by permission of the publisher.

An Invitation to Religious Education, by Harold W. Burgess, copyright © 1975 by Religious Education Press, used by permission of the publisher.

The Story of Philosophy, by Will Durant, Copyright © 1926, 1927, 1933, 1954, 1955, 1961 by Will Durant, reprinted by permission of Simon & Schuster, a division of Gulf & Western Corporation.

The New Testament: An Introduction to Its Literature and History, by J. G. Machen, copyright © 1976 by Banner of Truth, used by permission of the publisher.

How Should We Then Live?, by Francis A. Schaeffer, copyright © 1976 by Francis A. Schaeffer, published by Fleming H. Revell Co., used by permission of Franky Schaeffer V Productions, Los Gatos, Calif.

Mark A. Noll, and Nathan O. Hatch, used by permission of Zondervan Publishing House.

"Education as Artifact: Ben Franklin and Instruction of 'A Rising People,'" by David Tyack (Vol. 6, Spring 1966), copyright © 1966 by *The History of Education Quarterly*, used by permission of the publisher.

"Why We Need a Christian Philosophy," by J. Oliver Buswell (November 1961), reprinted by permission of *Eternity* Magazine, copyright © 1961, Evangelical Ministries Inc., 1716 Spruce Street, Philadelphia, PA 19103.

"The Legacy of John Amos Comenius," by Eve Chybova Bock (November 6, 1970), copyright © 1970 by *Christianity Today*, used by permission of the publisher.

"The Concerns and Considerations of Carl F. H. Henry" (March 13, 1981), copyright © 1981 by *Christianity Today*, used by permission of the publisher.

"The Chicago Statement on Biblical Inerrancy," used by permission of the International Council on Biblical Inerrancy, Oakland, Calif.

The Search for a Christian Education-Since 1940, by Kendig Brubaker Cully. Copyright © MCMLXV W. L. Jenkins. Used by permission of The Westminster Press.

Basic Writings in Christian Education, edited by Kendig Brubaker Cully. Copyright © MCMLX W. L. Jenkins. Used by permission of The Westminster Press.

Preaching and Teaching in the Earliest Church, by Robert C. Worley. Copyright © MCMLXVII The Westminster Press. Used by permission.

We also wish to thank the following people for their help in the preparation of this book: Mr. Frederick D. McCormick, minister of education at the Park Street Church, Boston, Massachusetts, for his extensive assistance on Chapter 11; Dr. Perry G. Downs, Trinity Evangelical Divinity School, Deerfield, Illinois, for the section on Horace Bushnell in Chapter 12; Dr. Gerald L. Gutek, Dean of the Graduate School of Education, Loyola University of Chicago, and Dr. Raymond A. Nighan, for their criticisms and suggestions; Dr. Marcos Ramos, Professor Charles Schauffel, Dr. D. Campbell Wyckoff, manuscript typists Ruth Braun and Marjorie Wells, and the 1981 history and philosophy of education class at Miami Christian College, to whom the entire book was taught during its preparation stage.

Contents

Introduction

A history of Christian education must not be confused with a record of the achievements of the Sunday school. The discipline has advanced well beyond that stage, and today's sophisticated students fully understand that no proper concept of the history and philosophy of Christian education can be gained without seeing all the ramifications, implications, and influences that have affected it from pre-Christian times to the present.

We have attempted to make this volume both logical and readable—logical in the sense that the best approach to analysis of thought-flow seems to be a combination of chronology and biography. Obviously there are overlaps when it is necessary to allow for different developments in different parts of the world during the same time period.

The volume is designed to be readable for both graduate and undergraduate students in that it emphasizes the fact that *people* influence thought and make history. Each chapter focuses on the views of those persons who influenced or were influenced by educational concepts that are Christian. Readers are asked to keep in mind the assumption that a gradual development and clarification of ideas over the years is essential. How did we get from Plato to Pietism? What is the connection between Aristotle and Augustine or between Augustine and Aquinas? What is there about the Renaissance, the Reformation, and the Enlightenment periods that offers essential patterns of understanding for the analysis of the late twentieth-century world? Those kinds of questions make a history of educational ideas intensely important.

It is unfortunate that both history and philosophy have often been thought dull and ponderous subjects by many students. Apart from theology, they are the very foundational disciplines upon which all other thought is based. Clichés abound and many of them are true, such as the one suggesting that he who ignores the errors of the past is bound to repeat them. Futhermore, Christians should be lovers of wisdom, the very meaning of the word *philosophy.* At times the concepts of philosophical writers are difficult to understand, but it is the pattern, *the flow of thought,* that is essential. As you read, pay less attention to the pieces of the puzzle than you do to the picture that emerges as the pieces are interlocked.

APPROACHES TO HISTORY

The very concept of a "flow" suggests that the authors are committed to a linear rather than cyclical view of history. To be sure, Arnold Toynbee offers some brilliant insights into the recurrence of events. His work is a masterful treatment of Herodotus, for whom history was a repetitive pattern regulated by the cosmic law of compensation. Thucydides varied from the scheme of Herodotus only slightly. Polybius did take a linear view, but saw all world events leading up to the domination of Rome.

Alexis de Tocqueville came close to a Christian analysis by suggesting, "the gradual development of the equality of conditions is . . . a providential fact, and it possesses all the characteristics of a divine decree: it is universal, it is durable, it constantly eludes all human interference, and all events as well as men minister to its development."[1]

Of all modern historians we are probably most deeply indebted to Jakob Burckhardt, who "was completely free of modern prejudice . . . who saw in history a cumulative process of progressive development, realizing more and more the idea of Christianity in the secular world of history."[2]

Because the authors are neither theologians nor philosophers, but educators, we resist the argument of whether there is a distinctly "Christian philosophy of history" or even a "theology of history." It is presupposed in this volume, however, that the linear view is most positively correlated with biblical Christianity and its strong emphasis on the doctrine of creation, the cataclysmic significance of the incarnation, and the movement toward a God-designed end of the world. It is Christocentric, as Reinhold Niebuhr definitively states: "The Christian faith finds the final clue to the meaning of life and history in the Christ whose goodness is at once the virtue which man ought, but does not, achieve in history, and the revelation of a divine mercy which understands and resolves the perpetual contradictions in which history is involved, even on the highest reaches of human achievements."[3]

DEFINITION OF TERMS

Exhaustive treatment of our subject would require a mul-tivolume series, totally unsuitable for purposes of a college and seminary textbook. However, such condensation as that which we have done leaves us with the problem of some unproved assumptions and unstated presuppositions. Perhaps we can clear up a portion of that problem by defining words that appear with some regularity throughout the book.

SECULAR

Most of the men whose writings have left an impact on the flow of philosophy were not Christians. Some were religious, and some were *secular*. The term was first applied to the ethics of Holyoake in the late nineteenth century because of his commit-ment to the idea that mankind could better itself without refer-ence to religion or theology. Warren Young tells us, "Today sec-ularism is the integration of life around the spirit of a specific age rather than around God. It is living as if the material order were supreme and as if God did not exist. While secularism may not indicate theoretical atheism, it certainly does represent practical atheism."[4]

The importance of secular thought in an analysis of a Christian philosophy of education is based on the premise that all truth is God's truth wherever it is found and by whomever it is spoken. Consequently, we measure the philosophical viewpoints of the secularist against the opposite polarity, Christianity, and, more specifically, evangelical Christianity.

CHRISTIAN

Widely bandied about in our day, the term *Christian* is used in this volume to describe biblical Christianity, a commitment to Jesus Christ and the Scriptures. We assume the credibility of the Christian position, namely, that there are good reasons for believ-ing it. Here is the eloquence of Carl F. H. Henry:

> Against any view that faith is merely a leap in the dark, I insist on the reasonableness of Christian faith and the "rationality" of the living, self-revealed God. I maintain that God creates and pre-serves the universe through the agency of the Logos, that man by creation bears the moral and rational (as opposed to irrational) image of his Maker, that despite the fall, man is still responsible for knowing God. I believe that divine revelation is rational, that the inspired biblical canon is a consistent and coherent whole,

that genuine faith seeks understanding, that the Holy Spirit uses truth as a means of persuasion, that logical consistency is a test of truth, and that saving trust in Christ necessarily involves acceptance of certain revealed propositions about Him.[5]

Henry's words describe more than just the word *Christian*. He speaks to the point of historic, evangelical, and biblical theism.

EVANGELICAL

The authors are committed to the inerrancy and authority of the Scriptures, both Old and New Testaments. Obviously, therefore, our point of view in perceiving facts has a significant bearing on the interpretation of those facts. The Christian will view history and philosophy quite differently from the secularist. And the evangelical Christian, because of his allegiance to the Word of God, will allow that divine revelation to provide the critical methodology in approaching both history and philosophy. John W. Montgomery offers six principles:

1. On the basis of accepted principles of textual and historical analysis, the Gospel records are found to be trustworthy historical documents — primary source evidence for the life of Christ.
2. In these records Jesus exercises divine prerogatives and claims to be God in human flesh. He rests His claims on His forthcoming resurrection.
3. In all four Gospels, Christ's bodily resurrection is described in minute detail; Christ's resurrection evidences His deity.
4. The fact of the resurrection cannot be discounted on a priori, philosophical grounds; miracles are impossible only if one so defines them — but such definition rules out proper historical investigation.
5. If Christ is God, then He speaks the truth concerning the absolute divine authority of the Old Testament and of the soon-to-be-written, apostolic New Testament; concerning His death for the sins of the world; and concerning the nature of man and of history.
6. It follows from the preceding that all biblical assertions bearing on philosophy of history are to be regarded as revealed truth, and that all human attempts at historical interpretation are to be judged for truth value on the basis of harmony with scriptural revelation.[6]

LIMITATIONS OF THE STUDY

Though we have already spoken to this issue in brief, further specification may be helpful. We will no doubt receive criticism (just as we have given it) for our omission or insufficient treatment of some of the great thinkers of history. At the same time some will wonder why we have given so many paragraphs or pages to other writers. Perhaps criteria of selection/rejection might be helpful in offering an ipso facto rationale.

1. We attempted to select persons whose authority and influence made a significant contribution to what Christian education is today even if at the time of their lives and writings that contribution may not have been obvious.
2. We have attempted to make our way back to what that authority really said, and in most cases, within what context. For the benefit of the student we have at times elected to use secondary sources. For this sin we expect judgment from some professional colleagues and offer as atonement only our interest in *writing for the student rather than for other professors.*
3. We are committed to the educational principle of integration. No thought, no idea, no person is rejected because of his life or viewpoint. In biblical history God used pagan kings and spoke through demon voices. We are far more concerned about how an idea fits into a wholistic world view that is both bibliocentric and Christocentric than whether it was said or written by a "good person." By the same token we reject that which does not positively correlate.
4. Finally, we have not intended to produce a "philosophy of Christian education." The student is referred to volumes such as Herbert Byrne's *A Christian Approach to Education* (Rev. ed. [Milford, Mich.: Mott Media] 1977), Frank E. Gaebelein's classic *The Pattern of God's Truth* (Chicago: Moody, 1968), and other volumes cited throughout the book.

Certainly a point of view will emerge throughout the book, and in the chronological approach it should narrow with the passing of the chapters. But the suggestion that we have prepared a definitive philosophy fits neither claim nor purpose. We propose only to trace in history the flow of thought that has affected and continues to affect the development of a distinctly evangelical philosophy of education.

Kenneth O. Gangel, Ph.D.
Warren S. Benson, Ph.D.

Notes

1. Alexis de Tocqueville, *Democracy in America,* cited in Karl Löwith, *Meaning in History* (Chicago: U. of Chicago, 1949), p. 11.

2. Löwith, p. 31.
3. Reinhold Niebuhr, *The Children of Light and the Children of Darkness: A Vindication of Democracy and a Critique of its Traditional Defense* (New York: Scribner's, 1944), p. 188.
4. Warner C. Young, "Secularism," in *Baker's Dictionary of Theology* (Grand Rapids: Baker, 1960), p. 477.
5. Carl F. H. Henry, "The Concerns and Considerations of Carl F. H. Henry," *Christianity Today*, 13 March 1981, p. 21.
6. John W. Montgomery, *Where Is History Going?* (Grand Rapids: Zondervan, 1969), p. 35.

1

The Debt of Christian Education to Old Testament Theology and Pedagogy

During one of the postresurrection appearances described in the last chapter of Luke, Jesus visited with the disciples and ate a piece of broiled fish to demonstrate the reality of His resurrection body. Immediately after eating, He affirmed again the importance of fulfilling everything written in the Old Testament Scriptures—the law of Moses, the prophets, and the psalms. "Then He opened their minds [so they could] understand the Scriptures" (Luke 24:45). We are not told in the passage everything the Lord shared with the disciples that day, but He certainly indicated how His own life, death, and resurrection were the key to grasping the essential unity between the Old Testament and the New Testament.

It is virtually impossible to approach a Christian philosophy of education without acknowledging our debt to the Hebrew educational system and especially to Old Testament revelation. The law, the prophets, and the psalms—all must be fulfilled, none is set aside. The Christian commitment to absolute revelation is foundational to building an understanding not only of the Judeo-Christian heritage of our culture in general, but of a biblical and evangelical philosophy of education specifically.

How different is that kind of commitment from the contemporary attitude toward the history of philosophy. There was a time in the history of learning when all sciences were a part of philosophy's domain, but gradually each became an independent discipline. And philosophy itself has revolted against its own past, its time-honored function to explore and affirm not only logic, but also the values and ethics of life. Donald Kalish speaks for many of his colleagues when he says, "There is no system of philosophy to spin out. There are no ethical truths; there are just clarifications of particular ethical problems. Take advantage of these clarifications and work out your own existence. You are mistaken to think that anyone ever had the answers. There are no answers. Be brave and face up to it."[1]

Perhaps, before exploring the components of Hebrew education itself, there may be some merit in identifying the differences that marked it as unique among the philosophies of the Orient. Certainly, its foremost distinction was *the acknowledgment of and commitment to a speaking God.* The centrality of revelation and the hermeneutical principle of progressive revelation are basic to a grasp of Hebrew as well as Christian education. Other oriental faiths regarded God as some kind of cosmic principle, and some (such as Buddhism) even denied the existence of any kind of supreme being. For the Hebrews, history was indeed His story.

Like other orientals, the Hebrews made much of their own history, but they were even more concerned with the personal faith of the moment. Whereas the objective of Chinese education was generally to preserve the past as a way of honoring ancestors to the point of worship, Hebrew education focused on the present and the worship of God alone. The teachings of Confucius emphasized noble living, horizontal human relations, the cultivation of the cardinal virtues, and other factors that focused on the man-to-man level. Hebrew education always placed the vertical before the horizontal, relation man to God before concerning itself with the human level.

Although recognizing the sovereignty of the God of heaven, Hebrew theology was less deterministic than other oriental faiths. In the Hebrew view, man chose to honor God or to reject Him, and man's character was not fixed by a series of transmigrations.

Still another difference was *the serious biblical concept of sin.* Secular philosopher Frederick Mayer puts it this way: "While in Oriental religion, the failings of man are mostly regarded as the products of ignorance, in Hebrew religion, sin is viewed as a conscious defiance of the will of God—an action which merits harsh punishment. This sense of sin is intensely emotional in Hebrew religion and it results in the abasement of the individual before his creator."[2]

Mayer goes on to talk about how both the philosophy and educational practices of the Hebrews were derived from concepts of God borrowed from Midianite culture, explaining that

Jehovah "was a God of fertility who inhabited fiery volcanoes." The Christian senses immediately the antisupernatural presuppositionalism of such a stance. He fully understands the "givens" of Hebrew education — how the Scriptures can begin with a simple statement of the existence of God with seemingly no concern for arguing that existence.

Egypt may have been the gift of the Nile, but Israel was the gift of God. The centricity of Hebrew education is unashamedly and explicitly theistic, as is evidenced in the famous *shema* passage of Deuteronomy 6:4-5: "Hear, O Israel: The LORD is our God, the LORD is one! And you shall love the LORD your God with all your heart and with all your soul and with all your might."

Education was always a passion with the Hebrews, so the Scripture is full of pedagogical concepts. The curriculum was the Scripture — first the Torah, then later the prophets and the writings. Later was added the Mishna, the oral tradition handed down from generation to generation and finally written in the Talmud. In the synagogues during the postexilic era, the Apocrypha and Pseudepigrapha were added to the learning experience of the Hebrew child. Recitation, storytelling, symbolism, question and answer — those and other methods built a cultural consciousness, a unit of custom based upon the Old Testament concept of an omnipotent God. Monotheism reigned supreme and dominated the educational patterns as well as all facets of the life of the Hebrew people.

EDUCATION IN THE FAMILY

From the earliest days of the human race in the Garden of Eden the family has been the most important educational agency on earth. It is so designed by God, and the Hebrews never got away from the centrality of the home in the educational experience.

Well before the law was given it was crucial for children in a godly family to understand the nature of their God. Before the time of Abraham one can hardly refer to Hebrew "education," but the principle was already there — God the personal, living, eternal, holy, gracious, mighty Creator; entirely self-sustaining and perfect in every way; spiritual and changeless in His nature; timeless in His existence; truthful, merciful, just, and sometimes inscrutable in His dealings with men. Not a convenient idea of men's minds, no psychological image conjured up to meet the demands of a superstitious society, the eternal God and His message to His world was the bull's-eye on the educational target.

Hebrew education technically began with Abraham and the covenant. The covenant was national and personal with profound educational implications. It was a contract between the Hebrews and God, but also between each individual Hebrew and God. Every person in the nation had an individual obligation to God, to his family, and to his nation.

But how was that obligation to be communicated? How was it to be maintained as the nomadic families and tribes of the patriarchs wandered across the sun-baked plains of the land we now call Israel? Perhaps it survived because that most crucial of all educational elements—aim, or objective—was never distorted or diminished in the minds of Hebrew parents. Theirs was the task of training the next generation, and failure in that task would not be taken lightly by the God who had called them to it. Elmer H. Wilds and Kenneth V. Lottich spell it out well: "The greatest lesson to be drawn from the history of this people is that a strict adherence to an educational system based on a peculiarly high religious and moral ideal has preserved their unity in a way that no political system could approximate. The salvation of this people, at least, has been due to its education."[3]

Certainly the informal educational process of the patriarchs was not without its faults and failures, but its fruit is also obvious in the lives of some of the members of the fourth generation. Joseph, who never once deviated from his absolute commitment to the God of his fathers, reiterated the covenant of his brothers in his 110th year: "God will surely take care of you, and bring you up from this land to the land which He promised on oath to Abraham, to Isaac and to Jacob" (Genesis 50:24).

During the bondage in Egypt the Scriptures record that the Hebrew midwives "feared God" (Exodus 1:17). When the suffering became so severe that they could stand in their own strength no longer, the entire nation cried before the Lord, "and God saw the sons of Israel, and God took notice of them" (Exodus 2:25).

EDUCATION AT THE TABERNACLE

We should never forget that the children of Israel were delivered from Egyptian bondage not by a great military leader or seasoned politician, but by an educator-turned-shepherd. Stephen tells us, "Moses was educated in all the learning of the Egyptians, and he was a man of power in words and deeds" (Acts 7:22). It is not our purpose here to review the history of the deliverance, but rather to note that once in the wilderness, the people were immediately instructed by Jehovah in the processes of the perpetuation of truth. Indeed, the teaching role of the family emerges with great strength in the book of Deuteronomy. Rather than taking away from the family's responsibility, the formal center of worship merely became the mortar for attaching the bricks of parental efforts. No one understood this better than Moses, who specified it clearly in Deuteronomy 6:7-9.

> This passage contains a great deal more than just the injunction to carry out the educational task of the family. It contains, through the use of the Hebrew word *shanan*, a strong hint as to the methodology. The word literally means "to whet or sharpen" and appears here in the present tense. In other words, Hebrew parents were continually to whet the intellectual appetites of their children. . . . They were to sharpen their minds, prompting questions which would create teachable moments so that instruction in the faith of Israel might be given.[4]

THE LAW

It is very difficult for us in Western culture to understand the dynamic of the Torah in ancient Hebrew education, or even in orthodox Jewish education of our own day. Its unity, its revelatory impact, its involvement with every aspect of life makes it unique among national documents in history. The Torah was far more to Israel than the Constitution has been to the United States, a distinction that shows up nowhere more clearly than in the matter of education. Few American children or teenagers can recite major portions of the Constitution unless preparing for some fine arts festival, but a Hebrew boy who scarcely walked heard and repeated the Torah until it was woven into the very fabric of his life. Lewis Sherrill describes the instructional character of the Mosaic law:

> "Torah" is one of the great words of the Old Testament and of Judaism. It is from a root meaning to throw, or to cast as with lots; we have already referred to this method of seeking to discover the divine will. Torah itself means teaching, that is, instruction, the thing taught. It might be such instruction as that of a mother or father, or sage, or a poet. It may mean *divine* instruction as given through God's approved servants. At times it appears to mean the body of prophetic teachings. Torah often means *special* laws, as for example regarding a feast or the Sabbath; or it may mean *codes* of law. In these latter uses the term Torah embodies the belief that the Law is God's answer, through an approved spokesman, to

man's questions about rights and duties. This is well shown in the Exodus account of Moses' work as a judge and law giver. A similar conception of Law is set forth in other places. Torah, then, is content of teaching.[5]

Things were at a spiritual, cultural, educational, and emotional low point in the twelfth century B.C. when the godly family of Elkanah of Ephraim went regularly to the Tabernacle at Shiloh to worship. Of course, the genuine heroine in the story is Hannah, whose earnest prayer for a son was answered by Jehovah. In return she surrendered that son to the service of the Lord "as long as he lives" (1 Samuel 1:28). The intent of bringing Samuel to the Tabernacle was to have him trained by the high priest Eli, who made a very special personal project out of the child's nurture and development. The Bible writer tells us, "the boy Samuel grew before the LORD" (1 Samuel 2:21b).

The history of the priesthood in Israel began at the time of the exodus. A distinct transfer of educational responsibility from patriarchs to priests took place after the founding of the Aaronic order, recorded in Exodus 28:29 (see also Leviticus 8). The primary office of the priest is essentially mediatorial, standing between Jehovah and the congregation, arranging communications between God and His people, offering the sacrifices, and leading other forms of worship. But in addition to the mediatorial calling, the priest is also a teacher and interpreter of the law. Ezekiel 44:23 is very clear: "They shall teach My people the difference between the holy and the profane, and cause them to discern between the unclean and the clean."

The priests communicated the letter and meaning of the law and were responsible for delivering into the hands of the people a knowledge of the meaningful religious rituals and patterns of ancient Israel. Notice that the priests were responsible for teaching parents, since almost all education in Israel was adult education, at least until the synagogue schools of the postexilic time. The home was never forgotten as the central place of instruction, but it was supplemented by the work of the priests at the Tabernacle. In the theocratic concept of the Tabernacle era, the educational program consisted of far more than what we would call spiritual or moral instruction. It was also a solid dose of general human ethics, civil law, and the relationship of family to family, tribe to tribe, and Israel to the other nations.

RELIGIOUS RITUAL

Contemporary Christians have hardly paid sufficient attention to the significant educational value of Old Testament ritual. C. B. Eavey does not exaggerate when he states, "Every sacrifice, symbol, and ceremony was a basis for a feeling and an attitude toward God and an effective means of teaching some belief, conception, or law. By the procedures connected with the tabernacle worship especially, the people were taught the holiness of God, the importance of faithfulness to Him, the way He regarded sin and the need for repentance."[6]

JOSHUA AND JUDGES

Though there was never any question in the mind of a sincere son of Abraham that God controlled the events of history, a serious philosophy of history did not emerge until the days of Joshua. Greek historians like Thucydides may offer a thoroughly naturalistic account of historical events, relating them exclusively to economic and political factors. The Hebrew historian, however, always looks upon the events of the world as being guided by Jehovah. Karl Löwith asserts the kind of meaning in history that has characterized both Hebrew and Christian thought from the early Old Testament to the present.

> The modern over-emphasis on secular history as the scene of man's destiny is a product of our alienation from the natural theology of antiquity and from the supernatural theology of Christianity. It is foreign to wisdom and faith. Classical antiquity believed that human nature and history imitate the nature of the cosmos; the Old Testament teaches that man is created in the image of God; and the Christian teaching is focused on the imitation of Christ. According to the New Testament view, the advent of Christ is not a particular, though outstanding, fact within the continuity of secular history but the unique event that shattered once and for all the whole frame of history by breaking into its natural course, which is a course of sin and death. The importance of secular history decreased in direct proportion to the intensity of man's concern with God and himself.[7]

Education hit a low during the period of the judges. The nation was occupied with survival, but there was no consistent central authority, and all forms of culture and development suffered. The authority of Samuel, who was at the same time the last judge and first prophet, was not a great deal better. Spiritual development and purity in worship certainly improved under

Samuel's leadership, but there is little record that much serious education took place. Samuel did gather around himself a prophetic band, and the era of prophetic instruction actually received its beginning with the sage from Ramah (1 Samuel 19:18-24).

EDUCATION DURING THE MONARCHY

The first king of Israel was hardly a schoolmaster at heart. A courageous warrior who led his nation in numerous military victories, Saul more or less depended on Samuel for any ongoing nurture the nation might experience during his reign. There were prophets, priests, parents, and wisemen, but all of those various educational officers operated in such a militaristic setting that nurture seemed to be of minimal importance. Of course, the feasts continued along with the sacrifices and later the Temple worship.

> Jewish law laid it down that a father must explain the great festivals to his son. When a son asked the meaning of "the testimonies, the statutes, and the judgments" his father must be ready with an explanation. Now, what is not sufficiently realized is that these great festivals had not only an *historical* significance; they had also an *agricultural* significance. They did not only commemorate events in history; they also marked out the cycle of the agricultural year; and it may well be true that their agricultural significance was more primitive than the historical significance which was attached to them. Their historical significance was as follows: The Passover commemorated the deliverance of the Jewish people from slavery and bondage in Egypt; Pentecost commemorated the giving of the Law on Mount Sinai; the Festival of Tabernacles with its living in booths made from branches, commemorated the journey through the wilderness to the promised land.[8]

Though a military genius who surely spent the majority of his time and effort in that dimension of monarchial activity, David was really a sensitive scholar at heart. As musician and lyricist, he is unexcelled in Old Testament literature. Though he himself was not allowed by Jehovah to build the Temple, he certainly made elaborate provisions because of his deep love for the Lord and concern for the purity of worship. David was also responsible for expanding the worship system of Israel to elaborate proportions. Toward the end of his reign a complete system of levitical services was organized, arranging thirty-eight thousand Levites into various job responsibilities and developing singers and minstrels, Temple servants and doorkeepers, to prepare for the Temple that his son would build.

Perhaps David's greatest contribution to godly education was the example of his own life. This is how Gustav Oehler describes it in his classic *Old Testament Theology:*

> The *contrast between sin and grace*, which it is the object of the pedagogy of the law to bring to light, appeared in all its sharpness in his inner life; and that life brings to view, as its external course advanced in a state of continual conflict, both the deep degradation of the fallen, sin-burdened man, and the elevation of a spirit richly endowed with Divine grace. To a greater degree than any other Old Testament character, he experienced the restlessness and desolation of a soul-burdened with a consciousness of guilt, the longing after reconcilation with God, the struggle after purity and renovation of heart, the joy of forgiven sin, the heroic, all-conquering power of confidence in God, the ardent love of a gracious heart for God; and has given in his Psalms imperishable testimony as to what is the fruit of the law and what is the fruit of faith in man.[9]

Of course, education in the monarchy must take into consideration the tremendous instructional capacity of Solomon. Even if we recognize the strong possibility that Solomon did not write Ecclesiastes, the educational value of the book of Proverbs alone is unsurpassed for both its elevation and distribution of wisdom. Notice how education takes on a much more personal dimension in the writings of Solomon. Earlier instructional content centered essentially on the history of the Hebrew people and how their God had dealt with them, explanation of the feasts and festivals, interpretation of the law, and, in David's time, a new awakening of the educational value of hymnody. But Solomon spoke in terms that are still relevant and usable in today's family life. It is a return again to the father-son relationship and deals with matters of economics, moral behavior, and development of the mind.

During the divided monarchy, the dominance of the prophets came to the fore. To be sure, having begun with Samuel they exerted some influence during the days of David and Solomon. Now that the nation was in military and economic turmoil, however, the prophets became the center of Hebrew education right up to the time of Jerusalem's fall. One notable exception would be the itinerating teachers sent out by Jehoshaphat in the third year of his reign. Officials, Levites, and priests "went throughout all the cities of Judah and taught among the people" (2 Chronicles 17:7-9).

The very place of education changed. Rather than the people's coming to a central location such as the Tabernacle or Temple, the prophets were intinerating preachers taking God's message wherever they could find people who would listen. Their messages were highly ethical as well as theological and focused more often than not on the relationship of God's holy people to the pagan nations all around. Justice and mercy dominated their sermons as they called a nation back to the original provisions of the covenant.

> "Behold, days are coming," declares the LORD, "when I will make a new covenant with the house of Israel and with the house of Judah, not like the covenant which I made with their fathers in the day I took them by the hand to bring them out of the land of Egypt, My covenant which they broke, although I was a husband to them," declares the LORD. "But this is the covenant which I will make with the house of Israel after those days," declares the LORD, "I will put My law within them, and on their heart I will write it; and I will be their God, and they shall be My people" (Jeremiah 31:31-33).

Secular historians see a new message and even a new concept of God in the prophets. But a thoroughly evangelical view of the unity of Old and New Testaments will not permit any bifurcation between the God of Moses and the God of Micah. Progressive revelation certainly was at work, and new insights into the meaning of the law were offered. One can hardly argue that Isaiah 53 does not represent a new level in the nation's understanding of the coming Messiah.

Educational process among the prophets was geared to deepen religious insight, increase its fervor, and develop a better and more intimate knowledge of Jehovah, which would ultimately consummate in a personal righteousness. Unfortunately, most of their efforts were unsuccessful, and God's judgment had to fall when His people would not heed the message of His teachers.

EDUCATION IN EXILE

Of course, the prophets transcend the period of the monarchy and follow their people into the exile. The kingdom divided approximately 931 B.C. with Ahijah, Shemaiah, and Iddo serving as God's prophets at that time. By the fall of Jerusalem in 586, God had raised up the more familiar Jeremiah and Ezekiel. Other writers have spent a great deal of time on the messages of the prophets, and we are reminded here that this book is a history of educational thought, not a theology of Old Testament prophetic Scriptures. Suffice it to say that during the period of exile a whole new realm of prophetic theology emerged. There was a balance between an immediate trust in God for deliverance from the present, and the promise of a glorious future that could be realized through repentance and obedience.

Of great importance during this era was the development of the schools of the prophets mainly associated with the ministry of Elijah and Elisha (2 Kings 2:3-5; 4:38; 6:1). Scholars do not suggest that those two nonwriting prophets were the founders of the schools since there seemed to be groups of prophets studying under Samuel many years before. One can probably conjecture with some accuracy that the so-called schools were informal disciple bands, not unlike those men who lived and learned with Jesus during the three and a half years of His earthly ministry. Samuel and the others were not instructors in homiletics, but by watching and learning from the dynamic propheticism of men like Samuel, Elijah, and Elisha, the young prophets undeniably enjoyed an educative process.

We have spoken of the aims of Hebrew education, its content, and its agencies. Perhaps it is important to mention once again the complete intertwining of the theocratic concept in Hebrew learning. Even after the people rejected Jehovah as their king and accepted earthly leaders, it never occurred to any Israeli educator to separate civic from religious responsibility in the learning process. Duty to God was the only vehicle for duty to man, and the latter could not be properly carried out unless the former was in strict accord with the law, which ever-dominated Hebrew life in the Old Testament.

Maintenance of faith and learning during the exile was a major problem, but hardly impossible when we look at examples like Daniel and Nehemiah. A careful system of nurture did enable the people of God to sing the Lord's song in a strange land. Perhaps the greatest learning experience in Babylon was the cultivation of absolute aversion to idolatry. God's people had played with idols for years, contrary to the warning of priests and prophets. Now in Babylon they were surrounded by the ultimate in pagan idolatry, and by the time Persia became an international power under Cyrus the Great (during the mid-sixth century B.C.), the

Jews were ready to give up idolatry forever—they had learned their lesson.

Meanwhile, the ruins of Jerusalem stood as a constant reminder for seventy years that God's people had been unfaithful to their Lord.

> In spite of the warnings they had confidence that God would not permit his temple to be destroyed. As custodians of the Law these people did not believe God would let them go into captivity. Now, in comparing the Solomonic glory and international fame of Israel with the ruins of Jerusalem, many gave vent to their shame and sorrow. The book of Lamentations vividly deplores the fact that Jerusalem had become an international spectacle. Daniel acknowledged in his prayer that his people had become a reproach and a byword among the nations (Dan. 6:16). Such suffering was more burdensome to the captives who were concerned about Israel's future than any physical hardship they had to endure in the land of their exile.[10]

EDUCATION IN THE SYNAGOGUE SYSTEM

During the fifth century B.C. the synagogue became the central place of instruction in Hebrew theology. The Torah reigned supreme again, although Aramaic instead of Hebrew became the spoken language of the people. Because of the necessity of reading theological books in Hebrew, however, that language became a major subject of instruction for students who would serve in some kind of official religious capacity. Other kinds of schools emerged, more as defense against the encroaching pagan Greek culture than for any other reason. Elementary schools called "houses of the book" were established during the first century to provide formal training for children outside the home.

The synagogue itself really became the first formal educational institution the Hebrews had developed. The Torah emerged in written form in the Talmud, and high qualifications were required for all teaching. Robert Ulich describes the system of education that emerged from the synagogue pattern.

> Since, like the Christians and Moslems, the Jews possessed their revelation in written form, much emphasis was laid on the art of reading, though the Old Testament contains no reference to formal schooling. Nevertheless, Ezra the priest (Ca. 536-456) was called "the scribe of the law of the God of heaven." Nehemiah and others of the school of scribes formed an aristocracy of teachers and established their special houses of learning. Regular instruc-

tion in the Law was given in the halls of the outer temple, as we know especially from the New Testament (Matt. 21:23; 26:25; Mark 14:49; Luke 2:46; 20:1; 21:37; John 18:20).

During the Second Commonwealth (515 B.C.—A.D. 70) a great number of schools for adolescent youth or institutions, which we might call secondary, must have existed throughout Israel. They prepared those of their pupils who wished to go further for the college of advanced theological studies at Jerusalem. At the same time, probably in consequence of foreign influences to which Israel became increasingly exposed, the old custom of teaching children within the family seems to have degenerated without formal and elementary education taking its place, until Rabbi Joshua ben Gamala corrected the defect.[11]

Methodology was largely oral with strong emphasis on memorization and recitation. The dialogue technique made postexilic Hebrew education quite progressive by the standards of earlier centuries. Teachers like Hillel and Gamaliel demonstrated the quality of instruction maintained in the Hebrew system, and other historical evidence suggests the involvement of such contemporary factors as interest, socialization, and a concern for individual differences.

Nathan Drazin talks about three ideals or goals that dominated Jewish education just before the time of Christ. The first centered on *nationalism* and emphasized how education would hold the nation together despite its constant batterings from other powers and philosophies. But, of course, there was also a *religious* goal since God was always the center of Jewish education. Strict obedience to the Torah was demanded, and that brought about clear-cut domestic and civic responsibilities as well. Third, according to Drazin, was a concept of *universalization*. Earlier only the privileged few had opportunity to be involved in formal education, but now everyone must learn. Every Jew should internalize his faith and be able to communicate it to others.[12]

Perhaps no national history on earth exhibits the power of education more clearly than that of the Jews. Their very existence at the time of Christ—their very existence today—demonstrates how essential is the transmission of truth to the maintenance of national or familial identity. Dispossessed, dispersed, fragmented, and broken, the nation returned to its battered land to regather itself in front of a wooden pulpit constructed by Ezra for the purpose of *teaching*.

Christian educators owe an incalculable debt to Hebrew education and Old Testament theology. All the doctrines of the New Testament find their roots in some way in the Old, and the preservation of God's truth through prophets, priests, and kings enables evangelical educators today to deal with the whole inscripturated truth of God. Jews and Christians share a reverence for the Old Testament, a healthy respect for the history of Israel, and a strong biblical commitment to the responsibility and privilege of education.

NOTES

1. Donald Kalish, "What (If Anything) to Expect from Today's Philosophers," *Time*, 7 January 1966, p. 24.
2. Frederick Mayer, *A History of Educational Thought* (Columbus, Ohio: Merrill, 1960), p. 80.
3. Elmer H. Wilds and Kenneth V. Lottich, *The Foundations of Modern Education*, 3d ed. (New York: Holt, Rinehart and Winston, 1961), p. 46.
4. Kenneth O. Gangel, "Toward a Biblical Theology of Marriage and Family," *Journal of Psychology and Theology* 5 (Winter, 1977): 60.
5. Lewis J. Sherrill, *The Rise of Christian Education* (New York: Macmillan, 1944), pp. 41-42.
6. C. B. Eavey, *History of Christian Education* (Chicago: Moody, 1964), p. 55.
7. Karl Löwith, *Meaning in History* (Chicago: U. of Chicago, 1949), pp. 192-93.
8. William Barclay, *Educational Ideals in the Ancient World* (Grand Rapids: Baker, 1974), pp. 19-20.
9. Gustav F. Oehler, *Theology of the Old Testament* (New York: Funk and Wagnalls, 1883), p. 373.
10. Samuel J. Schultz, *The Old Testament Speaks* (New York: Harper, 1960), pp. 252-53.
11. Robert Ulich, *A History of Religious Education* (New York: New York U., 1968), p. 13.
12. Nathan Drazin, *History of Jewish Education From 515 B.C.E. to 220 C.E.* (Baltimore: Johns Hopkins, 1940), pp. 15-23.

2

Greek Philosophy and Its Impact on Christian Thought

The trial started almost 2,380 years ago and continues to engulf Western civilization to the present hour. The issues before the judges on the hill at Athens involved the nature of truth, how it is discovered, whether or not there is a supreme good, the significance of tribal deities, and tolerance versus intolerance.

Amazing, is it not, that in over two millennia educators have still not been able to resolve the issues grappled with at the trial of Socrates? In this last quarter of the twentieth century the world is still marked by intellectual confusion, economic and social disunity, and international chaos. The curse of Babel prevails with obstinacy, estrangement, and discord reigning on thrones that should be occupied by flexibility, unity, and harmony.

The spirit of Athens in 400 B.C. is impossible to understand apart from the political make-up of the city-state. With a population of about 100,000 freemen, 65,000 slaves, and 45,000 foreigners, the landed aristocracy gave way to primitive democracy after the Peloponnesian War. It was the constant threat of anarchy due to the conflict between the remaining artistocracy and the dissatisfied lower classes that led both Plato and Aristotle to prefer the government of the middle class and to be more empirical and democratic in their political ideals.

It is interesting that Athenian boys were educated much as are American boys in the late twentieth century. Studying at home until the age of six, they then entered formal schools for physical exercise and instruction in the arts, sciences, humanities, and general metaphysical philosophy intended to enable them to fit into the cultural setting of the city.

At the secondary level, grammar was emphasized along with arithmetic, geometry, and, later, the military arts. In 335 B.C the city passed a law making military training compulsory for all boys at the age of eighteen, after which they served the state for two years. All of that should sound familiar—a secular state holding virtual monopoly on early education and military service.

Higher education was marked by the queen of Athenian studies, philosophy. Essentially, four schools were discernible: The Academy, where Plato taught, emphasized mathematics and literary studies; Aristotle's Lyceum stressed the biological sciences; the school founded by Epicurus stressed ethics. Contrary to the reputation Epicureanism gained from the followers of the founder, it originally emphasized that the highest place was that of the mind. Finally, there were the Stoics. Founded by Zeno, stoicism brought a bit of Spartan mentality to Athens, emphasizing the resignation of fleshly desire and a high level of self-control.

During an era in which Athenian life was shifting from agrarian to commercial economics, the Sophists emerged with their commitment to the relativity of truth and their challenge to any absolute standards of morality. Of them Will Durant writes,

> The most characteristic and fertile developments of Greek philosophy took form with the Sophists, traveling teachers of wisdom, who looked within upon their own thought and nature, rather than out upon the world of things. They were all clever men (Gorgias and Hippias, for example), and many of them were profound (Protagoras, Prodicus); there is hardly a problem or a solution in our current philosophy of mind and conduct which they did not realize and discuss. They asked questions about anything; they stood unafraid in the presence of religious or political taboos; and boldly subpoenaed every creed and institution to appear before the judgment seat of reason.[1]

Protagoras argued that one could never have certain knowledge regarding the existence of the gods. He refused to affirm or deny the existence of religious truth, and he believed that man is ultimately the measure of all things—the father of secular humanism predating Socrates himself.

Meanwhile, Gorgias was teaching a similar rejection of absolutism.

1. Nothing (absolute) exists.
2. Even if it existed, it could not be known.
3. Even if it could be known, it could not be communicated.

Into such a vacuum of truth entered the father of philosophy, urging his students to "know thyself" and arguing that the unexamined life is not worth living. Why did they kill him?

SOCRATES AND MORALISM

"Barefoot in Athens" he wandered among his students, ever questioning, ever insisting upon reason, ever pressing the issues of the nature of man. Socrates sounded a bit like the apostle James when he argued that the teacher is the leader of civilization with an absolute responsibility to pursue truth despite how his contemporaries oppose or abuse him.

What was it about the master that so attracted students of all kinds and classes? Certainly it was not his physical appearance, if we can render judgment from seeing the bust of Socrates, which is our heritage from the physical ruins of ancient Athens. It was hardly his aristocratic bearing, for he lived in careless poverty. Indeed, he was rather like John the Baptist or even Jesus in his attitude toward the things of this world. Certainly it was not his distinctive achievement as a father, for he never worked, he neglected his wife and children, and, according to Xanthippe, he brought his family more notoriety than food. Perhaps it was his humble approach to the wisdom that he loved so dearly, his self-abnegation of the knowledge that so obviously flowed from his fertile mind. Said he, "One thing only I know, and that is that I know nothing."

Socrates irritated establishment politicians by arguing that many Athenian leaders were ignorant and guided by irrational idols. On the other hand, he fought the dangers of anarchy, because government of the people would surely be constantly swayed by their emotions and therefore be ever unstable. Socrates lived 1,500 years too early to enjoy the Renaissance, but he was a true Renaissance man except for his disavowal of the importance of science. In his view, the function of a teacher was to stir the thinking of the average man, shake him out of his lethargy, straighten out his irrationality, and drag him out of the cave of tribal superstition. Of course, a social value ultimately emerges from such education since society is changed when morality and intelligence are combined. The teacher was to be the conscience of his time, cherishing the ideals of knowledge.

Hardly a Christian in his understanding of the God of creation, Socrates was nevertheless committed to a universe that reflected a moral order and a definite purpose. The agnosticism of the Sophists was blasphemy to him, for only the truly moral man could exhibit true knowledge. We should not be confused by the similarities between Socrates and Jesus, thereby reading a biblical element into the philosophy of the Greek. Though denying

Sophism, Socrates remained a true rationalist, finding the ultimate approach to education and reason in the methodology of his now-famous dialectic.

The dialectic was used by Jesus as well, but the purpose was not to lead to ultimate reason or an *end* of self-examination, but rather to ultimate faith and, *through* self-examination, to a commitment to the God of heaven. The philosophy of Socrates is not so much an argument for freedom of speech as it is a historic lesson in the need for tolerance of ideas. Socrates was killed by bigots, jealous and envious men, representing the poets, artisans, and orators desperate in their defense of the old system to which, in their opinion, Socrates presented an unforgivable threat.

Prejudice is a judgment or opinion formed without due examination. It is sometimes excused by unthinking Christians as "faith," but hardly the kind of faith called for by Jesus, Paul, and James. As in Athens, so today, prejudice arises from fear. Socrates said to his judges: "I did not think it right to behave through fear unlike a free-born man." The kind of mob rule that Socrates deplored runs rampant in world society today in the form of terrorism. Whether Arab, Italian, Japanese, African, or American—terrorism is the curse of the modern world.

The opposite of intolerance, prejudice, and dogmatism is tolerance—a cordial and positive effort to understand another's beliefs, practices, and habits without necessarily accepting them. The tolerant thinker makes allowances for errors in thought and act. Though he was not privileged to participate in them, Socrates believed that mercy and truth are an integral part of justice.

So the scheduled trial was enacted, and Socrates was convicted by thirty votes before the Tribunal of the Five Hundred. As every student of philosophy or history knows, he drank the hemlock and died, but not before making it clear that he marched to the beat of a different drummer and would not yield to the pressures of the mob or the state.

> Athenians, I hold you in much affection and esteem; but I will obey heaven rather than you, and, so long as breath and strength are in me, I will never cease from seeking wisdom or from exhorting you and pointing out the truth to any of you whom I may chance to meet, in my accustomed words: "My good friend, you're a citizen of Athens, a great city famous for wisdom and strength; are you not ashamed to spend so much trouble upon heaping up riches and honour and reputation, while you care nothing for wisdom and truth and the perfection of your soul?" And if he

protests that he does care for these things, I shall not immediately release him and go my way; I shall question and cross examine and test him, and if I think he does not possess the virtue he affects, I shall reproach him for holding the most precious things cheap, and worthless things dear. . . .

For I have no other business but to go about persuading you all, both young and old, to care less for your bodies and your wealth than for the perfection of your souls, and to make that your first concern, and telling you that goodness does not come from wealth, but wealth and every other good thing, public or private, comes to mankind from goodness.[2]

Thus died the one whom Plato called "our friend . . . the wisest, the justest, and best of all the men whom I have ever known." The world was never the same again. One writer reminds us of the relevance of the Athenian master for today:

Those who display intolerance are pushing time back a thousand years, though they think of themselves as being *avant-garde*. The Athenians repented their sentence on Socrates when it was too late. They punished his accusers, and erected a statue of bronze in one of the most public parts of the city. But they could neither halt the enlightenment he had started nor make amends for their own intolerance.[3]

PLATO AND IDEALISM

Plato is probably the most significant philosopher of ancient Greece. He was born in the year 427 B.C. and died in 347 at the age of eighty. His parents were members of an old and distinguished Athenian family, and his two brothers, Glaucon and Adeimantus, both play important roles in *The Republic*. Plato was likely the greatest student of Socrates and, although giving some new interpretation to his mentor's thoughts, never departed from his overwhelming respect for the master.

Plato's real name was Aristocles. We are told that he was both handsome and intelligent. The name *Plato* means "the broad" and was quite possibly adopted in recognition of its user's philosophic conceptualizations. Mayer, though writing from the secular viewpoint, demonstrates how Plato's philosophy is inseparably linked to theology.

The philosophy of Plato rests upon his belief in the immortality of the soul. How do we know that the soul is immortal? How can we be certain that it will not perish through death? Plato argues that the soul is not dependent upon the body, rather it is the dominant force in the body. The soul is unalterable and cannot be destroyed through successive reincarnations. The central idea of the soul is that of life, which excludes the idea of death. From a logical standpoint, Plato appeals to the identity of opposites. The existence of life demands the existence of death, whereas the existence of death demands the existence of life. Also, death can only touch those substances which are composites; it cannot touch a simple substance—the soul. The soul, imprisoned in the body, longs for eternal union; it naturally transcends the limitations of human existence.[4]

That particular quotation, though not from Plato himself, appropriately demonstrates Platonic idealism with its dualism of mind and body: the struggle between good mental concepts and the bad concepts of the flesh; the struggle between those who have achieved the ascendancy of the mind (and therefore are in charge of directing the affairs of the state) and those who have not.

Like mind and body, the universe is also dualistic in character. Truth becomes a property of the intellect, gathered through revelation or intuitive reasoning, but it is always a thing of the mind and should not be confused with material substance. It can neither be gained from an examination of physical characteristics of the universe nor tested in material things. Can we believe in God? Plato would argue that the universal acceptance of the existence of God indicates its definite empirical foundation and followed what contemporary theologians would call a teleological approach in attempting to understand the universe.

What about morality, a subject that so occupied the teaching of Socrates, as Plato records it?

> Morality is the adherence to rules and decrees imposed by the outside source. These rules, as has been noted, are perceived through revelation and intuition. Compliance to these rules brings rewards, and transgressors are punished. Such rewards and punishments are always imposed in supernatural ways. As is necessary from the logic of the system, education is viewed as the instrumentality for transmitting to the new generation the truths that have been gathered in the past and for training the mind to understand, expand, and illuminate these truths so as to pave the way for the discovery of the new truth which must always be compatible with those truths already apprehended.[5]

That is an oversimplification of idealism, and is perhaps not exactly the way Plato himself would have put it, but readers are urged to remember that the purpose of this volume is an analysis of the flow of educational thought and not an in-depth critique of philosophy itself.

PLATONIC PHILOSOPHY

Let us get on then to some basic principles for understanding Plato's educational philosophy. Here are four suggestions:

1. Plato cannot be properly understood without some grasp of the influence of Socrates on his life. He became a disciple of the master at age twenty, and after Socrates's death traveled around the Mediterranean world before founding The Academy in 386 B.C. He taught there for the rest of his life. Plato was fond of saying, "I thank God that I was born Greek and not barbarian; free man and not slave; man and not woman; but above all, that I was born in the age of Socrates."

2. Plato's philosophy cannot be understood apart from his interest in politics and the political situation in Greece at the time he lived. For Plato education was a means to an end, namely, social and political reform. We shall return to the political overtones in Plato in just a moment.

3. An understanding of Plato's philosophy rests on a comprehension of his comparison of the individual with the state. For Plato, the state represented the highest interests of the individual. It would therefore establish educational standards and could use any means (even immoral ones) to indoctrinate its citizens. There were obvious Machiavellian overtones in Plato's thinking, and it is probably not incorrect to say that he was even more influenced by the educational standards of Sparta than was Socrates.

4. Plato was a thoroughgoing idealist with an extreme emphasis on mind and reason. His system of truth-searching centered on reason to the exclusion of revelation. We have already noted that above, but it may well be grasped more clearly when stated as a separate principle.

> Plato began his thinking with the educational problem of the teachableness of virtue, but he soon discovered that to solve the educational problem, he must understand the nature of man and of the world and the relation of one to the other. With great boldness he outlined theories that still retain the admiration of mankind.[6]

Let us return for a moment to Plato's great concern for the state. We have already noted that it is precisely that issue that prompted his development of an integrated educational philosophy. An admittedly oversimplified diagram of his approach might look something like that in figure 3.1.

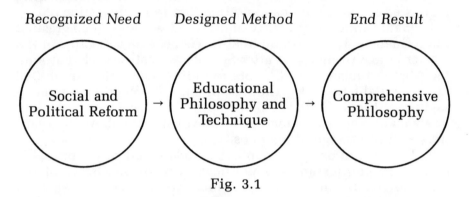

Recognized Need   *Designed Method*   *End Result*

Social and Political Reform → Educational Philosophy and Technique → Comprehensive Philosophy

Fig. 3.1

Plato argued that there are four virtues possessed by man and the state—wisdom, courage, temperance, and justice. All the citizens of any society are divided into four categories that, incidentally, have nothing to do with the four virtues possessed by the state. The first two categories are part of the world of appearances and deal with images and visible things. The other two categories are part of the intelligible world and include such matters as mathematical objects and forms of thought. The educational process carries one through those four states, if indeed one can possibly attain as high as the fourth.

1. *The category of imagination or fiction.* Children and ignorant people inhabit this area. Their ideas of things are individual and therefore in relativity cannot be considered "wrong" but merely irrelevant to the real intelligible world. They deal in realms of fiction. Persons in this category have only a subjective viewpoint of society and truth.

2. *The category of belief.* The attention here is on visible things, the way one thinks of things that he sees. This is a Platonic social generalization—a tree is a tree because the learner's idea of "tree" agrees with society's idea of "tree." He has now moved from a personal viewpoint to a public viewpoint. Though still a common person, the learner in category 2 has

shown some advance, because this category has moved from that personal viewpoint of society and truth to a greater concern for the "know-how" of life.

3. *The category of thought.* Here we have the guardians of the state, soldiers who are not only concerned with knowing *how* but also knowing *why.* Abstractions begin to form at this stage, and the learner is able to perceive things not in the world of appearances.

4. *The category of knowledge.* Finally, we arrive at the philosopher-kings concerned neither with knowing how nor why, but just with *knowing.* There is a "wholeness" in education for those in level 4. Having begun with imagining, they have proceeded upward to knowing and therefore are now prepared to govern the state.

What we know about Plato's philosophy we know from his dialogues, of which there are over twenty. The most famous is *The Republic.* Not a play or novel focusing on plot or characters, *The Republic* is rather a platform for the demonstration of educational ideas and arguments. Contemporary readers should not take the word *republic* in its modern sense. The Greek term simply means *state* or *society,* and it is Plato's goal to tell us how the ideal state is, in reality, more like an enlightened monarchy than the Athenian democracy that formed the womb out of which he wrote.

> Although his societal model is elitist, Plato did not conceive of the Republic as a fascist, dictatorial, or otherwise coercive state. He assumed that each component class in the polis would fulfill a necessary socioeconomic function by contributing to the life and harmony of the community and did not conceive of a situation developing in which the ruling elite would coerce the masses or a spirit of rebellion would be present in a seething proletariat. In contrast, he believed that the integrated society was a just one and that justice would emerge from the harmonious relationships of all classes. The Republic must be integrated in the same way that the rational, volitional, and appetitive elements in human nature are integrated in the properly balanced individual. The Republic was a scheme designed to achieve a socially integrated polity at a time of acute social disequilibrium.[7]

PLATONIC EDUCATION

Of all the parts of *The Republic,* the cave allegory is perhaps most pertinent to educational philosophy. Plato believed that men are bound to a false concept of reality and must therefore be converted or released from that bondage. The release involves turning one's love from the deceptive sphere of operation, in which sense data provide knowledge and principles for living, to the divine sphere of operation, in which innate knowledge and intellect give the true picture of reality.

The cave represents false reality as most people see it. Within the cave, men are compelled to sit and look forward while behind them on a raised level is a large fire. Between them and the fire, objects cast a shadow on the wall before them, so all they can see are shadows, a likeness of reality. How can the prisoners be pulled closer to the light? It is a painful process indeed, and massive changes must be made, but closeness to the light is the ultimate cause for all; the wisdom gained is highly prized, and the ones who have made the ascent pity their companions who are still imprisoned in the cave.

It might be well to note here that this concept of imprisonment and enforced movement toward the light is the principal reason Plato believed the state must control education. Those in charge

> will begin by sending out into the country all the inhabitants of the city who are more than ten years old, and will take possession of their children, who will be unaffected by the habits of their parents; these they will train in their own habits and laws, I mean in the laws which we have given them: and in this way the state and constitution of which we were speaking will soonest and most easily attain happiness, and the nation which has such a constitution will gain most.[8]

The Platonic system of schooling is compartmentalized into nine eras charted in detail by Frederick Eby and Charles Arrowood. From infancy (birth to three) the child moves through a system of education that ultimately brings him to the beloved dialectic between ages thirty and thirty-five. Here he emphasizes philosophy, psychology, sociology, governmental law, and education, and at thirty-five is then ready to be of service to the state.

What is the dialectic? Let Plato explain it.

> And so, Glaucon, I said, we have at last arrived at the hem of dialectic. This is that strain which the faculty of sight will nevertheless be found to imitate; for sight as you may remember, was imagined by us after a while to behold the real animals and stars, and last of all, the sun himself (sun symbolizes absolute truth). And so with dialectic; when a person starts on a discovery of the absolute by the light of reason only, and without any assis-

tance of sense, and perseveres until by pure intelligence he arrives at the perception of the absolute good, he at last finds himself at the end of the intellectual world, and in the case of sight at the end of the visible.[9]

What positive values does the Christian educator find in Plato? Certainly his metaphysic is preferable to most secular philosophy of the day such as logical positivism or secular humanism. He taught there are values above and beyond the physical world and that the world of appearance is not always the world of truth.

Furthermore, the idea of dialectic borrowed from Socrates is surely a legitimate means of a search for truth. It is a method of instruction, though hardly a guarantor for the achieving of faith.

Plato comes close to the "image of God" concept with his ideas of self-realization and at times sounds a bit like John Calvin, advocating the control of the theocratic state. But attaining a renewed "image of God" through regeneration is hardly what Plato had in mind. The Christian educator also appreciates Plato's concern for the education of all individuals and his recognition of individual differences, an important feature in all respectable education today.

On the *negative side,* we surely understand that Plato had no place for the God of the Bible or even a supreme being that approximates the Creator. He might claim that the universal acceptance of the existence of God is empirically based, but Plato's god is not the God of the Bible. We may be assured that Plato would be just as vigorously opposed to the self-revealed God of orthodox Christianity as he was to the gods of the Greek Pantheon and Homeric mythology.

The Christian also cannot accept Plato's excessive idealism in its glorification of the mind of man. In fact, good and truth are *not* impersonal; they are *not* arrived at because a man has learned to think his way through. Thinking is important for any Christian in the educational process, but ultimately faith and truth are gifts from above, not some extension of the idea of good in the life of the individual and the state.

Plato also placed no stock in the doctrine of original sin. To be sure, he did not hold a very high view of people in the lower stages of life and learning. In reality, the ultimate development of the Logos had nothing to do with the Christian understanding of that term, as used by John, but rather was a refining of basic knowledge contained within the citizen all the time. It merely took the proper process of education to unleash it. That process was "habituation," the only way to achieve knowledge, with the state all the time guarding the molding process.

Add to those deficiencies Plato's acceptance of reincarnation, his inability to shake aristocratic pride, and his patently unbiblical denial of family control and supremacy, and we see the system weakening.

In the final analysis, Plato's system crumbles because of his absolute insistence on making all things subservient to the state. Despite Harold L. Gutek's evaluation quoted earlier, we believe Plato was actually a totalitarian with contempt for the masses. The lovely individualism of Socrates had to be sacrificed in order to achieve immediate ends in behalf of the state. The common people dare not lie, but on occasion philosopher-kings may have to lie to protect the common people. Such axiological confusion denies the absolutes that Socrates held and Plato claimed.

Unlike his mentor, Plato passed into history quietly. Will Durant tells the story in his inimitable style.

> One of his pupils, facing that great abyss called marriage, invited the Master to his wedding feast. Plato came, rich with his eighty years, and joined the merry-makers gladly. But as the hours laughed themselves away, the old philosopher retired into a quiet corner of the house, and sat down on a chair to win a little sleep. In the morning, when the feast was over, the tired revellers came to wake him. They found that during the night, quietly and without adieu, he had passed from a little sleep to an endless one. All Athens followed him to the grave.[10]

ARISTOTLE AND REALISM

Some wag has said, "Aristotle is a classic philosopher—everyone respects him, but nobody needs him." Though purists would fume, the beginning student of educational philosophy grappling with the mystical Macedonian might tend to agree for several reasons: First of all, Aristotle is extremely difficult to read; second, there is really no clear interpretation of his key book *(Politics)*; and third, he had no really discernible philosophy of education. Our approach to a study of Aristotle, therefore, must be one of pulling out ideas and concepts rather than unveiling a structured philosophic system. Like Paul, we must be *spermologi* in Athens, picking up seeds as best we can in order to grow a philosophic garden. Such eclecticism is common as the Christian confronts secular work in almost any academic realm.

Just as Plato was the pupil of Socrates, Aristotle (384-322 B.C.) was the pupil of Plato. There were some likenesses between teacher and student, but many more differences as Aristotle demonstrated early by his disavowal of Plato's idealism and his founding of what we have to call historic realism. Ralph L. Pounds states it simply.

> He agreed basically on most matters with Plato, but he had more interest in the things of the physical world than in immaterial things. In the first place, Aristotle was actively a great scientist. He wrote voluminously upon all matters which are now embodied in the various fields of knowledge. The modern organization of these fields of knowledge follows fairly closely that which was made by Aristotle in the fourth century B.C. Aristotle was primarily a collector of facts and a classifier of knowledge.[11]

Aristotle's criticism of Plato particularly rejected the concept that knowledge is a priori. He argued that there is no referenced knowledge outside of experience, and therefore rejected Plato's dislocation of "objects" from one world, putting them in another world where they could not be contemplated. Rather than thinking about things that the common person could not understand (as Plato argued philosopher-kings should do), Aristotle countered that it should be the function of leaders in society to provide a straightforward description of the objects about them; hence the difference between classic idealism and classic realism. Perhaps we should stay with that differentiation a moment longer.

Realism tends to reject idealistic dualism and argues that the universe is monistic, like a giant machine set up to run in accordance with certain inexorable laws. Truth becomes the discovery of those laws by objective observation, sampling, empirical description, and statistical analysis. One cannot thwart the natural laws, so society becomes a matter of setting up human organizations so they can best function in accordance with the absolute laws of the universe.

Adam Smith's argument that supply and demand will govern the distribution of goods, and the now-famous Malthusian theory that the working population must remain at a starvation level in order to keep society from overrunning the supply of food are spin-offs from original Aristotelian logic. Roald Campbell and Russel Gregg offer a simple paragraph of definition.

> Thus, from the point of view of realism, morality is getting in step

with the natural laws of the universe. The immoral person is one who does not understand or accept the natural laws, or who tries to deviate from them when he does understand. Education is largely a matter of training people to accommodate themselves to the inevitable. Here again is a slight dualism since it is recognized that the human organism is quite prone to disregard the natural laws and thus must be trained in the strict sense of the word to obey without question. Educators, of course, will be well-versed in the application of the laws of learning as they apply to the development of the "right" specific habits in individuals; or, to say the same in other fashion, they will be well-versed in helping the individual develop appropriate S→R bonds.[12]

ARISTOTELIAN EDUCATION

Education for Aristotle was an achievement of *happiness* and *virtue*, two key words in Aristotelian thought. We must not understand his "happiness" in our contemporary idea of comfort and freedom from care, but rather the original meaning of good spirit and form of activity. One develops a sense of doing good and thereby receiving the praise of men. Such a process results in happiness. But how is that accomplished? The most obvious way is to subordinate all thoughts and actions to reasonable or rational principles; hence "the Golden Mean."

Such a life of moderation is learned by habituation and repeated practice. When related to education, we might say that Aristotle argued that the actual *doing* of something was much more important than thinking about it. Resolution to do good is powerless against the crushing weight of the act. Is classroom instruction then not important? Oh, indeed, but habit is molded much quicker and more firmly by *doing*. As in most educational philosophy, it is impossible to understand Aristotelian educational concepts without some grasp of his view of man. We like the way James L. Jarrett summarizes it:

> The man who has not greatly cultivated his mind is like a fruitless apple tree or a weak-backed ox, missing his only claim to distinctiveness. A measure of Aristotle's respect for the intellectual powers is the fact that when he asked what God's activity, the divine process, must be, his answer was, inevitably, thinking. God thinks. And to the best of our ability so should we. . . .
>
> Even more famous is Aristotle's pronouncement that man is a political animal. The formal study of ethics and politics, he taught, is not for children, simply because it takes an accumulation of experience and a certain maturity to deal intellectually

with these complex problems. Nevertheless, education is bound to be shaped by the particular state that provides it; the virtues it will try to inculcate will be consonant with its own sort of political philosophy. Aristotle was no utopist.[13]

So education leads to control of one's self and one's environment, achieved through rational and virtuous thinking. But Aristotle's use of the word *virtue* is not consonant with our present understanding of the term. He had in mind *excellence* or *perfection* in the intellectual sphere. Virtue is always built on knowledge and always results in doing all things in moderation. The world needed a new birth of knowledge, but not one built on authority, such as Plato argued. Rather, man must take thought and inquire into its application into life—human effort in its own behalf.

What signs are there that we are indeed rational beings? First of all, we can think abstractly. We can determine "good." Furthermore, we can think discursively with an ability to put ideas into a system in some kind of cognitive design. Third, we have some intellectual intuition, a faculty in man that makes it possible for him to grasp principles. The Golden Mean is accomplished by making right choices. One right choice brings about improved environment, thereby leading to another right choice, and so on, until the Golden Mean is achieved.

What does the Christian say to all of this? Well, for one thing, he might express relief at being rid of Plato's totalitarianism. Aristotle also seemed much more concerned with the development of character through right behavior rather than just contemplative thinking, and his concept of education was considerably more rounded than that of Socrates or Plato, particularly in his emphasis on natural science, music, art, and the humanities, in order to achieve his beloved Golden Mean.

On the negative side of the slate, we must recognize that Aristotle, though more flexible than Plato, was hardly a true liberal in the good educational sense of that term. He had a low opinion of women, he defended slavery, and he had nothing but contempt for other nations. He also was concerned that the state retain its control of education much in the way Plato suggested.

> That education should be regulated by law and should be an affair of state is not to be denied, but what should be the character of this public education, and how young persons should be educated, are questions which remain to be considered. For mankind

are by no means agreed about the things to be taught, whether we look to virtue or the best life.[14]

Since Aristotle himself was not settled on a satisfactory approach to education, we should not be surprised to discover a vagueness in his metaphysics and epistemology. It is one thing to say that the end of education is to guide children to love what they ought to love and hate what they ought to hate. It is considerably different to identify and define what it is that they are to love or hate. Though he was interested in religion, Aristotle viewed God as completely impersonal rather than the loving heavenly Father described in the Scriptures.

We have come a long way from Jerusalem to Athens, the classic contrast between faith and reason that has dominated symbolic philosophy through the ages. While Hebrew parents taught the law of Moses at home and sent their children to the synagogue for formal instruction, Aristotle was turning the minds of Athenians from a dependence on God to a dependence on man. Education had become a psychological task, and the coronation of scientific empiricism was about to begin. To be sure, the dominance of Rome put an end to the emerging science of Aristotle, and it was not recaptured until the Renaissance, but, though a thousand years may separate their writings, we will look again at the Athenian logician through the writings of Thomas Aquinas.

BIRTH OF HELLENISM

The death of Aristotle in 322 B.C. closed the door on the Hellenic period of Greek history and opened the door on what we have commonly called the Hellenistic period. Arguments arose and conflicts developed between faith and reason, skepticism and religion. The Hellenists were far more concerned with the physical development of the state and had little time for either Plato's cave or Aristotle's Golden Mean. They were building cities like Alexandria and developing a culture that boasted Euclid, Appolonius, Hero, Strabo, Posidonius, Hipparchus, Aristarchus and, of course, Archimedes.

The amazing thing is that the emergent culture of Greece was so strong it survived even the crushing heel of the armies of Rome and became the cradle for Western civilization as well as early Christian thought. Paul may have walked on Roman roads and preached from Hebrew and Aramaic Scriptures, but the culture, the language, and the concepts of New Testament Christianity were Greek. In all the history of the world, there never was, nor likely ever again will be, an era like that of Socrates, Plato, and Aristotle.

NOTES

1. Will Durant, *The Story of Philosophy* (New York: Simon and Schuster, 1972), p. 7.
2. Plato *Apology.*
3. "An Unfinished Trial," *The Royal Bank of Canada Monthly Letter,* January 1970, p. 4.
4. Frederick Mayer, *A History of Educational Thought* (Columbus, Ohio: Merrill, 1960), pp. 96-97.
5. Roald F. Campbell and Russel T. Gregg, eds., *Administrative Behavior in Education* (New York: Harper and Brothers, 1957), p. 139.
6. Frederick Eby and Charles F. Arrowood, *The History and Philosophy of Education* (Englewood Cliffs, N.J.: Prentice-Hall, 1940), p. 349.
7. Gerald L. Gutek, *A History of the Western Educational Experience* (New York: Random House, 1972), pp. 37-38.
8. Plato *Republic.*
9. Ibid.
10. Durant, p. 47.
11. Ralph L. Pounds, *The Development of Education in Western Culture* (New York: Appleton-Century-Crofts, 1968), p. 40.
12. Campbell and Gregg, pp. 139-40.
13. James L. Jarrett, *Philosophy for the Study of Education* (Boston: Houghton Mifflin, 1969), p. 72.
14. Aristotle *Politics.*

3

Rome Versus Jesus:
New Testament
Principles of Education

Countries and eras are acclaimed for greatness when gifted thinkers and leaders appear. Yet none, not even the distinguished coterie of German philosophical giants—Kant, Hegel, Schelling, Marx, and Fichte—equaled the power and profundity of Socrates, Plato, and Aristotle. In Roman civilization, however, personages of reknown were not philosophers but rather military commanders and political dictators. The Roman genius for organization was concentrated in its military and political institutions rather than in an august academia.

The traditional date given for the founding of Rome, the city built on seven hills, is 753 B.C. Subsequently, the tribal life that had characterized the Italian peninsula gave way to organized political city-states much like those in Greece. A king would rule in conjunction with a senate made up of wealthy citizens called patricians. The patricians maintained exclusive control until the second-class citizens, the plebeians, rebelled and threatened to secede and establish their own city-state. As a consequence, the patricians were forced to grant political rights other than land grants for military service to the plebeians. Leaders or tribunes were elected to the governing body, which procedure assured better representation for the plebeians. The patricians, with the king, retained control of the government, and the plebeians began to earn and purchase some of the land, which eventually became a negotiating factor between the two social classes. But the stratification distinction remained.

The expulsion of the kings and the beginning of a republic under the leadership of consuls commenced in 509 B.C. The republic existed from the late sixth to the first century B.C. Rome succeeded in conquering neighboring city-states, and by the third century B.C. had become a military power. But culturally the

51

people had not progressed much above barbarism. Formal schools began about 250 B.C., and when they were established, they were under Greek influence and often with a Greek slave as the teacher.

THE SOCIAL SETTING OF ROMAN EDUCATION

To the practical Romans, education was not restricted to a formal institution. Their concern was one of building empires, not the building of culture. The Romans believed that the chief function of education was the training of a good citizen. Yet for all their practicality, they recognized a superiority in Greek culture and learning.

GREEK INFLUENCE ON ROMAN CULTURE

The full technical development of Roman education did not come until the end of the first century B.C., resulting primarily from their conquest of Greece. Actually, that process dated back to the beginning of Rome as a town. It was located on the apron, the very edge of the Greek world. The nearest Greek town, Cumae, a short distance away, affected the surrounding area. Rome was therefore never free from the impact of Hellenism. The Greeks themselves had been influenced by the Etruscans. Etruria had possession of an area between the Arno and Tiber rivers and inland to the Apennines in Italy through the fourth century B.C.

Greek cultural influence continued and increased as the Roman Empire grew. The area known as Greater Greece was conquered at Tarentum in 272. After a long series of eastern wars Macedonia was annexed in 168, as was the kingdom of Pergamus in 132. Historians correctly insist on the profound effects that that penetration of Hellenism had on Rome. Rome had won the military battles, but the Greeks triumphed in the "intellectual war."

Moses Hadas has stated, "the most significant characteristic of the Greeks is that no group of them settled anywhere without at once establishing a school, and organized education was the most important single factor in the process of hellenization and also to the resistance to that process."[1]

The intellectual impact of the Greeks moved almost irresistibly until vast parts of the civilized world could be identified as Hellenic and Hellenistic (roughly from 800 B.C. to A.D. 200).[2] It should be noted that the military conquests of Greek leaders such as Alexander the Great (d. 323 B.C.) were not incidental to that Hellenization, as their conquests provided a political framework. In essence, that unusual context originated from the base of the Grecian political, military and economic prowess, and from their language, literature, philosophy, knowledge, art, and life-style.

GREEK INFLUENCE ON ROMAN EDUCATION

Despite the fact that the Romans held the power, the Greeks knew they had the superior culture. A land that dreamed of philosopher-kings and utopias probably saw little worth in a military society. The Greeks viewed the Roman mind as being noncurious, quite unlike their own creative, speculative powers. They were aware that after only a brief struggle their culture was eagerly sought by the Romans. Cicero, the learned and politically astute Roman, spent several years translating Plato and the Greek moralists into Latin.

Greek education was theoretical and designed, in Matthew Arnold's phrase, to cultivate the "circle of knowledge." Emphasis was not only placed on rhetoric. Educators such as Plato, Aristotle, and Isocrates concerned themselves as well with questions of virtue, ethics, music, and the foundation of the medieval liberal arts curriculum—grammar, logic, and rhetoric. Greek education was humanistically oriented and not well organized. The "school" was where the teacher happened to be.

Roman education, in contrast to the aesthetic and warm Greeks, was somewhat pedantic and more practical. Where the Greeks learned a poem, the Romans learned the laws of the city. The single improvement made by Rome over Greece was that Rome formalized education by developing an academic assessment system. The Romans developed a three-rung ladder system: elementary, secondary, and rhetorical (somewhat like junior college) schools.

FAMILY EDUCATION

Let us go back to basics by looking at the role of the family in the educational process. Early Roman life was integrated upon the core of tradition, and it was the father's responsibility, as head of the family, to transmit the values, obligations, and rituals of that tradition to the child. In Greece the early education of a child was in the hands of a slave or pedagogue.

During Early Roman education (c. 750-200 B.C.) the backbone of education was the family. Until the age of seven the child was educated by the mother. "Even in the greatest families she considered it an honor to stay at home so that she could do her duty and be as it were a servant to her children. The mother's influence lasted a lifetime."[3]

Marrou continues: "When the mother was unable to do her job properly, a governess was chosen to look after the children, and she was always a relative, a woman of experience whom all the family respected, and a person who knew how to maintain an atmosphere of severity and a high moral tone—even when the children were playing games."[4]

Legal historians emphasize the unusual strength of the Roman family by citing the respect accorded the mother and her devotion to the children. It should be noted that the mother was not a doormat upon which the children might freely walk. On the contrary, she exuded a genuine love for them and a concern that they would be disciplined properly. Part of love for one's children is the responsibility of loving discipline. Even during those earliest years under the care of the mother, the father was held responsible and given absolute authority.

At seven years of age the boy came under the direct supervision of his father, who was acknowledged as the "child's real teacher." Later on, the trained teachers or literators of the *ludus* (elementary schools) were expected to take on more or less the role of a father. The appearance of the literator weakened the concept of the father's role in education. The same may be true of the pedagogue, a slave who accompanied the child to school in both Greek and Roman contexts. He was to keep the child from getting into trouble and to insist that the child finish his academic assignments. Understandably, the pedagogue incurred resentment from his charge during the adolescent years. It is to that custodian, not to the schoolteacher, that the apostle Paul compared the law in Galatians 3:24.[5]

The Roman father was to work diligently in his teaching responsibilities rather than emulate the careless and incompetent Greek fathers who appear in Plato's *Laches*. On the boy's turning sixteen his home education was to be terminated. To finish his "education" he entered military service and spent usually one year preparing for a vocational pursuit.

ROMAN EDUCATIONAL SYSTEM

As the Roman Empire expanded, the Greek system provided a model for the Roman educational program. The *ludus*, or elementary school, was for children ages seven to ten or eleven; the *grammatikus*, or grammar school, was for those ten to sixteen years; and the rhetorical school was for sixteen-to eighteen-year-olds.

ELEMENTARY SCHOOLS

Elementary schools appeared at the end of the fourth century B.C. At first they supplemented the efforts of the home, but in time they supplanted it. The Greek ideal was the well-rounded person. Initially, the emphasis in the *ludus* was literacy. As it became more formal, memorization of the Laws of the Twelve Tables was replaced by the reading of Homer's *Odyssey*. The major Roman educational methods, however, remained those of memorization, drill, and discipline.

SECONDARY SCHOOLS

By the third century B.C. the grammar (secondary) school had been imported from and influenced by Hellenistic literature, philosophy, science, and religion.

> Beginning as a result of the very practical need to meet Greek traders on even terms, the desire to learn the Greek language grew apace, until at length Greek scholars and teachers began to pour into Rome. Of course, there was opposition to the Greek influence by such men as Cato the Elder, who saw nothing but evil for sturdy Rome in effete Greek culture; but even he capitulated finally. In general, most Roman intellectuals of the later Republic and early Empire were nourished on Greek thought.[6]

The Hellenizing of the West was accomplished by Roman economic, political, and cultural contact with Greece. The thrust of teaching Greek grammar and literature was, in effect, choosing the best of academic achievements provided by the Hellenistic East. But the Romans responded with an attempt to make Latin the national language by requiring that it be taught in the grammar school.

Marrou maintains that the creation of Latin poetry was due to the demand that a Latin secondary school teach something comparable to the Greek poets studied in the Greek secondary schools. "Latin poetry came into existence so that teachers should have something to argue about, probably as a result of national pride, for Rome would not have gone on being satisfied for long with an education that was solely given in Greek."[7]

The first secondary schools in Rome were foreign language

schools. Latin had a difficult struggle in competition with Greek, but eventually Latin provided as valuable an educational experience as did Greek. The first secondary schools among English-speaking peoples such as the American colonists were Latin grammar schools. It is important to remember, "The belief that someone else's language is better than one's own for educative purposes has had a long tradition. It is especially characteristic of a formative period of education. Once a people arrives at the florescent stage, they feel at home with their own language; in fact they begin to feel that they should disseminate it to others."[8]

Before we move on to the rhetorical schools the subject of discipline must receive at least brief treatment. Previous to and during the time of Quintilian (A.D. 35-95) corporal punishment was the common practice. Herodes, writing in the third century B.C., vividly described a typical flogging. Hebrew schools used brutality as well. Quintilian strongly disapproved of flogging and stressed that teachers do all in their powers to create a stimulating educational experience.

RHETORICAL SCHOOLS

During the republican period the upper-class Roman youth of sixteen continued his education with two or three years of study at the rhetorical or philosophical schools in Alexandria, Athens, or other Hellenistic centers of the East. Training in Greek rhetoric was highly prized by the Romans. Greek was the international language of diplomacy, and rhetoric was useful to the politician. By the third century B.C. Greek-language rhetorical schools appeared in Rome, but eventually the Roman senate expelled the Greek philosophers and rhetoricians because of their sharp differences in moral standards. From Cicero (106-43 B.C.) through the beginning of the Empire Latin rhetorical schools compared favorably, with rhetoric being taught in Greek by Roman literators. Rhetoric dominated Roman higher education to such an extent that Greek philosophy and science were never pursued wholeheartedly by Romans at home.

This is not to say that interaction with Greek culture had a negative effect on Roman education. On the contrary, although many Romans (e.g., Cato) objected strenuously to the impact of the Greeks on them, they could neither suppress nor deny the profundity of its thrust. The earliest Roman historians wrote their accounts in Greek. The apostle Paul addressed the church at Rome, Hadrian wrote his epigrams, and Marcus Aurelius his

Meditations all in Greek. In the first century A.D. Quintilian recommended that Roman schoolboys begin their studies with
Greek before Latin. Greek had conquered almost every walk of
life.

The rhetorical schools began in the first century B.C. with the
purpose of producing orators and statesmen. They combined the
Greek model of the educated man with the Roman proclivity for
practicality. The Romans saw the practical value of oratory in
terms of gaining control of a crowd, influencing voting, and in-
spiring the military. But the study of rhetoric led the Romans to
other aspects of Greek culture. The rhetorical schools purported
to teach rhetoric and declamation, but the boundaries or curricula of the grammar and rhetorical academies were not clear.
As a result the grammar schools often trespassed into the province of the other. Rhetorical education included music, mathematics, history, and law in addition to rhetoric. Such corollary
subjects were essential for a nation that stressed civic responsibility as an important goal. Speeches dealt with policy, law, and
the eulogy.

Without doubt, rhetoric remained the single most useful instrument for public recognition and advancement. This was true
during the republican period when education was primarily a
private matter in which the state exercised little control. During
the Empire, however, the emperors gradually exerted their influence and authority over education by subsidizing teachers and
schools. Emperor Vespasian (A.D. 69-79) was particularly aggressive in this regard as he "introduced taxation benefits and
exemptions to attract Greek teachers, established library
facilities, and provided endowments for distinguished rhetoricians."[9]

That financial and political support was not without its problems. Roman education began to decline in quality as the Empire
became decadent. Despotic emperors from Nero to Hitler have
never been enthusiastic about public debate over their policies.
Rhetoric was given a severe blow with the loss of political freedom. Previously rhetoric was based on reality-oriented themes,
particularly dealing with government. Rhetoric became more
formalized and ornate, consisting of compilations of adjectives
of praise. The schools distanced themselves from reality.

Later, as the Empire began to crumble, the schools became
even more formal. Greek disappeared, and the Christian church,
stressing faith and morals versus humanistic education, began

the transition to the Middle Ages. Education became the toy of the idle rich—the masses could not afford it because of the enormous tax burden placed on them by the emperors.

QUINTILIAN

Marcus Fabius Quintilianus (A.D. 35-95) was a Spaniard and may well have been educated in Spain, one of the cultural centers of the first-century world. He was appointed to the chair of Greek and Latin rhetoric at Rome by Emperor Vespasian. Quintilian became the most famous teacher and theoretician in Rome. He distinguished himself as a lawyer as well, but teaching was his great love.

Quintilian's educational aim was to produce the perfect orator, and he insisted that the first essential was that he be a good man. To Quintilian, oratory without character is a prostitution of the process. Fluency of speech would then be "the accomplice of crime, the betrayer of innocence, the enemy of truth."[10] He requested his students to speak on virtues such as courage, justice, and self-control, knowing that those virtues touch so much of life. Gifts of speech were not to take precedence over excellence of character.

ROLE OF THE TEACHER

Quintilian realized that a crucial part of the teaching-learning process was the spotless character of the teacher. Inevitably he would produce students who emulated and imitated their teacher (Luke 6:40; 1 Thessalonians 1:5-8). The teacher was to be a father to his students, aware that he was taking the place of the parent (in loco parentis). He was to study each child, becoming knowledgeable of each one's abilities and character, in order to match his style and content to the child's needs. Even the nurse and pedagogue were to be carefully scrutinized to determine the purity of their persons in light of the student's power of imitation.

METHODOLOGY

Quintilian was a pedagogic revolutionary. He was aware of the value of play in early childhood and the importance of early influences in life. The child's nurse should ideally be a philosopher of good character who spoke the language with precision because of the difficulty of correcting first impressions. The mind of the child should not lie fallow until seven years of age.

The unusual early powers of memory should be employed with a literary as well as moral education.

Learning was to be made interesting (Proverbs 15:2), and control of the educational environment was to be without corporal punishment.

> His studies must be made an amusement: he must be questioned and praised and taught to rejoice when he has done well; sometimes too, when he refuses instruction, it should be given to some other to excite his envy; at times also he must be engaged in competition and should be allowed to believe himself successful more often than not, while he should be encouraged to do his best by such rewards as may appeal to his tender years.[11]

CHILD DEVELOPMENT

Quintilian was a prophetic voice. Unlike Cicero, who was actively engaged in politics, Quintilian gave himself to the teaching task and the development of an educational theory. As a precursor of Erikson, Piaget, Kohlberg, and Fowler, he identified three stages of human development. Although lacking the sophistication of our contemporary developmentalists, he indicated the following stages: birth to age seven; seven to fourteen years of age; fourteen to seventeen. Quintilian believed that curriculum should be established in light of those stages. For example, from ages seven to fourteen the child learns from sense experiences, forms clear ideas, and memory is at its peak. Writing and reading were to be taught at the ability level of the individual child as much as possible.

Quintilian has been described as "one of the most enlightened educators of all time."[12] That gifted educator addressed himself to many theoretical and practical problems currently under discussion, issues that will continue to be high on the educational agenda. He emphasized the cruciality of understanding individual differences in the readiness and abilities of the student. He looked for the capacity in a teacher to stimulate and excite students about learning. Group situations were to be preferred to the tutorial approach because they enhance social skills and development. Quintilian believed there is a relationship between moral and cognitive learnings, and therefore, early childhood educational possibilities were to be appropriated. Only much later were Quintilian's contributions recognized. "When the Greek and Roman literatures were rediscovered by the Renaissance humanist educators, Quintilian's ideas assumed a new currency. His ideas on liberal culture, individual differences, interest and motivation were rediscovered by Vittorino da Feltre, who used them to educate the Renaissance man."[13]

The rhetorical schools were the province of wealthy families whose sons gave promise of a career in politics and public service. Unfortunately, those schools that emphasized Latin were not common until after the republic had ceased and the professional outlet for the schools had largely vanished.

> By the time the rhetorical schools were well established the opportunities for guiding the destinies of the state through public oratory had practically disappeared with the passing of the Republic; their usefulness had virtually been outlived before they began to function. In the hands of Quintilian the rhetorical school offered much more than simply the study and practice of rhetoric. He designed its course of study to include all the major fields of knowledge as a means of developing a person of broad understanding and good practical judgment . . . No other writer of the imperial period approached Quintilian in the scope or details of his proposals for education.[14]

Did Jesus Christ the Master Teacher have an impact on this Roman educator? Although Quintilian recognized that education could not do everything and that unless "Nature helps, all instructions will be useless,"[15] there was no direct acknowledgment of his awareness of the "teacher come from God."

MATRIX FOR THE INCARNATION

> Christianity is a gift of God. It came into the world from outside. But it came at a definite point in the world's history, and it cannot be fully understood without a study of the conditions that prevailed among its adherents. These conditions, as well as Christianity itself, were the work of God. The manner of his working was different in the two cases. The historical conditions under which Christianity arose are works of providence; Christianity itself is a new creation. But both are works of God. Both should be studied with reverence.[16]

Christianity began within the climate of the powerful Roman Empire. Therefore Rome must be understood if we are to interpret Christianity properly. The last monarch mentioned by name in the Old Testament is Darius (Nehemiah 12:22), the last king of Persia. The world power dominating the Near East and, in fact, the whole Mediterranean world at the beginning of the New Testament was the Roman Empire. The political struggle of the

Jewish people was devastating and humiliating. When Christ was born, a key to the geographical movement of his parents was a decree issued by "Caesar Augustus . . . that a census be taken of all the inhabited earth. . . . everyone [went] to his own city" (Luke 2:1, 3). Paying taxes to the Romans was a lively political and theological issue in the years of Christ's youth. A Roman magistrate sentenced Him to die, and a Roman form of execution was utilized in His death. The persecution of Rome was a reality to the Jews.

POLITICAL PEACE

From the last king of Persia to the growth of Roman rule over the Near East, the Mediterranean world was dominated by the Greco-Macedonian Empire of Alexander the Great and his successors. Within three years Alexander had conquered the entire Persian Empire, and in the following years he added the territories we now know as Afghanistan and Pakistan. Although his political empire did not survive his death (323 B.C.), the cultural empire of the Greeks remained for almost a thousand years until the rise of Islam and the Arab conquests of the seventh century A.D.

After Alexander's death his generals divided the empire and founded dynasties. A measure of autonomy was given to Judea under first the Ptolemaic and then the Seleucid dynasties. The Seleucids were routed by the Romans in 190 B.C. The sacrilegious Antiochus Epiphanes and his successors had provided a less than satisfactory context for the Jewish people. After a civil war Julius Caesar gained power in 48 B.C. By 27 B.C. Octavian (later known as Caesar Augustus) became the undisputed ruler of the Roman Empire on defeating Antony and Cleopatra. He established the *Pax Romana* and appointed procurators over Judea. The year 27 B.C. is generally accepted as the beginning of the Roman Empire.

The Roman occupation forces were hated by the Jews because they threatened the Jewish national heritage and aspirations. However, the Jews were allowed considerable freedom of self-government. Much of the government of Palestine was in the hands of the ruling religious party and was conducted in accordance with Old Testament principles. The central council (Sanhedrin) in Jerusalem and various local councils were allowed to exert some leadership.

Within the Empire a good degree of political stability was

established under the competent rule of Augustus. That stability provided the Romans with an opportunity to achieve consolidation in the realms of administration and jurisdiction. The most turbulent of their subjects were the Jews because of their religious peculiarities, strong isolationism, and nationalistic aspirations. Pilate, probably the worst of the procurators during that time, committed many atrocities against the Jews and was administratively inept. Previous to the trial of Jesus, Pilate had bungled a situation to which Caesar responded positively when the Jews appealed. To the Jews it was a time of uneasiness, but in the Empire at large, peace—*Pax Romana*—reigned. The Roman Empire was an instrument in the hand of God.

CULTURAL CONTEXT

Alexander failed to found an enduring empire, but his conquests accomplished one of the most important things in world history. They were a major cause of the dissemination of Greek culture over the entire Eastern world. Hellenistic thought permeated the northern district of Palestine. The Qumran literature indicates that even the Jewish culture was not impervious to Hellenistic ideas, which penetrated the narrow exclusiveness of the Jews in Jesus' day. There is little doubt that many used the Greek language in addition to the Aramaic. Jesus was undoubtedly aware of Greek modes of thought.

The Romans, on finding the Greek language dominant when they conquered the East, did not attempt to eliminate it. That would have been contrary to their principle of toleration when taking control. As we have discussed at length in this chapter, the Romans were profoundly influenced by Greek culture. Greek continued to be not only the language of the educated person, but was also the language of trade, international diplomacy and, along with Latin, the language of governmental administration. It was the language of the common man and understood by almost everyone. It was therefore the language of the New Testament, a vehicle whereby the gospel could be disseminated much more rapidly. In discussing the decline of Rome Mayer asserts, "while Rome was creative in its system of government and laws, it lacked imagination in its education and in its philosophical speculations. Roman education was far more limited than that of Athens. Ultimately, Rome paid the price for being too practical. It was seduced by foreign ideologies, first by Greek philosophies, then by mystery cults."[17]

The Roman Empire, then, was united not only politically but linguistically.

"This remarkable uniformity of language is of obvious importance for the early history of Christianity. Without it, the Christian mission would have encountered serious difficulties. With every extension of the field new languages would have had to be learned. As it was, the Roman world formed in some sort one community. A religion which arose in one part could spread rapidly to the whole."[18]

RELIGION—GOD AND GODS

The Greco-Roman world was in need of Jesus Christ. Paul presents an awesome picture of the spiritual needs of the people in Romans 1. In spite of the superb achievements of the philosophical Greeks and the pragmatic Romans the sinfulness of them and us is obvious. The impact of Greece is felt once again in the area of religion.

As non-Greek religions continued to be practiced in the Empire, some of them became Hellenized. The religion of Greece from the time of Homer could be described as an artistic polytheism. Unlike the sacerdotal elements of the Hebrews and the Persians, the Greek religion reflected the nation's unique philosophical bent. With the Greeks there was no Semitic fear, no Egyptian awe, no bowing.

> The gods were conceived of as living in a lofty region of light and gladness. They had passions like men, they engaged in strife and deceit. Greek religion, in its characteristic form, was aesthetic rather than moral; it was based upon the sense of beauty rather than upon the conscience. Its characteristics appear most clearly in the beautiful images of the gods—those unequalled masterpieces which are the wonder and delight of the civilized world. Beauty of form, but no satisfaction for the deepest needs of the soul.[19]

The "mysteries" of Greek religion go beyond the Olympian gods. They indicate a desire, however vague and imperfect, for liberation from this present evil world. But the solutions presented are unsatisfying and sometimes depraved. During the second century there was a growing number of mystery religions in the western half of the Empire that speak of the religious need of that period. The gods of Olympus were inadequate. For instance, the misdeeds of Zeus were excused and interpreted so as not to admit their full-scale immorality. Philosophers sought one common principle that would explain the facts of the world. They were discontented with the gods, and their speculation was open to monotheism.

The Romans worshiped an impersonal force that permeated nature and had its base in agriculture. They believed they had to appease the gods by their work and sacrifices to the images of those gods. During the Roman Republic (509 B.C.-27 B.C.) they adopted Greek myths and identified their own gods with the Greek gods. Jupiter (Greek god Zeus) was their chief god, and a large temple was erected in his behalf. Juno (Greek, Hera), Neptune (Greek, Poseidon), and Mercury (Greek, Hermes) were other well-known gods. They put a significant stress on the prediction of future events and the interpretation of past occurrences. No military campaigns would be initiated until the will of the gods was discovered by some act of divination.

The apostle Paul appealed to the religious nature and milieu of the people of Athens as he preached (Acts 17). He was aware of the vague monotheism of the poets ("unknown god," 17:23) and related to the needs of the people. God, in His wisdom and providence, had shaped the course of history so that the message of His Son Jesus Christ would be heard and understood in a responsive and receptive cultural setting.

NEW TESTAMENT PRINCIPLES FOR EDUCATION

Recent scholarship in the field of history has been in a state of flux. A generation ago historians wrote synthetic works that pulled many strands together into one fabric. Interpretive and descriptive histories wove remarkable intellectual tapestries. In the judgment of Bernard Bailyn, current historians have become specialists, and their writings are narrow with a disconnected effect that has majored in *how* with an inadequate emphasis on *why.*[20] The traditional justification for the study of history has been that in order to know where we are, we must know where we have been. In understanding history, then, we should look for personages and movements that have shaped the present. To Christians and non-Christians, Jesus Christ is the nonpareil hinge of history. He is the axis on which the spokes of history revolve. Jesus Christ is interwoven into the fabric of the Old and New Testaments. For Christians He is not only the Messiah, the Savior of those who place their trust in Him, but also the touchstone of history. His words and actions give us a philosophy of life and mission.

Although the New Testament was not written as an educational treatise, it is indeed "a mine of educational truth which is of the finest quality and of inestimable value."[21] The one constant in the field of education is that of change, and the Scriptures constitute the one educational handbook that will not change or go out of style. Its principles are eternal, whereas books in educational psychology and even foundations of education are abruptly and carelessly discarded. The New Testament records the ministry of the Master and the young church that emerged in the middle half of the first century A.D. A book remains to be written that examines the educational philosophy of the Savior in light of recent developments in the fields of education, educational psychology, and sociology of education.[22]

Because of the relative size of this section of the chapter only a few basic, briefly stated principles will be given regarding the educational ministries of our Lord, the apostle Paul, and the early church.

PURPOSES AND OBJECTIVES

The church must be scrupulously precise in determining its purposes and objectives, which of necessity must emerge from the Scriptures. Hayes cautions,

> evangelical Christian education is proceeding into the late summer of the twentieth century without clearly defined statements of purpose. Local church educational endeavors, at best, tend to revolve around a simplistic set of objectives which utterly fail to denote theological intent and educational methodology. Devoid of comprehensive statements of educational objectives, evangelical church education is in danger of being driven further and further into frantic activism.[23]

Gaebelein provides a general answer to that dilemma: "Scripture makes plain that the church is to be a worshipping body, committed to 'show forth the praises of him who hath called (it) out of darkness into his marvelous light;' that it is to proclaim the saving Gospel of Jesus Christ to all the world; and that it is to obey all the teaching of Jesus Christ, its great head and Lord."[24]

The means for attaining those goals are the access we have to God through the mediatorial work of Christ, the Holy Spirit as the source of our power (John 14, 16), and the Scriptures as the basis of our instruction (2 Timothy 3:16-17).

The church is responsible for fostering a climate for worship

(Ephesians 1:12, 14; 3:21; 5:19-20), providing a setting for fellowship (John 13:34-35; Galatians 6:2; 1 Thessalonians 2:7-12; 1 John 1:3), developing a concern for and involvement in evangelism (Matthew 28:19-20; Acts 1:8), and constructing formal and informal programs of instruction (Matthew 28:19-20; Ephesians 4:11-16; 1 Timothy 4:11-16). The New Testament has a strong emphasis on Christians employing their spiritual gifts and enlarging and enhancing the body of Christ by the utilization of those gifts (Romans 12:5-6; 1 Corinthians 12:7; Ephesians 4:7; 1 Peter 4:10). Those purposes are summarized in Acts 2:41-47 and Ephesians 4:11-16.

JESUS AS EDUCATOR AND LEADER

A perennial problem of secular educationists writing on the subject of Jesus as a teacher and educator is a failure to discern who Jesus was. He was more than one of the three greatest teachers who ever lived (joining Socrates and Gautama Buddha, in the opinion of Wilds and Lottich).[25] He should be acknowledged as the incarnate Son of God, Master, Lord, God (John 1:1-18; 3:2; 8:48-59). His unique perspective as very God enabled Him to understand people in a different dimension. When He responded to a person's need He could readily move beyond the felt need to what that individual needed in actuality (Matthew 9:16-22; Luke 11:1; John 2:24).

Jesus Christ was maladjusted to the educational status quo of His day. Initially, it was fashionable and intellectually stimulating to hear Christ speak because of His wisdom and winsome words. But He would not cater to popular taste, and He spoke authoritatively rather than accommodatingly to society's whims. That style of teaching was antithetical to that of the scribes, who lacked authority (Matthew 7:29). To the question of whether the approach of Jesus is relevant for today, Guthrie suggests,

> To assume that it is, one must show that the modern outlook is identical with that of the first century. The crux of the matter lies in the attitude toward authority. In Jesus' time on earth, children learned to respect the authority of their elders, and pupils the authority of their teachers. In the modern age, when authority has been so widely overthrown, educators are faced with a different problem. Yet it cannot for this reason be assumed that the approach of Jesus is obsolete. The modern rejection of authority is due to a lack of respect for its source, rather than a rejection of authority itself. In any age and among all peoples, there has al-

ways been a readiness to heed those whose stature is sufficient to command respect. Twentieth-century man, with all his technological achievements, is not different in his moral needs from first-century man. The methods of Jesus are not irrelevant. In this respect He is unique among those who have sought to educate people in the religious sphere. The superlative greatness of Jesus among all others is the timelessness of His approach. If it was true in the first century, as His contemporaries acknowledged, that no one taught as authoritatively as He, it is no less true today. Truth carries its own authority.[26]

It seems quite clear that the ministry of the Master had a much greater teaching than preaching thrust to it. Such an assertion cannot be made solely on the basis of the greater number of times Christ was addressed by the terms *teacher* or *teaching* as over against the words *preach* or *preaching,* which also described His style of ministry. But only a cursory reading of the gospels indicates that much of Jesus' recorded ministry was in a teaching context. The apostle Paul's work was heavily of a teaching character as well. It is readily apparent that education was of paramount importance in the New Testament.

Worley has spoken cogently to the educational community within the church in regard to our tendency to attempt to analyze too precisely the educational role regarding teaching and preaching.

> Our practice today of separating preaching and teaching into distinct functions with distinct officers for each function cannot be justified from early church practices. The larger purpose of preaching-teaching in the early church overshadowed and made any distinctions that did exist subservient to that purpose.
>
> This larger purpose was the communication of the postresurrection faith of the church. . . . Among church educators there is confusion about the purpose and direction of church education. Much of this confusion is related to the fact that we look for simple, neat distinctions between preaching and teaching a single content of teaching and a single educational theory and method. This study has shown that no simple distinctions were made between preaching and teaching. There was no single content or theological interest except the desire of teacher-preachers to communicate their postresurrection faith. There were multiple theories and methods at work.[27]

Jesus was the very source of truth (John 14:6). He taught courageously and forthrightly, and on occasion His words bit and stung. Whereas He was moved with compassion and deeply sensitive to the needs of people, Jesus would not compromise the truth (Matthew 9:36; 15:1-20; John 8:3-11; 11:35). The uniqueness of Christ as the God-man is intimately tied in with this style of teaching. He is the only teacher who set a high standard of ethics and perfectly fulfilled it. Christ was the embodiment of what He taught. Yet the sinless one washed the disciples' feet with tenderness and abject humility (John 13:1-17).

When the apostle Paul calls the Thessalonians to imitate and follow his pattern as a fellow believer it is from a different base of authority. Paul willingly states his sinfulness, but he was aware that his modeling behavior was of a quality worthy of emulation (Romans 7; 1 Thessalonians 1:6-7; 2 Thessalonians 3:7, 9). There is a spirit of Paul's servanthood in leadership that should characterize our ministries of education. This crucial concept must not be lost in the midst of the potpourri of educational ideas.

The mother of James and John had high maternal expectations. She wanted places of recognition for her sons. When the other ten disciples heard of her play for power they were indignant, and Christ seized that unique teachable moment. Jesus contrasted the leadership style and method of secular leaders with the leadership style and method He desired in His Body, the church. "You know that the rulers of the Gentiles lord it over them, and their great men exercise authority over them. It is not so among you, but whoever wishes to become great among you shall be your servant, and whoever wishes to be first among you shall be your slave; just as the Son of Man did not come to be served, but to serve, and to give His life as a ransom for many" (Matthew 20:25-28).

Models conflict because secular leaders exercise authority over others, whereas Christian leaders are not *over* but *among*. The servant-leader is to expend his life on behalf of others. His primary concern and ministry is the building up of the Body of Christ. That does not imply that Christian leaders are a group of weak people who neither lead nor assert authority. The godly leader is to set an example by his life, and the quality of that model will draw others to him. Christian leadership is not to be grasped but rather given. Spirit-filled leaders will be recognized by the people of God for what they are, and the church will respond by seeking the leadership of such individuals.

The specific task of leaders is to serve fellow Christians by equipping the saints to do the work of the ministry (Ephesians

4:12). Through the educational processes of identification and modeling Christians will become more like their leaders, and therefore like Jesus Christ (Luke 6:40; 1 Thessalonians 1:5-8; 2:7-12; 2 Thessalonians 3:7, 9). Lawrence O. Richards has well said that "spiritual leaders who minister in this way will have no need to worry about their 'authority.' God will open hearts in the Body to respond to them (cf. 1 Peter 5:5)."[28] Again, this does not imply that a leader in the church is to capitulate to every voice heard within the body. Rather, he is called to give leadership that is sensitive to the people and their needs, and his method is that of service. Power politics and political maneuvering are antithetical to servant leadership.

The Master taught profoundly by His life and example. He knew the power of modeling the truth and that inevitably His disciples would become like Himself. Lee Magness has given an interesting purpose statement of Jesus' teaching:

> One statement of Jesus, almost an understatement, may provide the clearest insight into the purposeful way Jesus taught and the objective he had in mind: 'A learner is not superior to the teacher nor is a slave superior to his master. It is sufficient for the learner to become like his teacher, and the slave like his master' (Mt. 10:24-25, par.). Learning was the means of relating to Jesus, but the goal was broader than the assimilation of facts, the adoption of a body of tradition, or even identification with a philosophical position. For the disciples, learning was living, living with and like Jesus. Perhaps, we should interpret more literally: learning was becoming, being like Jesus. Education in Christ was not even merely the mimicry of Jesus' habits; it was growth into a state of being which was Christ-like.[29]

Christ taught from an educational strategy that included a ministry to the masses of people, the seventy, the twelve disciples (Mark 3:13-15), and also to Peter, James, and John (e.g., Mark 14:33; Luke 9:28). His peripatetic teaching of the twelve constituted the greatest educational situation ever to exist. Christ recognized that the ministry He modeled with the small group and the large group would be perpetuated by the church. However, church history is replete with instances and even eras when His methodology was forgotten or prostituted. Currently, parts of the church are coming back to biblical principles for doing the work of the ministry.

The Savior and Paul utilized the principle of involvement and participation with great skill. After demonstrating how to do the ministry with people and delivering the cognitive data necessary to feel comfortable with the content to be preached, Christ sent out the twelve (Mark 6:7-13, 30-34). He was precise and lucid in His instructions to them. Christ was careful, too, to debrief them and hear their reports of what had taken place. Christ gave them verbal instruction, demonstrated exactly what was to be done, presented them with an opportunity in which to report, and finally, evaluated the ministries. That training resulted in the disciples' being equipped to make strides toward the carrying out of the Great Commission of evangelism and edification.

The traveling commune that joined Paul was given the same type of teaching and ministry opportunities that Christ offered. No one traveled with Paul on a permanent basis, but all were provided an adequate set of time frames to observe Paul's work and be taught theological constructs individually and collectively. The colleagues of Jesus and Paul were given a type of in-service training. The apostles of Jesus learned the meaning of God's initiative of love, not from a textbook, but by accompanying Him among people. When Paul taught that the gospel was to eliminate the ancient divisions between Jew and Gentile, it was not just words. Paul traveled with a Gentile named Titus so that the churches could see the first example of a Gentile-Jewish community in action.

The Savior often ministered to the multitudes, but a particularly dynamic factor in His teaching effectiveness and that of the early church was the small group. Jesus called a limited number of disciples. His approach was not toward mass production but toward the building of a mature, solidly constructed group of disciples (Colossians 1:28-29). That type of maturity demands intense exposure and close contact. Neither Jesus nor Paul shied away from letting people be close to them, for they knew that community life is the best environment for learning. In this atmosphere the essential elements for growth, care, mutual responsibility, and accountability are most effective. Community enhances authentic Christian teaching. The church will inevitably produce after its kind. And that is an awesome prospect.

The community aspect of Jesus' mode of teaching brings another strategy to the fore. Rabbinic teaching in Jesus' day was stuffy, rigid, and based on rote exercises. To repeat the rabbis' words without error resulted in the highest praise. When we read the gospels, as if for the first time, we are struck with the

freshness and creativity of Jesus' words. We do not find Him
drilling the disciples on His material. Although there are powerful lectures in the gospels that may have been given on a number
of occasions (e.g., Matthew 5-7), the virility and spontaneity of
His speech is amazing. Almost every page vibrates with vivid
metaphors, similes, and hyperbole. Along the road, in a home,
with a little group in a boat are the prosaic locations of His
encounters with people having all kinds of needs and problems.
Sometimes His teaching came in response to questions. Christ
delighted in dialogue. For Him, every event and conversation
was an important learning situation. That creativity was something one could not teach by example alone. It was caught by the
contagion of being His companion. "The Good News was to
travel from person to person through enthusiastic live communication."[30] As they waited and reflected in the upper room after
His crucifixion, how quickly His actions and words must have
come to mind because of the vitality of His words.

When Christ was in the upper room with the disciples He
indicated that He would be leaving them. But Christ's departure
was to hail the arrival of the Holy Spirit in a new dimension of
ministry to them. Pentecost signaled the birth of the church and
the coming of the Spirit to reside in all believers. The Holy Spirit
came as the divine Counselor and Teacher who led the believers
into all truth and reminded them of what Christ had said to them
(John 14, 16). So although His words were readily remembered
because of their spontaneity and profundity, the Holy Spirit
came to assist them in the interpretation and memory process.
The Spirit came to teach and to present a spiritual gift or gifts to
every believer in Jesus Christ.

The pastor-teachers are responsible from the human dimension to equip Christians to do the work of the ministry (Ephesians 4:11-16). Through the equipping process, those and other
leaders whose primary task is education (Romans 12:6-8; 1 Corinthians 12:4-10, 27-31; 1 Timothy 3:13; Titus 1:7-9) are to work
with the Holy Spirit in producing Christians who are spiritual
(1 Corinthians 2:14-16), mature (Ephesians 4:13), loving
(1 Thessalonians 3:12; 1 Timothy 1:5), and reproductive
(Matthew 28:19-20; 2 Timothy 2:2).

Christians should be encouraged to exercise their spiritual
gifts. Lawrence Richards lists four principles to be considered in
regard to the Body of Christ exercising its gifts:

1. An awareness of the living presence of the Holy Spirit and our relationship to Him is the basic UNDERSTANDING the body needs to move toward the exercise of its giftedness.
2. Learning to sense the Spirit's leading and to respond obediently to His voice is the basic TRAINING the body needs to move toward the exercise of its giftedness.
3. Catching a vision of the many purposes God intends to accomplish through the living church is the basic ORIENTATION TO MINISTRY that the body needs to move toward the exercise of its giftedness.
4. Realizing that God the Spirit ministers to others through us as we come to know them and sense a call to serve them is the basic RELATIONAL COMMITMENT that the body needs to move toward the exercise of its giftedness.[31]

As those ideas become part of the experience of the members of Christ's Body, believers will increasingly desire to serve others, and the Spirit will be allowed to guide them into personal ministries in which those gifts will function and develop.

Jesus Christ was the greatest teacher. His mission was primarily that of presenting Himself as the Son of God who came to earth to die to bring about the possibility of our justification by faith. He desired that our attitudes and conduct would conform to His Father's will. Christ presented His message by teaching far more than He did by preaching. In His teaching the individual was given central priority.

> He stressed the personal touch, not mass following. Each soul stood alone, had eternal value, and was worthy of the teacher's supreme attention. Each person had to have specific instruction in the truth of God. Over and over He talked with individuals, drawing out the best in them, working on their conscience, teaching them the requirements of God, and showing them how to become children of God. Even when He talked to a group, it seemed as if He directed His teaching first to one, then to another, with a view to meeting the needs of individuals. Much of what is recorded of His teachings would not be in the Gospels had He not given primary attention to the individual.[32]

Christ deftly discerned where the person was and established contact. Because of who He was and His awareness of where they were, they responded eagerly to Him. His manner was gracious, and His content was presented attractively. Christ was concerned with imparting information, but His major thrust was meeting the needs of people.

The apostle Paul used a variety of strategies as well. William Barclay states that "in his approach Paul had no set scheme and formula; his approach was completely flexible. He began where his audience was."[33] When Paul preached he declared the gospel and gave a careful and concise explanation and defense of it. And argumentation and debate were part of his strategy at Damascus, Athens, Corinth, and Ephesus. But he did not engage in argument for argument's sake. He began at the point of common agreement and omitted arguments that would needlessly cause offense and thereby "exhibited his pastoral principle of being 'all things to all men.' Here is legitimate flexibility of approach and elasticity of attitude that should characterize every Christian pastor, teacher, missionary, scholar and statesman."[34]

The discussion of New Testament principles of education was predicated on the premise that those principles were of eternal value and would not be rendered obsolete. As those principles are of a permanent quality, so are the moral needs of twentieth-century people when compared with those of people in the first century. The methods of Jesus are not irrelevant. "In this respect He is unique among those who have sought to educate people in the religious sphere. The superlative greatness of Jesus among all others is the timelessness of His approach."[35]

The Scriptures are a seedbed of enduring educational principles from which we have offered only a superficial sampling. However, it is to be noted that it is the Word of God, the written and the living Word (Christ), that changes people's lives. When an individual places his faith and trust in Jesus Christ as Savior and Lord he becomes a new creation (2 Corinthians 5:17). When a Christian studies Holy Scripture individually and/or in a group setting the power of that book becomes effective. "All Scripture is inspired by God and profitable for teaching, for reproof, for correction, for training in righteousness; that the man of God may be adequate, equipped for every good work" (2 Timothy 3:16-17). "The word of God is living and active and sharper than any two-edged sword, and piercing as far as the division of soul and spirit, of both joints and marrow, and able to judge the thoughts and intentions of the heart" (Hebrews 4:12).

NOTES

1. Moses Hadas, *Hellenistic Culture: Fusion and Diffusion* (New York: Columbia U., 1959), p. 59. Cited in R. Freeman Butts, *The Education of the West* (New York: McGraw-Hill, 1973), p. 103.

2. Butts, p. 103. Francis Henry Sandback denotes "Hellenistic" as that period of Greek history extending from the conquests of Alexander (323 B.C.) to the Roman takeover of the kingdoms that Alexander's successors established, a process virtually completed by the subjugation of Cleopatra's Egypt (30 B.C.). See Paul Edwards, The Encyclopedia of Philosophy, 4 vols. (New York: Free Press, 1973), 3:469.

3. H. I. Marrou, A History of Education in Antiquity (New York: Sheed and Ward, 1956), p. 232.

4. Ibid.

5. John T. Townsend in Stephen Benko and John J. O'Rourke, eds., The Catacombs and the Colosseum (Valley Forge, Pa.: Judson, 1971), p. 144. Townsend claims that both boys and girls attended the primary-elementary schools, but he gives no date.

6. Butts, p. 117.

7. Marrou, p. 336.

8. Butts, p. 119.

9. Gerald L. Gutek, A History of the Western Educational Experience (New York: Random House, 1971), pp. 54-55.

10. Quintilian Institutio Oratoria 1. 12. 20.

11. Quintilian 1. 1. 20.

12. William Barclay, Educational Ideals in the Ancient World (Grand Rapids: Baker, 1974), pp. 165-66.

13. Gutek, p. 60.

14. Butts, pp. 122, 127.

15. S. S. Laurie, Historical Survey of Pre-Christian Education (St. Clair Shores, Mich.: Scholarly Press, 1970). This was originally published in 1907 and was Laurie's summary of a passage written in Latin by Quintilian.

16. J. Gresham Machen, The New Testament: An Introduction to Its Literature and History (Carlisle, Pa.: Banner of Truth, 1976), p. 20.

17. Frederick Mayer, A History of Educational Thought, 2d ed. (Columbus, Ohio: Merrill, 1966), p. 121.

18. Machen, p. 29.

19. Ibid.

20. Karen J. Winkler, "Wanted: A History That Pulls Things Together," The Chronicle of Higher Education 20, no. 19 (7 July 1980): 3.

21. Harry Angier Hoffner, Jr., "The Teacher-Pupil Relationship in Pauline Pedagogy" (Master's thesis, Dallas Theological Seminary, 1960), p. 10.

22. One reason no one has attempted this is that the aforementioned fields are constantly in a state of flux so that a book written from a contemporary perspective would be out of date rather soon. Among the worthy recent contributions on Christ's teaching methods and ministry are Clifford A. Wilson, Jesus the Master Teacher (Grand Rapids: Baker, 1974); Joseph A. Grassi, Jesus As Teacher: A New Testament Guide to Learning the Way (Winona, Minn.: St. Mary's, 1978); and Carl W. Wilson, With Christ in the School of Disciple-Building (Grand Rapids: Zondervan, 1976). Lawrence O. Richards's A Theology of Christian Education (Grand Rapids: Zondervan, 1975) is one of the best evangelical treatments of Christian education. But it does not purport to be exhaustive on the teaching ministry of Jesus. The seminal book by Lois E. LeBar, Education That Is Christian, rev. ed. (Old Tappan, N.J.: Revell, 1981), is a first-quality work on the methods of the Master.

23. Edward L. Hayes, "Reconstruction in Christian Education—A Problem of Purpose," Action, September 1966, p. 11.

24. Frank E. Gaebelein, A Varied Harvest (Grand Rapids: Eerdmans, 1967), p. 160.

25. Elmer H. Wilds and Kenneth V. Lottich, The Foundations of Modern Education, 3d ed. (New York: Holt, Rinehart, and Winston, 1961), p. 103.

26. Donald Guthrie, "Jesus," in Elmer L. Towns, ed., A History of Religious Educators (Grand Rapids: Baker, 1975), p. 36.

27. Robert C. Worley, *Preaching and Teaching in the Earliest Church* (Philadelphia: Westminster, 1967), pp. 135, 142. See also Klaus Wegenast, "Teach," in Colin Brown, ed., *New International Dictionary of New Testament Theology*, 3 vols. (Grand Rapids: Zondervan, 1978), 3:7640.

28. Lawrence O. Richards, *A Theology of Christian Education* (Grand Rapids: Zondervan, 1975), pp. 132-35; and Lawrence O. Richards and Clyde Hoeltdke, *A Theology of Church Leadership* (Grand Rapids: Zondervan, 1980), pp. 103-10.

29. Lee Magness, "Teaching and Learning in the Gospels: The Biblical Basis of Christian Education," *Religious Education* 70, no. 6 (November-December 1975): 629-35.

30. Grassi, *Jesus As Teacher*, p. 61.

31. Richards and Hoeldtke, p. 260.

32. C. B. Eavey, *History of Christian Education* (Chicago: Moody, 1964), pp. 80-81.

33. William Barclay, "A Comparison of Paul's Missionary Preaching and Preaching to the Church," in W. W. Gasque and R. P. Martin, eds., *Apostolic History and the Gospel* (Grand Rapids: Eerdmans, 1970), pp. 165-70.

34. Richard N. Longenecker, "Paul," in Towns, p. 51.

35. Guthrie, in Towns, p. 37.

4

Christian Education
in the Early Church

The church Fathers and the early Christian apologists took a deep and practical interest in education. Christ had commanded the church to teach and spread the good news. The followers of Jesus were to go, make disciples of all nations, baptize, and teach (Matthew 28:19-20). Making disciples was the central imperative among going, baptizing, and teaching, which were descriptive of what is involved in the making of disciples. The Master was explicit in stating that believers were to carry out that mission under the direction and empowering of the Holy Spirit. They did so with such enthusiasm and abandon that many of them lost their lives for the faith. The apostle Peter had warned them not to put down their stakes too deeply; to remember that they were to live as aliens and strangers in this world (1 Peter 1:17; 2:11).

However it should also be recognized that breaking the umbilical cord of Judaism was a colossal struggle. After a brief but intense encounter, the gospel and its freedom-producing teaching (John 8:32) spread, irrespective of race or rank.

> Some members of the new Christian communities were aristocrats, people of wealth and culture, in high positions, even in the imperial household. On the other hand, many were poor, coming from the ranks of slavery or from the soldiery of the Roman army. Women took a leading part, as well as men. For the Gospel was universal; not for men as against women, not for Jew as against Gentile, neither for wealthy nor poor as such, but for persons, whoever and wherever they might be. . . . The new communities of Christians were scenes of tremendous spiritual experiences. Men and women, stripped bare of accidental trappings such as color, race, class, possessions, and prestige, stood open to the inrush of powers which hitherto they and their kind had never known. The primitive church, say until about A.D. 125, was in the first flush of the Christian experiments with liberty, and two of their first dis-

coveries were this equality of which we just spoke, and this new sense of power. The earliest New Testament documents abound with echoes of the power and manner of its coming. The Gospel had come 'in power and in the Holy Spirit.'[1]

Liberty in Jesus Christ was and is an exhilarating experience. The early Christian society was intensely dynamic, and the Old Testament was of only partial value as a manual of operation. Hundreds of questions arose almost overnight. How was the community of Christians to live? Should communal living be the pattern? What organizational structures were to be accepted? What relationship should they have in the synagogue? With Christ's return being imminent, was it wise to marry? Did Christian liberty mean they were free from the laws of the Sabbath and the tithe?

Wrestling with those questions and many others formed much of the body of the New Testament epistles and other early Christian writings. When new Christians in the first century faced those issues with no precedents to guide them, the teaching and preaching in the early church took on new perspective and importance. Excesses of all descriptions arose in the congregations. But those intemperate actions were not unique to their time alone. The epistles are timeless in their relevance for the contemporary church.

The apostles of Christ played a very strategic role in that problematic but dynamic period. Paul, the brilliant theologian prepared by God in such a unique manner, was of consummate significance to the infant church. His singleness and availability for travel, his understanding of the Old Testament through the instruction of the gifted Gamaliel, his total dedication to Jesus Christ, and the revelatory work of the Spirit in his own experience aptly fitted Paul for his role of teacher-theologian in the church.

The teaching of the other apostles gave particular theological stability and guidance to the infant church, serving as a necessary complement to the evangelization process carried on by preaching and personal witness. But Worley should be heeded once again when we think of the relationship of teaching to preaching. In critiquing C. H. Dodd's theory of preaching as an exclusive primitive missionary activity, Worley suggests that a radical separation between teaching and preaching cannot be justified from the practices of the earliest church.

Early church leaders and intertestamental Jews before them used the words 'preaching' and 'teaching' interchangeably to refer to a large variety of activities, one of which was missionary proselytizing. Both teaching and preaching activities as occurred in synagogues, temples, homes, vineyards, streets, on mountains, and by the lakeside. Study of word usage of preaching and teaching has shown that a substantive case can be made for understanding teaching as a missionary activity and as a more inclusive word that encompasses the meaning of preaching within its general meaning. Significant distinctions in the content of preaching and teaching were not found.[2]

With the contemporary church's penchant for teaching content it must not permit evangelism to become of secondary significance. The young church did not lose that delicate balance that today seems so difficult to achieve.

It is the element of evangelizing, which is most readily and frequently omitted in the separation of preaching and teaching. It is this activity which ought to be central to the activity of teaching-preaching in our culture. . . .

Teacher-preachers of the early church were not concerned primarily with educating a person in the facts of the faith. Something more was at stake than the communication of the sayings of Jesus, or the stories about Jesus. Teaching-preaching was the way of communicating Christianity to believers and unbelievers in different contexts through the interpretation of tradition, and the interpretation of the work, person and sayings of Jesus, using a variety of methods, ideas and practices from different sources to the end that those heard would receive life . . . in Christ, in the postresurrection Christian community.[3]

EDUCATION AND THE APOSTLES

First-century teaching occurred in two places: the Christian meeting and the Christian home. The believers gathered in three kinds of meetings. The first of those was for the teaching of Scripture for the purpose of edification. Edification denotes the elements of worship, instruction, and fellowship. Prayer, hymns, the reading of apostolic letters, teaching, and, on occasion, prophetic revelations, constituted those gatherings.

A second kind of meeting was the common meal or love feast, which was followed by the Lord's Supper. The meal was an expression of fellowship and concern for one another. Worship was the major thrust of the Lord's Supper since the breaking of bread in holy communion was the climax of congregational worship.

Though solemnity characterized the Lord's Table, it was an occasion for joyful celebration and thanksgiving, and it was admirably suited for teaching since the apostles understood worship in teaching terms, not aesthetic terms. A third type of meeting took place when the Christian community had business to transact. Church discipline, which was not incidental to the strength and purity of the fellowship, was also a part of the business session.

The Christian family was the second of the two foci in which teaching received a place of prominence. The first-century Christian family was richly influenced by Old Testament teachings. We must dip back briefly into the centuries before Christ to sense the *Sitz im Leben* (contextual situation).

No nation has ever set the child at center stage as did the Jews. The child was the most important person in the community. Rabbi Judah the Holy said: "The world exists only by the breath of school children."[4] The Jew was sure that of all people the child was dearest to God. Therefore education was high on the list of their priorities. Josephus wrote: "Our ground is good, and we work it to the utmost, but our chief ambition is for the education of our children."[5] Jewish education was all-encompassing religious education. The Scriptures were the only textbook, all primary education was preparation for reading the Book, and all higher education was concerned with the reading and study of the law.

But centuries before and during the advent of the Messiah the most crucial concept of Jewish education was this: the home is the absolute center of education. Schools were important to the Jews, but the home was without parallel in its cruciality. Isidore Epstein writes: "In no other religion has the duty of the parents to instruct their children been more stressed than in Judaism." In his judgment, the school remains "an auxiliary home."[6] So then, the responsibility of educating the child was laid squarely on the shoulders of the parents when there were schools as well as before they came into being (Deuteronomy 4:9; 6:7, 20; 11:19; Proverbs 1:8; 6:20). There was no shortage of schools, but that did not absolve the parents of their responsibility to rear their children to be servants of God.

Early Christian education developed in a world in which the cultural forms were predominantly Hellenic and the political organization was Roman. With the Old Testament exhortations regarding child training ringing in their ears, their educational task was twofold: (1) to provide instruction that would initiate their children and converts in Christian doctrine, Weltanschauung, and way of life; and (2) to help them assess and synthesize their Christian life with the best of the secular culture embodied in the rhetorical and philosophical studies of the pagan schools.[7]

The second part of the task was complicated because the pagan schools were normally the only ones available to urban Christian families. That is one of the reasons the words of Peter regarding their "strangers" status in a pagan culture were particularly poignant. The writer of Hebrews reminded his readers that Abraham was an "alien . . . in a foreign country" (11:9-10). Educationally and religiously, that was the plight of the Christians.

There is another dimension to this discussion. Paul speaks in 1 Thessalonians 4:11-18 and 1 Corinthians 7:29-32 regarding the transitoriness of life and the imminency of the coming of Christ. The Thessalonians had abandoned the ordinary activities of life, and Paul chastened them for their "other world" attitude. He instructed them to get back to work without discounting the continuing possibility of the Lord's return.

The early Christians did not usually withdraw from the world. Christians were found in every walk of life, but there was a reticence to get involved in public life and accept public office. Although they did not withdraw from society they did not feel themselves to be fully members of it. Only infrequently did one of them become involved in public administration. That attitude acutely affected their view of the education that secular society offered.

EDUCATION AND THE CHURCH FATHERS

Unfortunately, and as a defensive mechanism, there developed a pride in this deliberate anti-intellectualism. Unwillingly, Origen had to admit Celsus's charge that Christians consisted of the "uninstructed, the servile and the ignorant."[8] Justin Martyr claimed that the deepest things can be learned from the unlettered, who are wise and trust God.[9] Tatian, who detested Greek culture, insisted that Christians had rejected conclusions based on human wisdom alone.[10] Irenaeus reminded the flock of God that it was not the chief priests and rulers who turned to Christ but rather the beggars, the deaf, and the blind.[11] Tertullian declared that when Plato said that the maker of the universe is not easily found, and, when found, is with difficulty explained to the people, "any Christian laborer both finds and sets forth God."[12] So, for a period of time, the Christians were perceived as humble and uneducated. They endured the criticisms of the crowd and even welcomed them. The words of Paul regarding the wisdom of the world were repeatedly quoted. Not many of them were wise by human standards, influential, or of noble birth (1 Corinthians 1:19-20, 26-29).

But that is not the full story. The fact that Christianity can be understood and appropriated by the humblest and simplest saint is part of the genius of the gospel. However, some church leaders such as Origen were not entirely pleased with the nonintellectual image of Christianity. Origen would have been happier had all men like him become philosophers in the true sense of that term. He did not have contempt for learning, nor did he take pride in ignorance. In fact, when the apologists are read critically, they show that they themselves had a substantial education in the classics they condemned.

One of the factors encouraging the growth of Christianity was the unified language and culture, at least in the cities, from Italy to India. Paul and the other early Christians were able to use Greek in the spread of the Good News. Three hundred years of peace, the *Pax Romana*, permitted freedom of travel on Roman roads and under Roman protection. Because simple and uneducated people could understand and believe the gospel it spread to all social levels. This concept also relieved the young church of depending exclusively on a professional clergy. Indeed, great impetus came to the movement through the persecution at Jerusalem that forced so many of the Christians to leave the city while the apostles remained in Jerusalem (Acts 8:2-3).

Initially, the Christians were looked on as a Jewish sect and in fact, they utilized the synagogues, both inside and outside Judea, as a primary center for evangelism. Each Christian was both minister and missionary. The early Christians were known for their strong and lucid doctrinal and ethical convictions despite the graphic and pointed denunciations by Paul in some of his epistles.

But potent and unsavory forces militated against Christianity. Paganism retained its substantial presence and hold on people. Moral corruption continued to flourish. Jesus, Paul, and Peter had been executed by the civil government, and those who joined them in death for the faith were numerous. The persecutions grew even greater in the second and third centuries A.D., but in spite of them the church grew.

While paganism and moral corruption were thriving in society outside the church, pernicious doctrinal views began to arise early in the second century inside the church. Sin and error within the fellowship have always been more to be feared than evil without. Gnosticism, Marcionism, and Arianism were some of the controversial movements that threatened the church. As the church grew, people from diverse backgrounds had to cope with a multiplicity of thought patterns, customs, and cultures. In the providence of God, unusually gifted persons became Christians and vigorously opposed those corrupting influences. Those thinkers and writers defended the faith against popular attacks and more sophisticated accusations. A brief presentation follows that highlights some of the contributions of those Fathers, apologists, and defenders of the faith. Only four have been chosen, but they are representative.

IRENAEUS (c. 140-c. 200)

Irenaeus became the bishop of Lyons in South Gaul. Polycarp of Smyrna, who claimed the apostle John as his mentor, was the teacher of Irenaeus. On at least two occasions he lived up to his name — "peacemaker" — first by pleading on behalf of the fanatical but not heretical Montanists and later by urging the need for restraint and toleration over the debate regarding the date of Easter.

Irenaeus never lost touch with his function as a missionary pastor or his responsibility as a theologian. Some have thought of him as a dull establishment figure because of his tiresome detail in refuting the Gnostics. Nevertheless, his five monumental volumes against Gnosticism and his *Proof of the Apostolic Preaching*, an instructional book describing how the Christian faith fulfilled the Old Testament, were very important doctrinal contributions. He perceived that the gospel and human ideas of any age were incompatible and that the divine revelation was not to be accommodated or compromised. As a pastor and theologian he knew that the facts of the faith had to be safeguarded, and he therefore laid great stress on the historical basis of the New Testament documents. He was committed to the ministry of teaching as the instrument for building the church.

Bromiley judges that Irenaeus might credibly be called the first theologian of stature in the postapostolic church.

> He packs more food for thought in many of his brief chapters than later writers do in the much lengthier chapters of their time. Even

though one might not accept what he says or like the way he says it, he leaves us in no doubt that his theme is in fact that which has to be pondered and expounded. . . . He wins through to an exciting theological construction which has stimulated thinkers of status across the centuries and the church.[13]

JUSTIN MARTYR (c. 100-165)

As a young man, Justin searched for the truth in philosophy. In his *Dialogue With Trypho* he outlines his spiritual pilgrimage and includes his unique philosophical background. Before becoming a Christian, philosophy was the greatest of his possessions, and philosophers were the true holy men to him. After thorough dialogue with a Stoic, then someone he identifies as a Peripatetic, then a Pythagorean, and finally a Platonist, he felt he was getting nearer to the truth. At least the Platonist spoke of the vision of God. But an elderly Christian undermined his Platonism by showing Justin that Christ was spoken of in the Old Testament. Through his conversion at about thirty years of age he felt that in Christ he had come to a more perfect philosophy.

Although this rich background provided him with tools, techniques, and arguments, he was constantly tempted to "philosophize the gospel or at least put it in the dangerous framework of philosophical understanding and presentation."[14]

Justin's philosophy was eclectic, not in the sense of seeking to reconcile everything, but in taking the biblical revelation as the criterion of truth and welcoming all philosophy congruent with it. He did not adopt a deliberate theological strategem of accommodating his message to his hearers, but his missionary zeal tended to outrun his theological discretion.[15] For instance, he attempted to show that Plato had learned from Moses the mystery of the Trinity, and that pagan parallels of biblical truth can be explained as devilish imitations.

The writings of Justin are powerful and ardent. They appeal to reason but bear the stamp of the ominous threat of persecution. His *First Apology* was addressed to the emperor. It attempted to clarify the doctrinal claims and ethics of Christianity.[16] No one can accuse him of diluting the gospel. He taught and preached it with enthusiasm and employed the style of presentation with which he was most familiar. His teaching provides excellent examples of the way early Christians interpreted the Bible. We are not told much about the catechetical school in Rome at which he taught. He must have been a compelling instructor.

Justin was the chief apologist of the early church. He was in the bloom of his ministry when he was martyred in Rome about 165.

TERTULLIAN (c. 160-c. 220)

As passionately as Justin Martyr defended utilizing philosophy in theological discussion, so Tertullian vehemently opposed it. Only Tatian was more outspokenly critical of philosophy. Here is his manner of stating the cleavage:

> What likeness is there between the philosopher and the Christian, the disciple of Greece and the disciple of heaven, the trader in reputation and the trader in salvation, the doer of words and the worker of deeds, the builder up and the destroyer of things, the friend and the enemy of error, the corrupter and the restorer and exponent of truth, its thief and its guardian?[17]

Tertullian continues his denunciation of philosophy with this famous paragraph:

> What indeed has Athens to do with Jerusalem? What concord is there between the Academy and the Church? What between heretics and Christians? . . . Away with all the attempts to produce a mottled Christianity of Stoic, Platonic and dialectic composition! We want no curious disputation after possessing Jesus Christ, no inquisition after enjoying the gospel! With our faith we desire no further belief![18]

Quintus Septimus Florens Tertullian was a man of extremes. Although he wrote vigorously in opposition to the philosophers, his own works demonstrated how familiar he was with their literature. He delighted in answering them with his witty and, on occasion, very profound and scholarly acumen. Barclay was speaking of men like Tertullian when he said, "It is well to remind ourselves of the at first astonishing fact that there was no better educated group of men in the Roman Empire than the Christian apologists. There is scarcely one of them who could not have had a scintillating career in secular life, and there were many of them who actually had such a career."[19] Tertullian was a lawyer of excellent reputation when he came to Christ as a mature adult. His early years were marked by immorality and adultery, which may explain his ascetic and legalistic approach to Christian conduct. Indeed, his own strict views led him to join the Montanists.

Three themes dominated Tertullian's writings: the attitude of Christianity to the Roman state and society, a defense of orthodox theology against heresy, and the moral behavior of Christians. His *Apology* argued effectively for societal toleration toward the church. He scored Marcionism with five penetrating volumes. Tertullian faced squarely the question of a theological norm in contrast to vague and rudderless Gnosticism. He identified the touchstone through apostolic tradition in the foci of "Scripture, the rule of faith, and the teaching of the apostolic churches." For him, however, it rested finally on God's revelation in Christ.

Tertullian was controversial and uncompromising. He allowed the Christian child to go to the pagan school as a matter of necessity but refused to let Christians teach in those same schools. The church did not follow his advice to ban the teaching profession. He criticized the baptism of children, adopted an extreme asceticism, and forbade Christians to attend public amusements of all kinds. He vigorously contended for greater strictness in church discipline, remarriage, and fasting. Tertullian was a literary genius, a writer of marvelous fertility and inventiveness. Due to his proclivity for "overkill" in his writings, he must be read contextually, with understanding of his use of rhetorical hyperbole. Even allowing for that, he still was guilty of a number of extreme and biblically indefensible positions. Yet his writings were abundantly used by his immediate successors and the authors of later centuries.

ORIGEN (c. 185-254)

About 179, Pantaenus, a converted Stoic philosopher, opened a catechetical school in the great cosmopolitan Egyptian city Alexandria. This second largest metropolis in the Empire had one of the finest libraries of the ancient world. From the second through the seventh centuries it was the center of Greek-speaking Christianity. Initially, it was a "school of instruction" for those converts who were preparing for Christian baptism (catechumens). Later under Clement and Origen, advanced classes were added even in secular subjects for more highly educated students. The very gifted Clement became a Christian under Pantaenus after years of searching for truth. For Clement and Origen pagan learning could never be substituted for divine truth, but it had its place and was not to be hated or despised. The learned Clement, under pressure of persecution, had to leave Alexandria. His replacement, Origen, became the greatest scholar and most prolific author of the early church.

This profound thinker was born into a Christian family in the city of Alexandria. His father was a schoolteacher who grounded Origen in the Greek liberal sciences. Each day the son had to memorize portions of Scripture. When Origen was just sixteen his father died and, as the oldest of six children, he had to assume financial support for the family. He opened a school of grammar. His immense erudition was recognized immediately and his reputation grew. At eighteen he was appointed head of the school of Alexandria. Origen gave up his secular teaching and concentrated on his primary responsibility, the sacred writings. He also engaged in lay preaching. That and accepting ordination as a priest caused him to be censured by Bishop Demetrius. He left the catechetical school and began to teach at the school of Caesarea.

The breadth of Origen's learning and openness to the best of the secular culture was effectively communicated to his students. His extremely able pupil at Caesarea, Gregory Thaumaturgus, describes the broad curriculum available to the students and gives us a feel for Origen's philosophy of education.

> No subject was forbidden to us, nothing hidden or inaccessible. We were allowed to become acquainted with every doctrine, barbarian or Greek, with things spiritual and secular, divine and human, traversing with all confidence and investigating the whole circuit of knowledge, and satisfying ourselves with full enjoyment of all pleasures of the soul.[20]

In addition to that illuminating letter from Gregory to Origen we have one from Origen to Gregory. They clarify how a great teacher understood the process of inculcating in his students the "firm conviction that the Greek concept of education *(paideia)* is not only compatible with Christian revelation, but also finds in it its true fulfillment."[21] It is an interesting picture of the ways that outstanding Christian teachers introduce their students to great concepts. Origen knew how to motivate students.

Origen lived an ascetic existence. He had a prodigious capacity for work, and later in his life he wrote on a seemingly constant schedule. He designed curricula for the ordinary student as well as the advanced. Origen employed Clement's stages of faith, knowledge, and love, and his own theory of three levels of meaning in any biblical text: the literal sense, the moral application to the soul, and the allegorical or spiritual sense. Those stages and levels became known as the Alexandrian presentation, particularly Origen's allegorical theory of biblical interpretation. His allegorical interpretation theory has plagued the church ever since. Origen quoted Scripture extensively yet embarked on speculations for which only minimal support was available. He produced the *Hexapla*, the finest piece of biblical scholarship in the early church. His major work in theology, *First Principles*, introduced basic Christian doctrines in a systematic manner. The writings of Origen dominated the theological thinking of the third and fourth centuries. Not surprisingly though, he has been heralded as a contributor to orthodoxy and "condemned as a fountain of heresy."[22]

EDUCATION IN EARLY CHRISTIAN SCHOOLS

The apostle Paul admonished fathers not to exasperate their children but to "bring them up in the discipline and instruction of the Lord" (Ephesians 6:4). In the first decade of the second century Ignatius of Antioch echoed that advice and added that children were to be taught Scripture and a trade. Schools in that period were seldom found outside cities, were usually conducted by pagans, and were available only to boys of wealthy families. Ideally, then, education was to be given at home by the parents.

One should also remember that the first Christians brought from Judaism a respect for learning and tradition in which literacy was acquired primarily to study the Scriptures and secondarily for secular pursuits. The culture of the Mediterranean world, being heavily influenced by the Greeks and Romans, expressed pagan religious and philosophical positions.

CATECHUMENAL SCHOOLS

As adults became followers of Jesus Christ they had a significant need to be taught Bible doctrine. In time the church began to require new Christians to spend several probationary years before they received baptism and received the Lord's Supper. They were taught by elders, deacons, or laymen (e.g., Origen) usually in the homes of their teachers. Known as catechumenal schools, they paralleled the meeting of worship and teaching that, from the second century on, had two clearly differentiated segments. Charles Gresham has summarized it well:

> The first of these was known as the missa catechumenus, or the mass of the catechumens. This was a teaching service, patterned after the synagogue service of Judaism. Persons who were receiving instruction prior to baptism, known as catechumens, were

allowed to participate in this portion of the service. These catechumens were known as '*hearers*.' After this segment of the worship service, the '*hearers*' were dismissed and the baptized believers remained for the missa fidelium, the mass of the faithful. Here the sacrament of the Lord's Supper was celebrated.[23]

C. B. Eavey continues this discussion regarding the three classes or grades of catechumens, the first of which were the *hearers*, who received only elementary doctrinal training. The second grade was that of the *kneelers*,

> who remained for prayers after the hearers withdrew. They received more advanced instruction and had to prove by their manner of living that they were worthy of entering upon the last stage of their probationary period. Those in this third grade were called the *chosen* and were given intensive doctrinal, liturgical, and ascetical training in preparation for baptism.[24]

The catechumenal schools constituted the first formal education of the early church. The trainees or catechumens were the believers' children, adult Jews, and Gentile converts. The words *catechism* and *catechumen* come from a Greek word meaning "inform" or "instruct" (*katecheo*). Luke used the word four times with both meanings. Paul used it in Romans 2:18, 1 Corinthians 14:19, and Galatians 6:6 "exclusively in the sense of to instruct someone regarding the content of the faith."[25]

These schools gave systematic instruction to those preparing for Christian baptism. The curriculum consisted of the Didache, the Shepherd of Hermas, and many other writings of such men as Irenaeus, Cyprian, Justin Martyr, and Theophilus. Moreover, the spiritual and moral development of the catechumens was held to be of greater importance than the transmission of content. It was only when their lives evidenced maturity in the faith that they were accepted for baptism and numbered among the faithful.

Catechumenal teaching reached the zenith of its advanced form between 325 and 450 but continued into the fifth century.

> After 450 the teaching deteriorated. The growth of the practice of infant baptism accounted in large part for this deterioration. Infant baptism made for a change of the time of systematic instruction in basic Christian truth from before until after baptism. The church created no special agency for teaching those born in the church and baptized in infancy or childhood. It was deemed that the Christian home ought to perform this task. Many sermons and

tracts admonished parents concerning this duty. Some church
fathers went so far as to advise parents to have their children
educated in convents. Along with the change resulting from infant baptism, the difficulty of teaching adult converts increased as
an outcome of the alliance between state and church.[26]

Elements of catechumenal teaching have lingered with us
until the present day. Many mission areas of the world employ a
probationary period in which instruction is given and before
baptism is received. North American countries prepare new
Christians through the Sunday school and/or church membership classes. Unfortunately, however, the careful evaluation of
maturity of faith of the new Christian is often neglected, partly
because of fear of the process's subjectivity and the lack of
spiritual depth on the part of those who would make the evaluation.

CATECHETICAL SCHOOLS

A significant achievement was made when the Catechetical
School of Alexandria was established. Pantaenus, the founder,
gave it a healthy birthing. Clement and Origen, his successors,
were skilled in presenting the gospel in terms respectable to
people familiar with the highest forms of Greek culture. Intellectual respectability was established with culturally sophisticated
academicians.

The catechetical school represented the scientific approach to
Christianity. A wide-ranging curriculum was pursued in an atmosphere of freedom. This approach prepared the way for advanced thought and study in theology. In time, some of them
became seminaries engaged in training the clergy. In addition to
Alexandria, other well-known catechetical schools were located
in Antioch, Edessa, Caesarea, Nisibis, Jerusalem, and Carthage.
The principal names associated with the theology at Antioch
were Lucian, Diordorus, Theodore of Mopsuestia, John Chrysostom, and Theodoret, bishop of Cyrrhus.

Antioch represented the Aristotelian method of approach to
the problems of revelation in contrast to Alexandria, which had
its basis in the philosophy of Plato. The school of Antioch started
with the facts of experience, used the inductive method, gave
more attention to the historical Christ, and interpreted the Scripture from the historical rather than the allegorical vantage
point.[27]

The episcopal, cathedral, and monastic schools were tangential to the catechetical and catechumenal institutions. They form a part of the discussion found in a subsequent chapter.

The Roman Empire was far-reaching and powerful. One of its strategems was to tolerate the various religions and sects if those groups were willing to make an occasional gesture of adoration to the gods and the government. The emperors were piqued to find that, of all the heretics, only the Jews and the Christians refused to acquiesce to those regulations. However, except for the barbarous Nero and a few others, most magistrates were individuals of some culture and toleration. The opposition to the Christians came not from the magistrates in the main but from the people. The masses of the pagan population resented the "aloofness, superiority and certainty of the Christians, and called upon the authorities to punish these 'atheists' for insulting the gods. . . . From the time of Nero Roman law seems to have branded the profession of the Christian faith as a capital offense; but under most of the emperors this ordinance was enforced with deliberate negligence."[28] In the very early years of Christianity, the Christians enjoyed the exemption from emperor-worship that the Jews had, but when Christianity and Judaism diverged the special privilege was lost.

The Christians were subjected to a long series of well-known persecutions. As the church grew, so did the list of martyrs. The persecutions under Nero, Decius (244-251), Valerian (253-260), and Diocletian (284-305) were some of the most devastating. Diocletian issued four edicts that were political actions designed to gain more enthusiastic support from his army, whose members were strongly anti-Christian. His decrees of 303 and 304 "ordered the destruction of all church buildings, the confiscation of Christian books, the dismissal of Christians from the government and army, and the imprisonment of the clergy . . . and all Christians to offer sacrifices to the pagan gods."[29]

The Diocletian persecution was perhaps the greatest test and triumph of the church. For a period of time the church weakened, but soon those who had defaulted under pressure begged to be readmitted to the fold.

Durant commends the church:

> There is no greater drama in human record than the sight of a few Christians, scorned or oppressed by a succession of emperors, bearing all trials with a fierce tenacity, multiplying quietly, build-

ing order while their enemies generated chaos, fighting the sword with the Word, brutality with hope, and at last defeating the strongest state that history has known. Caesar and Christ had met in the arena, and Christ had won.[30]

Conversely, Diocletian accelerated the emphasis on scholarship and built extensive libraries. He also sent scholars to Alexandria to transcribe classical texts there and bring copies to the libraries of Rome. Diocletian reorganized the Empire along more autocratic lines in an attempt to protect the further erosion of the Greco-Roman culture, which had begun to crumble. The afore-mentioned edicts were part of that scheme. Diocletian divided the Empire into two parts, the East and the West, and established an administrative pattern for centuries to come that affected the church as well. That division precipitated a civil war.

With Diocletian retiring to Dalmatia (seacoast of modern Yugoslavia), Constantius succeeded Diocletian in the West and Galerius ruled the East. When his father died, Constantine took the leadership in the West. Maxentius, son of Constantius's predecessor, contended with Constantine and was defeated in a famous battle at the Milvian Bridge in 312.

In 313 Licinius, successor of Galerius, and Constantine issued the Edict of Milan, which proclaimed toleration for both pagan and Christian subjects. Subsequently, Licinius turned against the Christians, and Constantine used a series of incidents to provoke and defeat Licinius in battle. Constantine became the supreme ruler of the Empire (323) and continued his favorable treatment of the Christians. The sons of Constantine continued this attitude, and except for the break of Julian the Apostate (361-363), when pagan worship was restored all over the Empire, the Christian influence grew on the basis of political support. In 381 Theodosius I declared Christianity the state religion and outlawed heresy and pagan religions.

As one would expect, not all results from this turn in events were beneficial to the church. The disadvantages outweighed the advantages. Without question, the church had raised the moral tone of society: gladiatorial shows were barred from the Roman schedule of events, the dignity of women was heightened and enhanced, Roman legislation became more just, slaves were given better treatment, and the spread of missionary work increased. But the government, in exchange for power, protection, and financial assistance, demanded the privilege of interfering in spiritual and theological affairs.

The Council of Nicea in 325 was convened by Constantine, and it met in the imperial palace. Constantine concluded that the East and West were split over a "theological trifle" and desired that both halves of the Empire be equally represented. His ambitions were not realized when, of two hundred and twenty bishops attending, only a handful were from the West. Although the Council itself came to a favorable conclusion in its statement on the divinity of Christ in the Creed of Nicea, nevertheless Constantine was much more interested in the unity of his empire, and he attempted to effect a reconciliation with the heretical Arians despite theological differences. Nicea was followed by more than a half century of discord and disunity in the Eastern church. No doctrinal statement at Constantinople in 381 survived, but at the Council of Chalcedon in 451, the Nicene Creed (regarded as the Creed of Nicea appropriately modified after later controversy) was attributed to Chalcedon.

The creeds became imperial law. That accelerated the tendency for Christianity to assume nationalist forms rather than transcending political boundaries. There also emerged a political pressure on the private domain of one's thinking. Christianity took on a "loyalty to the state and to a state-approved interpretation of the faith."[31] Shortly after it had become the state religion, the state began to disintegrate. As Christianity disentangled itself from the world, it changed its contours and became a "bridge between an old world dying and a new one being born."[32]

NOTES

1. Lewis Joseph Sherrill, *The Rise of Christian Education* (New York: Macmillan, 1944), p. 137.
2. Robert C. Worley, *Preaching and Teaching in the Earliest Church* (Philadelphia: Westminster, 1967), pp. 132-33.
3. Ibid., pp. 135, 144-45.
4. Cited in William Barclay, *Educational Ideals in the Ancient World* (Grand Rapids: Baker, 1974), p. 11.
5. Josephus *Against Apion*, 1.12.
6. Isidore Epstein, *The Jewish Way of Life* (London: n.p., 1946), cited in Barclay, p. 15.
7. J. W. Donahue, "History of Education I," in *New Catholic Encyclopedia*, 17 vols. (New York: McGraw-Hill, 1967), 5:111.
8. Origen *Against Celsus*, 6.14.
9. Justin Martyr *Apology*, 1. 60.2.
10. Tatian *To the Greeks*, 32.1.
11. Irenaeus *Against Heresies*, 2.19.7.
12. Tertullian *Apology*, 46.
13. Geoffrey W. Bromiley, *Historical Theology—An Introduction* (Grand Rapids: Eerdmans, 1978), p. 26.
14. Ibid., p. 13.
15. Ibid., p. 17.

16. Colin J. Hemer, "Justin Martyr," in Tim Dowley, ed., *Eerdmans' Handbook to the History of Christianity* (Grand Rapids: Eerdmans, 1977), pp. 68, 70.
17. Tertullian *Apology*, 46.
18. Tertullian *Against Hermogenes*, 18.
19. Barclay, p. 210.
20. Gregory Thaumaturgus *Panegyric* 13.
21. Robert Ulich, *A History of Religious Education* (New York: New York U., 1968), p. 43. See also Gregory Thaumaturgus *Address to Origen*, trans. W. Metcalf (New York: Macmillan, 1920). It contains the reply of Origen as well.
22. Bromiley, p. 48.
23. Eleanor Daniel, John W. Wade, and Charles Gresham, *Introduction to Christian Education* (Cincinnati: Standard, 1980), pp. 36-37.
24. C. B. Eavey, *History of Christian Education* (Chicago: Moody, 1964), p. 85.
25. Klaus Wegenast, "Katecheo," in Colin Brown, ed., *The New International Dictionary of New Testament Theology*, 3 vols. (Grand Rapids: Zondervan, 1978), 3:771.
26. Eavey, pp. 86-87.
27. Sherrill, pp. 207-8.
28. Will Durant, *Caesar and Christ: A History of Roman Civilization from Its Beginnings to A.D. 337*, The Story of Civilization, vol. 3 (New York: Simon and Schuster, 1977), p. 647.
29. W. Ward Gasque, "Church Expands: Jerusalem to Rome," Dowley, p. 78.
30. Durant, p. 652.
31. David F. Wright, "Councils and Creeds," Dowley, p. 167.
32. Sherrill, p. 175.

5

Augustine to Aquinas: Medieval Education

During the first centuries of its existence Christianity was seen as being one of a number of Eastern religions. The message of Jesus Christ gained adherents throughout the Roman Empire, and as the church grew it came into conflict with other religions and political powers, with persecutions a direct result. Under Decius and Diocletian systematic attempts were made to rid the Empire of the Christians, but not surprisingly the church put down its roots and flourished. However the Greco-Roman soil was not the most fertile for the church.

Most of the finest minds in the church were educated in the literary schools from a distinctly pagan and secular point of view. The church did not develop a primary school system of its own. The family was responsible for the spiritual training of the child, and any special doctrinal instruction was the province of the clergy.

As the church was growing stronger, the Empire was weakening. Constantine and Galerius granted privileges to the church because they realized it was politically expedient to work with this burgeoning, but tightly-knit group. Concurrently the church leaders were becoming increasingly disenchanted with the literary schools, yet none of them dissuaded his people from attending, nor did the Fathers crusade for the church to establish its own literary program. Such a program was established only after the Roman and Hellenistic institutions ceased.

The church experimented with several approaches to Christian education during its first three centuries. The catechumenal school ministered to the converts in preparation for their admittance to baptism and church life, whereas catechetical schools provided advanced instruction. The catechetical schools of Clem-

95

I like this concept

ent, Origen, and Chrysostom promoted a spirit of inquiry and the pursuit of a refreshing range of liberal arts disciplines as well as Scripture and theology. Eventually the growing power of the bishops and their tendency toward a more provincial approach negated some of those thrusts while failing to provide an adequate institution for theological education.[1]

Doubtful

However, many of the less threatening elements of secular learning, after having been divested of their pagan trappings, were incorporated by the church. Disciplines such as law, architecture, medicine, and engineering were considered not only to be irrelevant but also detrimental to the theological concerns of the Christian school. Natural sciences and materialistic philosophies such as Aristotelian thought were viewed in the same light. Consequently, they declined from neglect during the fourth and fifth centuries.

How then did curricula evolve over the first four centuries? In the days of florescent Greece the liberal arts curriculum was on two levels. The basic disciplines were grammar, gymnastics, music, and, on occasion, drawing. The advanced level courses were logic, dialectics, geometry, rhetoric, arithmetic, astronomy, and musical harmony. These were the usual components of the standard curriculum and were widely known as the *enkuklios paideia.*

Roman scholars of the florescent period then fashioned their own liberal arts curriculum based on those Greek sources. Through Cicero and Varro in the first century B.C. they chose nine areas of study for the cultured Roman: logic, rhetoric, grammar, arithmetic, geometry, music, astronomy, medicine, and architecture.

During the dispersive era of the Roman Empire, Martianus Capella persuaded the educators to eliminate architecture and medicine. The remaining seven liberal arts then became known as the trivium (grammar, rhetoric, and logic) and the quadrivium (arithmetic, geometry, astronomy, and music). By the end of the fourth century those studies composed the scope of Western Europe's liberal arts curriculum. Although other subjects were studied, those seven gave guidance in the curricular emphases of the next thousand years. They were to be taught in Latin or Greek, or (preferably) in both. The educational model established would seem to have been engraved in stone. A literary or liberal arts schooling continues to be thought superior to one that is utilitarian.

THE DEMISE OF THE ROMAN EMPIRE

As the Roman Empire approached disintegration so did learning and scholarship. Although it kept learning alive the church also suffered from the intellectual stagnation of that period. Butts evaluates scholarship and learning in general in the later Empire:

> Not much more helpful were the bodies of organized knowledge that were formulated in the later Empire and dispersed from Roman schools to the European Middle Ages. Scholarship in both the Greek and Latin worlds lost its creativity in nearly all fields of knowledge, turning almost wholly to editing and digesting the works that had been codified and systematized in the earlier periods. It was almost as though the later imperial scholars saw hard times ahead and frantically sought to reduce knowledge to the compact forms of small compendiums, so that they might weather the rigors of the intellectual depressions to come. Only in the field of religious thought was the creative spirit alive in the Eastern and Western world as the Fathers of the Christian church sought to reconcile Greek philosophy with the doctrines of Christianity.[2]

The decline of vitality in secular thought was a contributing factor to the demise and capitulation of the Roman Empire. To hold that Christianity was the "chief cause of Rome's fall" is unacceptable. Edward Gibbon argued that Christianity decimated the very fabric that had "given moral character" to the Romans and strength to the Roman state. Gibbon further contended that Christianity brought a weakening mysticism into the realistic and practical stoicism of Roman concerns; it had altered their thinking from the realities of this world to an energy-consuming preparation for an eschatological event; and it had enticed them into the pursuit of "individual salvation through asceticism and prayer, rather than collective salvation through dedication to the state."[3]

Indeed, Gibbon's claim is not without some justification. In the second and third centuries Clement and Origen jolted the church into a greater openness to secular thought. During the fourth and fifth centuries the church tended to withdraw from society and turn inward. It mandated that no Christian should serve in a governmental administrative capacity.

But the Christian message and ethics eminently prepare one for the existential present as well as for the eschatological future. It is anything but a single dimensional faith. The rapid expansion of Christianity was more an effect than a cause of Rome's demise. The Empire was already in a death struggle. Moral decay began with the conquest of Greece and reached its zenith with Nero. Subsequently, positive moral gains were made in the Roman culture. In the later Empire it was probably no more immoral then during any other of its periods.

A very critical problem in the fall of Rome was that too many noncontributory members of society had to be fed by too few productive workers. The army and the bureaucracy had increased in size substantially. The number of clergy and monks had grown as well, and they were among the nonproducers to be supported by the diminishing resources of the Empire.[4]

In short, there are no easy answers to this complex question. There were many factors that were contributory. Without doubt the Christian church shared in the responsibility for the fall of the Western Empire, but by the fifth century the Empire might not have been worth saving anyway.

> It had proved itself unable to deal not only with the barbarian problem, but with political, social and economic problems as well. We may well regret the passing of 'the glory that was Greece and the grandeur that was Rome.' But the fall of the Western Empire was offset in the long run by the conversion of the barbarians of Western Europe to Christianity.[5]

THE FORMALIZATION OF DOCTRINE

We have attempted to trace the history of the development of Christian teaching and instruction *(paideia)*. From the function of teaching came the vitally important formulation of doctrine *(dogma)*. Robert Ulich comments further:

> It was understood and communicated, not as concepts born in the brains of men, but as the self revelation of God through Christ and the Spirit; and its understanding was considered necessary for salvation and life eternal. Herein lies the superiority of the Christian teachers to the ancient philosophers' philosophizing: they did not invent the truth, but they believed to have received it through supernatural grace.[6]

Two dynamic eras of theological controversy have left an indelible mark on Christianity. Doctrinal formulation was accomplished primarily in the periods of the Reformation and the ecumenical or universal councils. Although numerous councils of bishops were held, four councils—Nicea (which in 325 condemned Arianism, a heresy that denied the eternal deity of Christ. The council stated that Christ was always of one substance [*homoousia*] with God the Father.); Constantinople (which in 381 reaffirmed the Christological statement of Nicea and also affirmed the *homoousia* of the Holy Spirit.); Ephesus (which condemned Nestorianism in 431. Nestorianism has usually, but not always, been called a heresy because it tended to separate the divine and human natures of Christ.); and Chalcedon (which in 451 restated and expanded the doctrine that Christ incarnate had two distinct, perfect natures [fully God and fully man] that were at the same time in one personal union [*hypostasis*])—had a major binding effect on the Christian church.

Our contemporary scene is hesitant to use the word *dogma* because of the unfavorable connotations it conjures up. The word came through the Latin from the Greek word *dogma*, whose derivation is from the verb *dokeo*, which means "to think." The doctrines developed in these periods were formulated as a "result of intense thought and searching of the soul in order to interpret correctly the meaning of the Scriptures on the disputed points and to avoid the erroneous opinions *(doxai)* of the philosophers."[7] The discussion of theological doctrines did not take place during the first three centuries because of the threat and reality of persecution that kept in central focus one's commitment to Jesus Christ and to the written source of Christianity, the Scriptures. Theological precision arose as the focus on survival diminished.

In summary, the four ecumenical councils were effective in determining theological standards but they created significant ecclesiastical disjunction. The eastern Mediterranean area had been weakened and became vulnerable to the Muslim invaders. Doctrinal issues became inextricably interwoven with political affairs. A high cost was paid for greater theological clarity and precision.

JEROME (c. 345-419)

Jerome is best known for his translation of the Bible into Latin. Pope Damasus, for whom he is reported to have been a secretary, commissioned him to terminate the confusion that existed regarding the old manuscripts and produce that which later was called the Latin Vulgate. His rich background eminently prepared him for this unique contribution.

At the age of twelve Jerome went to Rome and began the study of Greek, Latin, rhetoric, and philosophy. Allegedly he went to the catacombs on Sundays and translated inscriptions. At nineteen he was baptized and subsequently joined a small group of ascetics. For a period of time he lived in a desert as an ascetic.

Jerome became a profound scholar of classical literature. In a letter to Heliodorus he quoted Themistocles, Plato, Isocrates, Pythagoras, Democritus, Xenocrates, Cleanthes, Homer, Hesiod, Simonides, Stesichorus, Sophocles, and Cato.[8] However, Jerome insisted that in a dream God remonstrated with him regarding his excessive devotion to pagan learning. Jerome responded by employing his scholarly gifts for Christian purposes.

At Antioch Jerome heard lectures by the controversial Appollinarius. He was ordained but was not given a pastoral responsibility, which proved providential. He traveled to Constantinople and studied under Gregory of Nyssa and Gregory of Nazianzus. While there he translated some of the works of Origen and Eusebius. In 382 he went back to Rome and stood firmly with the church during the Melitian dispute. After the pope's death he left for Bethlehem where he drafted his translation and wrote numerous commentaries on Scripture.

Among Jerome's accomplishments were letters that he wrote to important people on substantive themes. These often had theological material of significance. His letters to Laeta and Gaudentius concerning the education of girls are important documents for the history of Christian education.[9]

Early in his writing career Jerome utilized Origen's allegorical interpretation of Scripture. Later he moved to a more historical-grammatical method. He often engaged in debate and his writings bear out his penchant for the polemical genre. Jerome emphasized the ascetical and moral objectives of education at the expense of man's earthly concerns. He thereby influenced Christian monastic schools that came into being a short time later. Jerome emphasized the equality of man in the eyes of God, which led educators eventually to adopt the principle of universal education.

AUGUSTINE (354-430)

Aurelius Augustinus, Bishop of Hippo in North Africa, was the most illustrious of the Latin Fathers. Born of a pagan father and a Christian mother, Monica, he received an excellent literary education in his home city of Tagaste and in Madaura and Carthage. This "genius, second to none in the formation of the Christian world-view in the West, wrote in Latin and knew very little, if any, Greek."[10]

Augustine taught rhetoric at Carthage, Rome, and Milan. Cicero's *Hortensius* convinced him of the pursuit of wisdom in philosophy, and because he was disillusioned with the style and content of Scripture he converted to Manichaeism. Augustine followed that heresy for ten years. Still searching, he went to Milan with his son and the son's mother. He applied for the vacant chair of rhetoric, received the appointment, and achieved the pinnacle of success in his profession. Through reading some of the Neo-Platonists Augustine was emancipated from Manichaeism. Spiritually, he was influenced by the learned Bishop Ambrose. He went through a period of deep trauma and came to faith in Christ in a dramatic encounter in which Romans 13:13-14 provided solace as he wrestled with his immoral past. This took place in August, A.D. 386, and the following Easter he was baptized. On arriving back in Africa he spent three years in solitude and study. Augustine invested the rest of his life ministering in North Africa.

In 397 Augustine began his two major works, *Christian Education* and *Confessions*. *Christian Education* was written in two stages; the bulk of it that year and the last section much later, in 426-27. The objective of *Christian Education* was to provide a manual of instruction for the Christian teacher, whether layman or cleric. The first three books provide a philosophical base for interpreting Scripture and the fourth deals with the techniques of teaching. It was judged to be a work of considerable pedagogical importance, and it remained a classic for the Christian educator for centuries.

To a request from Deogratias, a deacon of Carthage, he responded with *Concerning the Instruction of the Uninstructed*. This is a handbook on methodology for the Christian teacher in the task of instructing candidates for baptism, and for those who seek information about the Christian faith. In the *Instruction of the Uninstructed* Augustine takes the scholarship of the teacher for granted and concentrates on the principles of pedagogy for presenting content to the student. *The Literal Interpretation of Genesis* is the last of his writings that are important to understanding his philosophy of education. In *Genesis* he discusses creation, the Fall of man and the origin of evil, and the will of man. Augustine riveted his attention on the will, inasmuch as it occupies a prominent place in his educational theories.

The quest for truth was seen by Augustine in terms of a progression that begins with sensory data and ends with an understanding of absolute truth and the nature of God. Man has been created by God in His image, possessing a measure of God's understanding and freedom of will. By employing his rational intelligence man can launch out on the difficult task of learning, with confidence in his inborn ability to reach the goal. Although man must put forth effort, it is only by the grace of God that knowledge is illuminated in his mind.

Augustine used some of the essential elements of Platonism to expound his own view of Christian theism. In the exposition of his view of God he would argue in this manner:

1. There are immutable truths common to all men (such as math, existence, and thought).
2. There must be a cause for all these truths.
3. This cause must be either equal to, inferior to, or superior to our minds.
4. This cause cannot be *equal* to our minds, since these truths are independent of our minds and our minds are subject to them (truth does not advance with our minds but remains stable).
5. These truths cannot be inferior to our minds, since our minds are subject to them.
6. Therefore, these truths must be *superior* to our mutable minds.
7. Whatever is superior to the mutable is immutable.
8. Therefore, there is an immutable Mind, which is the source of these immutable truths.[11]

To Augustine, the objectivity of truth is confirmed because different men see the same truth, even though they cannot cause this truth either in their own minds or in other minds. Therefore, whenever any person affirms truth, he is thereby (implicitly) affirming *the* truth (God). This approach to apologetics has been crucial to Christian theism from that time to the present.

Out of Augustine's synthesis of Platonism and Christianity there emerged an interesting ideal of teaching. It combined a respect for the intellect with a deep concern for the feelings and the unique personality of the student. He saw teaching in terms of encouragement and stimulation rather than coercion and authoritarian control. The teacher provides the stimulus for the student's personal exploration and discovery, which demands a high degree of professional skill.

In *Christian Education* Augustine states that the value of

pre-Christian thought is couched in the concept that all truth is God's truth. In his judgment every Christian should understand that wherever one may find truth, in the final analysis it has come from God.

Augustine states further:

> If those who are called philosophers, and especially the Platonists, have said anything that is true and in harmony with our faith, we are not only not to shrink from it, but to claim it for our use from those who have no lawful possession of it. . . . Now these are, so to speak, their gold and silver which they did not create themselves, but dug out of the mines of God's providence, which are everywhere scattered abroad, and are perversely and unlawfully prostituted to the worship of devils. These, therefore, the Christian, when he separates himself in spirit from the miserable fellowship of these men, ought to take away with him, and devote to their proper use in the preaching of the Gospel.[12]

The proposition that all truth is God's truth has enriched the whole Christian education enterprise. For those who take a high view of Scripture it has been of an immeasurable value in building a biblical philosophy of education.

As an educational thinker, Augustine transcended his generation to make an enduring contribution. His impact continues to be felt today. For example, his high view of the teacher reflects the educational thinking of Christ and Paul. The teacher is to offer himself for imitation and to display those qualities that his students must develop if they are to become mature persons. In effect, Augustine asserted that the teacher must be an educational philosopher and be able to lead his pupils into the good life in Jesus Christ. Augustine was the positive fulfillment of Alfred N. Whitehead's incisive critique of education, "In schools of antiquity philosophers aspired to impart wisdom; in modern colleges our humbler aim is to teach subjects."[13]

It is difficult to assess with accuracy the profound influence of the Bishop of Hippo. From his own period through the early Renaissance in the twelfth century Augustine was the dominating force in the development of thought. The abundant resources of his educational writings are mines that repeatedly have been explored, and his theories have been reinterpreted in relation to the needs and dilemmas of the centuries gone by since his death.

Augustine was the channel through which Greek philosophy flowed into the Middle Ages. His ideas regarding the seven liberal arts permeated the thinking of the brilliant Boethius, Cassidorus the Benedictine, Isidore of Seville, the Venerable Bede, and Alcuin of York.

ALCUIN (735-804)

Learning was at a low ebb in the three centuries prior to Charlemagne (742-812). The upheavals that characterized that period were not contributory to education for the general populace. The emperors in the West relied increasingly on the bishops to assist in civil matters. By 600, legislation and leadership was provided by the Christian clergy. As the Empire disappeared the church, and particularly the bishops of Rome and Constantinople, grew stronger.

The political power drifted northward as the Germanic invasions swept in and the Frankish kingdoms in France and Germany were gradually consolidated under the leadership of the Merovingian kings. When Charlemagne was crowned emperor of the Romans by the pope on Christmas day in 800, he became the legitimate successor to the emperors of the ancient Roman Empire. The successors of Charlemagne, however, quarreled among themselves for control of the new empire and in time it split into three parts: the eastern Frankish kingdom ultimately became Germany, the western became France, and the remainder Italy.

The Middle East felt a new threat from the growing Islamic influence that was being exerted in Europe, Africa, and much of western and southern Asia. Because of the superiority of the Arab horsemen, the caliphs who succeeded Mohammed after his death in 632 were able to exploit the military weakness of the Byzantine Empire. Islamic learning achieved its peak between the eighth and twelfth centuries and had an impact on the few centers of learning.

In the year 735 the Venerable Bede died in the monastery in Jarrow, England. Bede was the father of the Carolingian renaissance and the first great English historian and man of letters. Egbert, a student of Bede, became the Archbishop of York. Inspired by the educational thinking of his mentor, he began a school in which he was the instructor. Egbert was succeeded by Alcuin who later was invited by Charlemagne to give leadership at his palace school in Aachen and to provide direction for the cultural activities of the empire.

Initially Charlemagne had an ongoing need of trained administrative personnel and he had an interest in upgrading the educational level of the clergy. Literacy was now demanded of all clergy. The Frankish nobility of the imperial court attended at York as well. Both at York and Aachen Alcuin based his curriculum on the seven liberal arts, stating that the house of knowledge cannot be perfectly built "unless it is raised up on these seven columns or steps." Alcuin had a rich background of study in the sixth-century writings of Cassiodorus and Boethius and the Latin classics. He structured a curriculum built around the Latin materials. Encumbered by the alleged necessity of teaching Latin, Alcuin ventured only as far as developing question and answer dialogues. However, this attempt to break out of the medieval pedagogical mold had limited success in eliminating the illiteracy of his barbarian students. Later he encouraged Charlemagne to enact "educational legislation that required every abbey to conduct a school where boys might learn reading, writing, psalm singing, arithmetic and Latin grammar."[14]

Unfortunately the empire of Charlemagne died with him, but the renewal of education and religion associated with Alcuin and Charles the Great improved European culture throughout the bleak and chaotic period that followed. The "Carolingian Renaissance" returned to classical scholarship and also to early Christianity for its models. The intellectual vigor accelerated new theological activity. Monastic developments at this time were affirmed through the fresh impetus of Alcuin's work. Although Alcuin did not initiate a revival of learning in the humanist sense, he did launch an organized program of fundamental educational development upon which Western Christianity could build a sound superstructure, particularly of Latin scholarship in the coming centuries. The education given during Charlemagne's empire remains an excellent basis for evaluating the level of learning during the early Middle Ages. Alcuin scholar Eleanor Duckett assesses his work as follows:

> As a teacher and as Master in England and on the continent, he influenced numberless minds, and his work as organizer of education, as editor of textbooks, as student of ancient classic literature, of sacred writings and their truth, was to live on through the Middle Ages. Yet he himself contributed nothing original. Instead, he drew reverently, scrupulously, from the sources of older time, and by this very drawing conserved for future generations the wisdom of the past. He was in himself no philosopher; yet he did much to make ready the way for medieval scholasticism. . . .
> To all whom he met he gave fresh life, by his spoken or his written word, by stimulation of rebuke, of warning, of praise and of admi-

ration entirely generous; yet all his days were clouded by self-conscious diffidence in regard to himself. . . . He feared to initiate, and therefore he did much to further the rigid adherence to tradition characteristic of the medieval mind.[15]

ECCLESIASTICISM AND EDUCATION

In the fourth century Christianity had come of age and enjoyed a period of numerical growth and a new level of theological sophistication. The medieval Latin Catholic church of the West and the Eastern Orthodox church of the Byzantine Empire developed in this century. The institutional church had been enriched by the work of Ambrose, Augustine, and Pope Gregory I (540-604), the last of the church Fathers in the West. By the fifth century the clerical hierarchy, a greater emphasis on liturgical worship, and the greater prominence of baptism in the process of salvation had developed. The strength Christianity did possess was not sufficient to counteract the decadence of the Roman Empire.

Western civilization was in retreat during the next three centuries. Barbarian invaders swarmed into what had been the Roman Empire of the West. Islam became a formidable opponent, particularly in the East. The Middle East, central Asia, and North Africa were in its grasp. The patriarch at Constantinople came under the Eastern emperors but the pope eventually emerged after centuries of struggle as the most powerful religious and political leader.

A few people are noteworthy among those who kept the educational lamp burning in this somewhat discouraging period. Columba (521-597)[16] of Ireland ministered with significance at Iona, Scotland as a missionary educator. Boniface (680-754), "the Apostle to the Germans," was a force in uniting Christian Europe. But Christianity was essentially stagnating because it was fighting for its very life during this five-hundred-year period (500-1000).

Several informal educational agencies were in existence through the early and late Middle Ages. Much of the learning taking place among the masses who could not afford formal schooling (even if those rare possibilities were geographically close) was apprenticeship training. Later that training evolved into guilds, which were organizations of craftsmen for civil, economic, and educational interests. Their chief function was to establish an educational network to train new members in specific crafts. Generally, a boy would work with a master craftsman for seven years as an apprentice. He would later become a journeyman, then finally a master craftsman. The trainer of the apprentice was to establish a written contract with the boy. He was responsible to give moral guidance as well as practical training in a trade (which included the provision of food, lodging, and a small allowance).

Chivalric training bore similarities to that of craft training in the guilds. It was the process of education and training for knights. At about the age of seven an applicant would be accepted as a page into a knight's household. After serving seven years the page would become a squire and accompany the knight to the battlefield as an assistant. Meanwhile the squire would learn courtly manners; how to fight on horseback; the art of hunting; care of armor, weapons, and horses; singing, reciting, and composing verses; and storytelling. At twenty-one the squire would become a knight, a title that carried various obligations. The inclusion of Christian principles and rituals into the system of chivalry helped church influence to grow in the late Middle Ages.

MONASTERIES

With the founding of the monastery of Cluny in central France in 910, renewed vigor began to seep back into the church. The Cluny monks attempted to revive the best ideas and procedures from the first monastery in the West, begun by Benedict of Nursia (480-547). But unlike those Benedictines who separated themselves from the community at large, these tenth-century monks integrated monasticism with society. The Cluny monks took meaningful action to eliminate the buying and selling of church offices (simony), to re-establish the celibacy of the clergy, and to purge the church of corruption.

While the Egyptian Anthony (c. 250-350) is generally regarded as the father of Christian, and especially Eastern, monasticism, the patriarch of Western monasticism was Benedict of Nursia. He established a code of regulations at Monte Cassino that dealt with the duties of the abbott, worship, discipline, and the internal administration of the monastery. Each monastery was to constitute an independent community. The only bond between the monasteries was to be their allegiance to the pope. The most outstanding characteristic of each one was obedience. Origen and Jerome favored asceticism as a protest against worldliness and the monasteries provided the place of retreat for surrendering oneself to God.

From the very beginning monasticism concerned itself with education. Initially, monastic schools received boys who intended to enter the order but by the ninth century they also accepted those who just desired an education. The sole aim of education was religious. Discipline was harsh, fasting and prayer were obligatory. The language of instruction was Latin, which was learned by repetition. Following the learning of Latin, instruction began in the seven liberal arts, with grammar first. The two major benefits of monastic educational efforts were (1) knowledge was preserved for use in the Renaissance and (2) manuscripts were copied and retained. A negative aspect developed over the centuries when the monasteries became wealthy and controlled large tracts of land. Among the noted monastic schools were those of Tours in France, Fulda in Germany, Jarrow in northern England, Monte Cassino in Italy, Iona in Scotland, and Clonmacnois in Ireland. The monastic schools dominated the educational scene of Europe from the sixth to the tenth or eleventh centuries.

CATHEDRAL AND EPISCOPAL SCHOOLS

As bishops (*episcopus*) were appointed, the churches they served were identified as cathedrals. The bishops came to have authority over the local churches in their area. That geographical location became known as a bishopric and still later as a diocese. The schools at their churches were called episcopal or cathedral schools. The bishops would oversee their development and determine if they were operating according to the rules or canons of the church.

Initially the bishops were the instructors, but with the growth of the church in the fourth and fifth centuries the teaching was delegated to a special cleric called the *scholasticus*. Not uncommonly clerics were converted rhetoricians and grammarians who previously had been teachers in the public schools. With this development the curriculum was broadened beyond that initiated by Clement and Origen in the catechetical school at Alexandria. It later embraced the full range of the sacred sciences of Scripture and theology, the Latin and Greek classics, literary and philosophical studies, and mathematics. The school at York, one of the famous cathedral schools of England, offered instruction in the liberal arts and law.

Although many monastic schools such as Cluny continued to be important centers of learning, in the main they lost their educational leadership to the cathedral and professional schools. Those schools flourished with the expansion of the urban centers in which they were located. Cathedral schools such as Paris, Chartres, Orleans, Liege, Utrecht, and Toledo became well known in the eleventh and twelfth centuries. They not only educated clerics but also became training schools for teachers of the liberal arts and theology.

UNIVERSITIES

The leading cathedral and professional schools provided the impetus to the origination of the university. That process evolved in the late Middle Ages. As cathedral and professional schools grew larger, the bishops appointed a chancellor who supervised the teachers. The teachers and students sought more autonomy and security through the formations of guilds in such urban centers as Paris and Bologna. In time the term *guild* changed to *universitas*, which gradually applied exclusively to unions of faculties and students.

The following complex factors provided the indispensable seedbed for the university and for the eleventh-century intellectual renaissance: the Crusades, the revival of commerce, and Western contacts with Arabic scholarship. Between 1100 and 1200 a flood of ideas poured from the Moorish scholars of Spain. The mobility involved in the Crusades had created bridges to people, places, and concepts. With its affinity for Greek thinking, the Arab world had become a storehouse of philosophical and scientific materials. The Arabic commentaries of Averroes, including the complete writings of Aristotle, entered the intellectual mainstream of Europe.[17] These scholarly materials could not be disseminated fully within the strictures of the cathedral and monastic schools and therefore an additional stimulus came to the emerging concept of the university.

The Crusades, despite a number of negative aspects, were a stimulus for reviving commercial and urban life. The economic rejuvenation of the twelfth and thirteenth centuries produced a middle class that enabled more people to avail themselves of university training. Travel accelerated and a cosmopolitan spirit that facilitated scholarly interchange transcended the provincialism of the feudal mind-set.

The Roman Catholic Church dominated the scene of life and

learning in Western Europe. There was an almost clerical guardianship of the schools. The founding of mendicant (owning no property) religious orders such as the Dominicans, Franciscans, and Augustinians corresponded with the burgeoning commercial renewal. They produced a strong cadre of learned men such as Anselm, Abelard, Duns Scotus, and Thomas Aquinas. Doing the work of theology became a central concern of those medieval scholastics. Aquinas and other scholars attracted students to the University of Paris, which began through the cathedral school of Notre Dame. The University of Paris made theology the keystone of all university studies "with all other disciplines subordinate to it." Its faculty became the arbiter in theological matters "deciding disputes, defining heresy, and on occasion even correcting the theology of the pope himself."[18] By 1300, universities existed at Salerno, Bologna, Paris, Montpellier, Lisbon, Oxford, and Cambridge.

Gutek has ably summarized the origins of the medieval university by citing these trends:

1. Many of the universities evolved from and frequently absorbed the studia generalia (curricula) of the older cathedral schools.
2. The general stimulus emanating from the revival of learning contributed to the support and growth of the universities.
3. The introduction of new learning and the rediscovery of classical Greek rationalism created problems of synthesis for the scholastics who tried to reconcile these new intellectual sources with the corpus of Christian doctrine.
4. Revived commercial and city life produced a mobile and cosmopolitan body of scholars and students who populated the universities.
5. The faculties and students of the universities followed the examples of the existing guilds and assumed the powers of self-government, establishing internal structures and enacting internal regulations.
6. The medieval universities established specialized schools for one or more of the major professional studies of law, medicine and theology.[19]

TOWN AND PRIVATE SCHOOLS

Although the schools operated by the church maintained their place of ascendancy in education, kings and towns established more schools because of dissent, and political quarrels. Economic and political strength and development is inevitably tied to the power of education. Although this was not a time when comprehensive state school systems were established, the groundwork was being laid for national systems that would provide vernacular (elementary) schools for ordinary people and classical (secondary) schools for the upper class.

As cities grew it became obligatory to start schools in the outlying parishes and in various parts of towns. It was becoming more difficult for children to travel to the central church. Secular agencies began to vie with the clergy for the right to educate. Among those agencies were town governments, secular political figures, private teachers, and voluntary associations of persons who wished to endow schools for charitable purposes. Severe struggles emerged for town control of the schools in Germany. Even in Italy there was some agitation. Gradually the town control concept became a reality in Germany and in the Netherlands.

Therefore, in the later Middle Ages individuals and groups began to establish schools that were not directly responsible to public leaders or the church. The most important of those were the chantry or guild schools, often begun and endowed by a wealthy individual. With funding through a chantry foundation, the first public school in England was founded at Winchester in 1382 by William of Wykeham.

THOMAS AQUINAS (1224-1274) AND SCHOLASTICISM

Only in the late Middle Ages did schooling begin to slip out of the total grasp of the church as secular agencies made slight inroads. Most of the finest thinkers of the ninth to the fourteenth centuries were monks and clergymen, who had access to the best education. Their intellectual work was done against a background of the past—classical Greek philosophy, Scripture, theology, and the writings of the church Fathers. The Scholastics (teachers) put this content into a logical system.

A major factor in the rapid rise of Scholasticism was the philosophy of Aristotle. Averroes, the brilliant Arab philosopher, had translated his works and introduced the translations into the West through Spain. Concurrently, the famous Jewish philosopher Moses Maimonides's translations of Aristotle appeared in Paris. The development of the university provided an educational vehicle for this movement. Philosophy was in a dominant role once again.

In essence, "Scholasticism was the attempt to support the Christian creed by a philosophical structure of sufficient strength to withstand the ever rising doubts among Christian theologians who, partly because of Arabic influences, no longer felt safe in their faith as did their predecessors of earlier centuries."[20] This process of assimilating, reconciling, and redirecting Greco-Roman knowledge to make it conform to Christian theology demanded the finest minds available. Erigena, Anselm, Peter Abelard, Peter Lombard, Albert the Great, Thomas Aquinas, and Duns Scotus were among those gifted schoolmen. Scholasticism, then, was a method of selecting and classifying general statements taken from religious and classical authorities, critiquing and comparing those writers, devising a systematic commentary on those statements, examining the arguments on both sides of the question, and gathering evidence to support conclusions.

As Aquinas engaged in this style and manner of thinking he would pose a problem and then reproduce an authoritative statement that might be a text of Scripture, a passage from Clement of Alexandria, or a quotation from "the philosopher." The latter remained unnamed because invariably it was Aristotle. The Islamic philosophies of Averroes and Avicenna and contemporary Jewish scholars were considered. Following a careful assessment of all the evidence he would advance his solution. The logical and vigorous thought of Aquinas and his Scholastic colleagues was profound. However, they were attempting to reconcile Greek philosophy with Christian theology and most often something had to be compromised. Colin Brown evaluates the work of the Scholastics:

> Perhaps . . . they were operating with out-dated concepts. So many of the questions they wrestled with have turned out to be pseudo-questions, in the light of our scientific view of the world, and modern critical philosophy. In one sense the Middle Ages were an age of faith. The questions that the schoolmen asked all had a theological bearing. But ironically the questions which so preoccupied them were a hindrance to hearing the message of the Bible about God and his love in Christ.[21]

Although Thomas Aquinas did not focus on developing an educational philosophy per se, a fairly substantial theory of his views can be constructed. Being an individual of prodigious intellectual gifts, still he was indebted to Aristotle for philosophical structure. Like Aristotle, Aquinas taught that all human knowledge originates in the senses and that human understanding, through abstractions, is capable of building up knowledge of the forms of things. His work was concentrated on the question of how God may be known.

Thomas attempted to differentiate between doctrine and philosophy. He held that doctrine is derived from Scripture or the data of revelation and that philosophy grows out of accessible and acceptable data. The end of theology is God, who surpasses the comprehension of rational powers but whose existence can be established philosophically.

Evangelicals often differ substantially in their evaluation of the epistemology of Aquinas. Paul Helm states:

> It is a mistake to think of Aquinas as a Christian philosopher if by this is meant someone who elaborates answers to philosophical questions on the basis of Christian revelation. The different places assigned to philosophy and theology may be vividly illustrated by Thomas' view of creation. Philosophically, the universe might be eternal. But the Christian believes from revelation that creation is an act of God.[22]

Geoffrey W. Bromiley declares:

> Thomas has a clear understanding of what theology is and never confuses it with philosophy nor makes philosophy its basis. . . . It is not apparent that he subsumes theology under philosophy. Nor is it apparent that he makes philosophy the source, basis or even the starting point of faith. Nor does he seem at all to pursue an essentially rationalistic or apologetical theology.[23]

Aquinas believed that the first concepts of man's understanding were preexistent within him and that they could be known through the light of one's intellect. The student is to be in a constant quest for knowledge through good intellectual habits called virtues.

> Knowledge . . . preexists in the learner potentially, not, however, in the purely passive, but in the active, sense. Otherwise, man would not be able to acquire knowledge independently . . . there are two ways of acquiring knowledge. In one way, natural reason by itself reaches knowledge of unknown things, and this way is called *discovery*; in the other way, when someone else aids the learner's natural reason, and this is called *learning by instruction*.[24]

Thomas stressed that the teacher must be knowledgeable, be a skillful communicator, and view teaching as a calling by which mankind is served. Because instruction is a highly verbal process, the teacher is to choose carefully the words, phrases, examples, and analogies employed. The data base a student brings to the teaching-learning process is to be ascertained, built upon, and utilized to form a bridge to new truth. He believed teaching is to be a blending of the contemplative and active life that springs from a love of truth, a love of man, and a love of God. Adequate time is to be spent both in diligent research and involvement in the lives of students.

The educational philosophy associated with Thomism has influenced twentieth-century thinkers such as Robert Hutchins and Mortimer Adler. Whether lay or ecclesiastical Thomists, such thinkers accept the basic metaphysical and epistemological tenets of Aristotelian natural realism, advocate the primacy of the liberal arts and sciences in curriculum construction, and lean toward the employment of syllogistic reasoning.

One of the criticisms of Scholasticism was its tendency to over-stress the intellect and reason at the expense of meeting people's needs. Aquinas inadvertently contributed to this by making a careful distinction between *educatio*, informal schooling, and *disciplina*, formal schooling. Thomas equated informal schooling with all agencies or means that contributed to a person's virtue, excellence, and general formation. By formal schooling he identified the learning and training that comes from the deliberate instruction of teachers and schools. His disciples tended to separate these two and failed to observe the relationship between them in the total development of the individual.

Joan Ellen Duvall has summarized the key elements of Aquinas's philosophy of education:

> He held that the learner has the active potency to arrive at a knowledge of the unknown through discovery. All teaching must be guided by this principle. The signs and symbols that the teacher presents to the student must enable the latter to relate them to the first principles which support what he already knows. The teacher, then, must possess explicit knowledge of what he is teaching and be able to reduce that knowledge to those first principles. As for curriculum, since the learner's intellectual knowledge is rooted in sense knowledge, he must acquire a knowledge of the material world before advancing to the world of abstraction, such as mathematics, and the world of metaphysics, which considers beings that exist apart from matter—that is, pure forms. Truth is rooted in the existence of things, and therefore the path to truth is the order of existence as it is apprehended by man.[25]

Franciscan scholars Bonaventure (1222-1274), Duns Scotus (1266-1308), and William of Ockham (c. 1280-c. 1349) joined a group of scholars who criticized the Dominican Aquinas for his failure to recognize that reason and revelation on occasion contradict each other. They defended the faith by contending with the philosophy of Aristotle. Thirteenth-century systems of thought were based on Aristotelian realism. Realism, as it was conceived by the Scholastics, is the doctrine that universals have a real, objective existence and that sense-perceived objects have an existence independent of the act of perception. William, one of the most influential philosophers of the fourteenth century, advocated a radical empiricism. Nominalism holds that general or abstract words do not stand for objectively existing entities, and that universals are no more than names assigned to them. He taught a new form of Nominalist theory that "rejected the prevailing view that 'universals' really exist. He argued that they are simply artificial products of the human mind. . . . Only individual or 'particular' things have real existence. William's Nominalism became known as 'the modern way' (via moderna) over against the 'old way' (via antiqua) of Aquinas. Since knowledge was based on experience of individual things, natural science took on new significance."[26]

The learned William of Ockham also adversely criticized the philosophical proofs Aquinas advanced for the existence of God. In his judgment, God was beyond all knowledge, ruling out the assertion of the Thomists that He can be apprehended by reason, or by illumination as taught by the Augustinians, but that He could be known by faith alone. These and other emphases opened the door for Reformation theology several centuries later.

The millennium of the Middle Ages was not the utopia that the term implies. Nor was it the low point portrayed by historians of just thirty years ago. In the early Middle Ages the church was fighting for survival against an antagonistic society and perverse heresies. Fortunately for society the church remained the one bastion of educational interest. The church had its own considerable failings such as the abuse of power by the papacy, comparative wealth, and land control. For decades education languished because the Roman Catholic Church placed its emphasis on power. The positive elements of reform movements such as monasticism, asceticism, and scholasticism were not able to bring about needed changes. Society was ready for the resurgence of education brought by the Renaissance.

NOTES

1. Lewis J. Sherrill, *The Rise of Christian Education* (New York: Macmillan, 1944), p. 209.
2. R. Freeman Butts, *The Education of the West* (New York: McGraw-Hill, 1973), p. 129.
3. Will Durant's interpretation of Gibbon's argument. See Will Durant, *Caesar and Christ: A History of Roman Civilization from Its Beginnings to A.D. 337*, The Story of Civilization, vol. 3 (New York: Simon & Schuster, 1977), p. 667.
4. Richard A. Todd, "The Fall of the Roman Empire," in Tim Dowley, ed., *Eerdman's Handbook to the History of Christianity* (Grand Rapids: Eerdmans, 1977), p. 184.
5. Ibid., p. 185.
6. Robert Ulich, *The History of Religious Education* (New York: New York U., 1968), p. 50.
7. Earle E. Cairns, *Christianity Through the Centuries*, rev. ed. (Grand Rapids: Zondervan, 1967), p. 141.
8. Jerome *Epistle* 60, cited in William Barclay, *Educational Ideals in the Ancient World* (Grand Rapids: Baker, 1974), p. 213.
9. Cf. St. Jerome, in Nicene and Post-Nicene Fathers, Philip Schaff and Henry Ware, eds. 2d series, vol. 6 (New York: Christian Literature Co., 1893), p. 195; Henry Barnard, *American Journal of Education*, vol. 5, 1894, p. 594. See also Barclay, pp. 253-57 for an excellent discussion of the kind of education, from Jerome's medieval perspective, a child should have, particularly if he would eventually serve Christ in a vocational capacity.
10. Ulich, p. 46.
11. Norman L. Geisler, *Philosophy of Religion* (Grand Rapids: Zondervan, 1974), pp. 168-69.
12. Augustine *De Doctrina Christiana* 40, cited in Barclay, pp. 232-33.
13. Alfred N. Whitehead, *The Aims of Education and Other Essays* (London: Ernest Benn, 1962), p. 45.
14. Gerald L. Gutek, *A History of the Western Educational Experience* (New York: Random House, 1971), p. 69.
15. Eleanor Shipley Duckett, *Alcuin, Friend of Charlemagne* (New York: Macmillan, 1951), pp. 305-7.
16. John Woodbridge, "Columba," in Elmer L. Towns, ed., *A History of Religious Educators* (Grand Rapids: Baker, 1975), pp. 63-70.
17. Gutek, p. 84.
18. Butts, p. 173.
19. Gutek, p. 85.
20. Ulich, p. 70.
21. Colin Brown, "Scholasticism," in Dowley, pp. 278-79.
22. Paul Helm, "Thomas Aquinas," in J. D. Douglas, ed., *The New International Dictionary of the Christian Church*, rev. ed. (Grand Rapids: Zondervan, 1978), p. 60.
23. Geoffrey W. Bromiley, *Historical Theology—An Introduction* (Grand Rapids: Eerdmans, 1978), p. 200.
24. Thomas Aquinas *Truth*, trans. R. W. Mulligan, 3 vols. (Chicago: Regenery, 1952), Q. 11, A.1.
25. Joan Ellen Duvall, "Thomas Aquinas," in Towns, p. 80.
26. H. D. McDonald, "William of Ockham," in Dowley, p. 341.

6

Renaissance Man and Cultural Renewal

Francis Bacon was born on January 22, 1561, at Yorkhouse, London. Aristotle had died in 322 B.C. It is incredible, but true, that some who have chronicled philosophy's history have dismissed those 1,883 years in only a few pages! Given the cultural vacuum of Rome, one can understand a secular mind's passing over the Christian philosophy of Jesus and Paul—but Augustine, Bacon, Dante, daVinci, Copernicus, Galileo, Erasmus, Aquinas, and Luther—in a couple of paragraphs? Despite secular historians, this chapter and the next must be written if our grasp of the history of educational philosophy is to be in any measure accurate.

When did the Renaissance begin? Was there a specific act that ignited the period, such as Luther's nailing the theses to the door did the Reformation? Most historians are hesitant to identify a person or date because the Renaissance represented a gradual break with the traditionalism of the Middle Ages through a definitive move toward a man-centered world. It was, in short, the same kind of humanism that still dominates society in the late twentieth century.

Generally speaking, the Renaissance is dated through the fourteenth, fifteenth, and sixteenth centuries with a "beginning," if one must be identified, somewhere in the middle of the fourteenth century. Italy was certainly the cradle—because of its dominance of the Middle Ages it continued to be the center of world attention. The vehicle was primarily art (or perhaps one should say "the arts") and, to a lesser degree, the unwrapping of the age of science.

Some secular writers tend to include the Reformation with the Renaissance in bridging the gap between the medieval and modern periods of history. Obviously, this text must treat the Reformation separately, and therefore this chapter will deal only with 240 years of Renaissance history, from 1280 to 1520. Though hardly acceptable to professional historians who dislike the fixing of dates when discussing process movements, perhaps the beginning student of educational history and philosophy can be assisted by thinking of the Renaissance as being launched in philosophy by Thomas Aquinas (1225-1274); in science by Roger Bacon (c. 1214-1294); in literature by Dante (1264-1321); and in art by Giotto (c. 1267-1337).

Thomas Aquinas's Philosophy

Though not canonized by the church until 1323, Aquinas had already begun to shake up medieval philosophic thinking with his teaching at the University of Paris and writing of several volumes, notably *Truth* and *Summa Theologica*. But let us think of the major impact of Aquinas as occurring shortly before his death and the impact of Luther shortly after the significance of the ninety-five theses had been realized across Europe. This gives us a simplified two and one-half century handle on the Renaissance, from approximately A.D. 1270 to 1520. Our last chapter ended with Aquinas, so it is most appropriate to begin here with the indomitable Dominican who accomplished so much in less than fifty years of life.

Having studied at the University of Naples in Paris and having been greatly influenced by Albert the Great, Thomas applied his larger-than-life genius to "Christianizing" Aristotle. The influence of Thomas continues and is reflected in the evangelical writings of the noted apologist Norman L. Geisler. Without doubt, Aquinas was the outstanding theologian of his day. In his thirty volumes, he dealt with almost every aspect of theology, but none so significant as the doctrine of man. Francis Schaeffer sums it up:

> Aquinas's contribution to Western thought is, of course, much richer than we can discuss here, but his view of man demands our attention. Aquinas held that man had revolted against God and thus was fallen, but Aquinas had an incomplete view of the Fall. He thought that the Fall did not affect man as a whole but only in part. In his view, the world was fallen or corrupted, but the intellect was not affected. Thus people could rely on their own human wisdom, and this meant that people were free to mix the teachings of the Bible with the teachings of the non-Christian philosophers.[1]

However, we are most concerned with the educational influence of Thomas, an emphasis to be found with greatest impact in Question 11 ("The Teacher") of *Truth*. After recognizing that Thomas was much more concerned with theology than its communication through teaching, Joan Duvall does agree that a philosophy of education can be "constructed from Thomas's writings . . . if education be defined as man's development of his nature, his acquisition of knowledge, and his realization of his potential. In Thomas's metaphysics, psychology, epistemology, and moral philosophy, he developed principles which are, in fact, the first principles of education, and specifically of intellectual, rather than moral and religious, education."[2]

This volume is obviously an overview and therefore cannot go into detail on the educational philosophy of any individual. The student is referred to Duvall's treatment in the chapter cited above. It is important, however, to note that Aquinas represents a unification of faith and reason, science and theology, the present and the future. The orderliness and consistency of his mind has rarely been duplicated in the history of educational philosophy. He was a proponent of an orderly universe under the control of a personal God.

Like Aristotle, he believed that the main purpose of scientific inquiry was the explanation rather than the control of nature. He was a strong advocate of the family and, true to his loyalty to the church, a strong opponent of divorce and birth control. Unlike Machiavelli or Hobbes, Aquinas argued that power is not a goal in itself, that the end does not justify the means, and that the state must preserve the integrity of the citizens in order for morality to dominate all relationships within the society.

To *teach* then, for Aquinas, is to mediate between God and man, to pass on the ideals of the church, and to glorify God in the development of one's own intellectual capacity as well as that of others.

One of the favorite analogies used by Thomas was a comparison between the art of teaching and that of healing. Both doctor and teacher know what needs to be done in order to bring about healing or learning, but the doctor does not give his own health to the patient any more than the teacher assists the intellect to acquire knowledge in the soul of the student.

An interesting differential in the comparison is that Thomas saw teaching as even more important than healing since the first is an interaction between two minds whereas the second is an interaction between mind and body. Given his basic commitment to intellectualism of the Aristotelian school, Thomas obviously saw a living intellect patiently making his way to truth in public before his students as the higher of the two endeavors.

CHARACTERISTICS OF THE RENAISSANCE

In one sense we have contradicted ourselves in earlier paragraphs of this chapter by suggesting that the Renaissance was primarily an Italian event and then naming among the progenitors of the movement a theologian who taught in Paris and a scientist who researched in England. Ultimately, however, the Renaissance was a *cultural renewal*, and the center of culture in the fourteenth and fifteenth centuries was, without question, Italy. We have already noted *humanism* as one of the major characteristics that have profound effects on theology, education, and the arts. Another focal point is the *urban centricity* of cultural renewal. One would expect that phenomenon since the urban centers were the locations of the universities and Italy was essentially a land of cities. Paris also was involved, and, to a lesser extent, London, but the Renaissance essentially began in the urban cultures of Rome, Florence, Orleans, Naples, and Salerno.

There was also a secular spirit that dominated the Renaissance despite the continuing strength of the church and the influence of dominant personalities like Aquinas and Erasmus. By no means was atheism considered a valid option, but the hustle of the cities, new opportunities for the enjoyment of life, the satisfaction of aesthetic or intellectual tastes, and an increasing level of wealth among certain classes in the urban centers all contributed to a general forgetfulness of God in times of prosperity. *Man and his world rather than God and His heaven became the focal point of human interest.*

Still another characteristic of the Renaissance was an awakening emphasis on *individualism*. The feudal system was breaking up, and the church had lost some of its control because of scandals, created by schism and the Babylonian captivity, that surrounded the papacy. New careers appeared on the horizon and were thrown open to people with talent. In the changing world of politics, power was now available to those not of noble birth. Capitalism began to affect business practice and the patronage of those involved in the arts raised low-born people to fame beyond that which would have been possible a century earlier.

All of this created what was called "the Renaissance man," a new gentleman who enjoyed athletics, music, literature, and science with equal interest. Baldassare Castiglione tells us that toward the end of the era,

> The man who would make his way successfully into the highest ranks of society must now be not merely or necessarily, nobly born, though that is an advantage, nor a great warrior, though he should be skilled in arms, but a fully developed personality, an amateur of all arts and all branches of learning and a master of some, possessing, above all, grace, tact, good manners, and personal charm.[3]

Castiglione himself epitomized the Renaissance man, standing in stark contrast to the boisterous and sometimes brutal manners of the crusaders like Richard the Lion-Hearted or the medieval monks like Alcuin, Maurus, Isidore, or even Abelard.

The student of educational history in this era makes a common but dangerous mistake to characterize the Renaissance as either all good or all bad. Abelard (1079-1142), for example, possibly ranks among the great teachers of all time, though regarded in his day as a heretic by no less a theological giant than Bernard of Clairvaux. Obviously, the stranglehold the church held upon all of Europe had contributed to the slow development of theology and learning, creating what we now call, for lack of a better term, "The Dark Ages." The Renaissance was primarily a time of drastic and dramatic change. Ferguson and Bruun capture the idea in a brief paragraph.

> So far as it can be defined, the age of the Renaissance was an age of chaotic change, in which there was much that was still medieval, much that was recognizably modern, and much also that was peculiar to itself. It bridged the gap between the High Middle Ages and modern times, but it was also a cultural period in its own right, filled with a great political, social, and intellectual ferment.[4]

FORCES OF CULTURAL RENEWAL

Leading church theologians had made clear the idea that man's main purpose was to glorify God. Renaissance leaders now saw man's main purpose as glorifying human life and enjoying the world to the fullest. Emergence of a middle class, the rise of materialism as a world view, the invention of printing, the new prominence of women, and the unbounded spirit of confidence in man's ability brought about an optimism that had not been seen in the world since the boundless enthusiasm of the early Christians in the first century.

It will be our purpose in these next few paragraphs to focus on five forces of cultural renewal—areas in which the Renaissance brought new light and change of thought to the world of learning. Not all readers will be pleased with the representatives we have selected, but in any survey limitations force such narrowing of choices. Obviously, Aquinas spanned the fields of theology, philosophy, and education; and the impact of Erasmus was so great that we must deal with him in a separate section. We shall save theology, in the sense of the precursors of the Reformation, until another section and deal here specifically with art, architecture, literature, science, and education.

RENAISSANCE ART

Francis Schaeffer suggests that the positive side of the theology of Aquinas was felt in the art of *Giotto* who forsook Byzantine symbolism, which had marked Florentine painting for five hundred years, for a new emphasis on reality and particularly the reality of people. That was in keeping with the philosophy of humanism, which permeated the Renaissance.

> . . . Giotto took a huge step toward giving nature its rightful place. That is proper, for, because God made the world, nature is indeed important—and nature was now being portrayed more like it actually is. Giotto also began to show the versatility which was to characterize Renaissance man.[5]

Later *Masaccio* (1402-1429?), who painted *The Tribute Money* in the Brancacci Chapel in Florence about 1427, set a standard of technical perfection far ahead of his generation and certainly far beyond his youth. We hardly have time to mention van der Weyden, van Eyck, and other Dutch masters who by the first half of the fifteenth century had mastered problems of modeling and perspective. The Northern painters were different from the Italian painters. The former concentrated on infinitely minute detail (shown magnificently in Jon van Eyck's *Madonna of the Cannon van der Paele*), whereas the latter continued to reflect the dominance of the Roman church, modified by the simplicity brought about by the influence of monasticism and scholasticism.

Of course, the master artists of the Renaissance were the

Florentine *Leonardo da Vinci* (1452-1519) and *Michelangelo* (1475-1564). Da Vinci may very well have been the most versatile man of his age — poet, musician, chemist, architect, mechanical engineer, and artist. He filled dozens of notebooks with sketches of all sorts of mechanical devices, spurred on by a driving curiosity to discover what lay beneath the surface of things. Perhaps his most famous painting is the *Mona Lisa,* though Christians certainly honor *The Last Supper.* Schaeffer suggests that da Vinci "really grasped the problem of modern man . . . (he) anticipated where humanism would end." And again, ". . . in this he saw ahead to where our generation has come: Everything, including man, is the machine."[6]

Meanwhile Michelangelo, born twenty-three years later, gave us some of the most magnificent sculpture of all time before he turned painter in the decoration of the Sistine Chapel. Schaeffer sees in the sculpture of Michelangelo a startling statement of the humanism of the Renaissance: "Man will make himself great. Man as man is tearing himself out of the rock. Man by himself will tear himself out of nature and free himself from it. Man will be victorious."[7]

Another interesting observation suggests that the attempt on the part of Aquinas and others during the early years of the Renaissance to combine New Testament theology with Aristotelian philosophy had failed, and now later Renaissance forces — particularly artists, architects, and writers — went back to Plato in an attempt to syncretize the gospel in some form of neo-Platonism. The result again was failure since the Renaissance was not turning man back to God, but rather inward to himself.

RENAISSANCE ARCHITECTURE

Brunelleschi (1377-1446) designed the churches of San Larenzo and Santo Spirito in Florence, in addition to working on the Founding Hospital and the dome of the cathedral of Florence. Renaissance architecture broke with the grandeur of the Gothic cathedrals, a change reflected not only in the work of Brunelleschi but also in the work of Lombard architect *Bramante* (1444-1514) who drew the original plans for St. Peter's Cathedral in Rome (plans later altered by Michelangelo).

RENAISSANCE LITERATURE

A triumvirate of names dominates the literary language of Renaissance Italy — Dante, Petrarch, and Boccaccio. The first and greatest of the three, *Dante Alighieri* (1265-1321) truly bridged the gap between the Middle Ages and the Renaissance. Rather than bringing the light of the gospel to shine on the characteristics of his age, Dante mixed pagan and Christian thought in the greatest of all his works, *The Divine Comedy*, a breathtaking voyage through hell, purgatory, and paradise, which is, in reality, a panoramic survey of medieval thought. Dante was a layman, definitely a part of the secular urban society of Florence, and an advocate of the ultimate division of the sacred and secular, the two-story thinking that characterized Thomistic Renaissance philosophy.

Francesco Petrarch (1304-1374) is sometimes known as "the father of the New Humanism." His passion for the classics and love for ancient Rome combined with the new longing for fame and focus on human qualities. His lyric poems *To Laura* genuinely mark him as a man of the Renaissance.

Giovanni Boccaccio (1313-1375) could not match the romantic insight of Petrarch or spiritual depth of Dante, but perhaps was more typical of the worldly Renaissance civilization than either of his contemporaries. In *The Decameron*, he shaped an Italian prose style that formed a model for later novelists.

RENAISSANCE SCIENCE

It is typical of the Renaissance that the father of its scientific inquiry should have been a trained theologian. *Roger Bacon* (c. 1214-1294) was born in Ilchester, England and studied at Oxford and Paris, where he received his doctor of theology degree. Actually, therefore, the foundations of modern science were laid at Oxford rather than Paris or Rome because accompanying Bacon in the Oxford group was Robert Grosseteste, one of the first to challenge the thinking of Aristotle.

Bacon's most important work was entitled *Opus Majus* in which he pointed out the need of nature and science as subjects for study in the schools. In style it was an encyclopedia of science as well as a discussion of various scientific topics and how to teach them. Bacon was a man ahead of his time who dabbled in geography, astronomy, and alchemy (which accounted for the great suspicion with which the church regarded him). He actually had great contempt for the thinking of his own day and attempted to stay in contact with the man on the street from whom he thought he could learn more than from the reknowned scholars. Few students of history today recall that Roger Bacon predicted the invention of the airplane, the submarine, and the automobile, while avowing his main purpose in science was the substantiation of the truth of the Bible.

The scientific master of the Renaissance period was *Nicolaus Copernicus* (1475-1543), the Polish astronomer. He appears toward the end of the Renaissance period, but so pivotal is Copernicus to an understanding of modern science that we must mention him here. Actually his most important book concerning *The Revolutions of the Heavenly Bodies* appeared just before his death in 1543, which would carry his influence more into the Reformation period. But during the Renaissance years, he developed his intellectual interests during a ten-year stay in Italy when he studied medicine, mathematics, astronomy, and Canon law. He then retired to the country life in his native Frauenburg where sometime in the early sixteenth century he was allowed by a sovereign God to unravel the bewildering complexity of Ptolemaic epicycles with his heliocentric theory.

Though their impact on education may have seemed small at the time, the Renaissance explorers surely must come in for brief mention. Marco Polo's thirteenth-century trip to China; the Portuguese settlements in Madeira, the Azores, and around Africa to India; to say nothing of the voyages of Columbus and Magellan, all fit into the quarter of a millennium we have chosen to call the Renaissance period.

RENAISSANCE EDUCATION

Here is where our interest really lies. All of the above-mentioned topics must be treated, because education is profoundly affected by art, architecture, literature, and science, but what of the development or reform of educational thought during the Renaissance years? Apart from Aquinas and Erasmus, who are the notables whose names should be recognizable to students of the history of educational thought? In order to introduce beginning students to some of the educational impact of Renaissance times, let us list just three names from a far greater list.

We must begin with *Geert Groote* (1340-1384), Groote was the founder of the Brethren of the Common Life, forerunners of the pietistic movement that gave so much to Christianity when building practical New Testament principles upon the theology of the Reformation. Groote was a Dutch thinker, schooled in law and theology as well as the classics. His story is well told by Julia

Henkel, who identifies his educational goals in the following paragraph:

> The Brethren schools, whose policies and practices were firmly grounded in Groote's ideas, sought to make their pupils, above all else, good Christians, disciples whose primary desire was to imitate Christ and His apostles. Having a religious goal in education was not a new thing, but such a goal had usually been limited to the education of the clergy. The Brethren's concept of educating the common man, and of giving him a religious education at that, was unique. The burden of their teaching (and preaching) was more purity, more charity, more tolerance, more enlightenment, and more respect for human faculties. Their concern for the common man was behind their use of the vernacular—even to the point of translating parts of the Bible into Dutch, a move that was attacked by many in the Roman church. But the Brethren, despite their mystical orientation, did not limit their educational goals to the central religious one; they were also concerned about the intellectual, physical, and social lives of their pupils.[8]

The influence of Groote was hardly limited to his own teaching practices or writings. We can never forget that Erasmus of Rotterdam was educated at a school in Deventer operated by Groote's Brethren and that the influence of the Brethren eventually reached the shores of America with the landing of the Puritans and Dutch Calvinists. Their low profile servant mentality offered a refreshing glimpse of biblical education in the otherwise urbane and worldly environment of the Renaissance.

Vittoriano da Feltre (1378-1446) may have been the most important Italian educator of the Renaissance, a famed classical scholar and noted mathematician who found an influential homebase in the court school at Mantua. In contrast to the austere surroundings of medieval scholasticism, da Feltre called his school the "Pleasant House" and tried to develop a spirit of happiness, mutual concern, and unity; in short, a family atmosphere. He lived right with his students, modeling what he wanted them to learn in their daily classes and required chapel services. A genuine Christian humanist,

> Vittoriano believed that truth and appreciation of moral values could be derived not only from Christian authors but also from classical writings, if portions of the latter were expurgated. While the curriculum of his school retained the seven liberal arts, literature dominated, with dialectic and grammar wholly subordinated. Physical training received as full attention as intellectual educa-

tion, for Vittoriano considered such training an integral part of a complete education.[9]

Finally, we must take a brief look at *Francois Rabelais* (1483-1553), a French monk, priest, scholar, physician, and famous satirist, who authored *Life of Gargantua* and *Heroic Deeds of Pantagruel*. Rabelais was definitely a young upstart, even at the end of the Renaissance period. Among his many avant-garde ideas was the recruitment of fair, intelligent, and personable men and women students.

Rabelais would have been a hit at Berkeley in the mid-1960s — no rules, no coercion, no punishment, no concern for the past. Rabelais was an existential utilitarian in the midst of humanistic classicists. But then, when a revolution like the Renaissance breaks out, who can tell what an educator might say?

We have looked at three educators and three countries — the Netherlands, Italy, and France. Space will not allow us to consider contributions of the Spaniard Juan Louis Vives (1492-1540), England's Thomas Elyot (1492-1546), and the German Jacob Wimpfeling (1450-1528). But greater insight awaits as we turn to study in detail the life and teachings of Luther's gadfly, "The Precursor of the Reformation," Erasmus of Rotterdam.

ERASMUS AND HUMANISM

A classic example of how one can view the Renaissance from various angles is the space afforded Desiderius Erasmus in Francis Schaeffer's significant volume *How Should We Then Live*. Although tracing the implications of theology in art, architecture, and literature in great detail, Schaeffer mentions Erasmus in only one brief paragraph, while at the same time noting that the humanism so much a part of his chapter on the Renaissance "was exemplified most clearly by Erasmus at Rotterdam (1466?-1536)."[10]

ERASMUS: PRINCE OF THE HUMANISTS

Eby calls Erasmus "the most famous of all humanists and one of the most influential men of all time," and Robert Ulich, in one of the best monographs ever written on the educational beliefs of Erasmus, says,

> few men have molded European education as decisively as Erasmus. He encouraged a better method of teaching and a more understanding and tolerant attitude toward the pupil, and he in-

filtrated classical studies with a spirit of exactness, historical criticism and international perspective. This allowed ancient philosophy to dominate the humanities until the beginning of the 19th century.[11]

We have already mentioned that Erasmus was a product of the schools run by the Brethren of the Common Life in the Netherlands. Later, at the universities in Paris, Oxford, Germany, and Switzerland, Erasmus found a home with many scholars who could converse in classical Latin, which served almost as his mother tongue. In 1499, however, he returned to England where he met John Colet and Thomas More, who not only became his friends but also exerted profound theological influence on his life. From that time on, the chief aim of his work was the restoration of Christianity to its early foundations by editing the Greek text of the New Testament from the earliest available manuscripts, a volume finally published with extensive notations in 1516.

Erasmus was a diplomat, a peacemaker who, although critical of the stagnant theology of his day, never really broke with the Roman church. His life was marked by unquestioned integrity and morality, possibly learned during his early education with the Brethren of the Common Life. Like Aquinas, he wanted to reconcile faith and reason but, unlike Aquinas, he was willing to criticize the church openly and especially its Bible, the Latin Vulgate, which he considered to be untrustworthy, full of errors, and a rather inadequate translation of translations to begin with.

ERASMIAN THEOLOGY

Though hardly embracing the worldly humanism of his colleagues to the South, Erasmus was a thoroughgoing humanist who believed that man was the measure of all things. As such, man's nature is fundamentally good, in contrast to the Reformation teachings of total depravity. As important as Erasmus was to the history of education, indeed to the history of Christian education, we dare not think of him as "evangelical" in the modern sense.

> To Erasmus, Christianity was little more than a lofty humane morality, and he taught the Platonic Doctrine that men will live the good life if only they know what the good life is. Hence, there was the paramount need of education.[12]

Erasmus also rejected the idea of predestination and was a

strong advocate of free will. He deplored radicalism in religion or education, and was appalled by the ignorance and iconoclasm he thought he observed in the Protestant preachers of the Reformation. Not unlike Francis of Assisi, the prince of the humanists wanted to be a peacemaker, while at the same time wanting to bring about desperately needed theological reforms.

EDUCATIONAL AIMS

In the pattern of Plato, Erasmus placed great emphasis on the role of the state in the educational task. The prince should live close to his people; laws should serve the welfare of the nations; and war should be waged only for the protection of human rights. Such was not the case in the society Erasmus studied. He wrote in *Praise of Folly,*

> It is almost needless to insist upon the several professors of arts and sciences, who are all so egregiously conceited, but they would sooner give up their title to an estate in lands than part with the reversion of their wits; among these, more especially stage-players, musicians, orators, and poets, each of which, the more of duncery they have, and the more of pride, the greater is their ambition: and how notoriously so ever dull they be they meet with their admirers; nay, the more silly they are the higher they are extoled; Folly (as we have before intimated) never failing of respect and esteem. If, therefore, everyone, the more ignorant he is, the greater satisfaction he is to himself, and the more commended by others; to what purpose is it to sweat and toil in the pursuit of true learning, which shall cost so many grips and pangs of the brain to acquire, and when obtained, shall only make the laborious student more uneasy to himself and less acceptable to others?[13]

Classicist that he was, Erasmus would, of course, insist on a core curriculum that would develop intellect as the center of man—the classics, the writings of church Fathers, and the Bible. The Aristotelian philosophy of Erasmus is not only pre-Reformation, but also pre-Copernican and pre-Galilean (i.e., Galileo).

EDUCATIONAL METHODOLOGY

Ulich considers *Liberal Education of Boys* published in 1529 Erasmus's finest work on education. Methodologically, Desiderius emphasized the careful study of the child's nature well before that kind of enlightenment found popularity with Comenius, Froebel, and Pestalozzi. He was furious at the mistreatment of young students and stressed the important role of games and exercise in education, favoring praise and reward rather than even mild discipline to accomplish the goals of humanist education. The task of the teacher was to help his students, not to display his own erudition. With such a commitment, we should not be surprised that Erasmus became one of the first advocates of the systematic training of teachers.

OTHER IMPORTANT HUMANIST EDUCATORS

Perhaps the keynote of thought for the Northern humanists was a common reaction against medievalism. Of course, that could be said of their Parisian and Italian brethren as well. In the Netherlands and England, however, there seemed to be a stronger commitment to the Scriptures and the writings of the early church Fathers, particularly in their original form and language. Consequently, the humanists developed serious study in Greek and Hebrew as well as Latin, which brought them into violent conflict with the conservative theologians of the church who preferred the scholars of the Middle Ages to the original texts.

In Germany one of the outstanding Christian humanists was *Johann Reuchlin* (1455-1522), who had studied in Italy but returned to Germany to devote his life to the study of Hebrew in order to understand the Old Testament Scriptures thoroughly. In 1506 he published the first Hebrew grammar north of the Alps and was subsequently charged with heresy by the inquisitor of Cologne backed by the Dominican teachers there. In France, *Jacques LeFever d'Etaples* (c. 1455-1536) was as committed to the New Testament as Reuchlin was to the Old. He too had studied in Italy and then returned to his native Paris to discover the real meaning of the New Testament through serious exegesis. Doubtless the work of both Continental scholars significantly influenced Erasmus.

We have already called attention to the association of the prince of the humanists with the British brethren Colet and More. *John Colet* (1467-1519) was dean of St. Paul's Cathedral and founder of a theological school there. An administrator rather than a scholar, he directed the activity of humanist scholars studying at St. Paul's. His contemporary and friend was *Thomas More* (c. 1478-1535) whose *Utopia*, published in 1516, presented the humanist's picture of an ideal society and is still considered a classic in social reform.

It is probably impossible to assess the impact of Christian humanism on the Reformation. The first-year student of church history notes the impact of Erasmus, particularly on Luther, but what about Melancthon, Luther's personal theologian, who studied at Wittenberg with Reuchlin? How much of Colet's thinking or perhaps that of *William Grocyn* (1446-1514) created the base for the Reformation in the British Isles?

Let us not forget to separate Christian humanism from secular humanism in our study of the Renaissance, but, by the same token, let us not fail to offer tribute to whom tribute is due and acknowledge that much of what we are able to think and do today in evangelical Christianity came about because of Renaissance thinking.

> The Renaissance is closer to the twentieth century than almost any age. It posed severe dilemmas which still torture modern man: What is the relationship of knowledge to morality? What is more important: General education or specific knowledge? Which is to be the center of education: Science or Literature? What is the relationship between intellectual and esthetic excellence? All these questions are of perennial importance in the history of education.[14]

Meanwhile, there were other thinkers in the history of educational thought who, rather than enjoy the prestige of the universities and societies they served, were slain for their faith. To them, too, we owe the glory of the Reformation and offer now that recognition.

FORERUNNERS OF FREEDOM

We have already talked of the influence of the Brethren of the Common Life during the Renaissance, but we must add to that mention a reference to the Waldenses, a group of believers hidden in the alpine valleys of northern Italy and Switzerland, who silently protested and continued through the dark centuries to preach and teach the Scriptures. Persecuted, always driven about from place to place, they were almost completely annihilated by Innocent III in the thirteenth century. It was through them that the purity of New Testament Christianity passed on to these three "forerunners of freedom" whom we shall study briefly — John Wycliffe, John Huss, and Girolamo Savonarola.

John Wycliffe (1320-1384), commonly called "the Morning Star of the Reformation," was leader of the Lollards, a moderately militant group committed to divine sovereignty and opposed to many of the trappings of the medieval church such as prayers for the dead, absolution, and the worship of saints. Their primary contribution to the evangelical strain of education, which carried through all the years of the church from Christ to the present hour, was their irrevocable commitment to the Bible as the absolute authority. They refused the traditions of the church as a standard for Christians and carried out their educational ministry through writing and distributing literature called "tracts." In a sense they became the forerunners of the Christian literature coleportage efforts so popular in the late nineteenth and early twentieth centuries.

Meanwhile, Wycliffe's disciples were at work in Bohemia. John Huss (1369-1415) and the Hussites had printed the Scriptures in the vernacular before the time of Luther. They had developed a system of schools and an outstanding university for the purpose of promoting practical Christianity. If they had lived 150 years later they might have been part of the Anabaptist movement, rather like the Mennonites, stressing purity of conduct, self-denying love, and an absolute commitment to Scripture. Another very important educational group, the Moravians, were descendents of the Hussites.

Huss was summoned to the Council of Constance in 1415 on the promise of safe conduct. But, as many times before and yet in the future, the leaders of the church broke their pledged word. John Huss was incarcerated in a stone dungeon three feet by six feet by seven feet and then burned at the stake. The fire of Huss's flesh served as a guiding light for Martin Luther. In the words of Fisher, "in condemning Huss to the stake, the fathers of Constance roused the soul of a nation."[15]

However, it was an Italian whom Luther acclaimed protomartyr of the Reformation. *Girolamo Savonarola* (1452-1498) was at the center of the Renaissance in the height of the period—Florence in 1482. What he saw about him was not the freedom of spirit taught in the New Testament but rather an increasing worldliness and commitment to materialism. So in Florence itself a second John the Baptist began to preach in the cathedral, pleading for a return to the pure life of early Christianity. For twenty years until the turn of the century, the prophet attacked the sins of the church and the world, promising woe and intoning judgment like the ancient Jeremiah. Stevenson records the message offered by Michael de la Badoyere.

"Listen to me," he cried. "Or rather listen to the words that come from God. I cannot say other than 'Do penance. Come, sinners, come, for God is calling you'. . . . Oh Florence (like Babylon) you are sitting by the rivers of your sins. Make a river of your tears that you may purify yourselves in it."[16]

In 1498 Savonarola went too far, alienated papal powers, and lost his life in the cause of reform. Once again the blood of the martyr became the seed of the church, and the Reformation was to break forth both from and against the Renaissance.

But some have asked, How are the Renaissance and the Reformation different? Obviously, one was a cultural movement and the other theological, though theology is hardly separable from culture or culture from theology. The major difference, of course, was the difference between humanism and theism. Schaeffer describes it this way:

> But while the Reformation and the Renaissance overlapped historically, and while they dealt with the same basic questions, they gave completely different answers. You will remember that to Thomas Aquinas the *will* was fallen after man had revolted against God, but the *mind* was not. This eventually resulted in people believing they could think out the answers to all the great questions, beginning only from themselves, and on the basis of human reason alone think out the answers to the great questions which confront mankind.[17]

Man versus God, Cain versus Abel, Athens versus Jerusalem—the drama was now to be enacted in a contest between Rome and Wittenberg.

NOTES

1. Francis A. Schaeffer, *How Should We Then Live?* (Old Tappan, N.J.: Revell, 1976), pp. 51-52.
2. Joan Ellen Duvall, "Thomas Aquinas," in Elmer L. Towns, ed., *A History of Religious Educators* (Grand Rapids: Baker, 1975), p. 72.
3. Wallace K. Ferguson and Geoffrey Bruun, *A Survey of European Civilization* (New York: Houghton Mifflin, 1969), p. 311.
4. Ibid., p. 309.
5. Schaeffer, p. 57.
6. Ibid., p. 74.
7. Ibid., p. 71.
8. Julia Henkel, "Geert Groote," in Towns, p. 86.
9. Elmer H. Wilds and Kenneth Lee Lottich, *The Foundations of Modern Education*, 3d ed. (New York: Holt, Rinehart, and Winston, 1961), p. 203.
10. Schaeffer, p. 81.
11. Robert Ulich, "Erasmus," in Towns, p. 102.
12. William Stevenson, *The Story of the Reformation* (Richmond, Va.: John Knox, 1959), p. 25.

13. Frederick Mayer, *A History of Educational Thought*, 2d ed. (Columbus, Ohio: Merrill, 1966), p. 184.
14. Mayer, p. 192.
15. H. A. L. Fisher, *A History of Europe* (London: Edward Arnold, 1936), p. 356.
16. Stevenson, p. 23.
17. Schaeffer, p. 81.

7

Reformation Dawn and the Light of Christian Education

On October 31, 1517, a young Augustinian monk by the name of Martin Luther nailed ninety-five theses to the door of the Castle Church at Wittenberg, Germany. It was the eve of All Saints Day, and Luther was reacting against Pope Leo X's efforts to gather money for Rome's new cathedral of St. Peter's through the sale of indulgences. Of course, Luther's inner troubles did not begin in the year 1517. They had been going on since a bolt of lightning nearly struck him while out walking one day when he was twenty-one years old. Through all his training for the priesthood he continued to wrestle with the question: How can a man gain salvation and acceptance with God?

But now the blatant hawking of indulgences by the Dominican preacher John Tetzel across the river from Luther's parish had forced the issue to the forefront of his heart and mind. The answer, he was convinced, had to be through a free gift of God's grace received only through the medium of faith. With that newly lit conviction consuming him, Luther cried out against the blatant violation so obviously demonstrated in the sale of indulgences — a manmade means of "purchasing" eternal life. He chose the eve of All Saints Day to offer his public protest, hardly aware of the worldwide, historical significance of his act.

> In these Theses Luther insisted on the need of real penitence and contrition. He further maintained that there can be no human mediation between a man's soul and God. No Indulgence can absolve guilt: Forgiveness rests not with the pope but only with God. In the Theses themselves there was nothing antipapal, but the condition of Germany was such that only a spark was required to set it ablaze. The Ninety-five Theses struck the spark: The Reformation had begun.[1]

The student of educational history must understand that a dating of the Reformation period in this book will be significantly

135

different from a dating that might attempt to cover the entirety of church history. The latter would trace Reformation influences on through the Wesleys and Whitefield into the preaching of Jonathan Edwards in New England and indeed into the Reformed faith as it is exercised in a major branch of evangelicalism today. And, of course, there are educational implications all through those centuries. But it is essential for us to be more specific if we are to look at historical influences of education as "a history of Christian thought in education." Just as we narrowed our thinking on Renaissance dates to approximately two centuries, so we must identify some framework in which to study the Reformation contribution to Christian thought in education. Therefore, although it may be arbitrary, we have chosen the sixteenth century as the rough boundaries of that period.

LUTHERAN CONTRIBUTIONS TO EDUCATION

It is extremely tempting to explore the adventures of Luther as pastor, theologian, and apologist for the evangelical faith. We could talk about Pope Leo calling on Luther to recant at the Diet of Augsburg, followed by the Reformer's refusal and excommunication in 1521. How exciting to remember again Luther's defense before the emperor at the Diet of Worms in that same year and the uttering of those memorable words, "Here I stand, I cannot do otherwise. God help me. Amen"; his enforced seclusion at Wartburg Castle; his return to involvement with Hans Müller in the peasant revolts; his translation of the New Testament, and the involvement in the Schmalkaldic religious wars.

But volumes have been written on that aspect of Luther's life and ministry. In fact, his greatness as a religious reformer overshadows almost to exclusion his greatness as a religious educator.

EDUCATIONAL CONTEXT OF THE REFORMATION

The one man who spanned the transition between Renaissance and Reformation was the great humanist, Erasmus of Rotterdam. In 1516 at the age of fifty, Erasmus was the arbiter of all Europe, the most popular scholar on the Continent. Luther was profoundly affected by the humanist's translation of the New Testament as well as by his many satirical writings against the excesses of the Roman church. Likewise, Erasmus supported Luther until the Reformer appeared in the eyes of the more moderate Erasmus to be engaging in extreme behavior. Later, when the persecution of Lutherans began in the Netherlands, Erasmus was trapped because of his kind words about Luther. His response was a trip to Basel and efforts to mediate the Lutheran-Catholic conflict. Of course, both sides attacked Erasmus as a compromiser.

It is important to note that in the initial days of the Lutheran movement, Luther had no intention of separating from the Roman church. He wanted to reform it from within. The break between Luther and Erasmus came on this point as much as any other because Erasmus maintained that internal reform position throughout his life, whereas Luther eventually was forced to an open break with the church. Erasmus also publicly disagreed with Luther on the freedom of the will, although that may very well have been a mutual misunderstanding. Ultimately Luther publicly condemned Erasmus and his "theology of peace," but right up until his death the humanist continued correspondence with Luther's in-house theologian, Philip Melancthon.

The major difference in theology and educational philosophy between the Renaissance and the Reformation is the difference between humanism and evangelicalism. Schaeffer has a succinct paragraph articulating that difference.

> Because the Reformers could not mix humanism with their position, but took instead a serious view of the Bible, they had no problem of meaning for the individual things, the particulars; they had no nature-versus-grace problem. One could say that the Renaissance centered in autonomous man; while the Reformation centered in the infinite-personal God who had spoken in the Bible. In the answer the Reformation gave, the problem of meaning for individual things, including man, was so completely answered that the problem—as a problem—did not exist. The reason for this is that the Bible gives a unity to the universal and the particulars.[2]

During Luther's time almost all education was under the control of the state, and the level was quite poor. Remember, Luther never argued for a separation of church and state, but rather believed the princes were responsible for education in connection with their responsibilities for protecting the citizens.

At that time the universities, the Burgher schools, and the monolithic system of education for medieval knights were all subservient to the church, a problem that Luther challenged by developing the "two-sword theory," concluding that:

1. The hierarchy of the church was turning the kingdom of God into a kingdom of this world.
2. The church must always be understood as "the church under the cross" and therefore earthly power, or it is out of order.
3. The church dare not practice an attitude of "the church under glory" because that would be contrary to New Testament teaching.
4. The church needed to correct medieval theology, which had confused Christ with the church.

The result, of course, was a desire to rid education of the trappings of medieval scholasticism, which Luther said endangered the moral development of young people. Education should center in reading, writing, thinking, and the study of Scripture rather than the classics (another obvious disagreement with Erasmus). And since such an emphasis on the Bible could hardly be expected from the church, Luther said it remained the responsibility of the Reformed princes to insist that it take place.

SOCIOLOGICAL SETTING OF LUTHER'S TIME

The sociological matrix for education always affects the teaching-learning process, and that generalized rule was no different in Luther's day. In addition to all the complexities of the Renaissance, the early sixteenth century was also experiencing a transition from a race of "Christians" into a heterogeneous mass of mankind separated into multitudinous states and countries. Complete secularization had not yet taken place by any means, and the "statesman" of Luther's day considered himself a representative of God.

It was on that basis that Luther could appeal to the princes to do something about religious education as he understood it. The pastor and the prince should confront each other in dialogue, with the former admonishing the latter and the latter maintaining his control in civic matters. The statesman, just like the cleric, was answerable to God. For Luther church and state had to work together rather like husband and wife. In his speech to the mayors and aldermen of Germany, Luther said, "Therefore, it will be the duty of the mayors and councils to exercise the greatest care over the young. For since the happiness, honor, and life of the city are committed to their hands, they would be held recreant before God and the world, if they did not day and night, with all their power seek its welfare and improvement."[3]

LUTHER'S SOCIAL ETHIC

According to Luther, love was the sustaining norm of all human interrelations. The Christian should not limit his relationships to fellow Christians, but must extend out to all neighbors. The educational implications of the love ethic argue that all learning principles are good if they reveal God, and evil if they hide Him in any way. Since genuine love reveals God, it is an important aspect of education.

The Lutheran balance of law and gospel emerged early in Luther's thinking. Lutheran educators have historically argued that both law and gospel be distinguished in biblical content, that both be taught in proper relationship to each other, and that the law be used to serve the gospel in pointing out an awareness of sin, the need for the Savior, and by revealing the paths of righteousness.

God confronts all men in His universe and demands obedience to natural law and order, but the gospel cannot be used to rule; that is the role of law. The gospel is a freeing agency, not a ruling agency. All life is lived in the shadow of eternity, and therefore a genuinely Christian education must continually keep eternal values foremost. As Jahsmann puts it,

> Though Lutheran education is also interested in the development of man for a useful and good life on earth, it approaches this concern through the primary goal of eternal life with God. To realize the I-Thou relationship, Lutheran education uses chiefly what it calls the means of grace—the Word of God. This word is properly identified in Lutheran theology as *the Gospel of God's forgiving love in Christ*. It is the divine plan of salvation revealed in the Holy Scriptures and in the Sacraments of Holy Baptism and the Lord's Supper. In its broadest sense the term Word of God includes the whole Bible, because in the last analysis the entire Scriptures are the inspired revelation of God's will for His people as manifested by his "mighty acts" (cf. Psalms 78), the Hebrew *dabhar* here meaning both word and work.[4]

THE HOME—LUTHER'S PRIMARY FOCUS

The crux of Martin Luther's educational philosophy was domestic training. Family government was to be the root of all other government, and where the root is bad, he argued, the trunk cannot be good. Against the parental neglect Luther found everywhere in Germany, he argued that bringing up children in the fear and knowledge of God was more efficacious than pilgrimages, masses, or the building of churches. Said he, "In my judgment there is no other outward offense that in the sight of God so heavily burdens the world, and deserves such heavy chastisement, as the neglect to educate children."[5]

Luther was able to proceed in logical argument from parental responsibility to state responsibility on two counts. First of all, the total inadequacy of domestic training required that religious education be turned over to the state, hence his famous sermon, "The Duty of Sending Children to School." That did not free parents of responsibility since they were still required to supervise and aid the catechetical training of their children as well as make each home a genuine learning atmosphere. Exams were to be given in the home at least once a week.

The second argument had to do with the bypassing of the clergy. Our contemporary formula of priority in Christian education is home $\longrightarrow$ church $\longrightarrow$ school. But because of the theological deficiencies he sensed in the clergy, and because of their already heavy load of preaching, administering the sacraments, and carrying out of pastoral duties, Luther turned to the princes and city councils.

Luther's concerns were not just for children, but for the education of youth and adults as well, a point covered aptly by Harold Grimm in his essay on Luther in *A History of Religious Educators.*[6] We refer frequently to that volume and see no need to reproduce here many of the details available in its fine collection of essays.

LUTHER'S CURRICULUM

Luther was one of the first educators in history to emphasize the need for universal compulsory education, mainly because he was so concerned that every citizen be able to read the Bible. In addition to biblical studies, Luther urged concentration on languages, grammar, rhetoric, logic, literature, poetry, history, music, mathematics, gymnastics, and nature study.

But Luther's big guns of educational reform were reserved for the curricula of the monastic schools and universities. He was a strong critic of the classics and the mystics alike. Next to the Scripture, the catechisms were the most important item in the curriculum, for they explained such things as the Ten Commandments, the Lord's Prayer, the Apostles' Creed, and basic theological concepts. Unique in his day was Luther's emphasis on music, which he esteemed as second only to theology in importance. Historians tell us he had a good voice, played several instruments, and encouraged others to do so as well. He believed, "Satan is a great enemy to music. It is a good antidote against temptation and evil thoughts. . . . Music is a semi-disciplinarian and schoolmaster; it makes men more gentle and tender-hearted, more modest and discreet. . . . A schoolmaster must be able to sing, otherwise I will hear nothing of him.[7]

true

LUTHER'S EDUCATIONAL METHODOLOGY

A fine teacher himself, Luther made a tremendous contribution to the history of education by raising the status of the teaching profession. Next to the work of preaching, teaching was closest to the heart of God.

An important ingredient of teaching methodology was discipline, and Luther was a strong believer in obedience on the part of both children at home and students in the classroom. But contrary to the practice of his day, Luther taught that strict obedience was to be tempered with moderation and love. He was revolted by the severity of discipline in the monastic schools, where children were sometimes beaten nearly to death for failure to learn or behave properly.

discipline

He emphasized the use of imagery, illustration, and repetition. Although committed to memorization, Luther did not believe in information overload, but rather was greatly concerned that comprehension be a major goal of the educational process. Turning his back on Socrates and Plato, Luther believed children should not be presented with controversial or polemical matters, but should be taught positively to internalize the truth of God's Word and Christian theology. Learning should also be interesting, reinforced by concrete examples and communicated through observation rather than abstraction.

We are greatly indebted to Martin Luther for emphasizing education for the common people, a renewal of the emphasis on the home, a love-moderated discipline, and the centrality of the Scriptures in the curriculum. It would be an inadequate view of his work to end this treatment without noting his rather unrealistic view of the church and state relationship, a probable overemphasis on rote memory as a method, and a general hostility to the inductive process. When strengths and weaknesses are measured, however, Luther's positive imprint on the history of Christian thought in education is unmistakable and we rather agree with Harold Grimm that the former monk "became one of the greatest preachers and teachers of all time."[8]

PHILIP MELANCHTHON

If we were following a strictly chronological flow in this chapter, we would move immediately to Zwingli in Switzerland, deal with the work of Ignatius of Loyola, and only then come to Melanchthon. But geography is a better way to follow the flow of educational patterns in the Reformation, and therefore we will stay with Germany and Luther's associate, Philip Melanchthon.

If Erasmus bridged the gap between the Renaissance and the Reformation, Melanchthon bridged the gap between Erasmus and Luther. We have already indicated that long after Luther and Erasmus had made public breaks with each other, the humanist and the theologian maintained correspondence. How, we might ask, could Melanchthon be Luther's resident theologian and teacher of teachers, while at the same time espousing a position that could be called "Christian humanism"? The only possible answer is the continuing commitment of Philip Melanchthon to "the liberal arts" and the classics. "It is this program which identifies Melanchthon as a Christian humanist. Indeed, Melanchthon cannot be understood as an educator if he is not taken seriously as a Christian humanist. He spelled out these convictions in his inaugural address at the University of Wittenberg on 29 August 1518. In it, he made a strong plea for the study of the languages."[9]

One wonders how Luther and Melanchthon dealt with their differences "behind closed doors." Apparently, Philip was able to tone down his obvious love for a classical curriculum sufficiently for Martin to ignore the differences and emphasize his strengths as theologian and historian. Even secular educators recognize the brilliance of Melanchthon. Wilds and Lottich call him "the greatest scholar among the school organizers of the German Reformation" and applaud his reorganization of the school system in Saxony in 1527.

> This Saxony system was the first state school system of history, although it must be remembered that it dealt only with secondary school organization. According to this plan, the secondary schools, which were to be established in every town under the support and control of the civil authorities were to be organized on three levels. The first level is for beginners, who were to learn to read Latin; the second level was for the study of Latin grammar;

the third level was for the pursuit of more advanced linguistic studies, reading of classic authors, exercises in rhetoric, and the study of logic.[10]

But it is Philip Melanchthon the Christian educator with whom we are most concerned. His attitude toward Christian education is probably the clue to his long and happy association with Luther. Though they may have differed on the value of the classics, they were of one mind on the centricity of Scripture and theology in the curriculum of all ages. Meyer points out that Melanchthon was a strong churchman and always subordinated his humanist pursuits to the service of the church, insisting that its pastors must demonstrate holiness of life as well as solid erudition. All theological professors at the University of Wittenberg were pledged to teach in accordance with the Apostles' Creed, the Nicene Creed, the Athanasian Creed, and the Augsburg Confession of 1530. Of himself as educator, Melanchthon wrote,

> I apply myself solely to one thing, the defence of letters. By our example we must excite youth to the admiration of learning and induce them to love it for its own sake and not for the advantage that may be derived from it. The destruction of learning brings with it the ruin of everything that is good—religion, morals, and all things human and divine. The better a man is, the greater his ardor in the preservation of learning; he knows that of all plagues, ignorance is the pernicious. . . . To neglect the youth in our schools is just like taking the spring out of the year. They, indeed, take away the spring from the year who permit the schools to decline, because religion cannot be maintained without them. And a terrible darkness will fall upon society, if the study of the sciences should be neglected.[11]

HULDREICH ZWINGLI AND THE SWISS REFORMATION

The Reformation in Switzerland is generally dated from the year 1523, which began with the First Zurich Disputation between Zwingli and his Catholic opponent, John Faber. Before the end of the year came, the city council had voted to move carefully in the direction of the reforms recommended by Zwingli. The final phase of reform did not come about, however, until the late spring of 1524.

The eighteen-month time segment from early 1523 to mid-1524 is important in understanding Zwingli's perspective, which was conveyed to the Zurich city council. Rather than a radical overthrow, it was an educational process that brought reform to the city. Zwingli was the chief pedagogue and author of the *Short Christian Instruction,* which was utilized during the process period to instruct the pastors and the people in the Reformed position. Also in 1523, Zwingli authored a short essay entitled "On the Education of Youth," which still serves as the primary source of his views on education.

Since we have compared both Luther and Melanchthon with Erasmus, it may be of benefit to continue that point of reference. Of all the Reformers, Zwingli was probably the closest to Erasmus and therefore the most thoroughgoing humanist. Short of Luther's continual presence that honor might very well have gone to the brilliant Melanchthon, but, separated from the fiery monk by several hundred miles, Zwingli went about his Zurich reforms very much in the spirit of the prince of the humanists.

Like Erasmus, Zwingli wanted to work within the system, both civic and ecclesiastical, to create reforms that were entirely peaceful. But it was not to be. Already in 1523, the Anabaptists were breaking with Zwingli. By the end of 1524, they were forming their own churches. By early 1525, Zwingli and the city council had reached the conclusion that the Anabaptist movement must be crushed, and open persecution began. By the end of the third decade of the sixteenth century, Zwingli was hopelessly embroiled in international politics, and Switzerland was divided into Catholic cantons (provinces) and Zwinglian cantons. On October 9, 1531, the Zurichers and their allies were defeated by the forest cantons of the Catholics. Zwingli, along with five hundred of the Protestant leaders, was killed. The Reformer's body was cut to pieces and burned, and his ashes, mingled with those of swine, were scattered to the wind.

The ministry of a mere eight years seems like such a little impact when compared with Luther and Calvin, but in that short time Zwingli nearly transformed a city (and almost a nation) both theologically and educationally. He set up a theological institute, trained scores of ministers, and laid the groundwork for much more extensive Swiss reforms to come under the leadership of John Calvin at Geneva.

Perhaps Zwingli's greatest contribution was the participatory, nonauthoritarian educational style of his *Prophezei* (theological institute). It was a genuine community of scholars in which lecturers and students joined together to seek out truth. The atmosphere exemplified New Testament community and respect for student as well as content, a solid foundation for effective contemporary theological education.

JOHN CALVIN AND THE GENEVA THEOCRACY

Martin Luther may have a denomination named after him, but John Calvin has lent his name to an entire theological system. Indeed, Philip Melanchthon himself was the first to call Calvin "The Theologian," though the Geneva Reformer was much more than just a dogmatician.

After studies in theology at the Sorbonne and law at the University of Orleans, Calvin began preaching Reformation doctrine in Paris about 1533, three years before he completed his famous *Institutes of the Christian Religion.* In 1536 he arrived at Geneva and became the virtual moral dictator of that city. Calvin's first reforms in Geneva lacked the patience shown by Zwingli, though the intent was essentially the same. Within two years he and his colleague Guillaume Farel were expelled, only to be called back in 1541. Calvin then worked in Geneva until his death in 1564.

Calvin's theology centered on the sovereignty of God, the total depravity of man, and an insistence on predestination. This is a hopeless oversimplification of a grandiose theological scheme, but it is nevertheless important to the total system developed by the Reformer at Geneva. Theologically, Calvin was tied to Augustine much in the same way that Thomas Aquinas was tied to Aristotle. Calvinism became much more than a theological or educational system, it was a veritable way of life, a civil order that formed the basis for the life-style practiced by the Puritans in early colonial America.

> From an economic standpoint, the growth of Calvinism encouraged the rise of capitalism. Calvin himself believed that morality should govern business relations, but some of the Calvinistic preachers glorified success, and they identified wealth and virtue. Accordingly, they taught that the rich man received his material rewards because of superior ability and a moral earnestness, while the poor man was punished for his sloth.[12]

Towns tells us about Calvin's famous Geneva Academy founded in 1557 and staffed by many of the notable scholars of the day such as Theodorus Beza, Antoine Chevalier, and Jean Tagant.

> The academy was divided into a *Schola privata*, for children up to

about 16 years of age, and a *Schola publica,* the university. The latter offered only the arts and theology at first, but Calvin hoped to add law and medicine. The entire academy was run by the rector, who was appointed for a two-year term and whose responsibilities included admitting students and granting degrees. He personally supervised the Schola publica, while his assistant was principal of the Schola privata. Under the rector were the public professors of Hebrew, Greek, the Arts, and Theology. Under the principal were regents, or teachers.[13]

The *Schola publica* later gained renown as the University of Geneva.

Calvin's concepts of education exerted far more widespread influence than those of Luther. They went with John Knox to Scotland, were spread all over France by the Huguenots, were enforced in the Netherlands by the Prince of Orange, (later known as William the Silent), and were carried to the new world by the Puritans.

Peter DeJong takes the position that the very popularity of Calvin's *Institutes* tends to obscure his significant role as educator. His entire life was involved with academic pursuits, and he was the quintessential teaching pastor at both Geneva and Strasbourg.

> He called the church back to its official task of teaching the children committed to its care and provided for this a pattern in which it could function with a high degree of effectiveness. Systematic and sustained instruction by pastors might not be neglected. . . . The teaching of children is to be instruction in the life which is according to Godliness. They must learn what it means to be Christian, not simply by giving the right answers with mind and in words, but so appropriating God's message of redemption in Christ Jesus that all of life comes to be lived by them in obedience to the Scriptures. This response alone makes manifest that they have become wise unto salvation.[14]

In addition to the *Institutes* Calvin authored numerous tracts, articles, and catechisms, among which were *Instruction in Faith,* published early in 1537, the *Catechism of the Church at Geneva* in 1541, and numerous commentaries in both Old and New Testament books.

THE BRITISH ISLES — BANE AND BLESSING

In talking about the Reformation in the British Isles, one is drawn inevitably to the larger-than-life picture of Henry VIII (clearly a bane) whose enforced on-again, off-again commitment to Protestantism inaugurated the Reformation in England, which was really a subordination of the church to the state. In Scotland the splendor of John Knox, set on fire in Geneva by Calvin, was transforming his nation into theological sensitivity.

The only educational consequence of the Reformation in England came about through some of the literature produced by the Anglican church. The first prayer book of King Edward VI appeared in 1549 and a second in 1552. Then, after the return to Catholicism under Mary, the Elizabethan Settlement's attempt at compromise between Luther and Calvin was just getting underway when the Puritan uprising began.

Meanwhile, John Knox returned to Scotland in 1559, more than thirty years after the death of Patrick Hamilton the "protomartyr of the Scottish Reformation." By 1559 the constant conflict between Protestant and Catholic forces had brought the nation to a virtual civil war; and by August of the same year Romanism was abolished by a decree of Parliament.

Can we say that Knox actually contributed something to the history of Christian education? Insofar as it is impossible to further the Christian faith without educational processes of some kind, all the Reformers were educators. Like Luther, Knox emphasized education in the family, but Marshall Dendy reminds us,

> Knox's most important contribution to education was the scheme of national education which he instituted in Scotland. It consisted of a graduated system of elementary schools, secondary schools (colleges) and universities. The elementary schools were established and conducted by the church, which appointed the schoolmaster and paid him. Attendance was compulsory for girls and boys, rich and poor, for at least four years. The people met only once a week, the minister or reader was to take charge, teaching the youth at least the rudiments and the Catechism. Those who finished the elementary course and passed the final examination were compelled to attend the colleges, which were established in every famous town. Those who completed college, past final examination, and produced testimonials to their good character could enter one of six universities, located in St. Andrews, Glasgow, and Aberdeen.[15]

Knox's educational views published in his *Book of Discipline*, ultimately "caused the Scottish peasantry to be the best educated in the world."[16]

THE ANABAPTISTS — FORGOTTEN PEDAGOGUES OF THE PERIOD

The fine book *A History of Religious Educators* to which we have referred often, lists six educators in what we have called the Reformation Period—Luther, Zwingli, Ignatius of Loyola, Melanchthon, Knox, and Calvin. As in most histories of the Reformation, the Anabaptists are ignored. Part of the reason is the wide dispersal of their activities throughout various nations, a general disagreement and lack of unity in theological positions, and consistent harassment both by the Roman Catholic church and the mainline Reformation movements. Hyma and Stanton state the problem simply.

> Many of the new sects opposed infant baptism because infants could not yet understand. Historians categorized these believers in one group called the Anabaptists. They came from almost every country of Europe. This term means "those baptized again." It was used to describe the many adults who joined the Anabaptists and were baptized again as adults.
>
> Anabaptists, as a group, had widely differing Biblical interpretations and philosophies. They felt no need for a central clergy because they believed each person should follow his own "inner light." Often they were persecuted because they questioned many of the basic beliefs of both Protestantism and Catholicism. Anabaptists were tortured and even killed in Switzerland, Germany, the Netherlands, and Austria. They did, however, find some degree of religious freedom in Russia and Poland.[17]

Yet it is impossible to measure the extent to which twentieth-century "free church" movements in Europe and the United States have been influenced by this underrated group of Reformation saints. The Baptists, almost all kinds of Brethren, the Mennonites, and the Independent church movement, to say nothing of Amish, Dunkers, Quakers, and others, all have their roots in the Anabaptist movement.

But who were the significant educators among the Anabaptists of the mid-sixteenth century? What universities did they found, and what are the titles of some of their more important books? It is rather difficult to found universities and write treatises on theology while being persecuted and harassed on every side. It is perhaps not unfair to counter with the question, What great educational treatises were written by Jesus or His disciples? What universities were founded by the early church? It is our opinion that, whereas the major Reformation leaders gave us a definitive heritage of educational design, it is the Anabaptists who really showed the world how to live like Jesus.

That generalization does not fit all of the Anabaptists, of course, and the movement acquired a jaded reputation by the radicalism of the "kingdom of God" at Münster, the Zwickau prophets, and other fringe heresies. Surely a high point of the movement was in June 1524 when several Anabaptist groups met at the home of Balthazer Hubmaier and decided to leave the Catholic church. Hubmaier was a distinguished scholar, as was Hans Denck, completely committed to purity of life, purity of church membership, communal sharing of goods, opposition to war, a solid view of Christian liberty — all the while still sharing with their Reformed and Lutheran brethren a complete commitment to salvation by faith and the absolute authority of the Word of God. One must also mention the Dutchman Melchior Hoffman and the Swiss Menno Simons, the founder of the Mennonites, among leading Anabaptists.

Most of the emphasis of the Anabaptists on education was in congregations, a view that is increasingly popular toward the end of the twentieth century. Hubmaier was burned at the stake in 1528, hardly having had any time to write anything of significance. Denck died in 1527, but in the last two years of his life he did publish a large number of spiritual and eloquent writings representing evangelical mysticism within the Anabaptist movement. Menno Simons shook off the stigma of the Münster kingdom and drew his portion of the movement closer to the Waldensians of pre-Reformation times. Until his death in 1559, Menno represented Swiss antipedobaptism and rigorous disciplinary views. His descendants today certainly represent one of the most Christian-education-conscious branches of the evangelical movement in North America.

ROME'S RESPONSE — IGNATIUS OF LOYOLA

In 1545, Pope Paul III convened the Council of Trent to discuss reform in the Roman Catholic church as a response to the Protestant movement. The main concern, of course, was winning back territory influenced by Protestantism, but the result of the council was a reform movement within the church, in which it concerned itself with the life-style of clergymen but not with the revision of any doctrines. One reformer was Teresa of Avila, a Spanish nun who founded thirty-two convents while influencing other convents and monasteries toward reform.

But the heart of the Catholic Counter-Reformation was Ig-

natius of Loyola, the founder of the Jesuits. A contemporary
Jesuit priest refers to Ignatius as

> A deeply prayerful man, one of Christianity's greatest mystics. It
> was in his native Basque environment that he first inherited the
> Christian outlook on life, enveloped in sixteenth century trap-
> pings. Through extraordinary mystical experiences at Manresa, he
> gradually conceived a world view which was centered around the
> divine plan in creating and redeeming man, and he intensely de-
> sired to be intimately associated with Christ and to cooperate with
> Him in achieving that plan as it slowly unfolded in history. . . .
> as a result [of his concern for the glory of God] he employed the
> phrase "for the greater glory of God" (*ad majorem Dei gloriam*) so
> frequently that it became a motto of his order.[18]

Later generations of Jesuits would take a more militant response to the threat of Protestantism, but Ignatius was an educator. His was the first religious order that made the conducting of
Christian schools one of its major ministries. Like the more significant Protestant Reformers, he saw the task of renewal in the
Roman Catholic church as being carried out best through an
emphasis on theology and particularly theological education.
The Jesuits have not forgotten their educational roots. At the
beginning of the decade of the 1970s they operated eighteen
universities, ten colleges, and fifty-one secondary schools.
Teachers in the Jesuit schools had to study sixteen to nineteen
years before they could become instructors. Self-discipline is
probably the central theme of Jesuit education, and indeed the
hallmark of the order itself.

As the sixteenth century opened, religion presented a united
front to the world, though we know diversity existed under the
surface to a far greater degree than anyone then imagined. By the
beginning of the last quarter of that century, however, the entire
continent of Europe as well as all the British Isles were divided
into two major groups, Protestants and Roman Catholics.

The world was never the same again in theology or education.
Eavey states five results of the Protestant Reformation that had an
impact on the history of Christian education:

1. The translation of the Bible into the language of the people,
   followed by as wide a distribution as possible
2. A revival of biblical and doctrinal preaching
3. Universal teaching of the Bible in the family
4. The establishment of Christian schools for all the youth of the
   community

5. The adoption of the view that all education is or should be a unity[19]

The Reformation and Counter-Reformation may have been over by 1564, a year that saw the death of John Calvin and the birth of Galileo, a not insignificant relationship marking the entrance of a new era in the history of educational thought.

NOTES

1. William Stevenson, *The Story of the Reformation* (Richmond, Va.: John Knox, 1959), p. 34.
2. Francis Schaeffer, *How Should We Then Live?* (Old Tappan, N.J.: Revell, 1976), p. 84.
3. Martin Luther, "Letter to the Mayors and Aldermen of all the Cities of Germany in Behalf of Christian Schools," in F. V. N. Painter, *Great Pedagogical Essays* (New York: American Book, 1905).
4. Allan Hart Jahsmann, *What's Lutheran Education?* (St. Louis: Concordia, 1960), p. 48.
5. F. V. N. Painter, *Luther On Education* (St. Louis: Concordia, 1928), p. 129.
6. Harold J. Grimm, "Martin Luther," in Elmer L. Towns, ed., *A History of Religious Educators* (Grand Rapids: Baker, 1975), pp. 103-23.
7. Painter, p. 165.
8. Grimm, in Towns, p. 122.
9. Carl S. Meyer, "Philip Melanchthon," in Towns, pp. 145-46.
10. Elmer H. Wilds and Kenneth Lee Lottich, *The Foundations of Modern Education* (New York: Holt, Rinehart, and Winston, 1970), p. 188.
11. Cited in F. V. N. Painter, *A History of Education* (New York: Appleton, 1896), p. 150.
12. Frederick Mayer, *A History of Educational Thought* (Columbus, Ohio: Merrill, 1966), p. 205.
13. Elmer L. Towns, "John Calvin," in Towns, p. 170.
14. Peter Y. DeJong, "Calvin's Contributions to Christian Education," *Calvin Theological Journal*, November 1967, p. 200.
15. Marshall C. Dendy, "John Knox," in Towns, p. 1064.
16. A. M. Renwick, *The Story of the Scottish Reformation* (Grand Rapids: Eerdmans, 1960), p. 118.
17. Albert Hyma and Mary Stanton, *Streams of Civilization* (San Diego: Creation-Life, 1976), p. 381.
18. George E. Ganss, "Ignatius of Loyola," in Towns, pp. 137-38.
19. C. B. Eavey, *History of Christian Education* (Chicago: Moody, 1964), pp. 155-56.

8

Comenius and His Contemporaries

The year was 1592. Elizabeth I, daughter of Anne Boleyn and the last of the Tudors, was entering the last decade of her reign in England. War with Spain had started in 1587 when Philip reacted to Elizabeth's execution of Mary Stewart. Spain's ultimate demise as a world power was sealed by the dramatic defeat of the Armada in 1588.

On the Continent, France was ending the century ignominiously after decades of political wars with Italy and civil wars of religion, the worst of these civil wars being the war of the Henrys. Henry III was assassinated by a fanatic in 1589, and Henry of Navarre proclaimed himself king of France and took the name Henry IV. The new king was supported by the Huguenots but bitterly opposed by the extreme Catholic party known as the Catholic League headed by Henry of Guise. The situation in France was to improve dramatically under Henry IV (sometimes known as the "Protestant Prince of Bourbon"), but in 1592 he still had not been officially crowned because of fighting and confusion in the nation.

Meanwhile, the Holy Roman Empire, geographically divided into Austrian Hapsburg possessions and Spanish Hapsburg possessions, was much more religiously fragmented. The German states, Prussia, Brandenburg, and Saxony, were Lutheran. Portugal, Spain, Italy, and most of Poland and France were still Catholic. Switzerland was heavily Calvinistic with pockets of Catholicism, while Europe to the southeast had Greek Orthodox domains still under the control of the Islamic Ottoman Empire.

In that year, one hundred years after Columbus discovered the New World, John Amos Comenius was born in Nivnitz, a little village in western Moravia. He has been called "The First Modern Educator" and "The Prophet of Modern Education."

JOHN AMOS COMENIUS (1592-1670)

Just as the irritation of a grain of sand inside an oyster produces the pearl, so the desperation of the early seventeenth century produced the first man seriously to view teaching as a science. Though Comenius's work received insufficient notice in his day, and he was virtually forgotten for two hundred years after his death, he emerged in the twentieth century with praise from both Christian and secular quarters. In fact, Frederick Eby claims, "None of the great educators is so deservedly admired and so little criticized today as this erudite, wise, and benevolent bishop of an exterminated people. In the word of Comenius, one feels that a prophet is speaking; he was indeed a colossal figure, but only in recent years have his ideas received the respect they merit."[1]

PERSONAL HISTORY

On November 15, 1970, a West German postage stamp honoring Comenius was issued commemorating the three hundredth anniversary of his death. He is even better known in Czechoslovakia since Moravia is now a province of that nation. John's father was a prosperous miller, but both his parents died when he was twelve, and careless guardians did not see to a satisfactory early education. John did not begin studying Latin until he was sixteen, a very retarded progress rate for the Europe of his day. Perhaps it was the more mature observation of the difficulties of his younger classmates that made John determine to carry through with educational reform.

Between the ages of sixteen and twenty-two he had studied at the University of Prague and the University of Heidelberg, establishing at the latter institution a reputation for both wisdom and interest in the problems of education. In 1614, he returned to Moravia to rejoin the fellowship called *Unitas Fratrum*, the Unity of the Brethren, known in America today as the Moravian Church. He was ordained two years later and assumed a pastorate and leadership of a school.

He married a lady of some means and moved to the town of Fulnek to enjoy the freedom granted to the Brethren in 1609 when King Rudolf II issued the "Letter of Majesty." Surely he must have thought that the heartaches and trials of his childhood were over and that the future of his beloved country and church was most bright as he settled down to preaching, teaching, studying, and writing. But Eva Bock tells us of the agony that followed.

> ... within a few years, dark clouds started to gather not only over the Brethren but also over all non-Roman churches, indeed, over the whole land, and in 1618 that most cruel of all religious conflicts, the Thirty Years' War broke out. The Protestant army suffered a crushing defeat almost at the onset of the war. Protestant political leaders were executed, ministers of the non-Roman churches were jailed and killed, "heretical" books were burned by the thousands, and Catholicism was forced upon the whole population. In 1621 the Spanish Army, helping to support the Catholic cause in central Europe, invaded the town of Fulnek. Comenius, whose life was in grave danger because of his ministerial status, was forced to flee, leaving behind his pregnant wife and a small son. He never saw them again. Both of them, as well as the newborn baby, died of the plague brought to town by the soldiers.[2]

It was typical of the grief-stricken life of this great man that while in hiding for seven years and unaware of what was happening back in Fulnek, he wrote a booklet for his wife entitled *On Christian Perfection*. In it he set forth the premise that "the best thing a man can do is to follow God willingly, though it may be with tears, and accept from His hand with gratitude everything—fortune and misfortune, joy and sorrow, laughter and weeping." The messenger who delivered the booklet brought back news of the three deaths.

Comenius's tortured heart turned to ministry among the thousands of fugitives crowding the forests. Like the Hussites before him, he learned to minister "on the run," serving his motley congregation in caves, huts, and hiding places all across the countryside. It is incredible that all during these "seven years of tribulation," completely deprived of his library and resources, Comenius continued writing pamphlets, tracts, homilies, and even one of his most famous books, *The Labyrinth of the World and the Paradise of the Heart*.

Early in 1628 Comenius crossed the border into Poland and settled in Leszno with his second wife. There, with full expectation of returning again to his beloved Moravia and helping to rebuild that broken nation through education, he began work on his most well-known book, *The Great Didactic*.

The publication of *Didactic, Labyrinth*, and in 1622, *Janua Linguarum Reserata (The Gate of Languages Unlocked)* made him something of a celebrity around the world. The last volume was translated into sixteen languages, including Persian and Mongolian, and has appeared in over a hundred editions. The *Janua* was published almost a quarter of a century before the *Didactic*, though the latter volume may have been completed first. The *Janua*, therefore, was more responsible for the popularity of Comenius than the more familiar *Didactic* referred to by educators in our day.

Between the publication of *Janua* in 1633 and the burning of Leszno in 1659, Comenius traveled widely, including visits to England, Sweden, Hungary, and Holland. During most of those years he held to his treasured hope of returning someday to Moravia, but in 1648 the Peace of Westphalia gave his country to the Catholics. His dream was shattered; there would be no rebuilt Moravia.

> Nearer to despair than before, Comenius hardly knew what to attempt next. His beloved fatherland laid devastated in enemy hands; his church was in danger of extinction. Then his wife, a faithful companion throughout the bitter years of exile, fell ill and died. He found solace in writing. In a sorrowful, profoundly moving little book that he called *The Bequest of the Dying Mother, the Unity of Brethren,* he pictured his church as a mother calling her children to her deathbed and dividing among them "the treasures that God entrusted unto her."[3]

Comenius lived for eleven years after the sacking of Leszno, spending most of them in Amsterdam in reasonable comfort writing and publishing. He died on November 15, 1670, and was buried in Narrden.

Of interest to American students is the belief that Comenius was once offered the presidency of the first college established on these shores. Bock quotes Cotten Mather's *Marginalia:*

> That brave old man, Johannes Amos Comenius, the fame of whose worth has been trumpetted as far as more than three languages (whereof everyone is indebted to his Janua) could carry it, was agreed withall, by our Mr. Winthrop in his travels through the Low Countries, to come over into New England, and illuminate this Colledge and country in the quality of a President. But (because of) the solicitations of the Swedish Ambassador, diverting him another way, that incomparable Moravian became not an American.[4]

Most biographers agree that Mather refers to a trip Comenius made to Holland about 1642, because that is when he went to

Sweden, spending six years in reforming the national system of education.

BASIC BELIEFS

We have spoken of the negative influences in the life of Comenius, and it is a great mistake to minimize their impact on his philosophy of education. On the other hand, the positive influences were probably even more dominant. Certainly the Moravian church with its emphasis on holy living and practical Christianity was a significant factor. In science, Comenius was profoundly influenced by Francis Bacon, applying Bacon's inductive method in developing a science of education. In Germany, Comenius encountered John Henry Alsted and was introduced to the principles advocated by Wolfgang Ratke (Ratish), who opposed compulsion in the educational process, was experimenting with the use of vernacular language in some of the schools in Holland, and fascinated the Moravian with his great concern for interest and methodology in the educational process.

Comenius did not hold a strong Calvinistic viewpoint on the total depravity of man and therefore tended to be somewhat of an optimist regarding what could be accomplished in education. At the same time he must be identified with that school of educational philosophy we generalize as "Realism," an influence largely gathered from the works of Francis Bacon and Wolfgang Ratke. Of course, the Moravian brought to his educational philosophy a distinctive Christian theology missing in the work of both Bacon and Ratke. It can be said that he studied truth in both of God's books—nature and the Scriptures.

Comenius may very well have been the forerunner of what we call today the process of *integration*, "the teaching of all subjects as a part of the total truth of God, thereby enabling the student to see the unity of natural and special revelation."[5] Lois LeBar talks about "inner factors" and "outer factors" in the thinking of Comenius, pointing out that inner factors were almost entirely neglected in the educational processes of his day.

> "Development comes from within," he observed from watching the processes of nature. "Nature compels nothing to advance that has not driven forward by its own mature strength." He purposed to *work* with the processes of nature rather than *against* them. Because so little psychology had then been developed, Comenius overdid the use of analogies from nature, but Scripture often compares spiritual growth with natural growth (Psalm 1:3, Psalm

92:12, 14, Matthew 15:13, Mark 4:4-8, 28, John 15:2), and he saw many valid comparisons. Chief among these is the fact that one grows by his own activity. Teachers and books may help or hinder growth, but the learner must do his own growing. Genuine inward changes are essential for any type of progress for the pupils, "Outward ceremonies without inward truth are an abomination to God," said Comenius.[6]

Comenius believed in a relaxed but disciplined approach to learning, one that would help children and young people "quickly, pleasantly, thoroughly, become learned in the Sciences, pure in Morals, trained in piety, and in this manner instructed in all things necessary for the present and for the future life." He was committed to the inspiration of Scripture, the reality of personal salvation, and the process of spiritual growth whereby a person is made more like Jesus Christ.

The emphasis on "outer factors" came largely from the influence of the other realists. Realism was a rejection of idealism as taught by the classicists, particularly Plato.

> The sense realists aimed at the discovery and advancement of new knowledge rather than the mere learning from books. They sought this in the realm of nature. But they did not seek information about nature for the sake of knowledge as an end in itself, or to satisfy only curiosity. They were rather seeking power, with which to utilize nature's forces for the welfare of mankind. The sense realists—like the practical scientists of today—aimed at the discovery and utilization of the secrets of nature for the real and practical benefits they could bring to man in the everyday works of the world.[7]

The Moravian pastor argued that the human mind was like a spherical mirror suspended in a room, reflecting all images around it. The reality was not in the mind or its perception, but in the natural world. One is reminded of the famous limerick written by Monsignor Ronald A. Knotts.

> There once was a man who said,
> "God must think it exceedingly odd
>   If he finds that this tree
> Continues to be
>   When there's no one about in
> The quad."

When inserted in an English newspaper, this bit of philosophical verse elicited the following anonymous reply:

> "Dear Sir, your astonishment's odd.
> I am always about in the quad.
>   And that's why the tree
> Will continue to be,
>   Since observed by yours faithfully,
> God."[8]

EDUCATIONAL IDEALS

Despite his creative approach to education, Comenius could not shake the "grocery list" approach to expressing his ideas. Perhaps they are best identified by looking at four important institutions in his learning system.

Comenius believed in *four kinds of schools*. The first he called *the school of the mother's knee*, representing the training of a child by his parents at home. In this institution Comenius had captured the emphasis of the Scriptures, the Reformers, and his Brethren heritage. The second institution was *the Vernacular School*, in which the child would learn his mother tongue rather than that of the classics. Of course, the arts and sciences would not be neglected during those elementary years. A third kind of school was called *the Latin school*, operated for advanced students and stressing the classical languages (Greek, Latin, and Hebrew) as well as science, literature, and the arts. Finally, genuine scholars and those who could make a contribution to the life of the church and the community would attend *the School of University and Travel*. Here leaders were created through original investigation and exploration of the ideals and morals of various nations. Comenius is generally credited with being the first to emphasize the educational significance of early childhood.

A second set of numbers is the *nine principles* expressed in *The Great Didactic*. We shall just list them here without going into explanation. The advanced student is encouraged to study the original source.[9]

1. Nature observes a suitable time.
2. Nature prepares the material before she begins to give it form.
3. Nature chooses a fit subject to act upon, or first submits one to a suitable treatment in order to make it fit.

4. Nature is not confused in its operations, but in its forward progress advances distinctly from one point to another.
5. In all the operations of nature, development is from within.
6. Nature, in its formative processes, begins with the universal and ends with the particular.
7. Nature makes no leaps but proceeds step by step.
8. If nature commences anything, it does not leave off until the operation is completed.
9. Nature carefully avoids obstacles and things likely to cause hurt.

For each principle, Comenius had not only explanations but multiple examples. In each case he directed the schools to follow the leading of "nature" in developing their methodology.

Finally, there are the *eighteen aphorisms,* which constituted the basic philosophy behind a "grandiose scheme for teaching everyone everything, a plan he named *Pansophia* —that is, 'universal wisdom.' "

> He hoped to publish an encyclopedia of universal knowledge to which all European scientists would contribute. He also hoped to establish a *Pansophic* college, in which laboratories would encourage scientific research, and he sought a method of instruction which would enable every person, to the limit of his capacity, to avail himself of the benefits of knowledge of all sorts. All of these ideas grew out of his faith in the power of education to save mankind.[10]

Comenius lost his *Pansophic Encyclopedia* in the burning of Leszno, a loss he could hardly bear. The emphasis of the eighteen presuppositions is not unlike that of the principles, though the *Pansophia* contains more theological and philosophical content.

INNOVATIVE METHODOLOGY

It is interesting that Comenius, whose educational realism contradicted the classic idealism of Plato, shared with the great Greek a common dream of what education could do in society. Mystic that he was, Comenius nevertheless believed that it was the social function of education to *reform society.* Perhaps the horrors he both saw around him and experienced personally from childhood led him to strike out against ignorance and the sin that surrounded it.

> Comenius urged men of good-will to unite; teachers, ministers, statesmen, and merchants were to create a society based upon love

and charity. The human race was to be invigorated; a truly creative concept of life was to be established. Comenius urged that more money should be spent for schools, that the best investment of society lay in great teachers, and that aids for instruction, especially text-books, should be liberally provided. Religion is to govern the school system; it is to follow Jesus, not the dictates of orthodoxy.[11]

The magnificent Moravian was also innovative in his view concerning the *role of the teacher.* The wise teacher will ever be concerned about the practical application of truth in everyday life. It matters not what the subject, if relevance and practicality are ignored "the things that you are explaining will seem to be monsters from the new world, and the attitude of the pupil, who is indifferent whether they exist or no will be one of belief rather than of knowledge."

Comenius was opposed to corporal punishment, but of course he was reacting against the useless beatings he saw all around him in European schools of the seventeenth century. The motivating factor here is important: a high view of man as a creation of God. He took seriously Jesus' words that the kingdom of heaven was to be made up of children and emphasized the tremendous importance of teaching those little ones the truth. Incidentally, he felt precisely the same way about women. What could be more contemporary than the following paragraph describing his concern for teaching little girls.

> They are also formed in the image of God, and share in his grace and in the kingdom of the world to come. They are endowed with equal sharpness of mind and capacity for knowledge (often with more than the opposite sex), and they are able to attain the highest positions, since they have often been called by God Himself to rule over nations, give sound advice to kings and princes, to study medicine and other things that benefit the human race.[12]

Comenius was also innovative in his view of the *teaching process.* His textbooks (he wrote some two hundred works) stressed the importance of action—learning by doing was the key to his system. One learns to write by writing; one learns to think by thinking; and one learns to memorize by memorizing. He utilized object lessons and pictures to interest the child in what was to be learned.

As a matter of fact, it is most appropriate that this abused genius should be the one who wrote the first textbook applying pictures as a teaching device. *The World In Pictures (Orbis Pic-tus)* was first published in 1657. Each chapter began with a rather complicated picture in which numbers corresponded with num-bered lines in the text. The student would combine the verbal with the pictorial in order to have the concept fixed in his mind.

What tribute can we pay to a one such as this? What can be said of this giant in the history of Christian education? Perhaps the words of Bock come closest to what Comenius himself de-sired.

> Apart from his contribution to education and to reconciliation among churches and nations, Comenius left to mankind a pearl of great value in the example of his own life. A man of grief, he was also a man of hope. A man of sorrow, he was a man of faith. A man of poverty, he was a man of virtue. All his life, even under the most adverse circumstances, he served the Lord faithfully and in obedience. Protest and rebellion had no place in his heart. . . . The One Thing Needed, as he saw it was neither wealth nor secu-rity; it was the thing Mary chose, willingness to sit at Jesus' feet.[13]

RENE DESCARTES (1596-1650)

Secular readers would shake their heads in disgust at a chapter that gives more than half its space to Comenius and then skips lightly over three philosophical giants such as Rene Descartes, John Locke, and Baruch Spinoza. But this is a book about Chris-tian education, and the contributions of all three, mighty though they may have been, do not begin to approach the significance of Comenius in the development of evangelical educational thought.

Rene Descartes was born at Lahey in Touraine, France, and studied at Lafleche, one of the most celebrated Jesuit colleges in Europe, from which he was graduated in 1612. Four years later, in the year of William Shakespeare's death (1616), Descartes graduated with a degree in law from the University of Poitiers.

Born just four years after Comenius, Descartes lived in a com-pletely different part of Europe and was ever the product of Catholic scholasticism and the Jesuits. He was primarily a math-ematician who attempted to apply mathematics to education and set forth the beginnings of analytical geometry. Like Comenius, he was a realist who believed that mind was spiritual substance by means of which thinking was possible. Unlike Comenius, he could not bring the spiritual and physical dimensions of the world together with any kind of integration and therefore developed a philosophy of dualism that had its roots in both Platonic idealism and Aristotelian realism. Descartes left *mind* (the spiritual part of the world) to the theologians or philosophers while assigning to science complete supremacy in the realm of *matter.*

Descartes is most famous for his doubting and, next to Thomas the Twin (John 11:16), is probably history's greatest skeptic. The famous Cartesian inference, "I think, therefore, I am" is quickly learned by every beginning student of philosophy. One can see in the Cartesian inference and its implications not only a subjective tendency that focuses on the essence of the self, but the very seeds of twentieth-century existentialism.

Descartes followed the rationalism of Aristotle and Aquinas in making man rather than God the starting point of education. In dealing with the existence of God, Descartes resurrected the arguments of Anselm. Man has an idea of perfection, which idea would not be perfect unless perfection existed. Furthermore, man is finite and thus cannot be the author of an infinite idea. He was forced to the dualism spoken of earlier just as soon as he got beyond his own absolute (God). In addition, he saw the universe made up of two other substances, mind and matter, which are relative because they are created.

It was authors like Descartes who led eighteenth-century society to the view that the intellectual capacities of man were so well understood that he ultimately would discover within himself the inner order of the cosmic system. Since man was obviously a rational being, the universe too was a rational operation and therefore human society could be reformed and made to function in harmony with the rational laws of the cosmic system.

The educational ideas of Descartes emphasized that valid knowledge cannot be achieved without the purging of all prejudice. This demonstrates the scientific tone of Descartes' thinking and places him as a bridge between the Middle Ages and the scientific viewpoint of the modern scholar. Mayer reproduces Descartes' four rules for the achievement of real education from the philosopher's *Discourse on Methods, Part 2.*

> *The first* was never to accept anything for true which I did not clearly know to be such; that is to say, carefully to avoid precipitancy and prejudice, more in my judgment than what was presented to my mind and distinctly as to exclude all ground of doubt.
>
> *The second* to divide each of the difficulties under examination

into as many parts as possible, and as might be necessary for its adequate solution.

The third to conduct my thoughts in such order that, by commencing with objects the simplest and easiest to know, I might ascend by little and little, and, as it were, step by step, to the knowledge of the more complex; assigning in thought a certain order even to those objects which in their own nature do not stand in a relation to antecedence and sequence.

And the last, in every case, to make enumerations so complete, and reviews so general, that I might be assured that nothing was omitted.[14]

Like Comenius, Descartes was widely traveled, spending a decade between 1618 and 1628 traveling all over Europe and even serving in the armies of several countries. For many years, he lived secluded in Holland, but spent his final years in Sweden as an instructor to Queen Christina. It could very well be that his death from pneumonia in 1650 was caused by the damp, cold climate of that country (and the fact that the queen demanded classes at 5 A.M.).

Was Descartes a rationalist? Not in the technical sense, but his commitment to the use of reason in the educational process paved the way for the scientific rationalism of Spinoza. But before we can continue that path we must take a brief trip to the British Isles.

JOHN LOCKE (1732-1704)

John Locke and Baruch Spinoza were born in the same year, four decades after the birth of Comenius. Why would we include them as contemporaries with the Moravian pastor? For one thing, Spinoza died only seven years after Comenius; Locke, though outliving Comenius by thirty-four years, was nevertheless in the same time period. Linked as he was to the Puritan era the Englishman represents an obvious step in the movement of Christian educational thought.

Charles I had been on the throne for seven years when Locke was born. The Church of England, established by Henry VIII and advanced by "good Queen Bess" (Elizabeth I), had found some new enemies in a group of middle-class Calvinists called Puritans. They had no patience with medieval concepts like the divine right of kings and the limitation of freedom in political and religious affairs. That was the thinking of the aristocracy, which was obviously the thinking of King Charles as well.

The Puritan revolution ended the reign of Charles I in 1649 (he had actually surrendered in 1646). Oliver Cromwell and the army ran the country for the next eleven years through the Protectorate. Actually, Cromwell died in 1658, but Charles II did not restore the Stuart monarchy until 1660. The Anglican church was restored as well, and for a time it attempted to persecute its persecutors. However, the principle of religious freedom remained and the influence of men like Locke prevailed.

In his day, Locke was a political liberal who believed that when the ruler became a tyrant, the people had a right to rebel. In philosophy and education, however, he was a moderate, building the rational thinking Descartes called for into the milieu of Puritan theology nurtured on Calvin's *Institutes*.

A comparison of the men is fascinating. Descartes was a natural scientist, Locke a political scientist. Descartes is best remembered for his Cartesian inference and Locke for the theory of the "tabula rasa" (the mind is a blank tablet). Both lived through wars and revolutions and both felt the power of the established state church in their respective countries. Both attended the best schools of their day and were influenced by the great minds of their own and other countries. Locke was influenced especially by Montaigne and Samuel Hartlib, a distant disciple of Comenius.

They disagreed, however, in their evaluation of Aristotle. Locke hated the medieval scholastic system based on Aristotelian philosophy. Perhaps for this reason more than any other, he made a big distinction between *logic* and *reason*, opposing the former and advancing the latter. He spoke often of the science of words and could very well be called "the father of the science of semantics." But then he is also frequently called "the father of the science of human nature" and "the father of modern English education."

As to the central aim of education, Locke promoted a sound mind and a sound body brought about through self-control, reason, careful analysis of nature, and a loving teacher who helps the students. Since Locke was also a strong believer in God's revelation and its role in educational process, most modern Christian educators can identify quite positively with his position.

However, married to realism but still flirting with rationalism, Locke does not come across as a strict revelationist. In fact, one of his books, *The Reasonableness of Christianity*, argues that reason rather than revelation should form the basis of education. So although he might denounce the teachings of Aristotle and divorce himself from medieval scholasticism, he could not escape the trap of Aquinas. John Locke was the Renaissance man carried to a fault. He showed limited vision for the lower classes while greatly cherishing good breeding, dignity, and a blend of practical and classical education.

Locke also served as a bridge of a different kind. The writings of Descartes, Spinoza, and other scientific rationalists were beginning to shake up Christian educators, as well they might. One could smile one's way through a reading of *The Great Didactic* and appreciate freedom from the church of Rome, but a rejection of discipline, both mental and physical, was going a bit too far. The disciplinary theory of education arose as a defense against the excesses of secularistic realism. The doctrine of *rationalism* advocated an aristocracy of intellect, whereas the doctrine of *disciplinism* emphasized content and organization in curriculum.

Many public educators blame Locke for stemming the tide toward universal education and for swinging Western thought back to undesirable disciplinism. We have already seen that he could be accused of aristocratic rationalism and therefore "doubly faulted" for slowing down (if not shutting off) for several decades the drive toward universalism in education.

Christians view the situation in a different light. Although we recognize Locke's limitations in both theology and methodology, we suggest that he may have foreseen the logical excesses of thinking advanced by the rationalists. Just seven years after his death Hume was born, and one year later Rousseau, followed by Kant, Pestalozzi, Herbart, Froebel, and then Darwin. Rather than stemming or stopping a flow, Locke merely had a finger in the dike before an enlightened Europe took secularistic rationalism to its logical conclusions in the eighteenth and early nineteenth centuries.

The popularity of Locke rests in his *moderation*. He may not have been a man for all seasons, but he certainly was the right man for his season in seventeenth-century England. Robert Ulich asks "how it came about that for two centuries or more the ideas of the Commonwealth educators (William Petty, John Durie, Samuel Hartlib, and John Milton, for example) and of Comenius were condemned to oblivion, whereas John Locke's treatise *(Some Thoughts Concerning Education)* became a classic?"

Then Ulich goes on to suggest the simplest answer: "Locke provided for the educated Englishman of the 18th century the right mixture of progress and conservatism."[15]

Descartes had opened the door, and now Spinoza walked through it. Denying "revelation and the personality of God, making mind and matter elements in one and the same universe united in one Being, which is God . . . (Spinoza) merged the finite and the infinite into a transcendental pantheism."[16]

For Will Durant, Baruch Spinoza was a logical stepping stone from the religious idealism of the ancient Greeks to the practical naturalism of the modern Germans. The Jews built their first synagogue in Amsterdam in 1598, and forty-six years later Spinoza was presented there by his parents at the age of twelve. According to Durant, he was "the greatest Jew of modern times, and the greatest of modern philosophers, . . . and a favorite student of the synagogue."[17]

But the synagogue and its limitations on learning could not contain Spinoza's expanding mind. He made his way from Maimonides through Moses of Cordova via the Latin language all the way back to Socrates, Plato, Aristotle, and the Greek stoics. In the Frenchman Descartes he found that mind-matter dualism that challenged his innate Jewish urges toward unification. On July 27, 1656, the leaders of the synagogue excommunicated the young Baruch, believing that he was suggesting God might have a body, namely the world of matter; that angels might be hallucinations; that the soul might be merely life; and that the Old Testament said nothing of immortality.

It seems clear that Spinoza was not interested in the theological side of philosophy. He tried to disprove miracles not on theological grounds, but because he felt they negated the concept of a rational universe. Since beliefs are private, an individual cannot be forced to accept a certain theological system. Besides, dogmatism inevitably leads to the regression of science and education.

But what could he do about Descartes' dualism? By assuming as an essential principle that the language of the Bible is deliberately metaphorical or allegorical, he was able to argue in his first book *(Tractatus Theologico-Politicus)* for the monistic position—one substance—a God who is completely autonomous, eternal, and beyond space and time. But that "substance" was hardly the God of the Old Testament Hebrews. Spinoza's "God" is not a person at all and, strictly speaking, there is no creation. Any apparent relationship between God and nature is purely mathematical.

Spinoza's second book, *The Improvement of the Intellect,* underlines his complete commitment to philosophy. Only in knowledge lies power and freedom, and the only real happiness is the pursuit of knowledge and the thrill of understanding. Is the highest kind of knowledge an absolute revelation of God? Hardly, since one cannot even say that God is self-conscious, much less that He communicates. A self-conscious God would imply limitation and defy infinity. Who or what God is never really gets explained by Spinoza, but one thing is clear—everything in the universe is determined.

The highest form of knowledge has nothing to do with revelation but is rather deduction and perception, such as one encounters in the sophisticated science of mathematics. In the *Ethics,* Spinoza describes the basis of his entire philosophical system, a fundamental distinction between the "temporal order"—the "world" of things and incidents—and the "eternal order"—the world of laws and structure.[18] Spinoza's fourth book, *Tractatus Politicus,* emphasizes again the distinction between the natural and moral orders. Freedom, argued Spinoza, is the goal of the state because only in freedom can the state exercise its proper function of promoting growth. Here Spinoza came about as close to discussing education as any other place. He really made only indirect contributions to education as a whole and obviously no significant contribution to Christian education. But we include him here because of that "bridge effect" described earlier. It is always encouraging to see how the thinking of man has evolved from one set of ideas to another set that is seemingly contrary. And Spinoza's genius was so great that those "indirect contributions to education" are still highly prized today: freedom of inquiry; rejection of dogmatism; and a commitment to reason.

Spinoza also raised questions about the relationship between science and ethics—questions that are at the very forefront of society in the last quarter of the twentieth century. What ethical responsibility does the scientist have toward his profession and toward society? How does morality play a role in political affairs? Spinoza was right to understand that there can be no genuinely progressive state in which facts and values are separated.

Four names, four countries, four philosophies—hardly a unified view in this chapter, but nevertheless a fairly accurate picture of the status of philosophy and its bearing on education in the late 1600s. And as far as Europe was concerned, it was to get worse before it got better.

NOTES

1. Frederick Eby, *The Development of Modern Education* (New York: Prentice-Hall, 1955), p. 178.
2. Eva Chybova Bock, "The Legacy of John Amos Comenius," *Christianity Today*, 6 November 1970, p. 11.
3. Ibid., p. 13.
4. Ibid., p. 12.
5. Kenneth O. Gangel, "Integrating Faith and Learning: Principles and Process" in Paul Kienel, ed., *The Philosophy of Christian School Education* (Whittier, Calif.: Western Association of Christian Schools, n.d.), p. 30.
6. Lois LeBar, *Education That Is Christian* (Westwood, N.J.: Revell, 1958), p. 43.
7. Elmer H. Wilds and Kenneth Lee Lottich, *The Foundations of Modern Education,* 3d ed. (New York: Holt, Rinehart, and Winston, 1961), p. 215.
8. See *The Limerick,* Greenleaf Classics (1967 reprint ed.; Paris: n.p., 1953).
9. See John A. Comenius, *The Great Didactic,* ed. and trans. M. W. Keatinge (New York: Russell, 1967).
10. W. Warren Filkin, Jr., "John Amos Comenius," in Elmer L. Towns, ed., *A History of Religious Educators* (Grand Rapids: Baker, 1975), p. 180.
11. Frederick Mayer, *A History of Educational Thought,* 2d ed. (Columbus, Ohio: Merrill, 1966), p. 237.
12. Bock, p. 13.
13. Ibid., p. 14.
14. Mayer, p. 222.
15. Robert Ulich, *History of Educational Thought* (New York: American Book, 1950), p. 200.
16. Eby, p. 167.
17. Will Durant, *The Story of Philosophy* (New York: Simon and Schuster, 1972), p. 141.
18. Ibid., p. 158.

9

Pietism and the Moravians

It would be impossible to write a book dealing with Christian history of educational thought while ignoring Pietism and the Moravians.

> Pietism is the name given to a great religious awakening within the Protestant churches of the 17th and the 18th centuries in behalf of practical religion. From religious gatherings called *collegia pietatis*, the movement was nicknamed "pietism." This movement, combining the mystical and the practical tendencies within the Lutheran and the Reformed churches, came as a reaction against the inordinate stress of orthodoxy on pure doctrine and formalism.[1]

Though the movement known as Pietism actually was not discernible until about 1660, we must go back into the previous century to find its roots in the *Unitas Fratrum,* the same group of believers that gave us John Amos Comenius. Although the political history of the Moravian church may go back to Jan Augusta's presentation of a confession of faith to King Ferdinand in 1535, the rural ministry of the Bohemian Brethren may be traced at least back to John Huss, who was burned at the stake in 1415. Some suggest that the movement may go as far back as the ninth century. The Bohemian Brethren received the heritage of the Waldenses and Albigenses, passed it on to the Moravian church, and it came to fruition in the mid-seventeenth-century work of the Pietists.

Before Luther ever walked up to the Castle Church at Wittenberg, the Moravians were operating 300 churches and 300 schools with a denominational membership of 100,000 in Bohemia alone! That represented tremendous growth and health from the days of Huss, after a persecution that had pretty well diminished by 1467.

Relations between the Reformers and the Moravian church were quite positive at first, but that all ended with the Thirty Years War. When the Protestants were defeated at the Battle of

White Mountain in 1620 (the beginning of the war) the *Unitas Fratrum* was almost totally exterminated. They faded back into the hills for another hundred years until the day they wandered onto the estate of Count Nikolaus Ludwig von Zinzendorf. But that is getting ahead of the story.

In Germany Pietism, far from being a comfortable subculture within the Lutheran church, was actually a revolt against the kind of politicized Lutheranism that had emerged as a compromise ending the Thirty Years War.

> Pietism was a reaction of the spirit against the letter, a relegating of doctrine to a minor place and the exalting of the pure, simple, teaching of the Bible. It stood for a return to the Bible as a whole, with freedom from creed. It emphasized an acute realization of one's sinfulness, a personal spiritual experience, and a Holy life. It stressed self-examination, honest study of the Bible, and complete reliance on God. It made much of the work of the Holy Spirit in illuminating the Bible, giving the knowledge of Christ, producing a sense of forgiveness and peace, and effecting in the Christian good works, love, and sacrifice for others. It required the separation of the individual from the world and his avoidance of carnal pleasures.[2]

But as we have learned, movements do not just drop from the sky, they begin with the convictions and courage of individuals who then form groups and eventually institutions. The spirit of Pietism surely owes its heritage to the early Bohemian Brethren and Moravians, but it owes its organization to the work of Philip Jacob Spener.

PHILIP JACOB SPENER (1635-1705)

Born in Alsace, raised in a manner befitting the nobility of his neighborhood as the godson of Countess Agatha of Rappoltsweiler, and taught by Joachim Stoll, Philip Jacob Spener showed an early interest in devotional reading in the works of both German and English theologians. At the University of Strasburg he continued his reputation of a rigorous moral life and after graduating spent some months in Switzerland in what we would call "internship" with several leading Reformed ministers. Travels also took him to Lyons and several German universities. Spener spent three years in the pastorate in Strasburg, beginning at the age of twenty-seven. He showed immediate concern for the apparent lack of fruit in the lives of many who professed a regenerating experience.

By the year 1670 Spener was well established as senior pastor in Frankfurt, where his preaching rivaled that of modern renewal leaders. He called for lay involvement, concern with social issues, particularly poverty, strict spirituality in personal life, and serious concern for Bible study. To implement that, he began renewal groups that he called *Collegia Pietates*, which became very popular in Frankfurt and by 1675 used only the Bible as the basis for their meetings. Spener described that approach in *Pia Desederia* ("Pious Desires") published in 1675. The book called for a reformation of the Lutheran church through better knowledge of the Bible and more practical commitment to Christian life. It also complained about the classic theological training of the seminaries in the 1670s and urged that more emphasis be placed on devotion and less on doctrine.

Keep in mind that Spener did not intend to found a new denomination any more than Luther did 150 years earlier. But like the institutionalized Catholic church, the institutionalized Lutheran church had no room for reform from within, and official opposition to the groups was in full swing all over Germany. But the criticism could not squelch the living vitality of the groups or the popularity of their founder, who had an influential voice as well as a charter professoriate at the University of Halle, founded in 1694.

Spener's contributions to Christian education are simply not sufficiently recognized in evangelical literature. We have already mentioned his commitment to the centrality of the Scriptures, a postulate that every evangelical educator now recognizes as the absolute core of curriculum development. Always the pastor, Spener was disenchanted with a Protestant education he saw slipping back into the classicism of the Catholic scholastics. To him it emphasized the secular knowledge of the past and the present with too little commitment to the cultivation of vital Christian life and godliness. Too much time, he argued, was given to the learning of Latin and not enough to Hebrew and Greek so that exegesis of the Scriptures could be carried out. In short, there was too much dogma and too little devotion. According to Spener, Luther had simply not moved far enough away from Aristotle and Aquinas.

While at Dresden before moving to Halle, Spener showed great concern and insight into the Christian education of young people. Catechetical instruction had gone out of style, and he revived it with a new concern for practical Christian living as well as cognitive input. Spener seems to have mastered that fine line between legalism and mysticism that can only come by keeping the letter and the spirit of the law in proper balance.

And like the master teacher he was, Spener multiplied his ministry through his most important student—August Hermann Francke. In the year that Spener joined the faculty of Strasburg, August Hermann Francke was born in Lubeck.

AUGUST HERMANN FRANCKE (1663-1727)

Just over one hundred years ago Johns Hopkins University was founded at Baltimore, Maryland. The university was incorporated in 1867, and the first president, Daniel C. Gilman, was inaugurated in 1876. According to John S. Brubacher and Willis Rudy, "Johns Hopkins represents the most important innovation in graduate instruction launched during the whole period between the Civil War and the First World War. It was the first American institution to be founded as a university in the authentic American tradition."[3] Almost all educators recognize the prestigious nature of this American institution, but comparatively few are aware that it was a secular model of the Christian university founded at Halle, Germany by the eighteenth-century Pietists. Furthermore, the academic pattern at Halle was not a product of the collective efforts of noted European educators, but rather the work of one Christian leader. As Philip J. Schröder puts it, "Halle was Francke."[4]

The earliest influence on August Hermann Francke's life fit the pietistic pattern that his life was destined to follow. His parents impressed upon him early the importance of a devoted Christian life, and while still a boy he determined to devote his years to the gospel ministry. There is no question about the brilliance of young Francke, but Albert Newman suggests that "as a student his life was exemplary, but was possibly more ascetical than it was wholesome."[5] After some years of private instruction, Francke entered the gymnasium at Gotha and there came under the influence of the philosophy of Comenius. His unusual intellectual capacities enabled him to enter the University of Erfurt at the age of fourteen. Here the young man met several students of Spener and participated in Bible study clubs on that campus. Although he had taken work at the University of Kiel as well as Erfurt and Gotha, Francke earned his degree at the University of Leipzig in 1685.

After two years of teaching and two more years during which

Francke divorced himself from academic life in order to spend time in private study and the clarification of a personal philosophy of life and education, he returned to the faculty of Leipzig in February of 1669, an articulate spokesman for the principles of Pietism. Opposition was great, however, and he accepted a call to the chief pastorate in Erfurt just one year later. But the situation there was no more receptive to Francke's views. Students who had followed him from Leipzig stirred up opposition at the University of Erfurt, and their leader was pressured to leave his parish in that city in September 1691.

Under Spener's influence Francke was invited to a ministry in Berlin, which included appointment to a pastorate and an unsalaried position as chairman of the Department of Oriental Languages at the new University of Halle. Although he changed teaching fields to the Department of Theology (which he also chaired) in 1698, the remainder of Francke's life from 1691 to his death in 1727 was spent as an instructor at Halle and pastor of the church in nearby Glaucha.

The extent of Francke's educational ministry at Halle is almost unbelievable. Eby describes him as "the noblest example of the practical educator of Germany" and suggests that he may very well have been the most efficient representative of the Christian spirit in educational history![6]

Among Francke's notable achievements at Berlin were the opening of the elementary school at Glaucha for the education of the poor in 1692; the founding of the orphan school in 1695 which, like the elementary school, was supported by alms; the development of a school for teachers (*seminarium praeceptorum*) in 1705; a private boarding school for college preparation students; a publishing institute preparing biblical literature; an infirmary; a home for widows; a boarding house where students could get free lodging; and a number of other institutions. Qualben notes that "the University of Halle became the great Pietist center which supplied Europe with teachers, pastors, foreign missionaries, and influential laymen."[7]

> At his death (1727) twenty-two hundred children were receiving training in this institute, one hundred and thirty-four (orphans) under one hundred and sixty-seven male and female teachers, and two hundred and fifty university students were supplied with their dinners there. The pedagogical work was organized under eight inspectors, and this children's school was a valuable object lesson for the Christian world.[8]

THEOLOGICAL VIEWS

What did Francke really teach? In his book *Brief and Simple Treatise on Christian Education* Francke points out that the aim of education is to honor God. All good instruction must combine godliness and wisdom, which are taught by living the knowledge of Christ through piety, prayer, Bible study, and evangelism. He believed that all good students should learn these things regardless of their wealth and status. Furthermore, Francke seems to have understood the principle of the unity of all truth, for he said on one occasion, "All learning and knowledge is folly if it doesn't have as its foundation true and pure love toward God and man." The theological positions of Pietism are only correctly understood when one recognizes that they emerged not in a vacuum, but rather as a reaction against a scholastic Lutheranism.

As a reactionary movement, Pietism may have neglected satisfactory emphasis on systematic theology. It was for that omission, however, no less committed to a strong view of Scripture. Indeed, the return to direct study of the truth of God was one of the major contributions of the proponents of Pietism. Theirs was a church-centered theology with no concern to break away from Lutheranism, but rather an emphasis on the formation of *ecclesiolae* in *ecclesia* that would serve as a positive influence on the larger church body. There was a strong emphasis on dramatic conversion, which represented a departure from the Lutheran position.

The doctrine of separation was a crucial one at Halle because of the emphasis on holy living and disassociation with worldly activities such as "dances, cards, and the theater." Separation included educational detachment from state institutions, and Pietism became a sectarian reaction to institutionalism, both ecclesiastical and secular. Martin E. Marty notes that issues of church and state "could be offensive or irrelevant to Pietists."[9]

Because of Pietism's hesitation to spend time in systematic theology, it has been constantly criticized as a movement with glaring theological weakness. Although many historians adopt this negative view, Ulich defends Pietism by suggesting that it did not dilute theology but rather channeled it into more practical forms: "Theology, rather than being mere erudition and contemplation, should aim at discipline of the will and the affections with the purpose to improve men, not merely to teach them."[10]

Whether Pietism should be commended or condemned for its approach to theology, one thing is clear: the linkage of theology to educational philosophy was so obvious to Francke that he built his system of educational practice entirely on theological premises, stated or unstated.

Initially recognizing the necessity of conversion, Francke developed his educational programs around the concept that information about God's truth could bring his students to the point of regeneration and then build them up in the Christian faith. In *Pietas Hallensis* he states,

> The *End* we aim at, and the *Means* we make use of for obtaining the same, are all of a Piece. The Word of God is instilled into the Children from their Youth up. Unfeigned *Faith* in our *Lord Jesus Christ* is laid for a Foundation, and a real sense of *Godliness*, attended with a conscientious Behavior, are the most material Points, to the obtaining whereof, our earnest endeavors are constantly directed.[11]

The inseparable relationship of the head, heart, and hands in education marked the programs developed by Francke. In *Brief and Simple Treatise on Christian Education* he points out that the aim of education is to honor God. Children are taught by good example and by living the knowledge of Christ in everyday experiences. This truth must be taught to all, rich or poor, in the home or school. Francke was very home-centered in his approach to Christian education, frequently attributing the human degeneration and unhappiness he saw all around him to the tragic neglect of Christian training in the home.

THE ROLE OF THE TEACHER

The teacher is an integral part of Francke's educational system, and no aspect of the pedagogical role was more important to the Pietist professor than positive example.

> Especially must a teacher be careful that his pupils should not notice anything wicked in him. For children notice everything, whether good or bad. . . . Children who see their teachers or fathers drunk, angry, or unchaste and hear them swear and slander and observe through their example the vanity of the world and the pleasures of the flesh and luxurious life will thereafter not easily be brought to fundamental hatred for these vices.[12]

Love is central in the life of a teacher, and the doctrine of in loco parentis, generally rejected in higher education today, was very much a part of Francke's view. Discipline was important in Francke's schools, but the instructional process was not to be interrupted by the use of physical force or angry harshness: "Profane words and ridicule are absolutely not to be used with children, since they are more hurt then helped thereby. A teacher may not call them out of impatience oxen, asses, pigs, dogs, beasts, fools, scoundrels, swineherds, and so on, and still less, children of the devil."[13] Physical punishment may on occasion be necessary, but it must always be suited to the individual nature of the child and administered with the greatest care and discretion "for more children can be won with words than with blows."

Francke's concern for quality teaching was more obviously demonstrated by his influential teachers' seminary. Started as a special table in the dining room at the University of Halle, the institution grew until requirements for graduation included two years of instruction and three years of practice teaching. It was generally agreed that teachers who graduated from Francke's schools were of a much higher quality than any others in Germany at that time. His *Seminarium Praecepteorum* offered training for elementary schoolteachers, and the *Seminarium Inselectum* was for the training of secondary schoolteachers. Standards were rigid, and no teacher could violate the principles of moderate dress, temperate use of alcohol and tobacco, a serious commitment to teaching, and an affectionate patience with children.

CURRICULUM AND METHODOLOGY

The Holy Scriptures were the core of Francke's curriculum at all levels of instruction. In the *Memoirs*, Paul Beck tells us that "he made the Scriptures, in some form or other, the subject of most of his lectures, not merely giving a cold, and formal explanation of its truths, but applying them to the hearts and consciences of his pupils, and teaching them how they should apply the same truths to others."[14] The dominance of Scripture even at the elementary level is clearly seen in the following curriculum plan, which appears at the end of Cully's chapter on Francke.[15]

Hours	Weekdays	Sundays
7-8	Song, prayer and reading from the Bible repetition of the Catechism	Attendance at the morning service in church

8-9   ½ hour reading of Biblical
selections
½ hour catechism with the older
pupils

9-10   ½ hour explaining quotations and
proverbs to younger children
½ hour study of psalms and the
New Testament by the older
children

10-11   Writing hour

2-3   Prayer and Bible reading.   Attendance at the
Reading, music, and reading   afternoon services
for the smaller children, on   in church
different days

3-4   ½ hour reading by the younger
and study of quotations and
sayings by the older pupils
½ hour recitation of the sayings,
while the little children listen

4-5   Catechism

5-6   Evening prayers in the church

Francke recognized the importance of books in the educational process, but he also equipped his *paedogogium* with a botanical garden, a cabinet of natural history, a laboratory for the study of chemistry and anatomy, and a workshop for glass-cutting, copper engraving, and wood carving. Francke's commitment to biblical studies is further manifested by his involvement with the schools almost strictly in a superintending capacity except in the department of religious instruction: "This he made the grand object of attention: *The cultivation of the moral feelings of the pupils* was esteemed of paramount importance. To promote this, he used to catechise them."[16]

EDUCATIONAL GOALS

One might conclude from Francke's strong emphasis on individual Christian living that he had very little concern for the wider social implications of the gospel. But that would be a very unfortunate conclusion. In actuality, Francke was too idealistic regarding the power of education to change society. He hoped that through education at all levels of society, evil would eventually be eradicated. In *Pietas Hallensis* he muses that by such undertakings "the country will be cleared by degrees of suborn beggars, thieves, murderers, highwaymen, footpads, and the whole pack of loose and debauched people, who (as we may find if we search into the true reasons of such overflowing wickedness) commonly let loose the reins to disorder and impiety, because they never imbibed so much as the least tincture of a good education."[17]

Unlike Luther, Francke did not expect the state to support his religious education. Collection boxes were set up at the University of Halle and at his church in Glaucha. The provisions of the orphanage were all gathered on faith, and the building proceeded as funds were made available by interested donors.

While he was developing the curriculum in his children's schools and teachers' colleges, Francke was also reforming the theological curriculum at the University of Halle. There he emphasized the cognitive study of the biblical languages, the application of that study in the art of preaching, and the techniques of pastoral theology. Students in theological studies there received free board and lodging for a period of four to six years during which "they were required to read the Old and the New Testaments in the *Grundsprachen*, to write commentaries on all of the books of the Bible and to learn to use *die orientalischen Hilfssprachen* for a more thorough understanding of the Sacred Scriptures."[18] Scholarship and inductive Bible study produced a theological education that certainly rivaled any of his day and perhaps even our own.

The influence August Hermann Francke has had on Christian education up to the present is virtually immeasurable. The impact of the Halle pattern on Johns Hopkins University has already been noted. Add to that the promotion of interest in the Sunday school; his influence on John Wesley and the early Methodists; the contributions to the Moravian movement (particularly Count Zinzendorf); the development of the parish elementary school system; the impact of Franckean principles on Muhlenberg and Kunze; and, as Latourette points out, the influences of Pietism on the eighteenth-century Great Awakening.[19] What Luther was to the Reformation, Spener was to the development of personal, devotional Christianity. And what Melanchthon was to Luther, Francke was to Spener. It is difficult to imagine how Christian education would be different today had Francke never developed the program at Halle.

NIKOLAUS LUDWIG VON ZINZENDORF (1700-1760)

Count Nikolaus Ludwig von Zinzendorf has been referred to as the greatest evangelical since Luther and probably the most ecumenical thinker of his day. His ministry included poetry, hymn writing, pastoring, teaching theology, missionary service, and above all, a commitment to the union of believers based on a common love for the Savior.

Like true evangelical ecumenists today, Zinzendorf did not condemn the existence of denominations, but wished rather to see them working more closely together in one great commonwealth of faith with Jesus Christ as head. That basic concept had moved the Moravians from the beginning and was also dominant in the thinking of both Spener and Francke, so it was not surprising that a spark ignited in 1722 when a handful of Moravians built homes and settled down on Zinzendorf's estate in Saxony.

The arrival of the Brethren was not Nikolaus's first contact with Pietism. At the age of ten he had been sent to Halle and had spent six years studying Francke's system. There he had to work eleven hours a day—an unhappy experience that he later described as "slavery." Apparently, there was a breakdown in that aspect of educational philosophy between Comenius and Francke, a breech that was to be repaired by Zinzendorf.

Between 1722 and 1729 several hundred more refugees joined the initial two families of the "Hidden Seed" at the count's Saxony estate. Of course, they all could not be accommodated on Zinzendorf's grounds; however they began to settle around the area of Berthelsdorf and built a town called Herrnhut. A motley crowd they were—dropouts from the Lutheran church, Reformed communities, Anabaptist groups, and even some stray Catholics. If Zinzendorf believed in evangelical ecumenism, here was an ample opportunity to put it into practice.

After great difficulties and no small amount of bitterness, God laid His hand upon the community one evening at a communion service.

> A change came over the turbulent refugees, which in later days they could only explain by saying, "We learnt to love." Henceforward the *Gemeine*, as they called themselves (the Congregation, the Brotherhood), formed a happy band of Christians. Years afterwards a visitor described it as an earthly paradise. Zinzendorf eventually became the group's devoted leader.[20]

An 1848 book entitled *A History of the Bohemian and Mora-vian Brethren* gives some insight into the agreements that welded the Herrnhut community together.

> 1. Herrnhut is not to be considered as a rising town or village, so much as an establishment for the brethren.
> 2. A spirit of love towards the children of God, of all confessions, should be constantly maintained; not undertaking to judge of, nor entering into any dispute or controversy with persons of contrary sentiments, but seeking to preserve purity, simplicity, and the savour of the gospel.
> 3. He is not a brother who does not hold that the grace of God in Christ Jesus alone can effectually sanctify him, and that he stands in need of this grace every moment; and that the highest degree of holiness, if it were even attainable, without Christ and his meritorious intercession, is defilement in the sight of God, and can be acceptable only in the Lord Jesus. He is not a true brother, who does not prove by his conduct that he really desires to be delivered from sin, to become every day more and more like God, more detached from all sinful affections, vanity, and self-will, and to walk as Jesus walked, and to bear his reproach. But he who holds the faith of Jesus in a pure conscience, though he may not be wholly free from party spirit, fanaticism, or error, shall never be despised among us. Even if he should leave us, far from forsaking him, we will regard him as the object of our care, forbearing with him in love, kindness, and patience.
> 4. Those who are willing to comply with the forms of worship, as they exist amongst us, should not regard human institutions as unalterable; they are matters in which we should use our Christian liberty, in all humility, love, and submission one to another, waiting the direction of the Lord as to the time of making any changes. And in changes of this kind that may take place among us, we ought to do everything in simplicity, and for mutual edification.[21]

The community placed great emphasis on devotional exercises, such as fasting and prayer. The result of their long hours with God was a missionary vision to deliver the world and particularly Europe from its foggy shroud of Protestant scholasticism.

In 1731 the first Moravian missionaries went out to the West Indies, two men, each with half a guinea and three dollars in his pocket. Their purpose was to spread the gospel and set up a community of believers while earning their own living on location. During the first four years of Moravian missions, twenty-two of the Brethren died. They went into Greenland, Swedish Lapland, Russian Lapland, and even to North America to work among the Cherokee Indians in Georgia. By 1738, the Moravians had established communities in five other European countries and had extended their mission to include Norway, the Cape of Good Hope, Carolina, Russia, Lithuania, and the Dutch East Indies. By 1830 their missions were spread to dozens of countries, and their total mission program comprised some forty-four thousand hearers and fifteen thousand communicant members, with ten thousand people in twenty-three communities similar to Herrnhut.

It would be easy to devote the rest of this chapter just to the missionary efforts of the Moravians, for the connection between true Christian education and the missionary spirit is inseparable. But we must return to the educational practices of Zinzendorf himself, practices carried out in the Herrnhut community that he headed. Kinlock suggests three basic elements in the curriculum of Zinzendorf's educational program—the catechism, the hymnal, and the Bible. The catechism reflects Zinzendorf's love for the understanding of children. He attempted to see the world through a child's eyes and developed the catechism from that whole orientation. Although Zinzendorf actually published a catechism (entitled *Pure Milk*) consisting of seventy-eight questions and answers, he gradually lost interest in the catechetical approach, not only because of its abuse in the institutionalized church, but because he did not believe it really produced the practical Christian living the Moravians cared so much about.

Zinzendorf spoke often of the "liturgical method" of religious education, which emphasized strongly the relationship of hymns and Scriptures in the educational process. The Count wrote nearly two thousand hymns, but evangelicals today are not entirely enthusiastic about all the verbalizations he used. Apparently the Brethren movement fell into fanaticism by the mid-eighteenth century.

> The fanaticism "did not lead them into gross sins, but gave rise to the most extravagant conceptions, especially as regarded the atonement in general, and Christ's wounded side in particular; to the most sensuous, purile, and objectionable phraseology and hymns; and to religious services of the most reprehensible character. Such fanaticism Zinzendorf himself unwittingly originated in the fanciful and unwarranted ways in which he expressed the believer's joy and the love which the pardoned sinner bears to the

Savior" (De Schweinitz, a present-day bishop of the Brethren). Zinzendorf saw his mistake, and was afterward influential in eliminating fanaticism from the body. In 1749, the Saxon government rescinded its act of banishment and invited Zinzendorf to establish other communities like Herrnhut.[22]

Completely committed to the authority of Scripture and the educational process, Zinzendorf began a translation of the Bible into "modern speech," a task he never finished. In the school, however, Scripture was recited every day with 365 verses selected for each year as mottos around which the worship and learning of the day could develop.

Zinzendorf broke with Francke on the necessity of inculcating religious faith into one's children. Although he held a very high view of marriage and the home, he argued that the old have no right to impose their opinions on the young, and therefore parents should not demand that their particular form of religious experience be repeated in their children. All that was necessary is that the child learn to "walk with Christ." In that view Zinzendorf was revolutionary, more like the Enlightenment educators just about to break on the European scene in the mid-eighteenth century than like the Reformers or even his Pietist mentors.

> Zinzendorf, then, is in all educational matters an apostle of freedom, a convinced believer in individualism. Self-activity, directed by the Holy Spirit in a religious environment, is the best form of religious education. That which is inherent in the child, which develops from the child with the help of Christ, is the basis of all true religious education, rather than something imparted to the child in dogmatic form by older people.[23]

We could go on talking about the Pietist-Moravian contribution to Christian education — community service, graded choirs, concern for the problems of adolescents, love for one's students, and the development of a unique system of parochial schools through the work of Muhlenberg among Lutherans in Pennsylvania — those and many other contributions require the tributes paid in this chapter to three great men. Eavey sums it up.

> While Pietism lasted, it exerted highly important direct effects on life and education. Pietism showed afresh the reality of spiritual experience; it revealed the value of practical Bible study for Christian living; it gave birth to a powerful new interest in philanthropy and missionary work; it led to a new emphasis upon Chris-

tian education, making it a realistic training for practical life; and it directed attention to the need of all children for such education. Its indirect influence was to awaken men to a truer conception of God's revelation into a better idea concerning the form of worship. In Christian education, it served to emphasize the fact that God should be at the center of all instruction.[24]

CHRISTIAN EDUCATION AND THE TASK OF WORLD EVANGELIZATION

The best research available at present indicates that about 3 billion people live outside the circle of effective gospel witness[25] — in spite of fifty-four thousand Protestant missionaries in over one hundred countries of the world; even though North America alone invests over 1.148 billion a year in overseas ministries; even though the past thirty years have shown unbelievable advance in the science of missiology: Is it possible that one of the reasons for this incongruous situation we face in the last quarter of the twentieth century is that we have lost the beautiful balance between Christian education and missions that the Moravians showed us 250 years ago at Herrnhut?

The Christian education programs of local churches as well as the more informal but definitely more important nurturing surroundings of the Christian family need to emphasize the task of world evangelism as a part of the regular program of instruction. L. Ted Johnson suggests that we must be concerned with developing a missions education program that emphasizes "its biblical and theological base, a knowledge and understanding of people and their needs, changing attitudes, and learning experiences."

> Missions education is discovering individually and corporately a *global strategy* that puts us in touch with our world to win that world to Christ. . . . the cohesive that holds missions education together is lifestyle. Unless our lifestyle incorporates missions as a natural and indispensable ingredient, we are living at less than full potential.[26]

Perhaps it seems untoward to include some practical paragraphs regarding the church's missions education program in a book on philosophy. But it is precisely our debt to the Moravians that ought to call forth a much greater emphasis in missions education. Commitment to world evangelization is a part of the total educational philosophy that a wholistic evangelical framework espouses. More than ten years ago a group of top-level Christian educators and missions leaders met in Wheaton, Illinois, to discuss their mutual interests and draw up some "implications on recommendations for action." It seems appropriate to close our chapter with several of the recommendations that were directed at educators.

1. Re-evaluate the purposes and contents of missions in Christian education courses to determine if some need updating or restructuring.
2. Stress the importance of the future missionary fitting into the culture of the country where he is serving.
3. Consider sending selected students for a year to work, serve, and study in another country for the purpose of becoming oriented to another culture.
4. Encourage Missions students to take Christian Education courses and visa versa.
5. Provide more elasticity and variety in the content and instructional methodology in Missions and Christian Education courses.[27]

One can readily believe that Spener, Francke, and Zinzendorf would agree with these goals.

NOTES

1. Lars P. Qualben, *A History of the Christian Church* (New York: Nelson, 1942), p. 363.
2. C. B. Eavey, *History of Christian Education* (Chicago: Moody, 1964), p. 179.
3. John S. Brubacher and Willis Rudy, *Higher Education in Transition* (New York: Harper & Row, 1958), p. 176.
4. Philip J. Schroeder, "August Hermann Francke, 1664-1964," *Concordia Theological Monthly* 34 (November 1963):665.
5. Albert Henry Newman, *A Manual of Church History*, 2 vols. (Chicago: American Baptist Pub. Soc., 1902), 2:528.
6. Frederick Eby, *The Development of Modern Education* (Englewood Cliffs, N.J.: Prentice-Hall, 1952), p. 247.
7. Qualben, p. 365.
8. Newman, p. 529.
9. Martin E. Marty, *A Short History of Christianity* (Cleveland: World, 1959), p. 292. p. 292.
10. Robert Ulich, *A History of Religious Education* (New York: New York U., 1968), p. 138.
11. August Hermann Francke, *Pietas Hallensis or an Abstract of the Marvelous Footsteps of Divine Providence* (London: T. Downing, 1707), pp. 35-36.
12. Kendig Brubaker Cully, ed., *Basic Writings in Christian Education* (Philadelphia: Westminster, 1960), p. 225.
13. Ibid., p. 226.
14. Paul Beck, *The Memoirs of August Hermann Francke* (Philadelphia: Am. S. S. Union, 1831), p. 149.
15. Cully, p. 228.
16. Beck, p. 149.
17. Francke, p. 38.
18. Beck, p. 87.

19. Kenneth S. Latourette, *A History of Christianity* (New York: Harper & Row, 1953), p. 1018.
20. T. F. Kinloch, "Nicholas Ludwig Zinzendorf," in Elmer L. Towns, ed., *A History of Religious Educators* (Grand Rapids: Baker, 1975), p. 201.
21. Ami Bost, *A History of the Bohemian and Moravian Brethren* (London: Religious Tract Society, 1848), pp. 213-14.
22. Newman, 2:541.
23. Kinloch, in Towns, p. 205.
24. Eavey, p. 186.
25. See MARC Newsletter (World Vision: Monrovia, Calif.), November 1979.
26. L. Ted Johnson, "What Makes It Tick?" *The Standard*, 1 November 1973, pp. 25-26.
27. "Implications and Recommendations for Action." A summary report of Missions Seminar on Christian Education, Scripture Press Foundation, Wheaton, Illinois, 3-6 December 1969, p. 2.

10

Enlightened Europe in Post-Reformation Times

> In the evening I reached Bristol, and met Mr. Whitefield there. I could scarce reconcile myself at first to this strange way of preaching in the fields, of which he set me an example on Sunday: having been all my life (until very lately) so tenacious of every point relating to decency and order, that I should have thought the saving of souls almost a sin if it had not been done in a church.[1]

The following day, Monday, John Wesley reported:

> At four in the afternoon I submitted to be more vile, and proclaimed in the highways the glad tidings of salvation speaking from a little eminence in a ground adjoining to the city, to about three thousand people. The scripture on which I spoke was this, . . . "The Spirit of the Lord is upon Me, because He hath anointed Me to preach the gospel to the poor."[2]

The Church of England had fallen asleep, a victim of its suffocating institutionalism. Once again it was time for a radical reformation. To this scene came John and Charles Wesley and their friend George Whitefield. When not accepted in the church they preached in the fields. A radical context called for a radical methodology. That same year, 1739, David Hume anonymously published his famous volume *A Treatise of Human Nature*. The work aroused very little interest in the academic community and, in his own words, "fell dead-born from the press."

John Wesley and Whitefield were forced to preach in the fields because their biblical message was unwanted in the stagnant church. Hume published his book anonymously because its contents were too radical for the establishment, which included the church. Wesley and Whitefield preached the good news in Jesus Christ because they believed the Bible revealed that man was sinful and needed a Savior. Hume taught that man was perfectible and needed no savior other than himself. These two constructs, (1) the depravity of man whose need is met in Jesus Christ and (2) the goodness of man and his perfectibility, summarize the two solutions advanced in the period of the Enlightenment. It is paradoxical that the church was equally closed to two such opposite propositions.

The Enlightenment did not begin with Hume's *Treatise*, but his concepts were typical of the utopian position taken by the humanist philosophers who attacked the established ways of European life in the sixteenth and seventeenth centuries. By the nineteenth century the ideas of Hume occupied center stage in mid-Victorian England, caused significant debate in the universities of Germany, and, through Darwinian evolution, made a considerable impact on American thinking. Those same notions appeared in England in theoretical writings on religion, ethics, and natural law; in France in the works of the philosophers; and a century later fomented political revolutions in France and the United States. The years from 1500 to 1900 saw a number of profound changes. Two of those, a religious reformation and a scientific revolution, were occurring simultaneously.

The scientific revolution upset some of the provincialism of the church, and it destroyed society's dependence on the absurdities of an outmoded Greek and Roman science. With the motto *sapere aude* ("take courage to use your brain") becoming the watchword, the utopian dream of the Enlightenment was focused on the concepts of reason, science, happiness, progress, and natural rights. One of the great prophets of the new theories was Francis Bacon (1561-1626), who pointed the way to the movement by his statement "knowledge is power" and his scientific ideal of an objective, methodical investigation of nature.

Bacon, Johannes Kepler, Nicolaus Copernicus, and Isaac Newton were not attempting to scuttle the Christian faith. Bacon taught that the frame of reference found in the Scriptures was foundational to an understanding of science and art. Newton in his *Principia Mathematica* (1687) began with the theological construct of the existence of a personal God who utilized divinely ordered laws in the creation of the universe. A Lutheran prince, a Lutheran theologian, and a professor at the Reformer Melanchthon's Wittenberg University supported the publishing of the writings of Copernicus. Kepler was a devoted follower of Luther. During the seventeenth century the Calvinists and Lutherans aggressively supported scientific advances. A plausible case can be made for the statement that Protestantism "gave rise to modern science."[3]

DAVID HUME (1711-1776)

From the time David Hume entered Edinburgh University at age twelve he read voraciously in the philosophers, the scientists, and classical literature. Intellectually he was a radical and politically a conservative. His *Natural History of Religion* and *Dialogues Concerning Natural Religion* were so progressive that his friends advised him to publish them posthumously.

The writings of Rene Descartes (1596-1650) and other French philosophers we have studied intrigued him. Descartes had stated clearly his belief in the reality of the self when he said, "I think, therefore I am." Doubt, to Descartes, was a direct way toward discovery of self. Doubt is thought, and thought involves a thinker. But some joined Hume in his disagreement with Descartes' position that in man's doubt he has discovered the self-evident fact of his own reality. Hume was reflecting the changes taking place in the Enlightenment period.

The Renaissance witnessed the humanization of knowledge and a beginning of the reformation of the established church. In the middle of the sixteenth century the Copernican revolution began. The age of science and its attendant skepticism regarding revolution and Aristotelianism was exemplified by Kepler, Galileo, William Harvey, Descartes, and Newton. Using mathematical reasoning and systematic induction from observation of the natural world, those scientists achieved results that testified to the power of a new method of inquiry. Descartes, an orthodox Roman Catholic, managed to maintain an air of religious propriety that warded off the potential inquisitors. Newton spoke of his piety more than he did of calculus and the laws of motion. Gradually the scientific method developed and demonstrated its usefulness in one discipline after another, with the result that theology, once queen of the sciences, lost additional leverage in academic circles. Revealed religion was losing out to "natural" knowledge.

The philosophy of Hume is based on the methodology of John Locke and George Berkeley. It was Locke who spoke of the mind of the infant being a tabula rasa, a blank sheet inscribed by that which is experienced through the five senses. Hume reduced reason to a product of sensory experience and thus destroyed its claim to sole validity in the judgment of ideas.

Hume desired to emancipate philosophy and education from what he considered vagueness and obscurantism and to develop a new method that could be synchronized with science and separated from theology. He created uncertainty regarding proofs for the existence of God as developed by Anselm and Aquinas, claiming that the promise of the first cause was of little worth. Miracles were summarily dismissed for their failure to conform to natural law. His critique of miracles made some telling points, but the argument was far from conclusive.

> For when Hume talked about a 'firm and unalterable experience' establishing the laws of nature, he omitted to ask the question 'Whose experience?' If we take a sample selection of experience only from those who have no experience of miracles, then we are bound to conclude that miracles have not been experienced. But if we include evidence of contrary cases, we cannot say that miracles are automatically ruled out. They may be unusual and contrary to common experience. But we cannot rule them out on the grounds that they are at variance with all experience.[4]

David Hume constantly criticized religious institutions, whether Protestant or Roman Catholic. The deists were fair game as well, for he did not feel they could substantiate the conclusions of their nationally oriented religious beliefs. He railed against control of the schools by religious groups.

Although Hume was highly critical of education generally, he enthusiastically supported academic freedom and the liberty to read any book without censorship. He condemned the overuse of memorization and mindless repetition. He was best known for his *History of England* but felt that history was not to be taught in terms of events and dates. Instead the emphasis should be placed on cultural foundations and the ideas and constructs that gave form to how people thought and lived. Thus history and literature were seen to be interdependent, as literature was a key to understanding the ideals and wishes of people and therefore provided a "symbolic account of life."[5]

Bertrand Russell suggests that Hume demonstrated the inadequacies of eighteenth-century rationalism. John Wesley, Hume's contemporary, called him "the most insolent despiser of truth and virtue that ever appeared in the world."[6] In his journal entry of August 8, 1773, Wesley speaks of certain "menders of the Bible" and contends that "hereby they promote the cause of infidelity more effectually than either Hume or Voltaire."[7] To this day Hume is a folk hero for skeptics.

JEAN-JACQUES ROUSSEAU (1712-1778)

In the late eighteenth and early nineteenth centuries there arose a very determinative philosophy of education that could be termed *naturalism*. It formed the basis of modern educational theory and practice, and its emphasis upon individuality and freedom served as the rationale for American social thought.

It is interesting to note that Francis Schaeffer and Will and Ariel Durant agree that the Swiss-born, French-adopted Jean-Jacques Rousseau is the most important influence on modern thought. Schaeffer states, "Rousseau's concept of autonomous freedom led to the Bohemian ideal, in which the hero is the man who fights all of society's standards, values, and restraints."[8]

Rousseau was an enigmatic figure. Highly emotional, erratic, a creative genius, a man of reprobate and perverted nature, he was an idealist who was passionately devoted to the downtrodden and to liberty. His life was a psychological puzzle. Our thrust will major in his theories and ideas rather than his person. No one can be viewed apart from his historical context. Hume was part of that context. Both Hume and Rousseau emphasized experience rather than reason as the epistemological base for knowing truth. On the one occasion they were together they quarrelled so violently that Rousseau unexpectedly went back to France. In his later years he suffered from mental illness and while with Hume he imagined that everyone was persecuting him.

In 1762 Rousseau published his *Social Contract* and the educational novel *Emile*. Those books brought condemnation from the French monarchy and the church, but admiration from the literary and philosophical circles of Europe. To the present his writings have assured him a place in erudite centers of learning.

Three key words and phrases dominate the thinking of naturalism: *emotion, nature*, and the *goodness of man*. Naturalists stressed the role of feeling in the act of knowledge. Man is to experience fully the depth of emotion to understand nature. The statement "all things are good in a state of nature" is important to the romanticist. An individual should intuitively feel the natural phenomena around him. Nature is the highest value. Rousseau also emphasized man's inherent goodness and the corrupting influence of society, which he vehemently condemned.

Rousseau's approach to education was anti-intellectual in that he opposed bookishness and favored life experiences in the education of the child. He saw the primitive as innocent, and autonomous freedom as the final good that was reflected in his concept of the child as a "noble savage." That which is "natural" is morally good.

In the novel *Emile* Rousseau proposes a system whereby man can be rehabilitated even in the social climate in which he lives. Since society is evil and man is good (which is a contradiction), the chief aim of the carefully chosen tutor is to preserve Emile from any contact with society. His paradigm begins with the child as an orphan so that the teacher may remove him from society while very young. The child is left to his natural inclinations, and his innate goodness is cultivated and developed. Such an education supposedly provides an innoculation against the ill effects of life in an artificial society. Emile is given freedom within a prepared environment, a concept employed by Maria Montessori much later. Environmental forces help to shape the child's judgment. Emile's senses are to be educated — mere bookish learning would clutter his mind with useless knowledge. He is experiencing "life" directly. The teacher in the paradigm resembles today's progressive educationist who provides the best growth experiences, remains relatively inconspicuous, but never totally relinquishes the control of the learning environment. One of the most important lessons Emile learns is that his actions have consequences for which he is responsible. Profit and/or punishment are the result.

In his first twelve years Emile was to be kept from books as Rousseau believed that to substitute them for the products of sense experience would hinder the reasoning process. This time period stressed knowledge of the physical world and the development of a strong body. The extrinsic acceleration of the child by the teacher or parent is unacceptable, a concept he shares with Jean Piaget. A slow paced, natural progression in childhood tends to facilitate an emergence of curiosity, abilities, and intrinsic motivation. An important concept espoused by Rousseau is that the child is not a miniature adult.

Rousseau saw five stages of development: infancy, childhood, boyhood, adolescence, and youth. It is beyond the province of this volume to consider each in detail, but several pertinent points follow. Sensation is the basis for our knowledge. Objects and the physical environment are the facilitators used rather than words and books. During boyhood, ages twelve to fifteen, the first book was introduced to Emile. It was Daniel Defoe's *Robinson Crusoe,* which promoted an isolated natural environment and the aspect of dependence on one another (Robinson Crusoe and Friday). Because he did not acknowledge the depravity of man, Rousseau taught that one's first impulses are pure and would remain so if the tutor could keep the mind inactive.

In the period of adolescence, ages fifteen to eighteen, Emile would experience an awareness of sex. The tutor was to answer him plainly, without evasion or coarseness. Emile would now be taught about societal forces and have his aesthetic sensibilities enriched through visiting museums and theaters, learning languages, and reading books.

Emile had a significant impact on educational thought in the West. Johann Heinrich Pestalozzi attempted to take the educational philosophy of Rousseau and employ his doctrines in a group learning situation. Contact with Rousseau's naturalism influenced Pestalozzi's emphasis on sensation and the liberation of the child, though he found some of his doctrines theoretical and impractical.

The brilliant Rousseau was a strange combination of rationalist and romanticist. He was a devotee of Plato and valued the *Republic* as the single greatest work ever written on education. Yet he wanted to keep books and ideas away from children until adolescence. He idolized the innocence of primitive life in which he thought a slower maturation provided a context for building a resistance to the forces of society.

Rousseau was not a pure naturalist but rather a deist. He taught Emile a natural religion without creeds and dogmas, yet he believed in God and thought of nature as His creation. "Everything is good as it comes from the hands of the Maker of the world; everything degenerates in the hand of man."[9] Rousseau's naturalism was a revolt against the artificiality and corruption of human society. The revolutionaries of the nineteen sixties and early nineteen seventies found a ready-made folk hero in Jean-Jacques Rousseau. Possibly the finest contribution to education was his insistence on the importance of the study of the child. This prompted educators to focus on the characteristics and individual needs of the learner through the various stages of growth and change.

Rousseau's *La Nouvelle Heloise* propounded a natural religion necessary for morality. *Emile* and *Social Contract* addressed the problem man faces since he cannot return to a natural state. He must find ways to correct the vices of the society in which he must live in order to restore it to a state of virtue. The *Social Contract* states that free man must voluntarily surrender his will to the community and submit to its laws, which are based on the general will of the people. The state must protect man and preserve his original freedom. The state therefore is governed by a democracy since all laws are the direct expression of the general will.

One can readily see how educationists, the majority of whom

share Rousseau's disdain for the doctrine of the depravity of man, would react enthusiastically to his stance on the goodness of man, sensory education, the teacher as a facilitator, and his antipathy for the verbal methodologies of a classical content-centered philosophy. Rousseau had an impact on John Dewey and other progressivists regarding education that was based on the interests and natural activities of the child. Social Darwinist Herbert Spencer and utopian Robert Owen were among the many influenced by this enigmatic thinker. Because there are so many diverse—often contradictory—trends in Rousseau's writings, both reactionaries and progressives could use his arguments.

IMMANUEL KANT (1724-1804)

The day a copy of Rousseau's *Emile* arrived by mail, Immanuel Kant's neighbors noticed an exception in his habits. The neighbors could set their clocks by the punctuality of Kant's daily walk, but the day he received the *Emile* he was not seen at all. Rousseau was one of the two significant writers who marked the intellectual development of the great Kant. The man who seldom traveled beyond the county of Konigsberg, Germany, was an influential figure with those having philosophical proclivities in the Western world.

Kant was unlike Rousseau and Hume, the two who influenced him the most, in method, belief, and temperament. The empiricist Hume caused Kant to think carefully regarding his understanding of rationality and ultimate reality. Kant set out to give a defense of common sense notions about the world, which had been undermined by Hume. He came to the conclusion that phenomena such as causation, time, and space are a priori categories of the mind. Kant felt that empiricists failed to acknowledge that the human mind makes its own contributions to sense-based knowledge and imposes its subjective categories upon the world.

> The spatial, temporal, and causal order of experience represents universal ordering functions of the mind, and in this fact lies the possibility of making statements which are both certain and applicable to experience. That is, we can know a priori that every event occurred at some time and some place and on account of some cause, even though only through experience can we know the particulars.[10]

This reorientation of epistemology, or the theory of knowledge, had its effect upon the philosophy of education. Despite significant differences, Kant also was influenced by Rousseau. Kant was of the opinion that a school system should be based on moral law and the dignity of the individual and that work and discipline are means for reaching the highest goals.

> Discipline changes animal nature into human nature. Animals are by their instinct all that they ever can be; some other reason has provided everything for them at the outset. But man needs a reason of his own. Having no instinct, he has to work out a plan of conduct himself. Since, however, he is not able to do this all at once, but comes into the world undeveloped, others have to do it for him.
>
> All the natural endowments of mankind must be developed little by little out of man himself, through his own effort. One generation educates the next. The first beginnings of this process of educating may be looked for either in a rude and unformed, or in a fully developed condition of man. If we assume the latter to come first, man must at all events afterwards have degenerated and lapsed into barbarism.
>
> It is discipline, which prevents man from being turned aside by his animal impulses from humanity, his appointed end. Discipline, for instance, must restrain him from venturing wildly and rashly into danger. Discipline, thus, is merely negative, its action being to counteract man's natural unruliness. The positive part of education is instruction.[11]

It is through discipline that we become free, according to Kant. We become autonomous by gradually freeing our will from external control, in order to subject it to internal control.

> By discipline men are placed in subjection to the laws of mankind, and brought to feel their constraint. This, however, must be accomplished early. Children, for instance, are first sent to school, not so much with the object of their learning something, but rather that they may become use to sitting still and doing exactly as they are told. And thus to the end that in later life they should not wish to put actually and instantly into practice anything that strikes them.[12]

An important concept in Kant's lectures on education centered on morality. Men are to act, not as they want but as they ought. They are responsible for developing their own moral sensitivities, assisted in this process by education and culture. He reflected the thinking of the Enlightenment in his view of man's inherent goodness.

> Man must develop his tendency toward the good. Providence has not placed goodness ready formed in him, but merely as a tendency and without the distinction of moral law. Man's duty is to

improve himself; to cultivate his mind; and when he finds himself going astray, to bring the moral law to bear upon himself.

Man needs nurture and culture. Culture includes discipline and instruction. Man can only become man by education. He is merely what education makes of him. It is noticeable that man is only educated by man—that is, by men who have themselves been educated.[13]

JOHANN HEINRICH PESTALOZZI (1746-1827)

Whereas Rousseau and Kant were the able theoreticians, Johann Heinrich Pestalozzi was the competent practitioner. He took the ideas and concepts of Rousseau and modified them into a working philosophy of education that profoundly affected education in the West. Pestalozzi combined the naturalism of the Enlightenment and the romanticism of Rousseau. His career should be interpreted in light of the Swiss historical context in which he worked. Switzerland was an interesting composite of the European milieu in the latter half of the eighteenth and the early quarter of the nineteenth centuries. "The social, political, intellectual, and economic currents sweeping post-Enlightenment Europe had their effect on the Alpine cantons, which were a mosaic composed of rural-urban, feudal-democratic, Protestant-Catholic, and Teutonic-Romance conflicts."[14]

Switzerland, as all of Europe, was substantially influenced by the revolutionary climate in France. In 1798 the French invaded Switzerland. Pestalozzi applied for an educational position when a Swiss liberation movement called the Helvetian Republic came to power. He wrote propaganda materials for that new regime but lost what little political influence he had when Napoleon decreed further changes in the government.

The Enlightenment era was part of the intellectual shift from a theocentric world view to a humanistic Weltanschauung. Rationalism and romanticism were in vogue. In religious matters Switzerland courted both Roman Catholic and Reformed theology. Geneva was still strongly Calvinistic, whereas Zurich was both a Zwinglian and Calvinistic center. Economically, a transition from an almost totally agrarian to an industrial system was taking place. Handcraft arts were the first step in European industrialization.

When Pestalozzi was five his father died. His Italian family, living in the German-speaking city of Zurich, provided a warm, loving home dominated by his mother, an older sister, and Barbara Schmid, a family servant. Masculine influence was given through his grandfather, who lived in the canton of Zurich. Andreas Pestalozzi was a pastor, and Johann would occasionally accompany him on his visits to poor parishioners. This gave the boy a never-to-be-forgotten appreciation for the destitute and the culturally deprived. Johann grew up as a highly introspective, timid child who was socially isolated and somewhat incompetent in his peer relationships. Though he did not begin formal education until he was nine he received a good education in the elementary vernacular schools, classical Latin secondary schools, and the University of Zurich. Pestalozzi studied for the ministry, but his shyness and his first sermon (which was his last) changed his mind.

Hoping to alleviate the hardship of poverty, Pestalozzi purchased a farm at Neuhof in 1771 and began a social and educational experiment three years later by taking in orphaned and vagrant children. He taught them handcraft arts in an attempt to blend the teaching of vocational skills with moral and intellectual development. In rearing his own son Jean Jacques (whom he called Jacobli) by the methodology of Rousseau, Pestalozzi kept a diary recording his progress. For February 19, 1774, it reads,

> Whatever you can teach him from the nature of things themselves, do not teach him by words. Leave him to himself to see, hear, find, stumble, rise again, and be mistaken. Give no words when action, or deed is possible. What he can do for himself let him do. Let him be always occupied, ever active, and let the time when you do not worry him be by far the greatest part of his childhood. You will come to learn that nature teaches him better than men.[15]

The impact of Rousseau is readily seen. As Pestalozzi became more experienced in using the methods with his son and the school at Neuhof, adaptation and modification took place . He spent eighteen years (1780-1798) writing and theorizing. In 1781 he published his educational novel, *Leonard and Gertrude,* in which he attempted to show that social regeneration was possible through education. Unfortunately many missed its educational significance and regarded it only as a novel.

Leonard and Gertrude presented the school and the home as educational agencies and expounded the doctrines of Pestalozzian natural education:

1. Evil originates in a distorted social environment rather than in human nature.

2. Education is the surest means of securing both personal growth and social reform.
3. Genuine education should develop man's natural moral, intellectual, and physical powers.
4. Moral development begins in the home as the child responds to the mother's care and kindness.
5. Sensory and vocational education will train economically self-sufficient individuals.[16]

The novel brought him recognition but little financial assistance. The following year he wrote *Christopher and Elizabeth*, a series of dialogues based on *Leonard and Gertrude*. He later published *Inquiry*, but the effort was not well received. In 1801 his systematic discussion on education, *How Gertrude Teaches Her Children*, was released.

Following the devastation of the Swiss revolution Pestalozzi opened an orphanage at Stans. Limited funds and criticism of him as a radical and heretic caused it to be short-lived. However, it was there that he devised the concept of a home atmosphere of love and security that became prominent in his educational philosophy. He operated a school at Bergdorf (1800-1804), which he later moved to Yverdon (1805-1826). Herman Krusi, Johannes Niederer, and Joseph Neef joined him in this educational enterprise, which attracted international attention. Johann Friedrich Herbart, the educational philosopher; Friedrich Froebel, founder of the kindergarten; Robert Owen, utopian enthusiast for early childhood education; and Andrew Bell, developer of the monitorial method, were among those visiting Yverdon. That which could have become a monumental effort collapsed due to personality clashes and disagreements regarding methodology among the staff. Pestalozzi failed to give leadership in the decision-making process, and the gifted associates' skills were not maximized.

The educational philosophy of Pestalozzi is made up of a bewildering tangle of diversities such as "Enlightenment rationalism, naturalistic romanticism, German idealism, pietistical Christianity, social philanthropism, political reformism, and industrial liberalism."[17] One of the practical and determinative elements was the home in which he was reared. The basic relationship is that of the parent to the child. Pestalozzi's famous dictum "From the near to the far" is seen in the series of concentric circles or stages of educational development. It implies a continuity of experience whereby the immediate context relates to the large environment. Love was to be experienced from the teacher. It moved from the concrete to the abstract.

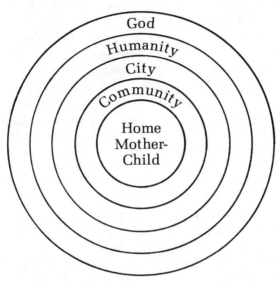

Fig. 10.1

The basic stage or relationship depicts the home as the place for creating a climate of emotional security. From the security of the family circle the child is gradually introduced to the larger community of society. As the child grows he becomes increasingly independent. Pestalozzi's emphasis on emotion and sensory experience was related to his conception of religion. His was a religion of the heart rather than of a doctrinal statement. Pestalozzi opposed religious education that was based on doctrine, dogma, and ritual. He rejected the doctrine of original sin and accepted that of innate human goodness. He followed Rousseau in his insistence that if the first environment (for Rousseau, isolation from society; for Pestalozzi it was the family) strengthens one, a person is enabled to resist corrupt society.

The implications of his attitude toward the nature of man and evil affected discipline, because external discipline would be necessary for a depraved child. But from his vantage point Pestalozzi felt that the discipline problem is substantially alleviated if a climate of affection and warmth was provided by the teacher.

Although the general method of Pestalozzi's philosophy centered in a context of love and an emotionally secure learning environment, the special method focused on visible objects. As a realist he based his epistemology on sense perception. One acquires knowledge through sensation that is refined into concepts. The curriculum was organized around "sensate" activities, that is, through direct experience. Demonstrations and field trips were to be favored over reading. Objects were to be brought to class. Pestalozzi declared:

> Strengthen and make clear the impression of important objects by bringing them near to you . . . and letting them affect you through different senses. Learn . . . the first law of physical mechanism, which makes the relative power of all influences of physical Nature depend on the physical nearness or distance of the object in contract with the senses. Never forget this physical nearness or distance has an immense effect in determining your positive opinions, conduct, duties, or even virtue.[18]

Pestalozzi would have approved John Dewey's concept that all learning should originate in the experience of the learner. He held that the student should be studied by the teacher so that individual differences would be recognized and adaptations made. Pestalozzi was an originator of the contemporary idea of "readiness."[19]

The teaching of Pestalozzi was remarkably influential. We have mentioned his impact on Herbart and Froebel in Germany. The Prussian government included aspects of his methodology in its educational reorganization in 1808. The English Pestalozzians, like so many of his followers, failed to generate the love environment of the general method. Among those were Charles and Elizabeth Mayo who further distorted his principles by formalizing the object lesson. In the United States Robert Owen and William Maclure, philanthropic industrialists, desired to develop a utopian community setting at New Harmony, Indiana. They purchased the small town and brought in Joseph Neef, a colleague of Pestalozzi at Yverdon, to give educational leadership. The communitarian social reform experiment lasted just over two years before disintegrating (1825-1828) because of internal strife and financial disputes between Owen and Maclure.

Henry Barnard was the first United States Commissioner of Education and editor of the substantial *Connecticut Common School Journal* (1838-1842). In advocating the establishment of the common or public school he promoted Pestalozzianism. The third phase of the movement in the United States was the work of Edward Sheldon and his associates at the Oswego (N.Y.) Normal School, who worked under the premise that knowledge comes from sense perception and that objects should be utilized. The full-blown development of the object lesson was the result. Unfortunately it became rigid and formal, thus departing from its original intent.

In effect, Pestalozzianism engaged in conflict with the advocates of traditional education and its emphasis on verbalization, memorization, and reading. The continuance of traditional education into the last decade of the 1800s in its Herbartian form successfully resisted progressivism until the powerful thrust of John Dewey was encountered. Dewey utilized a number of ideas conceived by Pestalozzi.

JOHANN FRIEDRICH HERBART (1776-1841)

When he took the chair of philosophy at Konigsberg once held by the great Immanuel Kant, Johann Friedrich Herbart was destined to live under the shadow of the idealist who wanted his stance to be known as "critical philosophy." This was the golden age of idealism in Germany, and Herbart was out of step with Kant, Hegel, Friedrich von Schelling, and Johann Gottlieb Fichte. As is the case with many thinkers, he did not live to receive the recognition due him, and it was not until the late nineteenth and early twentieth centuries that Herbart was appreciated. In order to get a better perspective of his life let us look at the educational climate in Europe in the nineteenth century.

The nineteenth century was one of great disparity and educational diversity. The various levels of growth reflected the variety of conditions produced by the Napoleonic wars. During the centuries previous to the wars education had remained in a stagnant condition. Differences between countries had been largely that of backwardness or progressiveness. During the first half of the nineteenth century each nation developed an independent plan and time schedule based on its own situation.

Germany (Prussia), the educational leader of Europe, engaged in an experiment of national education that was influenced by Pestalozzi and, in a secondary sense, by Froebel and Herbart. It was Fichte who contended for the adoption of Pestalozzianism in his "Address to the German Nation" in 1808. Switzerland also was enriched by the theorizing of Pestalozzi. All classes of society were influenced by him, but he worked most often with the poor and those without parents.

In France, the influence of Francois Guizot (1787-1874) and the Law of 1833 established a national system of primary education while still permitting private schools to continue. The work of Jean Marc Itard (1775-1838) and Edward Seguin (1812-1880) in mental retardation was pedagogical as well as medical, and from those two thinkers Maria Montessori derived many of her teaching principles.

In England primary education was available to all children, but it was not linked to secondary programs. Generally secondary education was the province of the upper and middle classes. Their famous public schools (private in North American nomenclature) were elitest. Winchester, the oldest of the nine "great schools," was founded in 1832. Thomas Arnold (1795-1842) and his son Matthew (1828-1888) were instrumental in modernizing and expanding the classical curriculum, but both advocated the traditional approach for a truly humane education. Herbert Spencer (1820-1903) combined the concepts of mental discipline and evolutionary development in his educational philosophy. He was opposed to governmental control of education. The influence of Rousseau can be seen on all of these educators.

Herbart was born in 1776, just seven years after Napoleon was born. Johann von Goethe, Kant, Friedrich von Schiller, and Mozart had already begun the German cultural renaissance. Herbart was a contemporary of Beethoven, Schelling, and Hegel. He was born of a passive, apathetic father and a very aggressive, domineering mother.

Herbart was tutored by his mother and Herman Uelzen, a graduate student who initiated his study of Greek, Latin, philosophy, and theology. Though a theologian, Uelzen did not use catechetical methods or teach dogmatically; rather he taught Johann how to think. Herbart's formal schooling did not begin until he was twelve, but the transition into the Latin school or gymnasium was made with ease. Herbart was bright, industrious, and musical. His precocity made him the youngest in his class. Casual relationships were difficult for the young man.

His mother also left Oldenburg to attend the university at Jena as his classmate. This dominating mother became a close friend of his philosophy professor, Johann Gottlieb Fichte, and Fichte's wife. Although he was Fichte's finest student, Herbart moved toward realism and away from the idealism of his professor. In 1796 while still Fichte's student he wrote:

> However many happy thoughts may be scattered about in Fichte's deductions regarding natural right and morality, I consider the fundamental points, i.e., his theory of the recognition of a reasoning being as such and his doctrine of freedom, as false.
>
> I am modest in my demands on human freedom. Leaving that to Schelling and to Fichte, I seek to determine a human being by the laws of his reason and nature, and to give him that which will enable him to make something of himself.[20]

Herbart gave early evidence of the conflict in his thinking as a philosopher and as an educator. He desired to reconcile the philosophical concept of unlimited freedom with the limitations educators know are there. His commitment to education directed him away from idealism to what Herbart judged to be a more accurate and realistic evaluation of man and his potential.

Herbart had entered the university as a law student, but philosophy became his prime interest. His mother, fearing that philosophy would not lead to a financially remunerative profession, urged him to become the tutor of the two older sons of the governor of Interlaken. (Abraham Friesen, Solomon Bluhm [*Encyclopedia of Education*] and Harry G. Good and James D. Teller hold to the position that Herbart tutored three sons of the von Steiger family rather than two. The bi-monthly written reports submitted to Herr von Steiger constitute an excellent source for discovering the evolution of Herbart's educational philosophy. Unfortunately only five of those reports are extant.) This was a common practice of graduate students. It gave them additional time for research and preparation for doctoral examinations.

Herbart's experience with the von Steiger family enabled him to formalize his philosophy of education. Although he remained with the von Steiger family only three years, his later writing and lectures reflected this teaching experience. Ludwig, the elder son, was lazy and an underachiever who leaned heavily on the wealth and position of his family. Herbart later would tell teachers that occasionally they must scrap their lesson plans and lower their expectations. The good teacher develops a unique program in line with the abilities and life situation of the student. However, the second son, Karl, was an excellent pupil with whom he sustained a continuing relationship through correspondence.

Herbart received his doctorate at Gottingen in 1802, but because his metaphysics were unacceptable to the idealists, he prudently began his university teaching career by lecturing on pedagogy, then ethics, and finally logic and metaphysics. He taught at Gottingen (1802-1809), Konigsberg (1809-1833), and, failing to secure the chair made vacant by Hegel's retirement at Berlin, he returned to Gottingen and remained there until his death. Despite Herbart's "politicking" he was passed over for an unknown Hegelian.[21]

The most prominent psychology of the mid-nineteenth century was associationism. John Stuart Mill and Herbart were the two leading exponents of this theory. Associationism was built on a realistic view of the world and took an empirical position regarding the nature of knowledge. It attempted to reduce all mental processes to those of association.

The aim of education, according to Herbart, takes its direction from ethics. The objective is strength of moral character. "The one and the whole work of education may be summed up in the concept-morality."[22] Thus, the goal of education is the development of a person with character and humane convictions who understands the art of constructive and integrated living. It is not simply to impart information but to produce a virtuous, compassionate, and refined person. To Herbart, the ultimate objective of "educative instruction" is the forming of character. Instruction enables the student to judge and choose discriminately on the basis of knowledge.

It follows then that what the student is taught is crucial. Morality is based on knowledge. It is possible that, having received proper training, an individual may not do the right thing even though he knows what the right thing is. "If inner assurance and personal interests are wanting, if the store of thought be meager, the ground lies open to the animal desires."[23] In another of his writings Herbart states: "Instruction will form the circle of thought and education of the character. The last is nothing without the first. Herein is contained the whole sum of my pedagogy."[24] This stagement is the key to understanding his philosophy of education. Content is crucial in the educational process.

Herbart differed with Mill and Mill's English associationist colleagues in that he saw the mind as a battleground of ideas or presentations.

> They [ideas] fight for dominance, and when they lose they become part of our subconscious. Consciousness is not a simple process; it

is like a stage play in which new actors constantly enter and occasionally the old performers reappear.

The mind . . . has three functions: it knows, feels and wills. However, the will is not a separate faculty; it is the desire which underlies our mental processes and our emotional reactions. The mind moves from sensation to memory, to imagination, and at last, to conceptual thinking, its highest sphere. When a new concept enters the mind it can be rejected, and thus find its way into the subconscious; or it can be accepted and assimilated with other presentations.[25]

The mind is built up from the "presentations" (performance, idea, notion, sensations, conception, or image) arising in it. The existing structure is continually altered by new presentations. Thus the apperceptive mass is continually being constructed. Dunkel discusses this concept as follows:

Let us begin with the simplest encounter—that between the first two presentations occurring in the mind. The two presentations—like two reals, like two forces—would in general oppose each other; but precisely what happens would depend on several factors. First, Herbart distinguished three categories of presentation: "similar," "dissimilar" (or disparate), and "contrary." The presentations could blend into fusions (Schmelzungen) or very tight combinations. Dissimilar ones, because of their very lack of similarity, would form less closely knit combinations, "complexions" (Complexionen). In the case of the two contrary propositions, it would be war; the stronger would succeed in wiping out the weaker in exact proportion to the extent it was stronger.[26]

Successive presentations become clusters of experience into which new presentations are assimilated. New experiences are always modified by what has been experienced previously. This was not a novel concept. Educators and philosophers such as Descartes, Leibnitz, Locke, Kant, Rousseau, and Pestalozzi had addressed the problem of the interaction between the human mind and external experience. Herbart was aware of their deliberations. His "conception of apperception, in which the new is and can only be perceived in terms of the old, is original with him and is the cornerstone of his theory of learning and method of instruction."[27]

Whatever the content to be taught or the methodology to be used, in order to hold the student's interest, the same sequence is to be followed. Herbart's four steps are clearness, association, system, and method, though at times he substituted other words for those four terms. The Herbartian movement, which began approximately twenty-five years after his death, modified those into five formal steps: preparation, association, generalization, and application. The five steps gained popularity because they provided a readily understood outline for the development of a lesson plan and gave clear direction to the teacher. This was the key to their wide acceptance among teachers in the late nineteenth and early twentieth centuries.

Tuiskon Ziller was the first Herbartian to expand Herbart's four into the five steps, but Wilhelm Rein articulated the five steps with the nomenclature used above.

> The most fundamental change, however, was that for most Herbartians instruction was no longer "educative" in Herbart's strict sense of that term; it no longer led to the formation of moral character through building the will. The aim was purely cognitive. The pupil was to be able to organize and structure his knowledge, with special emphasis on the development of general concepts or general ideas. But for most of the later Herbartians, the will was no longer the creature of the presentations. Consequently, though the end of education was claimed to be "morality" in some vague sense, instruction could no longer build moral strength of character in the way that Herbart had sought to build it. Apperception and the steps became merely a general theory of cognitive learning usable in all sorts of specializations. Herbart had not been opposed to such learning; he simply was not interested in it. Once instruction was declared unable to do what he had wanted it to do, he would have resigned from the local Herbart society.[28]

To Herbart the objective of education was sound moral development. This was attainable through the presentation of right ideas that captivated the interest of the student. He recommended the division of all subjects into the historical and the mathematical. The former included foreign languages, history, and geography; the latter mathematics and natural sciences. The "historical" provided the core around which the curriculum revolved because those disciplines, if studied in the proper manner, made a contribution to moral education. For example, after only a minimal preparation in Greek the student began to read Homer's *Odyssey*, as Herbart desired that the student understand the writing from an ethical standpoint. Because the aim was moral and not philological, the normal procedure of a detailed introduction to the forms and syntax of the language was secondary.

The curricular emphases of Herbart convey to the student a broad understanding of man and the cosmos. In his judgment, the development of the child's personality tends to follow the pattern by which the human race achieved its levels of culture. Rousseau had held this position, but Herbart's stance regarding the "culture epoch" theory had been influenced by Schiller at Jena. However, Herbart never developed it with precision or in detail. The Herbartians, particularly Tuiskon Ziller, improved what their mentor had done and cast into a dominant position the culture epoch approach to curriculum building. The theory suggests that "as the embryo retraces the biological evolution of the species, so the education of the child should recapitulate the major stages of man's intellectual and moral development."[29] Nowhere in his writings did Herbart specify exact stages as did his followers. The concepts of the culture epoch theory were rejected as being too rigid by educationists.

Herbart's ideas regarding the introduction of literature, history, geography, and other social studies in the lower grades of the elementary school were well received. He insisted that the correct methodology was crucial in the teaching of each discipline. His four formal steps, based on his theory of apperception, were to be followed.

J. F. Herbart was not evangelical in his theology. He thought that religious instruction should be given during the early years in order to foster religious consciousness.

> Education must look upon religion not as objective, but as subjective. Religion befriends and protects, but nevertheless it must not be given the child too circumstantially. Its work must be directing rather than teaching. It must never exhaust susceptibility, and therefore above all must not be prematurely made use of. It must not be given dogmatically to arouse doubt, but in union with knowledge of nature and the repression of egoism. It must ever point beyond, but never instruct beyond the bounds of knowledge, for then the paradox would follow, that instruction knows what it does not know; with the aid of the Bible it teaches historically and prepares the child for the church.[30]

The teacher, like the parent, was to encourage religious consciousness. But that consciousness was to be awakened initially by the parents in the home.

Herbartian thought has filtered into many educational institutions. Paul Monroe's almost sixty-year-old assessment is of interest: "No man has written with keener insight or with greater suggestiveness or with deeper philosophical penetration concerning the immediate work of instruction."[31] Tuiskon Ziller and Wilhelm Rein, both instrumental in reviving interest in the thought of Herbart, took great liberties with his material and recast much of it. As Americans went to Germany for doctoral and postdoctoral study in the latter part of the 1800s and the early 1900s, they were influenced by the impact of Herbartianism. In 1895, Americans Charles and Frank McMurry, and Charles De Garmo helped to establish the National Herbart Society for the Scientific Study of Education. In 1901 the society dropped "Herbart" from its name, indicating that it was no longer bound to his doctrines. John Dewey served on the executive committee, and Commissioner of Education William Torrey Harris and Colonel Francis W. Parker also attended the National Herbart Society meetings as they felt the movement was a useful stimulus to American educational thought. Dewey vigorously refuted Herbart's position on interest and the culture epoch theory. His critiques were published in the society's *Yearbooks*, in several articles, and in his *Lectures In the Philosophy of Education: 1899* and *Democracy and Education*, his magnum opus. Finally, the advancing scientific theories of psychologists Wilhelm Wundt and E. L. Thorndike made the Herbartians relics of another period. Nevertheless Herbart's influence remains in more than just a few pockets of the past. His clearly laid out lesson plans gave hope and direction to teachers.

FRIEDRICH FROEBEL (1782-1852)

Friedrich Wilhelm August Froebel, like all of us, was a product of his home life and societal setting. His mother died when he was nine months old, and his father, a Lutheran pastor in Germany, gave little time to young Friedrich. He was so deeply immersed in his pastoral duties that he tended to forget the needs of his son. Listen to the adult Friedrich reflecting on his early rearing:

> The care of five thousand souls, scattered over six or seven villages, devolved solely on my father. This work even to a man so active as my father, who was very conscientious in the fulfillment of his duty as minister, was all-absorbing; the more so since the custom of frequent services still prevailed. Besides all this, my father had undertaken to superintend the building of a large new church, which drew more and more from his home and his children.

> I was left to the care of the servants; but they, profiting by my father's absorption in his work, left me, fortunately for me, to my brothers, who were somewhat older than myself . . .
>
> My father was prevented by his manifold occupations from himself instructing me. Besides, he lost all further inclination to teach me, after the great trouble he found in teaching me to read—an art which came to me with great difficulty.[32]

His father remarried, but his stepmother also failed to give young Friedrich proper attention, choosing rather to invest her energies in her natural son. Separated emotionally from his parents and being much younger than his brothers, Friedrich was deprived of companionship and was forced to be dependent on his own resources. He grew melancholy, lonely, shy, and introspective and became maladjusted at school, home, and to society. Lacking proper supervision and encouragement, his weaknesses in personal discipline and perseverance may account for the variety of careers he pursued as an adult.

At age ten he went to live with his uncle in Switzerland. The five years with him were a positive experience for Froebel as this relative gave him love and understanding. Though his early education was fragmentary and disjointed, the period with his uncle was one of regular schooling, a supportive home, and normal peer relationships. It made such an impact on him that he was fond of recalling it for years. On returning to his home he found the atmosphere there had not changed. In frustration his father apprenticed him to a woodcutter. Two years away from society deepened his feelings of loneliness and isolation but opened up new vistas regarding creation and the Creator.

At seventeen he visited his medical student brother in Jena. He remained at the university for a year, captivated by the intellectual vitality and stimulation of academia. Lacking the classical preparation needed for the lectures, he was able to comprehend only the introductory and elementary lectures in philosophy, mathematics, physics, and chemistry. Fichte and Schelling influenced his thinking in those years. However, failure to pay his school bill landed him in the university jail. His father paid his debt, but only after Friedrich gave a written release relinquishing his share of the family inheritance. The next five years found him trying to succeed at farming, clerical work, forestry, architecture, and surveying. A brief stint at teaching drawing was partially successful.

After becoming a tutor of three boys, he took them to Yverdon, enrolled them in Pestalozzi's school, and apprenticed as a teacher there. He agreed with Pestalozzi that certain natural laws could be discovered and form the basis for educational principles. But he felt that Pestalozzi was insufficiently systematic and failed to provide an organic connection between the curriculum, the inner spiritual unity of the student, and the divine unity of God and the universe, which became one of Froebel's emphases. This will be discussed later.

In 1810 he returned to Frankfurt to tutor the three boys again but realized the paucity of his own educational background. In successive years he enrolled at the universities of Gottingen and Berlin, studying a broad range of subjects including philosophy and the natural sciences. Due to the Napoleonic threat he served in the army, where he met Heinrich Laugenthal and Wilhelm Middendorff, who later became his educational colleagues. When peace was declared he returned to Berlin and became the assistant curator at the university's minerological museum. Further research into the structure of crystals replicated for Froebel the structure of life. On being offered an academic post he refused, realizing he must proceed with his dream of the development of a school where he might test his emerging educational theories.

After the death of his brother in 1816 Froebel began tutoring his five nieces and nephews. His brother had been a pastor. The parish house at Griesheim was available, and a school was born. Another brother sent his two sons to Friedrich, and with additional enrollment he secured a farm at Keilha and called his school the "Universal German Education Institute." A Pestalozzian "family" situation was created when he enlisted a widowed sister-in-law as manager. Froebel filled the father role. The school grew to sixty students, but discord arose with the army friends who had joined him in this venture. Froebel arrogantly demanded compliance with his wishes, which resulted in his being forced out of the school's leadership. During that period he published The Education of Man (1826), a formal exposition of his theories.

From 1831 until 1835 Froebel carried on his work in Burgdorf, Switzerland at a school for parentless youngsters aged four to six in which he taught the children and trained the teachers concurrently on Pestalozzian lines. It was here that his fascination with early childhood years developed. He left Burgdorf and went back to Berlin to study the practices of the nursery schools. Froebel discovered that they were weak in the practice of training the instructors. At fifty-five, after failing at almost everything he had tried, he started a school for young children at Blankenburg that he called a *kindergarten* to convey the idea of an environment in which children could grow freely as plants, according to the nature of the child. It was here that he achieved success as a theoretician and practitioner.

The educational philosophy of Froebel was an attempt to bring together elements of idealism, Christianity, romanticism, naturalism, and science. Yet his thinking was not really philosophical or scientific but rather mystical and pragmatic. He defined education in the following terms: "Education consists in leading man, as a thinking, intelligent being, growing into self-consciousness, to a pure and unsullied, conscious and free representation of the inner law of Divine Unity, and in teaching him ways and means thereto."[33]

Thus, to Froebel, a spark of the divine existed in man, and it was the task of the educator to teach him how to discover it. Each person has an internal and an external dimension. The task of education is to help an individual become conscious of the internal or spiritual dimension so that he is aware of the inner law of divine unity. This "inner unfolding" of the child takes place through spontaneous and self-initiated activities.

Froebel failed to articulate a clear statement regarding the biblical concepts of God and the nature of man. It is generally accepted that his concept of God was pantheistic and that man was inherently good. His educational theorizing was also determined by his conviction of the mystical and ultimate oneness of life, nature, and spirit. "It is the destiny and life-work of all things to unfold their essence, hence their divine being, and therefore, the Divine Unity itself—to reveal God in their external and transient being."[34] Froebel was not a deist. He used the term *nature* as did American Transcendentalists Henry David Thoreau and Ralph Waldo Emerson. He viewed God as being immanent in nature.

A child has the potential within him for all he can become, and education must strive to unfold his being in conformity to that mystical plan of Divine Unity, according to Froebel. Through creative self-expression of those inner capacities and abilities the child develops into a fulfilled adult. The stimulation of self-activity and self-fulfillment is a prime requirement of instruction. Therefore, the felt need of the individual becomes the starting point of educational effort. The teacher may direct and stimulate the child toward certain goals, but no instruction is complete that does not result in self-active behavior.

To Froebel, children at play had a symbolic significance. It represented the fulfillment of their humanity, revealing peace, joy, harmony, and contentment with the world. Play is not only the child's primary learning medium, but also his work. Educators should cultivate this spirit of play in a child. This penchant for symbolism carried over to Froebel's attitude toward the object lesson. Thus the kindergarten was an important educational development. Children learn by playing with objects. The ball, for example, symbolized the spherical nature of the world and illustrated the unity of man with the Absolute. Such objects as the ball, cubes, spheres, and cylinders were called "gifts" by Froebel because he considered them gifts from God.

Other play materials such as clay, sand, and mud were called "occupations," and the child was encouraged to use imagination in shaping those malleable materials. In Froebel's mystical interpretation, the play-work symbolized the process of moving from an undifferentiated, unconscious unity to one that is clearly distinguished and purposeful. The use of those constructive activities would then prepare the child for his future vocation. Thus, play-work had distinct religious overtones.

> Play is the highest phase of child development . . . play is the purest, most spiritual activity of man at this stage, and at the same time, typical of human life as a whole—of the hidden natural life in man and in all things. . . . It holds the source of all that is good. A child that plays thoroughly, with self-active determination, perseveringly until physical fatigue forbids, will surely be a thorough, determined man, capable of self-sacrifice for the promotion of the welfare of himself and others. . . . It is highly serious and of deepest significance. . . . The plays of childhood are the germinal leaves of all later life. . . . His future relations to father and mother, to the members of the family, to society and mankind, to nature and God—in accordance with the natural and individual disposition and tendencies of the child—depend chiefly upon his mode of life at this period.[35]

An additional word is needed regarding the role of the teacher in the methodology of Froebel. The instructor functions as a stimulator and encourager in the unfolding of the divinely endowed nature of the child. Froebel advised educators to cooperate with the growth process:

1. Study the eternal laws of human development
2. Construct an educational theory that specifies the directions to be followed in cooperating with human development
3. Apply these directions actively to achieve the development of rational beings
4. Direct education to realize a faithful, pure, and holy life that actualizes the divinely implanted potentialities.[36]

The most dynamic contribution made to education by Froebel was the kindergarten and his influence was felt beyond the borders of Germany and Switzerland. The United States and England were eminently prepared for this new agency. In England the Froebel Society instituted its own kindergarten. France, Italy, Sweden, Finland, and the Netherlands did as well. Immigrants from Germany, led by Mrs. Carl Schurz, opened a German-speaking kindergarten in Watertown, Wisconsin in 1855. Elizabeth Peabody founded the first English-speaking kindergarten in Boston in 1860. Henry Barnard was an enthusiastic proponent of the new school. Nationally, the movement was furthered most by William Torrey Harris, who incorporated the kindergarten as part of the St. Louis school system in 1873. By 1900 it was an accepted part of American public education.

SOCIAL DARWINISM

An ongoing debate regarding education has continued from the time of the Greeks and the Romans. Greek educational philosophy postulated the cruciality of a classical approach to the curriculum. The Romans, being of a practical bent, had to acknowledge the superiority of the cultural level of Greek thought over their own, but hastened to develop pragmatic and utilitarian elements in conjunction with this theoretical and traditional stance.

In the nineteenth century Matthew Arnold and T. H. Huxley debated the relative merits of the classical and scientific curricula. Their distinguished reputations in English academia heightened the importance of their lively encounters, but, rather than a classicist, it was a scientist outside the academic establishment who profoundly affected Western thought and education.

Charles Darwin (1809-1882) published *On the Origin of Species by Means of Natural Selection* in November 1859. Darwin rocked the stability of nineteenth-century thinkers, for he believed that through the process of evolution only the strongest in a given species would survive. Herbert Spencer (1820-1903) first used the phrase "the survival of the fittest," which Darwin readily acknowledged to be apt. The essence of this survival was struggle or competition. Darwin's theories were founded on biological norms. However, philosophers observed that the principles of natural selection and survival of the fittest through competition also had implications for the societal context. Thus arose Social Darwinism.

Generally, the Social Darwinists believed that civilization and economic prosperity could best be ensured by competition between individuals and societies. Principles of hard work and dedication to excel would result in a superior product. The free enterprise system of laissez-faire capitalism was most conducive to this theory.

Spencer and Huxley were evolutionists who were bent on propagating and interpreting the foundational axioms in *Origin of Species*. But the interest of Spencer went well beyond the biological to a

> highly generalized theory of evolution as explanatory of change in everything from inorganic nature to human institutions. The schools will adopt a natural and evolutionary scheme, he argued, when they see the importance of proceeding from the simple to the complex, from the indefinite to the definite, and from the empirical to the rational. In short, the very processes of evolution are not only scientifically explained but also point to the triumph of the sciences in the curriculum and in life.[37]

Two of the leading figures of Social Darwinism were the Englishman Herbert Spencer and the American sociologist William Graham Sumner. Our discussion will center on Spencer due to his impact on educational theory. He achieved his greatest popularity in the decades following the American Civil War. The United States was being transformed into an industrial society. Factories in the North were producing weapons of war to defeat the agrarian South. In that setting, Spencer's philosophy fit well: "a system conceived in and dedicated to an age of steel and steam engines, competition, exploitation, and struggle."[38] He believed that society went through several stages in its struggle for perfection. As the final stage evolved, altruism would replace capitalism. "Evolution is an integration of matter and concomitant dissipation of motion; during which the matter passes from a relatively indefinite, incoherent homogeneity to a relatively definite, coherent heterogeneity. . . ."[39]

This principle is extremely important, for implicit in it is the concept of individual rights, "a society in which individual liberty is highly developed (coherent heterogeneity) is intrinsically more admirable and praiseworthy than a society in which there is less individual liberty" (incoherent homogeneity).[40] Individual ownership of property is seen to be essential, and the role of the state is one of negative value. The one thing the state must guarantee is the freedom of each individual to pursue whatever goals are desired, provided that others' rights are not violated. For Spencer, such a society cannot be achieved easily, for man must compete against man as well as the environment.

In terms of education, Spencer opposed all state aid, believing that each person was responsible to secure his own education. He encouraged individuals to develop schools and compete for students as businesses engage in competition, but resisted the right of the state to force parents to send their children to tax-supported schools.

From Spencer's view of the child we can derive his definition of education and its psychological implications. To him education is "a repetition of civilization in little, that it shall be as much as possible a process of self-evolution and that it shall be pleasurable."[41] He, like Dewey, stressed problem solving and learning by doing as opposed to "teacher talk." If those methods were used, Spencer believed that education would conform to the natural process of mental evolution. He felt "that there is a certain sequence in which the faculties spontaneously develop, and a certain kind of knowledge which each requires during this development; and that it is for us to ascertain this sequence, and supply this knowledge."[42]

As previously stated, Spencer spoke of evolution as progress from homogeneity to heterogeneity. The child therefore is to be educated in the same manner, from the simple to the complex, from the concrete to the abstract, and from the empirical to the rational. Above all, a child should be happy when learning, and he should internalize that which generates interest. In a sense then, the learner dictates the curriculum, "for a child's intellectual instincts are more trustworthy than . . . adult reasoning."[43]

In a famous essay entitled "What Knowledge Is of Most Worth" Spencer argued against the random selection of curriculum content: "Men read books on this topic, and attend lectures on that; decide that their children shall be instructed in those; all under the guidance of mere custom or liking, or prejudice."⁴⁴ Such an imposing problem motivated Spencer to evolve what he called a "rational curriculum." The criterion for determining what is to be taught is that which would best instruct man in learning "how to live completely."⁴⁵ The curriculum must attempt to serve needs most allied to the struggle for survival. In this regard he observed that parents were ineffective in giving their children the proper training because their own educations were irrelevant to their moral, intellectual, and physical needs. Spencer concluded that because education should proceed from the empirical to the rational, scientific studies should head the curriculum, classical knowledge should be subordinated, and the rote memorization of facts should be eliminated. Science, he reasoned, was the only means of providing the young with the necessary tools for survival. By appealing to the rational, scientific knowledge might teach proper moral conduct. It is interesting to note that Spencer did not see a dichotomy between a scientific curriculum and moral training:

> So far from science being irreligious, as many think, it is the neglect of science that is irreligious — it is the refusal to study the surrounding creation that is irreligious. Devotion to science, is a tacit worship — a tacit recognition of worth in the things studied; and by implication in their Cause.⁴⁶

When his essay was written in 1854, five years before Darwin's *Origin of Species*, it was prophetic. Spencer later recalled, "its leading thesis, that the teaching of the classics should give place to the teaching of science, was regarded by nine out of ten cultivated people as simply monstrous."⁴⁷ His thinking was a blend of old-fashioned classical liberalism, laissez-faire economic theory, antiestablishment nonconformism, and individualism.

The late nineteenth and early twentieth centuries witnessed the flourishing of capitalism, and consequently the United States grew as it never had before. Inventions such as the Bessemer process launched the age of steel. People became concerned with science and its effect on their own lives. Education allied itself with business interests. Evolutionary theory revolutionized educational psychology by emphasizing the concept of a changing society and the need of social studies to cope with it: "The theory of evolution pushed biology into the schools, stimulated the cult of child study, and virtually refashioned the psychology which had conditioned so much that was done in the classroom."⁴⁸

The influence of Herbert Spencer intensified the age-old debate between the traditional subjects and those of utilitarian value. The later Herbartians led in the criticism and reorganization of the classical curriculum in the 1980's, establishing a larger place for literature, history, and economics as well as the utilitarian subjects of typing and home economics. Fledgling educational philosophies emphasizing measurable results and social efficiency and change left traditionalism in disarray.

For the evangelical, the most distressing change in education over the last three centuries has been the constant drift away from biblical teaching. The Reformers' position on the doctrine of man has lost ground from Rousseau to the present. The doctrine of original sin has been roundly criticized as obscurantism. Although it was true that some educators who espoused Calvinism engaged in severe discipline of the child, the position must not be castigated or cavalierly dismissed because of the excesses of some. The biblical teaching that man is a sinner and stands before God in need of forgiveness remains categorically true. The grace of God, expressed in the substitutionary atonement of Jesus Christ, is man's only hope. Man is not inherently good, nor will he make inevitable progress. Unfortunately, all of the major educationists discussed in this chapter were defective on this crucial theological question. Although Froebel and Pestalozzi occasionally evidenced more than a little understanding of biblical truth, they, like so many insightful educators before and after them, capitulated to prevalent theorizing regarding the condition of man before God. The next chapter will deal with this from the context of Christian education in colonial America. The theological stance of the Puritans brought correctives and a certain rigidity to the New World.

NOTES

1. Nehemiah Curnock, ed., *The Journal of the Rev. John Wesley, A.M.* (1909-1916; reprint ed., London: Epworth, 1938), 2:167.
2. Ibid., 2:168.
3. See James R. Moore, "The Rise of Modern Science," in Tim Dowley, ed., *Eerdmans' Handbook to the History of Christianity* (Grand Rapids: Eerdmans, 1977), pp. 42-43 for additional information.
4. Colin Brown, "Reason and Unreason," in Dowley, pp. 488-89.
5. Frederick Mayer, *A History of Educational Thought*, 2d ed. (Columbus, Ohio: Merrill, 1966), p. 320.
6. *Journal of Wesley*, "May 29, 1745," 3:178.
7. Ibid.
8. Francis A. Schaeffer, *How Should We Then Live?* (Old Tappan, N.J.: Revell, 1976), p. 156.

9. Jean-Jacques Rousseau, *Emile, Julie and Other Writings*, ed. R. L. Archer (Woodbury, N.Y.: Barron's Educ. Series, 1964), p. 55.
10. James L. Jarrett, *Philosophy for the Study of Education* (Boston: Houghton-Mifflin, 1969), p. 251.
11. Immanuel Kant, *Kant on Education*, trans. Annette Churton (London: Kegan, Paul, Trench, Trubner, 1899). Cited in Jarrett, p. 271.
12. Ibid., in Jarrett, p. 271.
13. Ibid., in Jarrett, pp. 272-73.
14. Gerald L. Gutek, *Pestalozzi and Education* (New York: Random House, 1968), p. 3.
15. Ibid., p. 28.
16. Gerald L. Gutek, *A History of the Western Educational Experience* (New York: Random House, 1972), p. 194.
17. Gutek, *Pestalozzi and Education*, p. 4.
18. Johann Heinrich Pestalozzi, *How Gertrude Teaches Her Children* (Syracuse, N.Y.: C. W. Bardeen, 1915), p. 17. Cited in Gutek, *History*, p. 207.
19. Mayer, p. 286.
20. J. F. Herbart, *The Science of Education*, trans. H. Felkin and E. Felkin (Boston: Heath, 1896), p. 4.
21. Harold B. Dunkel, *Herbart and Education* (New York: Random House, 1969), p. 21.
22. Herbart, p. 57.
23. Ibid., p. 213.
24. J. F. Herbart, in A. Lange, *Herbart's Outlines of Educational Doctrine* (New York: Macmillan, 1901), p. 13.
25. Mayer, p. 296.
26. Dunkel, p. 55.
27. Solomon Bluhm, "Johann Friedrich Herbart," in Lee C. Deighton, ed., *The Encyclopedia of Education*, 10 vols. (New York: Macmillan, 1971), 4:350.
28. Dunkel, p. 117. See also pages 80-89 of Dunkel for a development of Herbart's approach to teaching mathematics and what role discipline played.
29. Ibid., p. 108.
30. J. F. Herbart, "Aphorismen zur Pädagogik," in F. Bartholomai, ed., *Pädagogische Schriften* (Langensalza: Beyer, 1906), p. 420.
31. Paul Monroe, *A Textbook in the History of Education* (New York: Macmillan, 1923), p. 638.
32. Friedrich W. A. Froebel, *Autobiography*, trans. and annot. Emilie Michaelis and Keatley Moore (Syracuse, N.Y.: C. W. Bardeen, 1890), cited in Robert Ulich, ed., *Three Thousand Years of Educational Wisdom: Selections from Great Documents* (Cambridge, Mass.: Harvard U., 1950), p. 524. Read this section in Ulich to sense Froebel's frustration with his father's inattention to him and to see his negative attitudes toward the ministry and orthodox theology. He developed such attitudes through listening to his father's counseling sessions with parishioners and from hearing theological discussions between his father and an older brother who was being taught liberal theology at the university. The fascinating data base provided gives one a much needed understanding of Froebel's personal development and the emergence of his educational philosophy. See also Robert B. Burns, *Friedrich Froebel* (Boston: Twayne, 1978).
33. Friedrich W. A. Froebel, *The Education of Man*, trans. W. N. Hailmann (New York: D. Appleton, 1887). Cited in Jarrett, p. 292.
34. Ibid., in Jarrett, p. 292.
35. Froebel, *The Education of Man*, in Ulich, ed., *Three Thousand Years*, pp. 573-74.
36. Gutek, *History*, p. 227.
37. Jarrett, p. 346.
38. Richard Hofstadter, *Social Darwinism in American Thought* (Boston: Beacon, 1955), p. 35.

39. Herbert Spencer, *First Principles,* in Frederick Copleston, *Bentham to Russell.* History of Philosophy, vol. 8 (Glen Rock, N.J.: Paulist-Newman, 1967), p. 149.
40. Ibid., in Copleston, 8:154.
41. Herbert Spencer, "Intellectual Education," in *Essays on Education.* Cited in Andreas M. Kazamias, *Herbert Spencer on Education* (New York: Columbia U., 1966), p. 177.
42. Ibid., in Kazamias, p. 163.
43. Ibid., in Kazamias, p. 170. This is not meant to imply that the child is left totally on his own. The parents of the child are responsible for providing physical and moral guidance and supplying satisfactory conditions for learning.
44. Ibid., "What Knowledge Is of Most Worth," in Kazamias, p. 123.
45. Ibid., in Kazamias, p. 125.
46. Ibid., in Kazamias, p. 156.
47. Ibid., in Kazamias, p. 121.
48. Merle Curti, *The Social Ideas of American Educators,* rev. ed. (Totawa, N.J.: Littlefield, Adams, 1971), p. 207.

11

New England and the Puritans

The exodus of the English Puritans to New England, 1629-1642, still is unique in the annals of migration:

> The most striking fact about this remarkable movement is that, once it got underway, by dint of able leadership, it quickly generated a dynamic momentum of its own. Here was no artificially stimulated, haphazard outpouring of individual Englishmen to serve mercantile ends. The massive religious concern of the English people, and of the Puritans in particular, impelled these emigrants to abandon England to save souls; only secondarily did economic or social considerations figure in their decisions. A majority of the rank and file, as well as the leaders, believed firmly that they had discovered the Northwest Passage to Utopia where they could be "merry in the Lord" and eventually attain salvation.[1]

Although Carl Bridenbaugh has caught the essence of the spiritual drive of the Puritans, his theological caricature is only partly correct. Those well-educated Christians were highly motivated to worship and work together. Part of the survival strategy of the Puritans was the desire to educate their children biblically so that their knowledge and value system would be perpetuated. But the Puritans, who dominated New England initially, were only part of the educational scene in colonial America.

The development of educational thought in colonial America in the seventeenth and eighteenth centuries was actually a product of Reformation thought carried from Europe to the colonies by those who came to seek political, ecclesiastical, and economic freedom. Because of the characteristically close alliance of the church and state in post-Reformation Europe in the sixteenth century, education involved an integration of "secular" and "Protestant Christian" teaching that resulted in an inextricable intertwining of political, religious, and economic aspects of European life.

Protestants living in that context of the Reformation developed an extreme intolerance of Catholicism and feared further Catholic conquest, as was the case in Central and South America during the Spanish expansion.[2] However, it would be erroneous to assert that the settlers of colonial America came seeking only religious freedom, as we are often so simplistically taught. The motivations that brought English, Spanish, French, Swedish, German, and Dutch settlers to North America are varied and complicated.[3] Some came, indeed, because of religious persecution and in search of an environment where proper religious expression and education of their children could take place. Others came to take advantage of opportunities for economic gain in a new environment where natural resources could be tapped and traded. Some came to further the political and economic interests of their homeland. There were also those who came to escape political situations with which they could not agree either in theory or practice.

Before we explore the development of education in the American colonies, it will be helpful to sketch briefly the historical development of the colonies' establishment and growth from sixteenth-century European roots through independence and into national identity. Then we will examine the development of education and Christian teaching in the New England, Middle, and Southern colonies, and the subsequent westward expansion of American culture and education.

COLONIAL GROWTH AND DEVELOPMENT

As noted earlier, the American colonies shared a strong European heritage that was part and parcel of their initial growth and development, even though they quickly began to develop and incorporate uniquely distinctive features into their models of government, education, economics, and the general cultural genre. R. Freeman Butts and Lawrence A. Cremin point out in their important work, *A History of Education in American Culture,*

> The foundations of American culture and education took their character in the colonial period largely from North European sources and particularly from the British Isles. This fact does not discount the contributions of other European peoples; it simply means that English institutions and ideas became, after a long struggle, the dominant pattern of life and thought along the eastern seaboard of America from Maine to Georgia.[4]

How then did this come to be, and what were those dominant patterns of thought and life that were established? During the sixteenth and seventeenth centuries the North American continent was a battleground of military and commercial interests among many of the great European powers. Spain laid hold of most of South and Central America and many portions of North America. This resulted in a long-term battle between Spain, France, and England for control of the eastern half of North America. France had actively sought to expand her fur trading interests south from Canadian territory into New England and to extend her territorial control of large areas of North America. Ultimately the English won control of this disputed area and the pact was sealed with the Treaty of Paris in 1763.[5]

By the end of the eighteenth century, Spain's dominance had been reduced to Florida and some areas west of the Mississippi River, while France had virtually no territory at all. Interestingly, during this time Canada also became partially aligned with Great Britain. Hence, colonial America, almost entirely throughout its history, was to be dominated by its relationship with England and its cultural roots in British life and thought.

THE POLITICAL GENRE

The formation of the colonies was the result of several factors. Many groups came in search of the religious and political freedom denied them by their homeland. The English Puritans, for example, who were Calvinistic separatists and came to settle primarily in Massachusetts, did so in order to escape the religious and political persecution by the Stuarts of England — specifically James I and Charles I. Others came seeking adventure and economic fortune in the New World, as was the case for the aristocratic Virginians who first settled in Jamestown in 1607. Education was certainly not high on the list of priorities for these spirited, class-conscious settlers; and as we shall discuss later, such an attitude resulted in inferior educational institutions and forms in the colonial South. Sir William Buckley's statement in 1671 well summarizes the educational values of those who came to America primarily for monetary gain and adventurism: "I thank God there are no free schools nor printing, and I hope we shall not have these for a hundred years; for learning has brought disobedience, and heresy and sects into the world, and printing has divulged them and libels against the best government. God keep us from both!"[6]

Many middle class and upper middle class Europeans came to America to administrate the large commercial and trading enterprises that England had initiated as a part of her vested interest in colonial expansion. However, there were also those lower class individuals, debtors, and "European social misfits," who came to the New World with aspirations of making a new beginning and developing a more satisfying, freer life.

Some of the colonies were formed under charter to British commercial stock companies, such as the Massachusetts Bay Company and the London Company, the latter of which pioneered the settlement of Jamestown, Virginia in 1607. Other charters were set up with individuals, many of whom disagreed with the current state of affairs in their colony and wished to draw up a new contract for self-government. This was the case for such offshoot groups as the one led by Roger Williams to Providence Plantation in Rhode Island in 1644, after a bitter disagreement with the Puritans of Massachusetts (specifically John Cotton) over separation of church and state. Williams believed it wrong that the church and government should be so closely allied (radical departure from his Calvinistic Puritan heritage) and spelled out his views in the book, *The Bloudy Tenent of Persecution for the Cause of Conscience Discussed,* in 1644. He strongly opposed tax-supported churches and required church attendance in order to obtain voting privileges in the colonial assembly.[7]

Another way in which colonies were formed was by proprietary grants of land by the crown. Maryland, Pennsylvania, New York, New Jersey, and Georgia were established on that basis. Georgia became the last colony to be settled. In 1732 it was endowed by philanthropists and humanitarians as a haven for Englishmen who were oppressed, poor indentured servants desirous of a new start.

The Continental Congress adopted the Declaration of Independence on July 4, 1776. Interestingly, each state formed its own "Bill of Rights" that served as a model for the federal constitution's Bill of Rights, formulated after the Revolutionary War. Another of the key results of the individual states' governments was the sense of responsibility that each accepted for education. Up to that time, education was either privately or religiously controlled—but all under the ultimate scrutiny and permission of the crown via royal governors and proprietors. This important change paved the way for later nineteenth-century movements, under such people as Horace Mann, toward public education as we know it today.

THE RELIGIOUS GENRE

The establishment of state governments represented a partial cause of the movement toward separation of church and state in the later colonial and early national period (1770-1800). The Enlightenment that gave birth to classical humanism in post-Reformation Europe through the naturalistic thought of Rousseau, Hume, Kant, Pestalozzi, and others began to be transmitted across the Atlantic to the American colonies by settlers educated in Britain. The impact of humanistic and naturalistic thought, not only through indirect contact with institutions but in the forming of them, moved the colonies toward an increasingly secularized and modernized society.[8]

The colonists brought their own established religious beliefs with them, and imported a close alliance of church and state, which was a product of the thinking of Luther, Calvin, and the other Reformers. The Dutch brought the Reformed Church to New Netherland, English Anglicans established the Church of England in Virginia and the Carolinas, the Swedes carried their Lutheranism into Delaware, the Quakers settled in Pennsylvania, and the Puritans brought their Calvinism to New England in the form of Congregationalism and Presbyterianism.[9] It became the norm for states to support the established church with taxes, thereby enforcing the worship and theology of that particular church. Laws were passed (Massachusetts, 1631; Virginia, 1607) requiring church membership to ensure voting privileges. Opposing views were not welcomed except in Rhode Island.

From that milieu came the struggle for free exercise of religion, including those who functioned from an "enlightenment orientation," such as Roger Williams and William Penn. The proliferation of protest groups brought about a gradual relaxation of such rules and an increased toleration for other organized churches within a specific governance. The constitutions of the individual states formed in 1776-1777 allowed for freedom of religious conscience, with the exception of qualifications for public offices in Delaware, Pennsylvania, New Jersey, North Carolina, South Carolina, and Maryland.[10] This freedom and tolerance was based on the humanistic ideal that man ought to be free to develop his full potential in any way he wished without external restriction.

Thus it became apparent that with the trend toward separation of church and state in the late eighteenth century, and with the state retaining legal rights to control education, religion no longer would have its strong grip on education as was the case in the earlier colonial period. The early colonial mind-set based on theological conceptions and enforced by religious sanctions evolved into nonreligious, governmental sanctions by the end of the eighteenth century. The move toward the Enlightenment was in motion. Butts and Cremin summarize it as follows:

> Especially during the eighteenth century proposals for change in the older ways of thinking and acting carried appeals to *human* reason rather than divine law, to *natural* rights rather than super-natural rights, to *scientific* method rather than established truths, to *social* agreements and *individual* freedom rather than authoritarian control, and to *humanitarian* and *democratic* faith rather than aristocratic privilege. The results of this shift in emphasis in intellectual sanctions were felt in theology and religion, in philosophy, and in political, economic, and social theory. They were likewise seen in the emergence of new forms of educational theory and proposals for educational change that eventually led to changes in educational practice.[11]

THE SOCIAL GENRE

Although the English feudal system was not carried in its entirety into the colonial social structure, social stratification was certainly present. Southern plantations serve as a prime example, with the ruling aristocratic land owner as the nobility, tenants who worked the land as the middle class, and slaves and indentured servants as the lower class. Fortunately, the American colonies were settled primarily by Northern Europeans who were in the process of throwing off the old feudal patterns of social stratification and lack of mobility between classes. Most of the colonists were "middle class" Europeans, many of whom were merchants attempting to expand trade and involve themselves in territorial colonization for the crown.

With the mushrooming development of mercantilism, the need for skilled labor grew significantly. Hence, there was a great demand for ambitious men to develop skills and trades. Because good skilled labor was scarce, the ambitious man could improve himself economically and socially. Upward social mobility became a reality for many because of freedom of land policies for those who wished to contribute to the merchants' businesses.

The school system tended to perpetuate the class distinctions in the colonies. Because of tuition expenses, grammar schools and early colleges were most available to the upper classes. For a period of time, even Harvard College distinguished between students of differing class status upon their entry.[12] Though there was public demand for skill development, manifested in the academies and in highly developed apprenticeship programs, many students received only a bare minimum of education. "Even in New England where schools were in operation by 1636, the level of instruction was low and not all children could attend. Before American independence, there were trends toward a more flexible and democratic school pattern but the rigid class system and the strong religious atmosphere continued to influence education until comparatively recent times."[13]

The center of the economic, political, and religious life of the New Englander was the town. The New England township was more than merely a congregating of people in a convenient place to live. It was a "gathered community" for political, social, and religious reasons in order to provide for mutual defense, establish local government, and provide for "Christian community" (an interesting phenomenon given the current emphasis on community). It was a commonwealth with a *paideia* (educational system) in which there was tremendous mutual influence, given the sharing of experiences, goals, desires, and religious ideals.[14]

EDUCATION IN NEW ENGLAND

The Puritan settlers who inhabited New England brought with them their own form of strong Calvinism in an attempt to establish a "community of saints" and to educate their children. Settling in Massachusetts, first with the establishment by the Pilgrims of Plymouth in 1620 and with subsequent arrivals of more colonists, they felt it their first responsibility to preserve Calvinistic doctrine and a strict separatistic life-style. They held to a "severe belief" in man's total depravity as a result of the Fall, unconditional election, limited atonement (Christ's death only for believers), irresistible grace, and the perseverance of the saints — the "Five Points of Calvinism as set down by the Synod at Dort in 1618."[15] They taught the need for spiritual conversion through coming to faith in Christ. This stood in opposition to the later development of the "Christian nurture" concept by Horace Bushnell, who saw no need for a radical conversion for children reared in a Christian home.

The educational interests of Puritan education stemmed from its understanding of the nature of man. Because man is inherently evil and fallen, he must be taught the Bible in order to be brought to a realization of his depravity and to be led to repentance. They believed that "only supernatural grace could overcome total depravity, but the ability to love and keep God's law indicated that a person was a child of God."[16] Although following the law did not save a person, a regenerated person would follow the law. Schools, then, were important as resources to teach children biblically and theologically. Education to them was not optional but mandatory. Severe discipline, frequent punishment, and low tolerance were Puritan bywords as children intentionally were treated like "little adults" and expected to act accordingly. The Puritans' prime concern was for literacy so that children could read the Bible, as was reflected in John Adams's statement in 1765: "All ranks and orders of our People, are intelligent, are accomplished-a native of America, especially of New England, who cannot read and wright is as rare a Phenomenon as a Comet."[17]

The Puritan settlers were themselves a highly educated community. Many had studied at Oxford or Cambridge and carried with them high values and expectations regarding education. The educational philosophy stemming from the formal European approach was combined with their extreme Calvinistic earnestness and asceticism. This produced an authoritarian approach that engendered fear, discipline, and obedience in children.

Perhaps one of the earliest spokesmen for a Puritan life-style and education was the Boston Congregationalist minister, John Cotton. In 1641 he wrote a catechism for his church entitled *Spiritual Milk for American Babes Drawn out of the Breasts of Both Testaments for their Souls' Nourishment,* in which he stressed the child's sin, corruption, and tendency to transgress God's laws. Part of this work appeared later in the *New England Primer.* The answer was to teach obedience to and reverence for all authority as the prime goal of education. His views were extreme, as is shown in the following proposal he submitted to the Massachusetts General Court for debate in 1641: "Rebellious children, whether they continue in riott or drunkenesse, after due correction from their parents, or whether they curse or smite their parents, to be put to death."[18]

One of the best known Puritan religious educators in the late seventeenth century was Cotton Mather (1663-1728), a grandson of John Cotton and a son of the Congregationalist minister and president of Harvard College, Increase Mather. Mather served to reemphasize Cotton's stern position in his *A Family Well Ordered*, written in 1699 while serving as associate pastor at Second Church in Boston with his father. In this volume, he addressed parents in the first section regarding their responsibilities to teach personal piety, obedience, salvation, and to have their children baptized in light of their depraved natures.

Despite this emphasis on discipline, Mather also stressed understanding on the part of teachers in a statement to tutors in his pamphlet, *A Brief Essay to Direct and Excite Family Religion:* "Tutors, be strict; but yet be gentle too; Don't by fierce cruelties fair hopes undo. Dream not, that they who are learning slow will mend by arguments in Ferio. . . . To carry on the discipline of the school, with Rewards, as well as Punishments, is most certainly very adviseable, very preferrible."[19] Mather emphasized the importance of learning to read, write, and express oneself well. Much of the spirit of Mather's educational philosophy and content also found its way into the *New England Primer*, which was the most widely used textbook in America through the eighteenth century.

Jonathan Edwards, who preached and wrote a few years after Mather, taught in his *Thoughts Concerning the Present Revival of Religion in New England* (1741, during the Great Awakening) that sinners (including children) ought to be faced with the harsh results of sin, as his "Sinners in the Hands of an Angry God" sermon so aptly portrayed.

Because of their intense Calvinism and desire to re-create Calvin's Geneva concept of a theocracy, the Puritans made the church and government closely related in New England. Thus, there was really no distinction between "parochial" and "public" schools. The schools were merely intended to supplement what the Puritans intended to be the ideal of education—a distinctively Christian education centering in the home. The teaching of children began in the home at a very early age and they received instruction a little at a time. Parents spoke with their children and observed the biblical directives:

Who is it he is trying to teach?
    To whom is he explaining his
        message?
To children weaned from the milk,
    to those just taken from the breast?
For it is:
    Do and do, do and do
    rule on rule, rule on rule;
        a little here, a little there,[Isa. 28:9-10, NIV]

The Puritans, of course, had not espoused the humanism that had had its incipient roots in the Enlightenment, nor had they employed "the religious humanism of an Erasmus of Rotterdam."[20] Thus their lives, though seeming to be often pharisaical, arrogant, and bigoted, were deeply committed to personal piety, hard work, and their faith in Christ.

Though the early Puritans shared such a commitment to education in the home, the close ties between church and state made government involvement in New England education inevitable. As early as 1636, the Massachusetts General Court appropriated 400 pounds toward the founding of a school to teach and train students for Christian ministry—Harvard College. In fact the first three American colleges, Harvard (1636), William and Mary (1693), and Yale (1701), were opened because of religious motivations. Yale was begun because Harvard was softening its stance on Calvinistic doctrines.

Apprenticeship had become a popular carry-over from Europe in New England as well as in the South in order to meet the growing need for a skilled labor force amid a burgeoning economy and mercantilism. In New England, apprenticeship took on an educational nature quite early, and training in a trade was not the only aspect of it. Law in Massachusetts in the late 1600s required that "masters give teaching in the liberal arts, sciences, the Christian religion and sound ethics. Thus apprenticeship was not merely a means of acquiring trade efficiency, but it was a preparation for citizenship and for life."[21] As was done early in the area of apprenticeship, colonial governments also took an active role in general educational requirements in New England, with Massachusetts taking the lead (Connecticut and New Hampshire soon followed). Often town meetings were given over to the discussion of education, and the first "town school" (the Massachusetts Bay School) was begun on April 13, 1635. The town decided that "our brother Philemon Pormont, shall be entreated to become schoolmaster for the teaching and nurturing of children with us."²² This set a precedent and within a year or two several other Massachusetts towns began some kind of formal school for their children.

Despite those initial actions taken toward the forming of schools, it was still strongly held that parents and masters were responsible to educate their own children in the home. However, it soon became apparent that this was not happening as it should, prompting the Massachusetts General Court to establish in 1641 a code called the "Body of Liberties," a part of which dealt with the liberties of children. In this code one can see a new thrust away from the Puritan concept of strict discipline and obedience to a liberal view of the child—a product of the Enlightenment itself.

From that first piece of legislation stemmed the General Court's Act of 1642 requiring that all parents and guardians provide for the education of the children under their authority or be subject to state-imposed fines. That ruling does reflect the Puritan emphasis on the role of the state to ensure religious education. The law did not in fact establish public schools, but it certainly paved the way for them as parents realized they could not provide adequately broad teaching in the home. The state sent representatives to the various towns to visit homes and businesses to see that the ruling was being honored. Many parents were fined, and children were apprenticed to masters who would teach them properly.

Obviously, there were a great many difficulties in enforcing such a law, and it was soon found to be inadequate. This prompted the General Court on November 11, 1647, to pass the famous Old Deluder Satan Act that served as the pivotal point in the establishment of public education in America:

> It being one chief project of that old deluder, Satan, to keep men from the knowledge of the Scriptures, as in former times by keeping them in an unknown tongue, so in these latter times by persuading from the use of tongues, that so at least the true sense and meaning of the original might be clouded by false glosses of saint-seeming deceivers, that learning may not be buried in the grave of our fathers in the church and commonwealth, the Lord assisting our endeavors, —
>
> It is therefore ordered, that every township in this jurisdiction, after the Lord hath increased them to the number of fifty householders, shall then forthwith appoint one within their town to teach all such children as shall resort to him to write and read,

whose wages shall be paid either by the parents or masters of such children or by the inhabitants in general by way of supply, as the major part of those that order the prudentials of the town shall appoint; provided, those that said their children be not oppressed by paying much more than they can have them taught for in other towns;

And it is further ordered, that where any town shall increase to the number of one hundred families or householders, they shall set up a grammar school, the master thereof being able to instruct youth so far as they may be fitted for the university.[23]

A number of other New England colonies followed Massachusetts's example and soon there were "common schools" opened in virtually all towns. Education was now available to all, though compulsory attendance was not yet established, which gave parents the freedom to educate their children or have them tutored.

Those schools were established as "public," but not in the sense that we use the term today. Schools were public in that they were established under the authority and supervision of the township. All parents had the right to send their children to them. However, they were *not* public in terms of free education. The school charged tuition to individual parents rather than deriving its support from public funds. Though some poor children were allowed to attend free of charge, most had to be channeled to other schools established by ministers in their churches, to endowed free schools, or to free schools established by other religious organizations.

DAME SCHOOLS

A number of educational patterns evolved from the Act of 1647 and subsequent rulings of the other New England colonies. Dame schools, which had arisen in England following the Reformation, were quite unstructured in nature and were dedicated to teaching children to read in the vernacular. A woman, perhaps a widow with children served as the teacher by taking in neighborhood children for a few hours each day. For a small stipend, she would instruct them in reading, occasionally writing, and the Puritan catechism, while she carried on her household duties. "Such enterprises were schools, to be sure, but they were also household activities, and the easy shading of one into the other is a significant educational fact of the seventeenth century."[24]

COMMON SCHOOLS

The common school made an important contribution to the history of American education. It provided a formal elementary education, and it was devoted to the cultivation of literacy and citizenship. The common school had a bona fide teacher and a building specifically used for classes.[25] This was the first kind of school provided for in the Old Deluder Satan Act (established in towns of fifty or more families). The Massachusetts law had far-reaching effects upon nearly every New England colony, including Connecticut, Maine, New Hampshire, and Vermont. Only Rhode Island with its "protest groups" remained unaffected by the act.

The school's curriculum was primarily confined to teaching the three r's in order to prepare the five-to-ten-year-old child both to read the Scriptures and to assume a place in the working world. Christian piety was heavily emphasized, requiring the teacher to be skilled not only in areas of literacy and mathematics, but also in the religious catechisms of the day. Memorization and recitation were the methodological approaches used to discipline students to take their study seriously.

The kinds of learning tools common today were of course nonexistent during colonial times. In fact, books themselves were rare. The *Shorter Catechism,* some of the pamphlets of religious leaders (e.g., John Cotton and Cotton Mather), the Psalter, and the Bible were the only written volumes available to the student, and those provided the primary sources for instruction.

The earliest tool placed in the hands of children in both the dame and common school was the "Hornbook" or "Battledore." It was actually not a book but a small paddle-shaped piece of wood with a sheet of paper attached to one side. The paper had on it printed letters, numbers, the Lord's Prayer, an apostolic benediction, as well as some other printed materials. The entire printed sheet was covered with transparent horn, hence the term *Hornbook.* The device was, of course, used to teach children the basics of reading and to prepare them to read passages from the Psalter, catechisms, and the Bible.

The Hornbook was replaced at the end of the 1600s by the famous *New England Primer.* Though there were many different primers available for reading instruction — most of them imported from England such as Edmund Cote's *The English Schoole-Maister* — the *New England Primer* quickly became the most commonly used book. Despite its name the book, with an estimated three million copies printed starting in 1690, gained a much broader exposure than merely in New England. In fact, it was used in virtually all schools except those under the control of the Anglican church.

The *Primer* was a small book, barely paperback in size, with only eighty-eight pages. However, its impact far exceeded its meager size. The book was thoroughly religious in content, using many selections from the Bible, the Lord's Prayer, the Apostles' Creed, a rhymed alphabet, prayers for children, and admonitions to children to seek diligently and reverently to know God and obey His Word. It also contained large excerpts from John Cotton's *Spiritual Milk for New England Babes,* John Rogers's *Advice to Children,* and the *Shorter Catechism.* One of its most well-known features was the rhymed alphabet that started:

> In Adam's fall
> We sinned all.

Hence, the book not only served the purposes of reading instruction, but it was intended to convey Christian moral truth at the same time. Besides in schools, the *Primer* could be found in homes, stores, and churches and was used to drill children and youth on their understanding of the catechism. It remained the primary reading tool of most colonial schools into the 1700s.

The common elementary schools also focused upon writing and arithmetic. Many of the resources were prepared by the teacher himself, although some books were available also for those tasks. Some spelling books were also used, starting with Coote's *English Schoole-Maister,* which was Christian in tone. Later spellers such as those by Quaker George Fox, Thomas Dilworth, and William Perry made way for Noah Webster's most famous spelling book, *The American Spelling Book,* published in 1783 as the first in a series of speller, grammar, and reader.

LATIN GRAMMAR SCHOOLS

In larger communities with 100 families or more, the Act of 1647 required that Latin grammar schools be instituted. Those were designed to pick up where the common schools left off. For the family desiring advanced education in the classics for their children, grammar school was the next step. The school's curriculum involved "a seven year sequence of studies of the Latin and Greek languages and literatures acquainting these lads with the tools necessary for an educated man." Hence, the common school provided education for the common man in a brief two- or three-year sequence, whereas the grammar school catered to the elite.

Latin grammar schools became the secondary school system of the time designed to prepare entering eight-year-old boys to assume places of leadership in politics, commerce, or the church. They were patterned after the English public or grammar schools that arose during the humanist revival of the Renaissance in fifteenth- and sixteenth-century Europe, during which time it was deemed necessary to have a background in classical languages and literature in order to attend the university and become a leader in civic or religious affairs. The religious emphasis came from the Protestant Reformation.[26] Interestingly Harvard College in 1642 required its incoming students to be well-versed in Latin and Greek, which demonstrated the need for Latin grammar schools and their preparatory nature. Thus, colonial grammar schools were instituted to preserve the religious and intellectual life of the community and to provide for well-informed, scholarly leadership in the church.

The curriculum in grammar schools generally began with the first two years devoted to basic principles of grammar and vocabulary in Latin and Greek. Latin was learned from a book called an "accidence," the most well-known including *Latin Accidence* by John Brinsley, *Orbis Pictus* by John Amos Comenius, and *The Common Rudiments of Latin Grammar* by Charles Hoole. Students then read and paraphrased such classics as Cato's *Distichs*, Aesop's *Fables*, and the *Colloquies* of Corderius. In the following years, students studied Horace, Erasmus, Ovid's *Metamorphoses*, Cicero's *Orations* and *Letters*, Virgil's *Aeneid*, Thomas Godwyn's *History of Rome*, Homer, Isocrates, the New Testament, and some Hebrew.[27]

It was a difficult program that demanded a great deal of discipline from the students and often ran from early morning to late afternoon six days a week. Classes were divided by year in the program, and classrooms were markedly improved with desks for the upper grades. Regulations were strict and rigidly enforced, with religious and catechetical instruction still a part of the curriculum.

One of the most noted schoolmasters in colonial history, Ezekiel Cheever, taught at the Boston Latin Grammar School.

Educated in England, he wrote a number of his own books including *Cheever's Accidence*. Perhaps the best tribute to Cheever was paid by Cotton Mather in a long verse elegy in which he penned:

> A learned master of languages
> Which to rich stores of learning are the keys . . .
> He taught us Lily, and he Gospel taught;
> And us poor children to our Saviour brought.[28]

Despite his modest salary, Cheever made teaching his full-time vocation and became the most highly respected educator throughout all of New England.

HIGHER EDUCATION

The Puritans' concern to perpetuate their beliefs and provide for well-trained, scholarly, intellectually astute clergy demonstrated itself in the early establishment of a number of colleges. The earliest was Harvard College, which was officially chartered in 1636 specifically for the training of ministers and Christian teachers. Its motto was inscribed over the first building's entrance and is still there today: *Pro Christo et Ecclesia* ("for Christ and the church"). The college was founded with an endowment from a young Congregationalist minister, John Harvard, who upon his death left his entire library and about 750 pounds to the establishment of such a school. Government tax support and land grants also served to bolster Harvard's financial condition.

Harvard's curriculum was thoroughly Christian and gave broad, comprehensive training to prospective ministers. It included six of the seven liberal arts of the cathedral schools of the Middle Ages:—grammar, rhetoric, logic, mathematics, geometry, and astronomy.[29] Only music was not a part of the program. There were also heavy doses of Aristotelian philosophy, Latin, Greek, Hebrew, and rigorous training in Protestant religious orthodoxy. Hence, the Puritan ministers and teachers were to be extremely well-rounded scholars in both secular and religious disciplines.

Harvard, as was the case with other Christian colleges of the day, was also a bulwark for the training in and practice of Christian piety. Twice daily, morning and evening, students were required to spend time in personal Scripture reading and private prayer. They were required to report to their tutors what new knowledge or insight into spiritual things they had received. After some initial struggles, Harvard graduated its first students in 1642. Growth was slow, but the college steadily increased to an enrollment of sixty by 1670. By the early 1700s, however, Harvard began to move more toward deism and unitarianism under Presidents John Leverett and Edward Holyoke and professors such as Edward Wigglesworth.[30]

Yale College, founded in 1701, was also established as a Congregational school strongly espousing Calvinistic theology. Increase and Cotton Mather were instrumental in Yale's founding in the midst of the liberal shift going on at Harvard. The New Haven, Connecticut school was dedicated to the preparation of ministers of the gospel as evidenced by Yale president Thomas Clap's 1754 statement: "Colleges are 'Religious Societies,' of a superior nature to all others. . . .Colleges are 'Societies of Ministers,' for training up persons for the work of the ministry."[31] Yale was initially chartered by the state of Connecticut; but later it established a board of eleven ministers as trustees under which it functioned. It was the first American college to rely upon self-governance as opposed to state control.

NOTES

1. Carl Bridenbaugh, *Vexed and Troubled Englishmen, 1590-1642* (New York: Oxford, 1968), pp. 434-35.
2. H. G. Good, *A History of American Education* (New York: Macmillan, 1956), p. 6.
3. Sydney E. Ahlstrom, *A Religious History of the American People* (New Haven, Conn.: Yale U., 1972), pp. 99-119.
4. R. Freeman Butts and Lawrence A. Cremin, *A History of Education in American Culture* (New York: Holt, Rinehart, and Winston, 1953), p. 4.
5. Ibid., p. 5.
6. Cited in F. V. N. Painter, *A History of Education* (New York: Appleton, 1896), p. 308.
7. Ahlstrom, pp. 166-71.
8. William W. Brickman, "Colonial American Education at the Dawn of Independence," *Intellect*, July-August 1976, p. 34.
9. Ahlstrom, pp. 105-15.
10. Butts and Cremin, p. 29.
11. Ibid., pp. 43-44.
12. John D. Pulliam, *History of Education in America* (Columbus, Ohio: Merrill, 1968), p. 14.
13. Ibid.
14. Lawrence A. Cremin, *American Education: The Colonial Experience, 1607-1783* (New York: Harper & Row, 1970), pp. 236-37.
15. Robert Ulich, *A History of Religious Education* (New York: New York U., 1968), pp. 146-47.
16. John D. Woodbridge, Mark A. Noll, and Nathan O. Hatch, *The Gospel in America* (Grand Rapids: Zondervan, 1979), p. 24.
17. Cited by Wilson Smith in "The Teacher in Puritan Culture," *Harvard Educational Review* 36 (Fall 1966): 395. From L. H. Butterfield, ed., *Diary and Autobiography of John Adams* (New York: Atheneum, 1964), section 1, p. 257.

18. Cited in Butts and Cremin, p. 67.
19. Cotton Mather, *Bonifacius: An Essay . . . To Do Good,* ed. Josephine K. Piercy (Gainesville, Fla.: Scholars' Facsimilies and Reprints, 1967), pp. 107, 112.
20. Ulich, p. 152.
21. Paul H. Douglas, *Apprenticeship as a Form of Education* (New York: Columbia U., n.d.), pp. 41-43.
22. Cited in Cremin, p. 180.
23. Frederick Mayer, *American Ideas and Education* (Columbus, Ohio: Merrill, 1964), p. 53. See also Nathaniel Shurtleff, ed., *Records of the Governor and Company of the Massachusetts Bay in New England* (Boston: n.p., 1853), 2:203 for the old English rendering.
24. Cremin, p. 129. See also "Extracts from the Diary of Josiah Cotton," *Publications of the Colonial Society of Massachusetts* 26 (1927): 278.
25. George M. Woytanowitz, "Education in Colonial America," *Education Digest,* October 1976, p. 33. Condensed from *Contemporary Education,* Spring 1976, pp. 125-29. Some historians state that common schools often shared the facilities of a church or town meeting hall.
26. Gerald L. Gutek, *An Historical Introduction to American Education* (New York: Crowell, 1970), p. 14.
27. Samuel Eliot Morison, *The Puritan Pronaos: Studies in the Intellectual Life of New England in the Seventeenth Century* (New York: New York U., 1936), pp. 102-3.
28. Cotton Mather, *Corderius Americanus: An Essay Upon the Good Education of Children* (Boston: John Allen, 1708), pp. 28-29.
29. Gutek, p. 15.
30. See Butts, pp. 289-91. See also Samuel Eliot Morison, *The Founding of Harvard College* (Cambridge, Mass.: Harvard U., 1935), p. 40 and Appendix B; Samuel Eliot Morison, *Harvard College in the Seventeenth Century,* 2 vols. (Cambridge, Mass.: Harvard U., 1936), vol. 1, chaps. 7-13.
31. Thomas Clap, *The Religious Constitution of Colleges, Especially of Yale College in New Haven* (New London, Conn.: T. Green, 1754), pp. 4, 12. Cited in Butts and Cremin, p. 81.

12

Denominationalism and Secularization

EDUCATION IN THE MIDDLE COLONIES

Education in the Middle colonies of New York, Pennsylvania, New Jersey, Delaware, and Maryland began in much the same way as did New England schools. Groups of German and Dutch Reformed, Quakers, Anglicans, Presbyterians, Methodists, Moravians, and many other settlers, each brought along its own unique theological presuppositions and educational patterns. The Middle colonies represented a great diversity in kinds of schools and curricula, and they have often been termed the "melting pot of colonial America." "Intellectual freedom and tolerance was possible in the central coastal cities to a degree unheard of in New England or the South."[1]

Because of the denominational plurality of the Middle colonies, state and public control of education was a much smaller factor than in New England. Although most of the central colonies' governing bodies issued some legislation requiring the institution of schools, few colonies were quick to follow through. This was most likely because of the sticky problem of a close alliance between church and state along with the great diversity in religious-ethnic groups. The question became, "Whose beliefs would then become the norm?" When Philadelphia was founded in 1683, provision was made for public education. However, it was not until 1711 when William Penn secured the charter for Philadelphia that any attempt was made to establish public schools. Penn made provision for public education in the charter:

> Where as the prosperity and welfare of any people depend, in a great measure, upon the good education of youth, and their early introduction in the principles of true religion and virtue, and qualifying them to serve their country and themselves by breeding them in reading, writing, and learning of languages and useful arts and sciences, suitable to their sex, age and degree—which cannot be effected, in any manner, so well as by erecting public schools for the purpose aforesaid.[2]

New York as well as Pennsylvania began with strong civil control over education, with the Dutch West India Company starting many schools. Its Dutch Reformed Church was Calvinistic, but not as sternly as were the Puritans. However, in 1644 when the English took control of New Netherland, there was no more "common religion," and the church schools were no longer considered town schools. Consequently, the colony moved toward predominantly private education.

Parochial or private education, then, was the prime educational pattern for the Middle colonies. The Dutch Reformed, Quakers, Anglicans, Presbyterians, and others set up schools in conjunction with each of their churches. Teachers were both well-trained schoolmasters and ministers in the early Middle colony schools. Interestingly, the Dutch government required that a schoolmaster and minister accompany every group of colonists that came to settle in America.

Settlers in the Middle colonies brought with them a very different view of the child than the Puritans to the north. Their more moderate Calvinistic influence and less separatistic mentality gave rise to a liberalizing view of the child in which he was to be treated as a person with individual rights. The child was expected to be just that—a child, not an adult. One easily can see how this outlook has affected twentieth-century progressive education with its strong emphasis on the freedom of the child, individual differences, and the dignity of the child's personhood. Thus, the emphasis suggested: "More genuine religious behavior could be achieved by methods that emphasize love rather than fear, tenderness and gentleness rather than harsh discipline, sympathy and understanding for childish weaknesses rather than vindictive authority and punishment, and learning through positive motivations of interest in a wider range of activities rather than through rote memorization of verbal symbols."[3]

Quaker thought emphasized this movement away from Puritan educational philosophy. William Penn in his *Reflections and Maxims* stressed that children have a natural propensity for "discovery learning" through observation of nature rather than rote learning. Hence Quakers sought to develop an approach to education that was enjoyable and interesting to the student rather than fearful, painful work.

The Anglicans who settled in the Middle colonies and the South also had a much more generous view of the child. One important religious organization that provided schools for the poor and underprivileged was a missionary arm of the Anglican church called the "Society for the Propagation of the Gospel in Foreign Parts." The SPGFP, organized in 1701 by Reverend Thomas Bray, had probably the most widespread influence of any organization in beginning schools, with its purpose being the enrichment of the ministry of Church of England clergyman and the establishment of an Anglican episcopacy in America. Their schoolmasters were told to use kind and reasonable methods and not to be vindictive. Punishment was not to be used to establish the teacher's authoritarian position. Samuel Johnson, influential Anglican minister and first president of King's College (later Columbia University), also stressed a much more humane tone in the catechisms he wrote.

Education in the Middle colonies was not only parochial in nature, but also tended to be intensely practical. William Penn was a vociferous opponent of the classical philosophy of education. He felt that all children ought to be taught a useful trade in addition to their academic learning and that children ought to be actively involved in studying the physical world around them. In *Reflections and Maxims* he states, "We press their memory too soon . . . we are at great pains to make them scholars but not men."[4] The ideas of Comenius had a profound impact on his views. Penn emphasized applied mathematics (navigation, shipbuilding, etc.) and agriculture as two important practical areas of study and work for children in the educational process. Interestingly, Penn attempted to push hard for state-controlled public education in the free sense of the term with what he believed would be a "useful and practical" curriculum.

A number of differing educational patterns grew out of the political, social, and religious environment of the Middle colonies. Schools varied highly in their style as the diverse philosophical and religious underpinnings gave the colonies a broad socioethnic constituency. Many of the schools were quite similar to New England schools in terms of curricula and methodology even though there was less civil control. However, there were also some developments in education unique to the Middle colonies' pattern.

ACADEMIES

Whereas New England schools focused on the importance of classical education, the mode in the Middle colonies was primarily vocational. Apprenticeship was very common to this area, with English poor laws of 1562 and 1601 requiring "work schools" and trade training. A number of academies were organized during the late 1600s and early 1700s to meet this need. Their popularity did not peak until early in the 1800s, but the impetus for the movement stemmed from the colonial period and the "private English school concept" to fill the void left between it and the Latin grammar school.

Academies were established as terminal secondary schools focusing primarily on the preparation of students for a specific vocation. There were classics and mathematics courses offered from the Latin grammar school model, but they were balanced with courses in English grammar, arithmetic, reading, writing, bookkeeping, merchandising, mechanics, and others. The schools were departmentalized in order to combine the values of classical Latin school education with pragmatic English school learning. Academies were open to girls, providing a unique opportunity for them that most Latin grammar schools did not afford because their enrollment was limited to boys. Children were permitted to live at the academy for a nominal fee, making the academies the first "boarding schools" in America.

Religious training in the academy included Bible study and memorization as a part of many schools' curricula, and children were expected to attend church every Sunday. English rather than Latin was the primary language because of the school's purpose as direct preparation for life and vocation. The academy thus served to broaden the scope of secondary education by dealing with the arts and sciences, music, modern languages, and applied disciplines.

Not surprisingly, one of the seminal thinkers in pragmatic education was Benjamin Franklin. Franklin was a brilliant, self-educated man who concerned himself a great deal with community structure and the role of education in social mobility within the community. "Academic custom, religion, and the established social structure—these were forces with which Franklin contended when he sought to design schools as efficient artifacts for the instruction of 'a rising people'. . . . With apparent casualness, Franklin cast aside two traditional guides in education—academic custom and religious orthodoxy—though he knew that thereby he invited reprisal."[5]

Though Franklin was self-educated, he was leary of such an approach for the masses because of its inefficient, sporadic nature. Hence, he believed in a structured school setting. Franklin asserted that the school should be "delightful, agreeable, entertaining and above all, 'useful.' "[6] His pragmatism was not simplistic, but carefully and thoughtfully designed to lead the child through progressive steps in learning. In 1749 Franklin made a reasoned attempt to design an academy to fulfill his educational ideals as he wrote *Proposals Relating to the Education of Youth in Pennsylvania*, which shortly thereafter resulted in the founding of the Philadelphia Academy.

In *Proposals*, and in his 1751 work *Ideas of the English School*, Franklin concluded, "Thus instructed, youth will come out of this school fitted for learning any business, calling or profession."[7] He too was influenced by the writings and thinking of John Locke. He proposed some twenty subjects with three major heads: English, mathematics, and history. History, however, was central in Franklin's thought, and all other subjects emanated from it. Writing ability was important as a vehicle to express in plain terms what was being learned. Rhetoric and logic were to be introduced as children grew to the age at which they began to grapple with moral questions of right and wrong. The sciences and physical education were also important in Franklin's proposal.

Although religion was playing a central role in other schools, Franklin believed it should not be the determining purpose of the school. Certainly his deistic leanings are apparent here. He considered religion important in public life and useful to individuals, but the school's thrust should be toward what he considered moral behavior not necessarily rooted in any theological or doctrinal ideals. He believed the child was neither inherently sinful nor inherently righteous — simply impressionable.[8] Consequently, it was the teacher's responsibility to imprint on the child's "tabula rasa" useful knowledge and good moral habits. Franklin believed that the academy ought also to be available to poor children who could never afford the luxury of the Latin grammar school, and he developed a plan of mutual aid through an organization he started called the "Junto."

Educational historian David Tyack says of Franklin: "His persistent keynote of utility, his advocacy of English over the classics, his stress on history and science — these clearly stem from his own experience. . . . Uninhibited by dogmatic religion, unimpaired by formal education, aided by social and economic opportunities, he was free to experiment, to test himself and his world by intellect and industry and humor."[9]

Academies gradually began to lose their place of prominence as public education grew in the nineteenth century. They began to take on a more classical flavor, and thus lost their unique educational thrust. However, in the academy we see the incipient roots of today's practical English education that is so much an integral part of the American public high school system.

LATIN GRAMMAR SCHOOLS

Secondary schools of the Latin grammar variety were not unique to New England. New York, Pennsylvania, New Jersey, and Maryland all had grammar schools in order to prepare students for college. New Jersey had a thriving grammar school as early as 1659, and it was common for the colonial governments as well as for denominational groups to give financial support to them. Sales taxes in Maryland, for example, were used to support the Latin schools.

The curriculum of Latin grammar schools in the Middle colonies was not all dissimilar to that of New England schools. Reading and writing of classical literature and languages was the core of study with an introduction to philosophical intellectual pursuits. Teachers in Middle colony grammar schools often were men who had begun ministerial training but had not finished college for one reason or another. The Society for the Propagation of the Gospel in Foreign Parts (Anglican), on the other hand, set rather high standards for their teachers, to be in keeping with the standards of the Church of England.[10]

DENOMINATIONAL SCHOOLS

The predominant educational pattern in the Middle colonies was parochial education undertaken by religious groups. Denominational schools were begun by churches in an effort to preserve the unity of their denomination and the essentials of their doctrinal beliefs. Though Pennsylvania had made strong attempts at organizing state-supported schools, denominational schools were by far the most common.

The Quakers established schools in Philadelphia and eastern Pennsylvania, a task made easier because of legislation that permitted churches to own property for the purpose of education. Quaker ministers were generally the teachers, thus having to divide their time between teaching, preaching, and pastoral duties. Other groups that settled in Pennsylvania also began their own schools. Among them were the Lutherans, German

Reformed, Mennonites, Moravians, and the Scots-Irish Presbyterians. Christopher Dock, well-known Moravian educator, established the Nazareth Hall School in 1759 and wrote widely in the field of education. His methods of gentleness and love serving as a motivating force were similar to those of Pestalozzi.

The SPGFP made perhaps the most organized and comprehensive effort to begin schools in the Middle and Southern colonies. Most of those were elementary schools designed to educate poor or underprivileged children in basic reading, writing, arithmetic, and Bible doctrine.

The Dutch Reformed Church, which was prevalent in New York where most of the Dutch settled, established a school in nearly every one of its churches. Even though the Dutch West Indian Company had begun schools in some nine villages, the Dutch people felt compelled to have their own denominational schools. They placed a strong emphasis on Christian education in the home through the study of catechisms led by parents. Only orthodox Christians were permitted to teach in the schools, and they were scrutinized carefully and placed by the church.

PRIVATE-VENTURE SCHOOLS

In addition to government-controlled schools and the many denominational schools established by churches and religious groups, there were a number of private-venture schools designed to provide training in areas not often offered in other schools. These schools were taught by instructors who believed they could better offer their expertise on a private basis and charge a certain fee. Their approach would be similar to a music teacher who offers lessons in his or her home, or in school, as an independent, self-employed instructor. More money could be made doing this and the teachers could specialize in their primary area of interest.

Dame schools in the Middle colonies were private-venture schools in which the teacher would use her own home as the classroom for instructing neighborhood children in reading, writing, and arithmetic. Some wealthy Middle colony families hired their own tutors to teach certain disciplines to their children on a strictly private basis with special fee arrrangements. Many teachers, however, established their own schools and buildings to which students came for specialized training in such areas as engineering, mathematics, navigation, classical training in Latin and Greek, surveying, bookkeeping, and others.

HIGHER EDUCATION

The Middle colonies were also very concerned with higher education, as were their neighbors in New England. Cultural and religious diversity gave rise to schools founded by various religious sectarian interests. Once again, the primary intention of these schools was thoroughly Christian, with a focus upon training young men for the ministry or teaching. They expected committed agreement to their orthodoxy from both teachers and students alike. The colleges also placed a high premium on personal piety through a structured daily prayer life.

The curricula of the Middle colony colleges were similar to those of New England schools. Aside from rigorous education in Bible and theology, there was exposure to history, literature, and philosophy in order to give prospective ministers and teachers the broadest education possible, and to preserve genuine biblical scholarship and critical intellectual thinking.

Kings College established in 1754 (later to become Columbia University) was perhaps the best known and most fully developed Middle colony college. It was founded by the Anglican church in New York City amid great controversy among the Anglicans, Dutch Reformed, and Presbyterians. Samuel Johnson, a former Calvinist who became an Anglican minister, was the school's first president. He openly and carefully stated that the school's purpose was not to teach merely one denominational point of view, but rather to provide Christian education for boys in areas of doctrine upon which all Protestant denominations could agree. The purpose of the school stated by Johnson reads: "The chief thing that is aimed at in this college is to teach the children to know God in Jesus Christ and to love and serve Him, in all sobriety, godliness, and righteousness of life, with a perfect heart, and a willing mind."[11]

Other schools also followed that pattern in the Middle colonies. The college of New Jersey (renamed Princeton in 1748) was founded in 1746 by the Presbyterians in response to what they felt was a need for their own school. Queens College (renamed Rutgers in 1774) was founded in 1766 at the request of a group of ministers and elders of the Dutch Reformed Church in order to provide "the education of youth in the learned languages, liberal and useful arts and sciences, and especially in divinity, preparing them for the ministry and other good office."[12]

Though most colonial colleges were small, often lacking

adequate finances and efficient equipment, they had a profound role in setting educational trends and shaping American Christian education. Because of their influence, churches and colleges today have been given a mandate for excellence in Christian education.

EDUCATION IN THE SOUTH

Educational patterns in the Southern colonies grew decisively out of the socio-political and economic patterns established during early colonization, beginning with the first settlement in Jamestown, Virginia, in 1607. It must be remembered that the settlement of the Southern colonies particularly, and Virginia especially, stemmed from interests of economic expansion and mercantilism.

Sprawling tobacco plantations sprang up all over the South as land grants were given to the wealthy by the crown. Those aristocratic land owners for the most part had been well educated in England, but they saw no need for universal education for the less-privileged general public. Consequently, the social class system that was so much a part of European feudal heritage was carried by them to the colonies. Class distinctions were sharply drawn. The wealthy plantation owners and merchants enjoyed the cultured life with much leisure time for gambling, dancing, poetry, literary societies, and book collecting.

On the other end of the spectrum, however, there were few opportunities for slaves, poor freemen, and indentured servants to grow culturally or intellectually. They were entirely dependent upon the powerful upper class for employment, financial support, and education. European provincialism, which provided no formal education for the poor, was a mind-set quite pervasive in the South, against which there were some struggles and battles won later in the 1600s. The state took little initiative, leaving the help of the poor to philanthropic efforts such as the Anglican SPGFP. State control in the South was, in fact, limited to apprenticeships and education of the poor, orphans, and illegitimate children.

The Church of England was the religious force behind Southern colonial development and education. Many Anglicans, seeking religious compatibility in an area where the Church of England was the established church, moved to the South from New England because of Puritan intolerance. There were a number of smaller religious sects in the South, but their impact on education was of little significance.

Even the attempts at parochial education by the Anglicans in the South were relatively small. Though they did establish separate private schools taught by the parish minister, only nine or ten schools were established in Virginia by the Church of England during the whole colonial period, and only seven out of ninety churches had their own schools. Poor children were given free instruction, and some of the schools admitted girls. Thus it becomes apparent that the bulk of educational responsibility in the South was considered private and left up to individual parents. Because of this factor, educational patterns in the South were diverse and moderately successful.

TUTORIAL SCHOOLS

The most common approach to education in the wealthy South was for plantation owners and merchants to hire private tutors for their children. The curriculum offered by most tutors was heavily classical after basic reading and writing were taught. Exposure to Latin and Greek grammar and literature was often sufficient training to qualify young people for higher education at Oxford and Cambridge in the mother country. Lily's *Grammar* was taught as preparatory for boys to enter private schools in England. In addition to classical subjects, practical ones such as applied mathematics, surveying, and specific trades were offered to boys and girls alike.

OTHER SCHOOL PATTERNS

A number of other kinds of schools were established in the colonial South. Dame schools were present in all of the colonies and were an integral part of education in the South. The women who taught children in their homes used Hornbooks, but were limited because of their own educational inadequacies.

Several "charity schools" were opened, most of which were established by the SPGFP. They provided textbooks, teachers, and necessary funds to start schools, particularly in the Middle and Southern colonies. The SPGFP played an important role in providing equal opportunity in education for the economically disadvantaged.

Finally, apprenticeships were probably more common in the South (especially Virginia) than in any of the other colonies. In such working and learning relationships, apprentices were taught to read, write, and do simple arithmetic. It was also required that some form of religious or moral education be provided by the master for his apprentices so that the child might become a model citizen and a productive part of society. Many Christian masters took great pains to see that the Scriptures were taught and that Jesus Christ and the gospel were directly presented to their worker/learners. Virginia issued a great deal of legislation to protect children "bound out" to landowners and to ensure that they were being properly treated and educated. This stems from the Anglican world view representing man in a much more positive light with the potential for growth, learning, and good. After apprenticing for about five years, most children moved into the trade in which they were trained. Only a few went on to get further education.

HIGHER EDUCATION

Many early attempts were made to establish institutions of higher learning in Virginia and throughout the South. Most met with failure because of lack of funding and support. In 1693 the College of William and Mary was begun as the first college in the South by the Anglican church after initially having been organized as a Latin grammar school. It is one of the few colonial colleges to maintain the same name today (along with Harvard, Yale, and Dartmouth). The Virginia assembly as early as 1661 began to call for the establishment of a college by declaring: "Whereas the want of able and faithful ministers of this country deprives us of those great blessings and mercies that always attend upon the service of God. . . .Bee it enacted, that for the advance of learning, education of youth, supply of ministry, and promotion of piety, there be land taken up or purchased for a colledge and free school."[13] When officially opened in 1693, following the groundwork laid by James Blair, the school was organized into four departments including sacred theology, philosophy, classical languages, and a department to teach the three r's to Indian children.

Rather than having to rely upon tuition and church offerings to support its educational endeavors, a great deal of public aid was supplied to William and Mary, making it unique among denominational colleges. This pattern and curriculum was maintained until after the Revolutionary War when Enlightenment thinking began to filter into American consciousness. In the late 1700s, Thomas Jefferson made some strong proposals for William and Mary that would radically alter its curriculum and purpose. More secular courses were to be added, including ethics, fine arts, law, history, mathematics, medicine, philosophy, ancient and modern languages. His proposal was rejected, most likely because the Anglican board of the school feared secularism and humanism that brought about change too quickly. As was the case in other colleges, William and Mary was committed to the training of Christian ministers and teachers.

Education in the Southern colonies was greatly limited by lack of public support and interest. The prevailing notion that education of one's children is a private affair did nothing to elicit public response to education. It only led to tutoring, aristocratic superiority, and more distinct social classes. Also, the sparseness of population with widely scattered towns and the bulk of the inhabitants living in a rural setting further inhibited public school expansion. Consequently almost no Latin grammar schools or academies were formed. Finally, the views of Southerners on the nature of man and education's role in salvation was different from New Englanders' views. Education was deemed not as important by Southerners; thus, it was not regarded by them as a Christian duty as it was by the Puritans.

WESTWARD EXPANSION AND SECULARIZATION

From the very start of the colonies, education in America was thoroughly Christian. Elementary schools were centers of reading and writing instruction so that children could read the Scriptures. Secondary education dealt with practical learning and classical studies to prepare the young student for college and the ministry. The aim of the colleges in the colonies could best be summed up in Harvard's motto, "For Christ and the Church," as they sought to train young men for Christian ministry and in the knowledge of God through Bible study and prayer.

The Bible and catechisms of various churches were perhaps the two most studied curricula in the colonies. Schools were looked upon as arms of the church for the Christian education of its youth, whether in the New England common schools and Latin grammar schools, the Middle colonies' private church schools, or Southern private education. Lutherans used Luther's *Short Catechism* and Anglicans used a catechism complete with the church's official Book of Prayer. Children were drilled in the catechisms and expected to memorize large sections of major doctrinal importance.

The colonial readers such as the *New England Primer* contained sections from Scripture as well as the catechism, so those books also served to teach the children to read. Obviously at that time there were no Sunday schools, so much of the responsibility for the inculcation of Christian doctrine and nurture was incumbent upon the schools as well as the home. It was hoped that such education coupled with a Christian home atmosphere would serve to instill piety in children.

WESTWARD EXPANSION

With the great influx of European settlers from 1700 onward, the colonies grew in population and political power. Westward expansion was inevitable. Frontier development was spurred by agricultural growth and the subsequent need for more land. Merchant traders desired to tap more of the nation's natural resources. This caused the adventurous to move westward into undeveloped frontier areas throughout the colonies. The need for great land holdings on tobacco plantations served to promote expansion specifically in the South. Small towns began to grow up in those areas, bringing more people to expand their businesses or begin new ones.

This westward expansion brought about a new pattern in education to meet the needs of a scattering, growing population. It became necessary to plant schools in those new areas of dispersed people, which areas then became school districts. Territories could be broken up and schools established in each area to meet the specific needs of the people. It would have been very difficult, if not impossible, for children of frontier settlers to attend schools in central towns and eastern seaboard cities. Hence, school districting was welcomed heartily by those settlers.

The schools were taught by traveling teachers who would move from district to district, staying long enough to cover a significant part of the curriculum and returning later to pick up where they had left off. Generally the teaching was more pragmatically oriented, since farmers and tradesmen saw little need for classical Latin grammar education for their children. They were more concerned with reading, writing, basic arithmetic, and other usable subjects for frontier life and existence. The central town still controlled the district schools, overseeing curriculum and teachers. Not until the late 1700s was full control given to individual districts by state legislatures.

After the Revolutionary War had secured independence for the colonies, the newly constituted federal government made a significant move in leaving the responsibility of education to the individual states. Shortly thereafter every new state had drawn up its own constitution, each of which made strong provisions for public education for all citizens. The state governments sought to work with church and religious groups already involved in the existent schools, but their control and authority became increasingly felt.

Education during the antebellum (pre-Civil War) years moved forward with great vigor, given the new spirit of national liberty and unity. Men such as George Washington, John Adams, and Thomas Jefferson were strong proponents of excellence in public education. Washington pushed hard for a "national university" and even willed fifty shares in his Potomac Company "toward the endowment of a university in the District of Columbia."

Thomas Jefferson was perhaps the loudest voice for public education, and early in the nineteenth century he made strong proposals for a system of publicly supported schools in Virginia (which ultimately proved unsuccessful). Shortly after the War, Jefferson wrote: "I look to the diffusion of light and education as the resources most to be relied upon for ameliorating the condition, promoting the virtue and advancing the happiness of man. A system of general instruction, which shall reach every description of our citizens, from the richest to the poorest, as it was the earliest, so shall it be the latest of all the public concerns in which I shall permit myself to take an interest."[14] We will look more closely at his philosophy in the next chapter.

SECULARIZATION

The Christian saturation of education in the early colonial period soon began to give way to a rise in secular thought that stemmed from the growing voice of the Enlightenment. Initially, the colonial outlook assumed a unity of church and state as a result of Reformation thinking, although there were smaller sectarian groups such as the Anabaptists who held to a separation of church and state. Thus, colonial governments chose to give strong support to churches and their schools just as churches gave strong support to the state in creating legislation regarding the education of children. This reciprocal relationship ensured a strong Christian emphasis in colonial education.

The part of the Enlightenment that began to alter American education was the rationalism of Descartes and the resultant emphasis on human reason in knowing (scientism). John Locke emphasized the importance of knowing through ideas that arise from sense perception (the "tabula rasa"). Locke borrowed from Francis Bacon, who believed that ideas are not innate but stem from observation of nature, collection of facts, and general propositions through the scientific method. Locke's notion was later termed "sense realism."

Thus there was a tremendous shift away from faith in epistemology to the empiricism of Locke and the rationalism of Descartes. Man, then, was to be studied in the same way as nature, and therefore he became explainable through natural laws. New views of the nature of man resulted from a rationalism that said man was innately good and perpetually moving toward ultimate goodness. Rousseau and other French humanists especially propounded this naturalistic view. Human society, then, could best be governed by such a philosophy, which sought to bring out the goodness already present in man. Christianity, which has its epistemological roots in faith, began to be ridiculed because of its "violation of natural law." Eventually scientism in the biological evolutionary concepts of Charles Darwin and the social-Darwinian, Herbert Spencer, became prominent.

Gradually with immigration to America in the late 1600s, the seeds of European Enlightenment thinking were sown in the colonies. Rationalism and humanism, with their emphases on individualism, human rights, and self-reliance, slowly began to break the grip of the church on education. One needs only to look at those concepts so clearly set forth in the Declaration of Independence to see how greatly America was and is affected by the Enlightenment. Revolutionary leaders including Washington, Madison, and Jefferson were greatly influenced by John Locke, whose popularity spread throughout all of the colonies. Locke had argued convincingly for the separation of church and state.

Consequently, legislation epitomized in the Constitution itself began to lay the groundwork for secular education. The First Amendment, which prevented the establishment of any one religion, began a new era of separation of church and state. Given the authority of the state over education, it became apparent that a de-emphasis of Christian teaching in schools was inevitable. As several have said, the intent was not to provide for freedom "from" religion, but to provide for freedom "of" religion. However, in order to please everyone, and so as not to impinge upon one's religious beliefs, an ultimate secularization of education was the only possible direction.

256   *Christian Education: Its History and Philosophy*

Unfortunately, the concept of the separation of church and state has been greatly misconstrued. The Constitutional intention was not to establish a nonreligious or atheistic state, but merely to ensure religious freedom and prevent certain beliefs from being foisted on people by government legislation. There were many bitter controversies in the late 1700s and early 1800s over what should or should not be taught in the schools. Various denominations and religious sects fought over standards and caused even more elimination of Christian emphasis in public education.

Ultimately, the Enlightenment emphases on reason, science, and humanism shifted the focus of education to a nonbiblical perspective in the teaching of history, science, and the arts. This shift eventually resulted in the present legislation prohibiting any religious education, Bible reading, and prayer in public schools. It is little wonder that the Sunday school movement spread so quickly across America during the 1800s in order to fill the gap created by a rapidly secularizing society.

NOTES

1. John D. Pulliam, *History of Education in America* (Columbus, Ohio: Merrill, 1968), pp. 18-19.
2. Cited in F. V. N. Painter, *A History of Education* (New York: Appleton, 1896), p. 314.
3. R. Freeman Butts and Lawrence A. Cremin, *A History of Education in American Culture* (New York: Holt, Rinehart, and Winston, 1953), p. 71.
4. H. G. Good, *A History of American Education* (New York: Macmillan, 1956), p. 65.
5. David Tyack, "Education as Artifact: Benjamin Franklin and Instruction of 'A Rising People,' " *History of Education Quarterly* 6 (Spring 1966) : 3-4.
6. Ibid., p. 7.
7. Ibid., p. 4.
8. Ibid., p. 8.
9. Ibid.
10. Butts and Cremin, pp. 131-33.
11. Edwin H. Rian, *Christianity and American Education* (San Antonio, Tex.: Naylor, 1949), p. 189.
12. Good, p. 62.
13. W. W. Hening, *Statutes at Large . . . of Virginia* (Richmond: n.p., 1809), 2:56. Cited in Butts and Cremin, p. 83.
14. Butts and Cremin, p. 315.

13

Thomas Jefferson and Horace Mann

The eighteenth century found Western Christendom engaged in a vigorous struggle with the Enlightenment. The age of reason, characterized by Baconian and Lockean empiricism, the rationalism of Descartes, and Newtonian physics, proved to be a formidable opponent. One of the central foci of Reformation thought was to formulate the meaning of the universe with God at the center, whereas the Enlightenment focused attention on a man-centered universe. The attacks on Christianity became increasingly more aggressive.

The evolution of an empiricism and a rationalism based on mathematical reasoning and sense experience left no room for the supernatural. Reason and revelation began to be thought of as antithetical. When man and his philosophies become the measure of all things, God becomes an anomaly.

As we begin this journey through the nineteenth century, it would be well to assess the state of evangelicalism at the beginning of that period. American theology then as now rested unequivocably upon a European base. It was heavily reflective of the Reformation. The earliest settlers were committed to that faith. Theologically they had a high view of God. He had spoken through the Bible. It constituted all they needed for developing a personal relationship with God, and it provided the guidance for establishing the church and a society that, while not entirely Christian, would make decisions that mirrored scriptural directives.

Mark A. Noll has summarized it in this manner:

> The New England Puritans, and to a lesser extent Reformed Christians in the other colonies, used a "covenantal" vocabulary to describe the relationship between God and man. They spoke of a mutual contract in which God and man fulfilled certain obligations to each other. From the Old Testament the Puritans saw that a covenant was sometimes a conditional agreement between God and man, sometimes an unconditional gift of God demanding a re-

sponse of obedience to God's law. The New Testament, the Puritans noted, spoke of a new covenant from God in Christ. Puritan theology adopted both the Old and New Testament concept of the covenant as a means to proclaim God's grace while maintaining the authority of His law . . . .

The virtue of a covenantal system in explaining the plan of salvation was twofold: it preserved the Reformed view of God's place while retaining an important place for the law. Only supernatural grace could overcome total depravity, but the ability to love and keep God's law indicated that a person was a child of God. Following the law did not save a person but a saved person did follow the law.[1]

Dissent from those high standards was inevitable with the immigration of many from various countries of differing views. In addition, the gradual dilution of Puritan thinking was characteristic of the second and third generations in New England as well as in the other colonies. Sturdy theologians began to appear on American soil in the seventeenth and eighteenth centuries. Yet it was the religious movement of the 1730s and the Great Awakening of the 1740s that brought new vitality to the teachings of the Puritans. Dutch Reformed Theodore Frelinghuysen (1691-1747), Presbyterian Gilbert Tennent (1703-1764), Congregationalist Jonathan Edwards (1703-1758), and itinerant preacher George Whitefield (1714-1770) made remarkable contributions to the thought, literature, and proclamation of the Great Awakening between 1730 and 1770. Edwards, to whose church came revival in 1734, was of particular significance: "Edwards' theological accomplishment was twofold: first, he restated the Calvinistic doctrine of salvation in terms that would dominate American theology for at least a century and influence it to the present. Second, he examined the nature of proper Christian behavior with the sophisticated categories of modern thought."[2]

Critics and detractors to such thinking were many, and the attacks came from the right and left. The movement away from evangelicalism was not necessarily consonant with the American Revolution, but the process of building the nation and the emerging ideas of a changing society adversely affected the evangelical movement. Noll outlines five major developments that changed the manner in which evangelicals perceived God and the way they communicated their thinking in society. First, the relative unity of Reformed theology was beginning to break up due to Arminianism on the right and liberalism on the left. Second, the "evangelical perspective was dominating American life less and less and cooperating with it more and more." American society continued as Christian for the first two-thirds of the nineteenth century. Third, the attitude of evangelicals was that America had been given a dispensation to be God's special agent for doing His work in the world. Without question, America had been favored in many ways. But such provincialism led to some Americans' developing an overconfidence in the "unquestionable truth of their doctrinal points of view. They often held them to be as uniquely blessed of God as their country was." Fourth, American evangelical theology was no longer setting the theological agenda. Edwards and other pastor-teacher-scholars had "set the tone for American intellectual life in the mid-eighteenth century," but by 1800, statesmen, political leaders, and scientists had assumed that role. "Theology . . . no longer reigned as 'queen of the sciences' in the American kingdom of thought."[3]

The Second Great Awakening beginning in the 1790s brought change to the theological scene. Presbyterian James McGready (1758?-1817) and Yale College president Timothy Dwight (1752-1817) were spearheads of revival, and Charles Hodge (1797-1878) of Princeton Seminary vigorously restated traditional Reformed theology. Meanwhile, Dwight's theology student, Nathaniel William Taylor (1786-1858), and the impact of John Wesley (1703-1791) and the English Methodists lifted Arminianism to new heights in this country. American Methodism was growing and by 1844 was this country's largest denominational body. Francis Asbury (1745-1816) and Peter Cartwright (1785-1872) provided distinguished leadership.

Charles G. Finney (1792-1875) combined strands of the Reformed theological tapestry with strands of Methodism and perfectionism. While joining the Presbyterians, he adopted some of the ideas of Nathaniel Taylor.

> In particular Finney was attracted to the idea that people had the ability within themselves to choose Christ and to choose to live the Christian life. Finney expounded this view during the "age of the common man" when Andrew Jackson publicized a new concern for the plain folks of the country. Much of what President Jackson was doing for politics, Finney was doing for theology. He brought the message of salvation into the highways and byways of "the common man." He proclaimed that energetic personal effort, with God's ready help, could overcome any obstacle to the life, liberty, and happiness of a Christian.[4]

The remarkable revivals of the eighteenth century, such as the Wesleyan renewal in England, made their way rapidly to North America. The revivals on both sides of the Atlantic set the scene for one of the most significant developments in the history of the church—the modern missionary movement. The evangelical and pietist awakenings spawned new efforts to bring the message of Christ to other countries, and tangential to revival and evangelism was the institution of the school, both the formal college and the informal Sunday school. Some of the Christian education innovations of Wesley are worthy of careful consideration.

THE WESLEYAN IMPACT ON CHURCH RENEWAL

The Wesleyan movement initiated many schools and colleges. One of its finest contributions was the pattern that John Wesley established for Methodism and one that has spilled over into some evangelical churches looking for renewal today. "The story of Wesley's life and ministry is the story of creating and adapting structures to serve the burgeoning revival movement. The system which emerged gave lie to the argument that you can't build a church on the poor and uneducated folk. Not only did Wesley reach the masses; he made leaders of thousands of them."[5]

Wesley developed three patterns in addition to the congregational meeting that he carried over from his Anglican heritage (though the conduct of the service was radically different). Those structures "composed a system of discipline-in-community." It was an immersion in close fellowship and strict discipline.

CLASS MEETING

The class meeting averaged twelve in number and met one evening each week. Each person reported on his spiritual progress. The church sustained itself financially from offerings received in this setting. The class leader knew each person well. The duties given each class leader were twofold:

> (1) To see each person in his class, once a week at the least, in order to inquire how their souls prosper; to advise, reprove, comfort, or exhort, as occasion may require; to receive what they are willing to give, toward the relief of the poor.
>
> (2) To meet the Minister and the Stewards of the society, in order to inform the Minister of any that are sick, or of any that are disorderly and will not be reproved; to pay the Stewards what they have received of their several classes in the week preceding.[6]

BAND SYSTEM

The idea of a band system came from Count Zinzendorf and the Moravians of Herrnhut. An average of six members would compose a band. They met weekly and confessed their faults to one another. Although the bands "caused some suspicion and the charge of 'popery' because of the practice of confession—they proved to be a useful means of spiritual growth."[7] They were to encourage spiritual progress and not to function mainly as disciplinary. The bands were restricted to those who had the assurance of the forgiveness of their sins. Traveling preachers examined each person.

SELECT SOCIETY

The select society was a group of people who "seemed to walk in the light of God." It was made up mainly of lay preachers. Those who had fallen into sin met "apart as penitents." There were three rules established for the select societies:

> (1) Let nothing spoken in this Society be spoken again; no, not even to the members of it.
> (2) Every member agrees absolutely to submit to his Minister in all indifferent things.
> (3) Every member, till we can have all things common, will bring once a week, bona fide, all he can spare to a common stock.[8]

The society-class-band system held together because of the itinerant system of traveling lay preachers. They were under Wesley's direct supervision and answered to him. Aspects of those ideas have been utilized in some evangelical groups. A key word in any healthy fellowship is *accountability*. Most react strenuously to the rigid, inflexible system used by the early Methodists. But many churches and groups have failed to arrive at any level of discipline and, because of that failure, are continually growing weaker. Some kind of accountability is mandatory for health in churches.

THE INDUSTRIAL REVOLUTION

While the Christian gospel was being received by some, tumultuous changes were going on in society. The Industrial Revolution was frightening and yet filled with possibilities for the church.

The age of reason was influential in the rise of a factory system that stressed capitalism. Technology and industry spawned the growth of cities and the development of the middle class manager. Newly invented machines eroded an economy in which each family supplied its own needs by handcrafted and homespun items. Markets for goods grew steadily with the emergence of an adequate transportation system and the arrival of a vast working pool of immigrants. The agrarian configuration of American society was beginning to change.

The factory system that modernized England resulted in greatly increased production and a new middle class that filled the gap between employer and employee. This upward mobility was unsettling to the upper class. The middle class, assisted by education, hesitatingly groped for its place on the social ladder as it continued to judge ideas pragmatically. In short, the Industrial Revolution revised the class structure in the United States, as the common school attempted to provide a culturally equalizing medium for the emerging nation.

Next we shall examine a small, seemingly insignificant educational effort that began concurrently with the Industrial Revolution and brought the children of the masses and upper classes together within a religious context.

THE BIG LITTLE SCHOOL

The Sunday school is American Protestantism's training ground. Denominations have established hundreds of colleges and universities, but the Sunday school is the BIG school in matters religious for the Protestant people—originally white people, though it has played a distinctive role in the religious experience and culture of black America. Compared to public education, Sunday school is marginal to American society, yet it is an important LITTLE school in the rearing of the whole nation. The Sunday school is the big little school of the United States.[9]

The Sunday school began as a protest and reform movement. When Robert Raikes started a school for poor children in Gloucester, England, during 1780 or 1781, an agency of the church was born.[10] However, over thirty-five years went by before the church embraced it. This was not Raikes's first attempt at reform. After becoming the publisher of the *Gloucester Journal* in 1757, he initiated prison reforms by calling for the moral education of criminals. Raikes's Sunday charity school worked toward the spiritual regeneration and the moral transformation of poor children from the following curious blend of supporters and motivation: "(1) an unusual adult interest and encouragement, (2) upper-class benevolence with its inevitable measures of condescension, bribery and social coercion, (3) the freedom to learn to read, a remarkable occurrence in the lives of the poor, and (4) a pervasive religious orientation."[11]

On the eve of the Industrial Revolution in England the social conditions of the poor provided a fertile seedbed for the founding of the Sunday school. With the children employed in the factories for long hours six days of the week, Sunday became a day of freedom and frequently delinquency. Another English layman, William Fox, started the first organization that promoted Sunday schools when he came to the realization "that in a Christian country, a Protestant country too, no provision would be made for the education of poor children, about whom the heathen take so much pain."[12]

Within the next fifty years, 1780-1830, the Sunday school moved across the Atlantic and participated in the early nineteenth-century new American awareness of children and childhood as a stage of life. From an agricultural economy, the United States was beginning to evolve into an urban and industrial nation. While children of lower class urban families remained as significant economic contributors in their homes, the role of middle class children was changing rapidly. Free of adult concerns as children, the teen years confronted young people with vocational choices never before encountered by adolescents.

The Sunday school in the United States grew rapidly. By 1790 there were Sunday schools in Boston, Philadelphia, and smaller towns such as Pawtucket, Rhode Island. The First Day Society of Philadelphia provided schools "for the benefit of such persons of either sex and of any age as cannot afford to educate themselves" and paid the teachers to instruct students in reading and copying the Bible. Between 1791 and 1800, their schools taught 1,224 boys and 903 girls.[13] The teachers, because of the illiteracy of their charges, taught reading and writing in addition to the Bible. However, by 1828 two-thirds of the children in the Sunday schools also attended weekday schools. The constituency of the Sunday schools now included middle class children, as well as a few upper class youngsters. Middle class parents were eager for their children to receive Christian teaching and the children themselves urged their parents to allow Sunday school attendance while the parents were in the worship service.

It should be noted carefully that the Sunday school was a lay movement. Initially, ministers from almost all Protestant denominations were unanimous in their derision of the Sunday school. Raikes, Fox, and the teachers they employed were not professional ministers. With the growth of the movement that included middle class children, an identification of individual Sunday schools with particular congregations took place. Slowly the clergy realized the potential of the Sunday schools as a growth force, and their attitudes began to change.

The history of nineteenth-century Sunday schools was one of guiding children to conversion. Anne M. Boylan states that from 1820 to 1830 the Sunday school progressed from "emphasizing students' prowess at memorization, to stressing the need to make students understand what they memorized, to pressing the importance of making students 'feel the truth' of their reading, to, finally, promoting the schools as forums for student conversions."[14] The teachers no longer were content to teach children to read or to listen to them recite. Conversion of the child to Christ was now envisioned as the primary result of teaching in the Sunday school.

In time some organizational improvements were made. Children were placed in classes on the basis of age rather than reading skills. Smaller classes of six to ten pupils were deemed a necessity. About age fourteen, the students thought they had outgrown Sunday school, so Bible classes were formed for teenage youth. Teaching biblical concepts to children ages four to six in "infant classes" also was initiated.[15] On reaching adulthood, the "children" of the Sunday school filtered back into the process of teaching others also (2 Tim. 2:2). The Sunday school was moving toward the biblical goal of bringing people to maturity in Christ (Eph. 4:13; Col. 1:28), which eventually led to their engaging in a ministry of spiritual reproduction and multiplication of themselves. The Sunday school was coming of age.

JEFFERSON AND CLASSICISM

Education in America in the nineteenth century reacted against the strong doctrines of Puritanism. Jonathan Edwards, Increase Mather, and Cotton Mather had taught the depravity of man, and the deists and the unitarians responded with their views regarding perfectibility. Edwards "influenced Congregational and Presbyterian theology in the United States for more than a century,"[16] but after the American Revolution, transcendentalism and unitarianism grew rapidly through the leadership of Ralph Waldo Emerson, Henry David Thoreau, and William E. Channing. When the divinity school of Harvard University was founded in 1816, it became the fountainhead of unitarian teaching.

Thomas Jefferson (1743-1826) was a deist and one of the most brilliant thinkers in the history of American educational theorists. He studied law at the College of William and Mary and moved into the political arena while still a young man. Jefferson is well known for his authorship of the Declaration of Independence as a member of the Continental Congress. He served successively and successfully in the following capacities: governor of Virginia, ambassador to France, secretary of state, vice-president and president of the United States.

From his youth Jefferson read voraciously in the classics, and he possessed an unusual capacity for work and study. To him education was of the utmost importance. He enthusiastically proposed education for the masses, because he believed it alone provided the best protection for liberty in the young nation. In his day that was a revolutionary concept. When he introduced a "Bill For the More General Diffusion of Knowledge," there were three assumptions implicit in his proposal: "first, that republican government and democratic decision-making required an educated and literate citizenry; second, that education should be political rather than a religious function; third, that education should be vested in state governments."[17] It is particularly crucial to note that Jefferson and Benjamin Franklin, both deists, proposed educational plans that shifted the emphasis from the "religiously oriented education of the colonial period to the more secular approach that characterized the later development of American public education.[18]

As he became known for his educational expertise, Jefferson was besieged by parents requesting advice regarding the instruction of their children. Fortunately, many of the letters he wrote are extant. They yield a veritable treasure regarding his opinions on a number of subjects.

Jefferson acknowledged that all people should be given the opportunity for some education. However, he was an elitest in terms of government and advanced education. Some of these attitudes emerge in a letter to John Adams.

> I agree with you that there is a natural aristocracy among men. The grounds of this are virtue and talents . . . there is also an artificial aristocracy, founded on wealth and birth, without either

virtue or talents, for with these it would belong to the first class. The natural aristocracy I consider as the most precious gift of nature for the instruction, the trusts, and the government of society. . . .May we not even say that that form of government is the best which provided the most effectually for a pure selection of these natural *aristoi* into the offices of government? The artificial aristocracy is a mischievous ingredient in government, and provision should be made to prevent its ascendancy.[19]

Adams felt that members of the artificial or pseudo-*aristoi* should be given legislative positions but that they should be put in a separate chamber of legislation where they could be "hindered from doing mischief." Jefferson countered by saying, "I think that to give them power in order to prevent them from doing mischief is arming them for it and increasing instead of remedying the evil."[20]

The theology espoused by Jefferson was a mixture of deism and unitarianism. To him, the "religion of Jesus" was clear and simple and was applicable to all. The following passage elucidates some of the planks in his theological platform.

1. That there is one only God, and He all perfect.
2. That there is a future state of rewards and punishments.
3. That to love God with all thy heart and thy neighbor as thyself, is the sum of all religion. These are the great points on which he endeavored to reform the religion of the Jews.

But compare with these the demoralizing dogmas of Calvin:

1. That there are three Gods.
2. That good works, or the love of your neighbors, are nothing.
3. That faith is everything, and the more incomprehensible the proposition, the more merit in its faith.
4. That reason in religion is of unlawful use.
5. That God, from the beginning, elected certain individuals to be saved, and certain others to be damned; and that no crimes of the former can damn them; no virtues of the latter save.[21]

Jefferson further attacked Calvin as having distorted the Christian faith, and in so doing articulated his own leanings toward unitarianism.

Had the doctrines of Jesus been preached always as pure as they came from his lips, the whole civilized world now would have been Christian. I rejoice that in this blessed country of free inquiry and belief, which has surrendered its creed and conscience to neither kings nor priests, the genuine doctrine of one only God is reviving, and I trust that there is not a young man now living in the United States who will not die an Unitarian.

But much I fear, that when this great truth shall be re-established its votaries will fall into the fatal error of fabricating formulas of creeds and confessions of faith, the engines which so soon destroyed the religion of Jesus, and made of Christendom a mere Aceldama.[22]

However, it should be made eminently clear that Jefferson, although not an evangelical Christian, was an individual of un-compromisingly high morals. In discussing the three important values of morality, health, and knowledge that should accrue from an education, he states: "The defect of these virtues can never be made up of all the other acquirements of body and mind. Make these, then, your first object. Give up money, give up fame, give up science, give up the earth itself and all it contains, rather than do an immoral act."[23]

Jefferson was committed to the proposition that all people should have at least a primary education. The objectives of elementary education were:

1. To give every citizen the information he needs to transact his own business.
2. To enable him to calculate for himself and to express and pre-serve his ideas, contracts and accounts in writing.
3. To improve, by reading, his faculties and morals.
4. To understand his duties to his neighbors and his country, and to discharge with competence the functions confided to him by either.
5. To know his rights; to exercise with order and justice those he retains; to choose with discretion the fiduciary of those he delegates.
6. And, in general to observe with intelligence and faithfulness all the social relations under which he shall be placed.[24]

The natural concomitant of the foregoing was Jefferson's plan, while governor of Virginia in 1779, called the "Bill for the More General Diffusion of Knowledge." While the bill did not pass the legislature of Virginia either time it was submitted (1779 and 1817), it was regarded as a forerunner of state-supported elemen-tary schools. He saw universal education as obligatory if a demo-cratic republicanism was to be a reality. Further, he projected that education could assist in breaking down class barriers. That aim took shape primarily in his quest for finding the brightest youths among the poor and providing advanced training at the College of William and Mary at public expense. He proposed the idea that has endured so persistently in American educational thought, that a single system of schools would assist in closing the chasm between the rich and the poor.

It should be noted that while "Jefferson kept alive for fifty years the ideal of universal elementary instruction, free to all alike and bearing no stigma of pauperism, and while in theory he regarded schools for the people as more important than a university, yet in actuality he devoted major efforts, particularly after his retirement to Monticello, to the founding of an essentially exclusive institution of higher learning."[25]

That institution was the University of Virginia. The College of William and Mary was limited in its curriculum and faculty and prepared no one directly for a vocation except those few studying for the ministry in the Church of England. To Jefferson, knowledge was of value only if it rendered the person more useful to himself and society. "The properly educated man was to be moral, healthy, and above all useful, capable of understanding the interests of his neighbors, his countrymen, and himself, and of working for their development."[26]

Communication with contemporaries, such as Benjamin Rush in the field of medicine and Thomas Paine in political theory, was engaged in with erudition and grace because he was so widely read. A general education in both the humanities and the sciences was highly prized by Jefferson. In his later years he still read the distinguished authors in the original languages of Greek, French, Latin, and Italian. But he deemed the enlightenment of the classics not to be of sufficient value in itself. Eventually he trumpeted science for its ability to shape the future.

At the time of Jefferson's death, his dream of the good society, made up of able and competent landholders, had not become a reality. He had misjudged the "significance of industrialization and urbanization" and had "failed to detect the direction Southern agrarianism was taking," for the South was increasingly "a section apart."[27] However, his powerful statement in the Declaration of Independence, "all men are created equal," was employed by the lower classes in their attempt to rise socially and economically. Jacksonian mass rule prodded the aristocrats and the political conservatives to act quickly toward publicly supported education, and in so doing provided an affirmative context for the common school movement led by Horace Mann.

HORACE MANN AND PUBLIC EDUCATION

At age fourteen, Horace Mann (1796-1858) had a traumatic experience that seemed to shape the religious views of his adult life. His seventeen-year-old brother died. At the funeral the family pastor stated that this brother, Horace's idol, was not a Christian, and therefore would experience eternal death. Horace Mann never forgot the groans of his mother, and from that time grew to hate the version of Calvinism in which the family was reared. His pastor, Nathaniel Emmons, was a stern, heavily didactic preacher who was a highly original and controversial theologian.[28]

In college Mann turned to the philosophy of John Locke, whose writings had influenced Jefferson and the fathers of the American Constitution. Locke argued that almost all knowledge comes by way of experiential perception. Mann retained a strong belief in God as creator of the world governed through benevolent laws, the immortality of the soul, and personal moral responsibility. He was an active and earnest churchman. Considering Calvinism to be sectarian, he became a unitarian.[29] Mann believed that religion was moralism and not piety, and that humankind was perfectible through the process of education. In short, Mann held to the primacy of human reason, believing that natural religion stood preeminent over revealed theology. Mann embraced the deism of his intellectual mentor, John Locke. However, that which motivated Mann most profoundly and was the driving force in his life was the need for universal education.

UNIVERSAL EDUCATION

All social and educational reformers in Horace Mann's day were enthusiastic proponents of universal education, but there was disagreement over the implementation of it. Three of the experiments engaged in were the aforementioned Sunday schools of Robert Raikes and other experiments that were charity enterprises with the goals of literacy and morality. A second approach was the monitorial approach of Joseph Lancaster (1778-1838), a Quaker schoolmaster, and Andrew Bell (1753-1832), an Anglican clergyman who had served as a missionary to India. In the monitorial system a master teacher would teach older students who would in turn teach their younger colleagues. The system operated on a reward/punishment basis and was highly competitive. The method was inexpensive (e.g., it used sand tables for writing). The system was effective for increasing literacy but it failed to fulfill expectations.

A third and fascinating venture at combating ignorance and promoting equality through education was by the communitarian socialists, Robert Owen and William Maclure. This 1825 experiment at New Harmony, Indiana, lasted just two years. Maclure believed the task of education was to develop "critical understanding" based on empirical facts. He argued for a flexible curriculum in which each student could pursue his own interest in a cooperative commonwealth. Owen favored social cohesion. He wanted a stable social order based on a curriculum that was broad enough to encompass both formal schooling and the environment, and which utilized a passive learning process. Educationally speaking, Maclure was a reconstructionist and Owen a reflectionist.

In Owen's judgment, education was the great equalizer in a period of social, cultural, and economic inequality. Both men had been markedly swayed by Johann Pestalozzi's opposition to a heavily structured curriculum and excessive verbalism as they had observed his work at Burgdorf. They had brought in Joseph Neef, Pestalozzi's trusted colleague, to assert educational leadership. However, because of mismanagement, diverse educational philosophies, and incompatible personalities, the experiment died.

There were four major reasons or arguments employed by those who were advocates of universal education:

> An important factor in the movement for universal education was the motivation of the reformers. Many of them were concerned with the people's need for political enlightenment. Democratic processes and procedures required an electorate capable of choosing its officials and an officialdom capable of governing.
>
> Equally important . . . was the increasing force of nationalism. Common schools could establish common values and loyalties and weld groups of diverse ethnic and religious backgrounds together into a common American identity.
>
> The rising middle and working classes wanted a more utilitarian education which would prepare skilled businessmen and workers.
>
> A fourth motive . . . was that Americans viewed education as a means of social improvement and economic advancement.[30]

In opposition to these reasons were some who viewed universal education as a way to obliterate class distinctions. Others held that it "violated the natural sanctity of property rights to tax one man in order to educate another's child." Some thought it was a movement by which one political party would be able to dominate another and thereby introduce its "political dogma into the curriculum in order to indoctrinate the young." Others feared that schools would become "godless and would dismiss religious values in favor of secular ones." Foreign language groups were afraid that their distinctives of language and custom would be obliterated.[31]

MANN'S PHILOSOPHY OF EDUCATION

In actuality, Horace Mann left no systematic treatment of his philosophy of education. As editor of the influential *Common School Journal,* he wrote prolifically and mostly in a popular manner. As the secretary of the Board of Education of Massachusetts, he was often thrust into the role of enthusiast, promoter, and even educational statesman rather than that of philosopher. He was an eclectic through whom five broad currents of thought ran: remnants of Calvinism, American transcendentalism, the republican-democratic ethic, industrial capitalism, and phrenology.[32] For Mann, any democratic concept of education rested on the principles of "natural ethics."

> The successive generations of men, taken collectively, constitute one great commonwealth. The property of this commonwealth is pledged for the education of all its youth, up to such a point as will save them from poverty and vice, and perhaps to prepare them for the adequate performance of their social and civil duties. The successive holders of this property are trustees, bound to the faithful execution of their trust by the most sacred obligations; and embezzlement and pillage from children and descendants have not less of criminality, and have more of meanness, than the same offences when perpetrated against contemporaries.[33]

The opening statement of this same "Tenth Annual Report" underscored the above principles, as follows:

> I believe in the existence of a great, immutable principle of natural law, or natural ethics, a principle antecedent to all human institutions and incapable of being abrogated by any ordinances of man, a principle of divine origin, clearly legible in the ways of Providence as those ways are manifested in the order of nature and in the history of the race, which proves the ABSOLUTE RIGHT of every human being that comes into the world to an education; and which of course, proves the correlative duty of every government to see that the means of that education are provided for all.[34]

Horace Mann believed in the stewardship theory of wealth, whereby people of financial means were to use a portion of their abundance for the public welfare and common good. If society were to produce greater wealth for more people, "intelligence is the grand condition." The machine for greater efficiency in the exploitation of natural resources was the common or public school.

> The common school is the greatest discovery ever made by man.
> . . .Other social organizations are curative and remedial; this is a
> preventive and an antidote; they come to heal diseases and
> wounds, this to make the physical and moral frame invulnerable
> to them. Let the common school be expanded to its capabilities, let
> it be worked with the efficiency of which it is susceptible, and
> nine-tenths of the crimes in the penal code would become obso-
> lete; the long catalogue of human ills would be abridged; men
> would walk more safely by day; every pillow would be more in-
> violable by night; property, life and character held by a stronger
> tenure; all rational hopes respecting the future brightened.[35]

Mann envisioned the school as the agency that could change society and bring in a utopian state. He entreated taxpayers to provide the funds necessary for this panacea for social ills.

Horace Mann believed that the common school would result in freedom for the people and would generate moral virtue. He began to project education as being messianic in its ability to deliver millennial qualities to society. It could bring in "the establishment of peace and righteousness upon earth, and . . . the enjoyment of glory and happiness in heaven."[36] Though he observed the weaknesses in a capitalism that could be unjust, Mann worked within the system toward greater social efficiency. He pointed out that it was in the best interest of the affluent to support the common school enterprise, because high on his educational agenda was respect for property and encouragement toward self-betterment by acquiring possessions. In effect, then, the "kingdom" could be brought in by education:

> For the creation of wealth, then, for the existence of a wealthy
> people and a wealthy nation, intelligence is the grand condition.
> The number of improvers will increase as the intellectual con-
> stituency, if I may so call it, increases. . . .The greatest of all arts in
> political economy is to change a consumer into a producer; and
> the next greatest is to increase the producer's producing power —
> an end to be directly attained by increasing his intelligence.[37]

A few of the ideas and concepts of Mann were of great significance in his time and are so at the present. However, it must be recognized that some of them were categorically incorrect. Without doubt, there were many values that accrued with the advent of universal or common schooling. But his faulty anthropology and utopian views are inextricably tied in with his theology. Knowledge is not moral virtue. The state (which is to control education) is not the basic institution in society and must not usurp the family's right to make decisions regarding the education of its young, though some federal or state legislation is necessary to protect the children. Although man was created in the image of God, sin has marred that image, and man is not perfectible (see Chapter 3). An educational system has to consider the sinfulness of man. It is a gross oversimplification to state that morality and intelligence are the products of education. Schooling is not the panacea for sin and the weaknesses of human nature, although education is important and contributes to the enhancement of societal values (be they good or not).

Because public education benefits children and youth of diverse backgrounds, there must be certain limits regarding the religious teaching given. Mann did not rule out the teaching of Christian principles in the school. Nor did he take the very secular viewpoint that now dominates some of contemporary public education. He suggested that the Bible be read without comment by either teacher or pupil.

> Moral education is a primal necessity of social existence. The unrestrained passions of men are not only homicidal, but suicidal; and a community without a conscience would soon extinguish itself. . . .But it will be said that this grand result in practical morals is a consummation of blessedness that can never be attained without religion, and that no community will ever be religious without religious education. Both these propositions I regard as eternal and immutable truths . . .
>
> I have felt bound to show, that so far from its being an irreligious, an anti-Christian, or an un-Christian system, it is a system which recognizes religious obligations in their fullest extent; that it is a system which involves a religious spirit, and can never be fully administered without such a spirit; that it inculcates the great commands upon which hang all the law and the prophets; that it welcomes the Bible, and therefore welcomes all the doctrines which the Bible really contains.
>
> It is a system, however, which leaves open all other means of

instruction—the pulpit, the Sunday schools, the Bible classes, the catechisms, of all denominations,—to be employed according to the preferences of individual parents. It is a system which restrains itself from teaching that what it does teach is all that needs to be taught, or that should be taught; but leaves this to be decided by each man for himself, according to the light of his reason and conscience, and on his responsibility to that Great Being, who, in holding him to account for the things done in the body, will hold him to the strictest account for the manner in which he has "trained up" his children.[38]

Horace Mann cannot be disassociated from his historical context, because he was affected by his generation. The Christian impact of the Puritans was still felt in New England and the other colonies. A religious aura was very much a part of America in that period. Even his journey from Calvinism to unitarianism could not have quelled his religious heritage entirely. Yet Mann should be interpreted in light of the base of natural theology that undergirded the unitarians. Their notion of inevitable progress decisively controlled their idea of human history and eschatology. The perfectibility of man and the transcendental view of God were the overarching concepts in their theology. The influence of Emerson, Thoreau, and Channing on Horace Mann was considerable.

Even though Mann encouraged the use of the Bible in the schools, he viewed it as promoting social efficiency and civic virtue rather than godliness. He made pragmatic use of religion with the focus on society rather than God. By "interpreting Christianity as freedom, and education as salvation, he undercut both Christianity and the republic."[39]

The Massachusetts law of 1827 and similar laws that prohibited the teaching of any religious tenet that would favor any sect were instrumental in aiding Mann, Henry Barnard (1811-1900), and James G. Carter (1795-1849) in the common school movement. Any belief held by one group and opposed by another was an issue upon which the school was to remain silent. Fortunately, compromises always were worked out and accepted by society. This system of compromises with respect to the religious issue, of which Mann was the principal advocate, set in motion a process that resulted in the legal secularization of most modern public school education.

Henry Barnard, although not the dominant figure of the common school movement, was a prominent commentator on educational affairs through his editorship of the *Connecticut Common School Journal* and the *American Journal of Education*, which was a thirty-one volume general encyclopedia of education. Through his writings, he introduced teachers to ideas of European educators such as Pestalozzi, Froebel, and Herbart. Barnard was the first secretary to the Board of Commissioners of Common Schools in Connecticut and the first United States Commissioner of Education. A fervent Episcopalian, he "associated his entire educational program with Christianity. He opposed the free-thinking and materialistic skepticism of some of the proponents of nonsectarian common-school education. . . . The Bible was to be used to bring about good character."[40] Barnard emphasized a utilitarian curriculum in light of the burgeoning industrialization and stressed the mastery of the English language—spelling, grammar, reading, composition, and speech.

The common school was conceived as a vehicle to reconstruct society and promote social harmony. It was supported by conservatives and liberals for decidedly different reasons. By the mid-nineteenth century, most people agreed with Horace Bushnell regarding common schools that "we must agree to have and maintain till the last day or latest day of our liberties."[41]

NOTES

 1. John D. Woodbridge, Mark A. Noll, and Nathan O. Hatch, *The Gospel in America* (Grand Rapids: Zondervan, 1979), p. 24.
 2. Ibid., p. 28.
 3. Ibid., pp. 32-33.
 4. Ibid., p. 37.
 5. Howard A. Snyder, *The Radical Wesley and Patterns of Church Renewal* (Downers Grove, Ill.: Inter-Varsity, 1980), p. 53.
 6. John Wesley, *The Works of John Wesley* (London: Wesleyan Conference Office, 1872), 8:253.
 7. Snyder, pp. 59-60.
 8. Ibid., p. 62.
 9. Robert W. Lynn and Elliott Wright, *The Big Little School*, rev. ed. (Birmingham, Ala.: Relig. Educ. Press, 1980), pp. 15-16.
10. Ibid., p. 23. It is likely that Raikes was not the first one to have made biblical instruction available for children on a scheduled basis on Sundays. Some suggest that Hannah Ball, an English Methodist, "gathered children in her home for Sunday instruction as early as 1763." Others contend that John Wesley instructed children on Sundays while a missionary in Georgia in 1735. Regardless, the critical issue is that a ministry in which the gospel was taught and children were assisted in learning to read was undertaken. See the chapter on Robert Raikes in Elmer L. Towns, ed., *A History of Religious Educators* (Grand Rapids: Baker, 1975).
11. Ibid., p. 26.
12. Joseph Ivimey, *Memoir of William Fox, Esq.* (London: George Wightman, 1831), p. 18.

13. First Day Society Minutes, 9 April 1800. Presbyterian Historical Society, Philadelphia, Pa. Cited in Anne M. Boylan, "Sunday Schools and Changing Evangelical Views of Children in the 1820s," *Church History* 48, no. 3 (1979): 321. (See also First Day Society Constitution, 1791.)
14. Boylan, p. 330.
15. Ibid., pp. 330-31.
16. Sydney E. Ahlstrom, *A Religious History of the American People* (New Haven, Conn.: Yale U., 1972), p. 311.
17. Gerald L. Gutek, *An Historical Introduction to American Education* (New York: Crowell, 1970), p. 34.
18. Ibid.
19. Letter to John Adams, 28 October 1813. Cited in Gerald N. Grob and Robert N. Beck, eds., *Ideas in America* (New York: Free Press, 1970), p. 120.
20. Ibid.
21. Letter to Benjamin Waterhouse, 26 June 1822. Cited in Frederick Mayer, *American Ideas and Education* (Columbus, Ohio: Merrill, 1964), p. 129.
22. Ibid.
23. Letter to Peter Carr, 19 August 1778. Cited in Robert M. Healy, *Jefferson on Religion in Public Education* (New Haven, Conn.: Yale U., 1962), p. 144.
24. Thomas Jefferson, *On the Objects of Primary Education*. Cited in Mayer, p. 133.
25. Merle E. Curti, *The Social Ideas of American Education* (Totowa, N.J.: Littlefield, Adams, 1954), p. 43.
26. Letter to David Williams, 14 November 1803. Cited in Healy, p. 145.
27. Clarence J. Karier, *Man, Society and Education* (Glenview, Ill.: Scott, Foresman, 1967), p. 46.
28. Somewhat different portraits of Emmons are painted by Ahlstrom, pp. 410-12, and Rousas J. Rushdoony, *The Messianic Character of American Education* (Nutley, N.J.: Craig, 1972), p. 19. Emmons served the rural pastorate for fifty-four years in Franklin, Massachusetts, where Mann was reared. Emmons wrote prolifically. "He chiefly extended and clarified the New England Theology" of Jonathan Edwards and trained eighty-seven students for the ministry. He took an extreme view of the "sole causality of God" (Ahlstrom). Rushdoony presents Emmons as a "kindly and genial man" and admits that his interpretation of Calvinism was "defective." But Rushdoony believes that "Mann's antagonism would have remained because he was a thorough believer in the doctrine of the 'perfectibility of man.'"
29. See Ahlstrom, pp. 401-2 and Rushdoony, pp. 19-20 for a helpful discussion of the Calvinism and unitarianism of that day. Neither form of these theologies, from a late eighteenth- and early nineteenth-century vantage point, coincides with our current understanding of the terms.
30. Gutek, p. 51.
31. Ibid., pp. 51-52.
32. Ibid., p. 54.
33. Horace Mann, *Life and Works*, 2:131; "Tenth Annual Report," 1846.
34. Ibid.
35. Mann, *Common School Journal*, 3:15, 1 January 1841 (introduction).
36. Mann, *Life and Works*, 3:466; "Eighth Annual Report," 1844. The messianic aspect was dominant.
37. Ibid., "Twelfth Annual Report," 1848.
38. Ibid.
39. Rushdoony, p. 31.
40. Gutek, p. 59.
41. Karier, p. 66.

14

Horace Bushnell and the Sunday School Movement

HORACE BUSHNELL AND RELIGIOUS EDUCATION

Horace Mann, "father of the American common school," and Horace Bushnell (1802-1875), "father of modern religious education," lived in New England during the same period. Both men struggled with the Calvinistic orthodoxy of New England and opposed its strong punishment for disobedience. However, while Mann disagreed with the Calvinistic position on the depravity of man, Bushnell did not.

> There are many who assume the radical goodness of human nature, and the work of Christian education is, in their view, only to educate and educe the good that is in us: Let no one be disturbed by the suspicion of a coincidence between what I have here said and such a theory. The natural depravity of man is plainly asserted in the Scriptures, and, if it were not, the familiar laws of physiology would require us to believe, what amounts to the same thing.[1]

Horace Bushnell was a Congregational pastor who served the North Church in Hartford, Connecticut. He was graduated from Yale College in 1827. In 1829 he returned to Yale to study law and to serve as a tutor at the college. As a result of the revival of 1831 at Yale, Bushnell dropped out of the law school and entered the theological school. Those studies concluded in 1833, and he was installed as the pastor of the North Church. This was to be his only pastorate, which he maintained until 1859 when he was forced to retire because of poor health.

The most well known of his many writings is the classic, *Christian Nurture*, which was published in its final form in 1861. This book was based on his two previous books: *Discourses on Christian Nurture* (April 1847), and *Views of Christian Nurture and Subjects Adjacent Thereto* (October 1847). The reason for this rather strange occurrence of events was that his ideas provoked a great deal of controversy among the theologians of his day. When the book was first published in 1847 by the Massachusetts Sabbath School Society, the ideas created such a stir that it was withdrawn from publication. Bushnell himself offered the second expanded edition of 1847 to defend his case and show that he was orthodox. The final edition of 1861 was published without much stir under the auspices of Charles Scribner and Sons of New York.

Bushnell's thesis was quite simple. He argued that "the child is to grow up a Christian and never know himself as being otherwise."[2] In other words, it was his desire to have Christian parents rear their children in such a way that the child could never remember having not been a Christian. He believed that from the child's earliest days, he should be taught to respond to God in faith and should love to do His will. As a result of this kind of training, Bushnell believed the child would therefore never have to experience a radical conversion of any kind. "The aim, effort, and expectation should be, not as is commonly assumed, that the child is to grow up in sin to be converted after he comes to a mature age; but that he is to open on the world as one that is spiritually renewed, not remembering the time when he went through a technical experience."[3]

The theological basis for Bushnell's reasoning was that he believed there was a "kind of organic connection" between the faith of the parents and their young child. He believed that "it is one of the grand distinctives of humanity that it has such a power to pass, and is set in such a duty of passing, its gifts, principles, and virtues, on the ages that come after."[4] Thus if a distinctive of humanity was to pass on to later generations its gifts, principles, and virtues, why not by the same process pass on its Christian faith?

The central idea of Bushnell's theory of Christian nurture was that the children of believers were to be considered as different from the children of unbelievers. The theological foundation offered for this concept was infant baptism. By this act Bushnell believed that children were being brought into the household of faith and, as baptized people, they should be treated and considered as different from children who were not baptized. He believed that Christian faith could be passed on to children as naturally and as easily as any other aspect of culture. But this process could only be achieved within the context of a truly Christian home.

Although his theory may not appear to be extremely radical today, when set in the theological climate of the early 1800s in New England, it was indeed quite radical. The predominant view of the day was revivalism. Based on a strong Calvinistic theology, the revivalists taught that a young child could not possibly be a Christian. Rather, the task of the parent was to teach his children that they could in no way please God. A young child was to be taught that he could not pray, that he could not read Scripture, and that he could not possibly please God in any way. This was based on the twofold understanding of (1) the seriousness of the depravity of man, and (2) the radical nature of the Christian faith. When a person was converted, he was to dedicate himself wholly to the Christian faith. Therefore, it was not believed that a child was capable of making such a Christian decision. The practical outcome of the foregoing beliefs was that parents were to teach their children that they were not Christians and that when they reached such an age as appropriate for deep conversion, they should then respond to Christ in faith. Prior to that time it was the parents' duty continually to point out the sinfulness of the child to him and to prepare him for conversion at a later date.

In reaction against those ideas, Bushnell suggested that the Christian parents should rear their children to be Christians from the earliest days. In effect, he was attempting by means of this theory of Christian nurture to prevent the necessity of a radical conversion later in life.

As might well be imagined, many theologians of his day were greatly disturbed by this theory. In the many published responses to his theory, the predominant complaint was that Bushnell did not believe in conversion. Also, he was soundly brought to task for presuming upon the sovereignty of God. The Calvinists argued that only God knew who the elect were and that it would be presumptuous of a Christian parent to assume that his child would be saved. In addition, Bushnell's teaching on infant baptism was vigorously attacked by Baptist theologians.

For Bushnell the foundation of his theory was the Christian life of the parents. He believed that the home could be the primary center for nurture and that God's grace could be communicated through the life of the parents. To the revivalists, the primary function of the parents was to teach their children regarding sin, whereas Bushnell contended that the parents should teach their children regarding faith. In effect, Bushnell wanted to make nurture a positive experience rather than a negative one.

The heart of the controversy surrounding Bushnell's theory was (and still remains) the nature of conversion. It is not accurate to charge that Bushnell did not believe in conversion. The issue is rather the kind of conversion that Bushnell was advocating. While the revivalists believed that conversion must be a crisis experience, Bushnell saw conversion to be much more a process experience. He stated:

> And this is the very idea of Christian education, that it begins with nurture or cultivation. And the intention is that the Christian life and spirit of the parents shall flow into the mind of the child, to blend with his incipient and half-formed exercises; that they shall thus beget their own good within him, their thoughts, opinion, faith and love, which are to become a little more, and yet a little more, his own separate exercise, but still the same in character.[5]

His desire was that parents would shape and form the minds of their children in such a way that faith and obedience to God was the natural outcome of their training.

Upon this theoretical basis Bushnell suggested some very practical guidelines for parents. He emphasized, for example, the idea of the parents' being a model to the children but cautioned the parents to be honest models. He advocated parents' admitting their own failures and shortcomings to their children so the child would not be discouraged by his own failures.

He also suggested that Bible stories, hymns, and theological lessons be reduced to language that was more appropriate to the age level of the child. He urged parents to listen to their children and to teach responsively to the interests and needs of their offspring. He envisioned Christian nurture as a natural and spontaneous kind of process, rather than a forced or negative experience for the child.

At times Bushnell suggested ideas that were years ahead of their time. He attempted to apply the rudimentary concept of heredity to Christian nuture by suggesting that there could actually be "ante-natal" nurture in which the parents would develop their own spiritual lives prior to the birth of children so that the child could actually be formed into some stage of faith prior to birth. He did not contend that this child would actually be a Christian, but he did believe that parents could and should prepare for their responsibility of nurture even prior to the birth of their children.

Bushnell wrote other theological works that cast serious doubts concerning his orthodoxy. Based on his unique view of the nature and function of language, and as a result of the strong influence of Coleridge's *Aids to Reflection,* Bushnell developed views regarding the idea of God in Christ and the sacrificial death of Christ that were deemed by orthodox contemporaries to be heretical. In *The Vicarious Sacrifice* (1866) he declared that Christ's atonement was a moral example or illustration of an eternal principle of love rather than a satisfaction by which God was reconciled to man. Because of such theological reasoning, he has been properly regarded as one of the fathers of American theological liberalism.

The effects of Bushnell's theory of Christian nurture cannot be over-emphasized. At the first meeting of the Religious Education Association in 1903, George Albert Coe, the leading theorist in liberal religious education circles during the first fifty years of the twentieth century, appealed to the writings of Horace Bushnell as the driving force behind that growing movement. Bushnell's theory that people could be educated into Christian faith with no need for conversion fit right in with modern religious education views.

His writings were not widely accepted while he was still living. But after his death, and on into the twentieth century, Horace Bushnell was and is considered one of the dominant forces in the development of Christian education as a separate discipline. Although his theological basis was questionable at best, his thesis that "a child should grow up a Christian" is still one of the most critical thoughts in the field of Christian education.

The theories of this intellectual giant "place Bushnell squarely at the head of the socialization approach to Christian formation."[6] He is the forerunner of George Albert Coe on the theological left, C. Ellis Nelson and John H. Westerhoff III in the middle, and Lawrence O. Richards on the right, in their emphasis on the socialization process. Interestingly, Bushnell influenced twentieth-century theoreticians more than nineteenth-century thinkers, as this comment by Lynn and Wright regarding the Sunday school indicates:

> Bushnell contributed little to the Sunday school movement in his day, 1802-1876, for his contention that children should be raised as if they had always been Christian flew in the face of Sunday school ideology in the mid-nineteenth century when youngsters were treated as "little adults needing conversion." By appealing

to Bushnell within a Sunday school context, religious educators gave their reforming ideas an undeserved appearance of maturity. They also created the impression, which too few historians have bothered to correct, that Bushnellian "Christian nurture" was an integral part of popular Protestant education.[7]

By the time of the founding of the Religious Education Association, there had developed, particularly among liberals, a curious blend of the methods of Pestalozzi and Froebel with John Dewey's social pragmatism, but the "classic expression of the movement's faith in the potency of education in the formation of Christian character" was Bushnell's *Christian Nurture*.[8] In reacting against the revivalism of his time, he may not have thought he was dismissing evangelicalism, but the theological and methodological stances he was taking were far more compatible with those on the left. They embraced him warmly as their champion. Some of his ideas, however, have become the property of all.

CIVIL WAR, RECONSTRUCTION, AND EDUCATION

On Palm Sunday, April 9, 1865, the Civil War guns became silent. Lee surrendered to Grant at Appomattox, and Jefferson Davis and his cabinet moved southward rapidly. On Good Friday, President Abraham Lincoln was shot and died the following day. Thoughtful people attempted to bring the nation to penitence, reformation, and only then to reconciliation. According to historian Sydney Ahlstrom, three of those who helped the nation in finding her way were Lincoln, whose Gettysburg Address and Second Inaugural Address were "supreme statements on the meaning of war"; the brilliant German-born church historian, Philip Schaff, who "interpreted the war in a larger sense as having readied America for its great role in the cause of human freedom"; and Horace Bushnell, who wrote his "*The Vicarious Sacrifice* as the nation bled on the battlefield" and who "dared to think that the war could be good in some way akin to the way in which Good Friday was good."[9]

Between the Civil War and the First World War the major period of development for the modern American school system occurred. But we need to step back to mention several events and legislative decisions that set the stage.

In 1812 New York state established the office of state superintendent of schools. Massachusetts created a state board of education with Horace Mann as secretary in 1837, and Connecticut had done the same in 1839 with Henry Barnard as secretary. Massachusetts passed a compulsory school attendance law in 1852 that other states began to follow.

Yet with all of this legislation a most basic problem lingered. The young nation could not and did not desire to deny its rich religious heritage. But what should be done about religious instruction being given in the public schools? The common schools attempted to find a universal religious outlook in the doctrines of Christianity. The Protestants felt that all sects would be satisfied. However, the country was becoming more diverse religiously, and understandably the Roman Catholics and Jews were having none of this so-called nonsectarian approach to religion. The Catholics launched their own school system and demanded a share in public tax funds, but most Protestants and Jews resisted the giving of public funds to parochial schools. The result was that many states prohibited any sectarian control over common schools and refused public money for private schools under sectarian control. "By the end of the first century of republican education, the general decision was that a free society was better served if the majority of children went to common, nonsectarian schools than if they went to separate, sectarian religious schools. This made it possible for the United States to build a system of free elementary schools sooner than any other country in the world."[10]

Abraham Lincoln's Emancipation Proclamation was officially issued on January 1, 1863, but the abolition of slavery did not become law until the passage of the Thirteenth Amendment, December 18, 1865. Congress established the Freedman's Bureau to try to begin making reparation to American blacks for 250 years of enslavement. In 1868 the Fourteenth Amendment was added to protect life, liberty, and property. The Fifteenth Amendment in 1870 was to guarantee civil rights. These were spelled out in greater detail in The Civil Rights Act of 1875. In actuality, integrated schools were few in number. Some efforts to integrate were made based on religious, philanthropic, and humanitarian motives. The American Missionary Society had a commitment to minister to nonwhites and at the end of the war had 528 missionaries and teachers at work in the South. "One of the noblest and least recognized chapters in Reconstruction history was written by these poorly paid educators, most of them women, as they struggled amid penury, ridicule, hostility, and sometimes outright violence to demonstrate their faith in the nation's ideals and in the Negro's natural capacity to enter fully into American life."[11] The reunion efforts of the Episcopal and the Roman Catholic churches were successful, but the other mainline denominations were less effective. The South went its own way religiously, and the rise of independent black churches, some with denominational names, gradually developed the "distinctive religious ethos which traditional denominational allegiances could neither submerge nor alter. Through a long and bitter century they became the chief bearers of the Afro-American heritage."[12]

The secondary and higher education scene was only slightly different. In 1819 the New Hampshire legislature ventured to transform Dartmouth College into a state university. The United States Supreme Court determined that the school was a private corporation and that its charter was a binding contract that the state could not alter unless "the funds of the college be public property." This decision protected the existence of the independent, privately controlled college. The number of private colleges immediately increased, most of them sponsored by Christian denominations. The advocates of public higher education intensified their efforts as well, so that by the Civil War twenty states had established universities. The earliest institutions under state control were in Georgia, North Carolina, and Vermont. They did not provide free tuition, and blacks were not permitted to attend.

Federal land grants authorized by the Morrill Act in 1862 accelerated the growth of state colleges and universities that were established specifically to further agricultural and industrial studies. The common schools were for everyone, but the academies, colleges, and universities primarily served the upper social classes. There were three goals of the Morrill Act: (1) to protect against the domination of the classics in higher education; (2) to develop practical instruction at the college level; and (3) to provide vocational training for the agricultural and industrial classes.

A central principle of education after the Civil War was that public education should be available to all. Repudiating the European dual system in which elementary education was for the common folk and secondary education was for the elite, the United States built a ladder system in which each person was free to begin at the lowest rung and advance on the basis of one's abilities. The financing of schools was the key issue in the implementation and functioning of the ladder system. In a suit brought by three taxpayers in Kalamazoo, Michigan in 1874, the state supreme court ruled that taxes could be collected to support public high schools. It was based on the obligation of the state not only to provide but also to maintain equal education for all. Because the state supported public elementary schools and colleges, it was determined that the middle rungs of the ladder ought to be put in place.

Christian Education Agencies

The 1828 presidential campaign between John Quincy Adams and Andrew Jackson was one of the bitterest in American history. When Jackson won, Adams refused to remain in Washington for the inauguration. Jackson's supporters left the White House in shambles following the inauguration, and he introduced the spoils system into national politics. Although the "mob rule" aspect has been overplayed, the common people were given greater opportunity for leadership under Jackson. The aristocrats were concerned as Jackson's star began to rise in the West. The Sunday school movement was reaching full stride and touching the lives of people in the growing rural West and the burgeoning urban areas. Some politicians saw the potential of the Sunday schools as a force for good. Men such as Theodore Freling-huysen, US senator from New Jersey, attempted to use this vital agency of evangelism and edification, and on occasion they were successful. The American Sunday School Union (now American Missionary Fellowship) was founded in 1824 (see Chapter 11). The Union expanded its ministry by the end of 1825 to twenty-two of the twenty-four states.[13] Where public schools had not been established, the Sunday school retained its "Raikes Approach" and taught reading and recitation. As late as 1858 the ASSU sold "hundreds of thousands" of its Spelling-Books. Their missionaries were often on the move because of the directives coming out of the headquarters in Philadelphia. They would leave "Sunday School Libraries" with the people they had taught. By 1959 there were 50,000 libraries in the country, and "30,000 of them were in Sunday schools, 18,000 in other schools and nearly 3,000 in city and town collections. That the Sunday school libraries were considered *public* is significant."[14] In many areas they were the only source of books available. A library was the mark of a bona fide Sunday school. The Union began to fill the void of juvenile literature and establish high character standards for itself.

After the Civil War, the Sunday School Union placed many of its missionaries in rural areas, whereas mainline denominations followed their migrating middle class constituencies. By the close of the century, ASSU forces were almost totally in rural ministry. Only in the last ten years has the American Missionary Fellowship deployed some of its forces to inner city and minority group ministry.

SUNDAY SCHOOL CONVENTIONS

Though conferences and conventions were held before 1820, the first convention at which a variety of groups and societies gathered was in Philadelphia in 1824 (when the American Sunday School Union was born). Stephen Paxson, one of the great heroes of Sunday school missionary work, succeeded in founding hundreds of schools and organizing associations. County, state, national, and even international conclaves began to emerge.

The Sunday school movement experienced still another surge forward following the Civil War. "The transformation of the Sunday school into the worldwide work of evangelical Protestantism was quite deliberately and thoroughly the work of an energetic group of men—the 'Illinois Band.' "[15] Dwight L. Moody was in the middle of the expansion. In June of 1865 Moody and William Reynolds of Peoria held an evangelistic crusade prior to the Illinois state Sunday school convention. A revival broke out, and the new impetus spilled over into conventions across North America. Joining Moody and Reynolds in the "Illinois Band" were Benjamin F. Jacobs, an affluent businessman; Edward Eggelston, an editor and later author of *The Hoosier Schoolmaster*; and John H. Vincent, a young Methodist pastor. Jacobs and Vincent were exceptionally gifted in organizational ability and were later joined by eastern entrepreneurs, H. J. Heinz and John Wanamaker. Their leadership skills were felt for the next twenty-five years.

At the Fifth National Convention in Indianapolis in 1872 a significant action was taken. A uniform lesson plan was devised, whereby the same lesson, departmentally graded, would be taught in all the participating churches on a given Sunday. "The plan encouraged interdenominational teachers' meetings, the expansion of supporting publications, and the foundation of teachers' institutes all across the country modeled on the Moody

Bible Institute of Chicago (1886)."[16] By 1900 three million English pupils and teachers were using them. The materials were utilized wherever British and American missionaries were working (e.g., India, Australia, Japan, New Zealand, and China). Uniform lessons were translated into more than forty languages.

Sydney Ahlstrom summarizes the position of the Sunday school during the fourth quarter of the nineteenth century:

> Revivals and revivalists would come and go, but the Sunday schools remained as a stabilizing force in the churches. In small towns and large cities they attracted dedicated lay leaders of great ability, helping to set the tone and temper of American Protestantism and providing an effective means of reaching the unchurched and unaffiliated—adults as well as children. Although they necessarily mirrored the country's values, the Sunday schools did produce a pious and knowledgeable laity on a scale unequaled anywhere in Christendom.[17]

For over one hundred years the Sunday school was the dominant and, exclusive of the home, almost the sole agency of Christian education of Protestant children and youth. The Presbyterian church failed in an attempt to establish parochial schools. The Reformed groups did succeed and continue to expand to the present. The Roman Catholic school movement began in Philadelphia in 1782 and has ebbed and flowed on the waves of immigrants coming to North America.[18]

EARLY PARA-CHURCH GROUPS AND BIBLE SCHOOLS

In the area of youth work, the Young Men's Christian Association (YMCA) was the pioneer. It began in England in 1844 and was introduced in America in 1851. The YWCA (Young Women's Christian Association) also was initiated in London and arrived in America in 1858. The early history of the YMCA was marked by aggressive evangelism and a solid Bible-study approach. Evangelical people such as D. L. Moody "received training as an evangelist and administrator in this movement."[19] Its fervor began to fade even in Moody's lifetime.

The United Society of Christian Endeavor commenced in 1881 under the leadership of Francis E. Clark in Portland, Maine. This nondenominational organization retained its zest for many decades. Often when denominational efforts spring up, transdenominational movements tend to institutionalize and die. However, American evangelicalism has spawned a number of para-church (alongside the church) organizations since 1940 that have remained fresh and forward thinking and often have set the pace for the churches.

In 1880 a Rhode Island church engaged in camping and began an important chapter in Christian education. The historical data base for this agency is a bit scanty.[20] Possibly it may be traced through the camp meeting movement that had its roots in Kentucky in 1799-1800. John H. Vincent founded Chautauqua (New York) as a "national Sunday school university" that served as a normal school or training program for lay teachers of the Bible. It also provided motivation for church camping.

Other agencies such as vacation Bible school and club programs for children and youth developed in the twentieth century, which moves them beyond the scope of this chapter.

Nineteenth-century Christian education reflected the pioneering that marked the progress of secular education. The spiritual awakenings opened fresh vistas for the teaching of the Bible and further evangelistic ministry. The Sunday school was a flexible, mobile medium with no traditions. It was a complementary vehicle for the revivalism of this period. "Revivalism and the Sunday school had much in common. They tended to read the future in the same stripped-down either/or fashion. They grew simultaneously, shared enemies, and embraced religion as an affair of the heart. . . .The involvement of the heart, especially in conversion, was essential to evangelicals.[21]

In the last third of the century progressive education received its first impetus. By 1900 John Dewey and George Albert Coe had vaulted to the forefront on the secular and religious education scenes. Their monumental influence remains to the present.

NOTES

1. Horace Bushnell, *Christian Nurture* (1861; reprint ed., Grand Rapids: Baker, 1979), p. 22.
2. Ibid., p. 10.
3. Ibid.
4. Ibid., p. 56.
5. Ibid., p. 30.
6. Thomas H. Groome, *Christian Religious Education* (New York: Harper & Row, 1980), p. 117.
7. Robert W. Lynn and Elliott Wright, *The Big Little School*, rev. ed. (Birmingham, Ala.: Relig. Educ. Press, 1980), pp. 121-22. According to Lynn's *Protestant Strategies in Education* (New York: Association, 1964), pp. 22-24, the Sunday school and the Second Great Awakening were so powerful that his emphasis on the home as the primary agency of Christian education received little attention.
8. Sydney E. Ahlstrom, *A Religious History of the American People* (New Haven, Conn.: Yale U., 1972), p. 781.

9. Ibid., p. 686.
10. R. Freeman Butts, "Search for Freedom: The Story of American Education," in Allan C. Ornstein and W. Eugene Hedley, eds., *Educational Foundations: Ideas and Issues* (Columbus, Ohio: Merrill, 1973), p. 86.
11. Ahlstrom, pp. 694-95.
12. Ibid., pp. 696-97.
13. C. B. Eavey, *History of Christian Education* (Chicago: Moody, 1964), p. 243. Lynn and Wright's *The Big Little School* and this volume provide extremely different perspectives of the Sunday school. Lynn and Wright's approach is from the sociological and political as well as the historical. Eavey gives the Sunday school history (chaps. 8-10) from the evangelical viewpoint with copious detail. For a balanced view, both sources should be used.
14. Lynn and Wright, p. 55.
15. Ibid., p. 90.
16. Ahlstrom, pp. 741-42.
17. Ibid., p. 742.
18. See Glen Gabert, *In Hoc Signo?: A Brief History of Catholic Parochial Education in America* (Port Washington, N.Y.: Kennikat, 1973).
19. Clifford V. Anderson, "Christian Education in Historical Perspective," in Werner C. Graendorf, ed., *Introduction to Biblical Christian Education* (Chicago: Moody, 1981), p. 48.
20. See Clifford V. Anderson, "Camping History," in Werner C. Graendorf and Lloyd D. Mattson, eds., *An Introduction to Christian Camping* (Chicago: Moody, 1979).
21. Lynn and Wright, p. 77.

15

Education American Style: John Dewey and George Albert Coe

In 1859 a mantle was transferred in New England. Horace Mann died in Massachusetts, and John Dewey was born in Vermont. It is very possible that those two men have been the most influential educational leaders in America from the day the Pilgrims first rowed ashore to the present hour.

American education is essentially the product of John Dewey's craftsmanship, but Dewey himself was influenced by forces before and during his time. For example, William James, psychologist and philosopher in New York City in 1842, is generally thought of as the originator of the philosophy of pragmatism. Dewey was thirty-one years old when James published *Principles of Psychology,* a two-volume work that linked the twin ideas of *pragmatism* and radical *empiricism.* Edward J. Power suggests, however, that pragmatism has an ancient philosophical history.

> The entire history of Pragmatism, beginning with Heraclitus and the Sophists, could be recited as having influenced Dewey, although one would hesitate to name the most critical elements in it. No one, and surely no philosopher, is immune to his philosophical past or the intellectual heritage of the race; on the other hand, it is unreasonable to suppose that every philosopher must in some way perpetuate in his own thinking the doctrines of the past. It was possible for Dewey to be keenly aware of the pragmatic tradition, diffused as it was, and not to follow it slavishly.[1]

James "improved upon" the relativism of Charles Sanders Peirce, arguing that values arise in the context of human experience, representing temperamental differences, and are therefore dependent on the way we feel and act at a given time. Absolute values for James represented a state of philosophical smugness and complacency. It might be noted that both Peirce and James stood in opposition to Harvard professor Josiah Royce, an exponent of absolute idealism and essentially a Hegelian.

The reader may wonder why the authors commit so much space to secular philosophers. Essentially there are two reasons: First of all, it is totally impossible for Christian educational philosophy to separate itself from the surrounding influences no matter how semireligious, secular, or pagan they might be. Second, most educational philosophers are espousing a theological base even if they do not admit it.

James did espouse a theological base and was very interested in religion, applying the philosophical ideas of pragmatism to religion in two separate books, *The Varieties of Religious Experience* and *The Will to Believe*. Of course for James there were no fixed theological values and he was therefore unconcerned with such matters as sin, salvation, the Trinity, eternal life, and the authority of the Bible. Religion aided education empirically because man was a creature guided by faith and sustained by hope. Though William James did not believe in an absolute God, he did believe in a God who gave man emotional sustenance in periods of chaos.

American education in the late nineteenth century was also strongly influenced by its European cousins whose views we have discussed in previous chapters. The fingerprints of Pestalozzi, Herbart, Froebel, and Rousseau are found again and again on the work of Dewey.

JOHN DEWEY AND PRAGMATISM

Like William James, John Dewey began with a theistic commitment. He earned his Ph.D. at Johns Hopkins University in 1884 and was influenced there by George Sylvester Morris, an idealist. J. Donald Butler suggests that after Dewey went to the University of Michigan, the changeover from idealism to instrumentalism (pragmatism) took place rather quickly, and was probably complete by 1892.[2]

The rejection of a "universal self" was based on Dewey's commitment to both behaviorism and Darwinian evolution. For him individuality was to be explained by the person's role in the physical-social phenomena surrounding him, without any connection with or interference from a supreme being. By the time Dewey reached the University of Chicago in 1894 he had the groundwork for godless pragmatism well laid out.

Cyril D. Garrett refers to John L. Childs (next to William H. Kilpatrick and Boyd H. Bode, perhaps the most authoritative exponent of pragmatism in the twentieth century) to explain the role of evolution in Dewey's educational philosophy.

> 1. It provides the theoretical structure for a universe with the "lid off," where everything is "ever-becoming" and undetermined. Instead of a system of status, fixed relationships, there is a change, novelty, and precariousness.
> 2. It brings man and all his cultural achievements within the natural process of development. Man is continuous with nature, not separate from it.
> 3. It permits a way of explaining the development of certain characteristics peculiar to man, i.e., mind, intelligence, selfhood, language, development of tools, without resorting to mind-body dualisms or matter-spirit dualisms.[3]

The very title of Garrett's article, "Democracy—The Religion of Dewey's Pragmatism," hints at the emphasis Dewey placed on the marriage of the American political system with its educational system, a view in which he was doubtless greatly influenced by Thomas Jefferson. The great pragmatist was primarily an educator and not a philosopher, though his confrontation with the Aristotelian realism of Frederick J. E. Woodbridge at Columbia University (where he spent most of his years, beginning in 1904) compelled him to face problems of metaphysics that had not troubled him in his days at Michigan and Chicago.

As in all aspects of education, Dewey's philosophy was concerned primarily with the activity of experiencing. The scientific method was to be carried over from the laboratory into the schoolroom and the philosophy library. Philosophy, therefore, becomes a tool of clarification used to give meaning to the activities of human existence. In *Democracy and Education*, Dewey devoted one of his chapters to "Philosophy of Education."

> Philosophy is thinking what the known demands of us—what responsive attitude it exacts. It is an idea of what is possible, not a record of accomplished fact. Hence it is hypothetical, like all thinking. It presents an assignment of something to be done—something to be tried. Its value lies not in furnishing solutions (which can be achieved only in action) but in defining difficulties and suggesting methods for dealing with them. Philosophy might almost be described as thinking which has become conscious of itself—which has generalized its place, function, and value in experience.[4]

METAPHYSICS

Dewey took violent exception with the many philosophers through history who had argued that both education and philosophy were inseparably related to metaphysical ideals. Being primarily a naturalist, he cared little for religious prejudice, which he believed was the molding factor of most metaphysics. We cannot look beyond our world for what is real but rather must confine ourselves to an understanding of reality in nature itself. Dewey believed that natural science is forced by its own development to abandon the assumption of fixity and to recognize that for it, process is the great universal. In this approach to metaphysics, Dewey's empiricism is even more radical than that of James.

In keeping with his Hegelian background, Dewey was in his early years concerned with metaphysics. But even then the relationship between the material universe and the nature of ultimate reality were apparent in his thinking. The title of one of his first publications, for example, was *The Metaphysical Assumptions of Materialism*. What Dewey failed to acknowledge in his later years was that metaphysics is inseparably connected with educational theory. One cannot begin to define the purpose of education unless one understands what about the universe is actually real and how reality affects the meaning of existence. Dewey's extreme relativism and preoccupation with change forced him to take an inadequate view of the importance of metaphysics.

In strict rejection of any kind of supernaturalism, Dewey rests man's purpose and possibility of survival upon his relationship to nature. In *Democracy and Education*, he wrote, "Man's power of deliberate control of his own affairs depends upon ability to direct natural energies to use: an ability which is in turn dependent upon insight into Nature's processes."[5] Dewey was quite confident that through the proper use of intelligence and scientific processes, man would do away with disease, poverty, and evils that we once thought inevitable. This concept of man in relation to the material world can only be described as naturalistic humanism.

EPISTEMOLOGY

In keeping with his emphasis on the process of change as inevitable, Dewey's concept of truth was extremely relativistic. An idea or a concept is not true because it properly discloses reality but because it happens to serve in a utilitarian way to enable the organism to adjust to its natural environment. The truth accumulated by previous generations is not a valid guide to contemporary life because of the phenomenal changes that have taken place between then and now. One wonders, therefore, what Dewey meant when he said, "Aristotle was certainly permanently right," when he uses that philosopher's concept of the separation between culture and utility to substantiate his own ideas on that subject. One also wonders if pragmatism itself can ever be considered true, because as Arthur W. Munk points out, "It does not work for nonpragmatists."[6]

Gordon Clark (to whom we are largely indebted for our understanding of Dewey) notes one of Dewey's favorite contrasts, that between certainty and security. Traditionally, says Dewey, men have always desired certainty. Plato's philosophy is a classic example of a quest for absolutes in the universe. Because modern science has shown us, however, that those cannot be had, we must concern ourselves with something that, in the final analysis, is really better — security. Science, for example, is not a discoverer of truth but rather a producer of truth. H_2O is not water, but rather describes a plan of action by which we utilize water for satisfactory purposes.

The value of science to produce usable items is not for one moment questioned by any intelligent person, but Clark puts his finger on the weakness of Dewey's view of science when he says: "It furnishes means to whatever a man may choose. But can it furnish any reason for choosing this [value] in preference to that?"[7] But this leads us to our next consideration.

AXIOLOGY

Like truth, value was also a relative item to Dewey. His classic expression of the instrumental concept of values is in a chapter in *Democracy and Education* entitled "Educational Values." In capsule, Dewey argued that every adult has acquired certain measures of the worth of different kinds of experience and has a tendency to pass those on to children. The danger involved here is that "standards so taught will be merely symbolic."[8] The norm of value then is an individual's own experience rather than some distinction placed upon an item by parents, teachers, or society in general. Dewey's conclusion was that there are no degrees of value and that we cannot put any particular order to values.

Dewey saw two possible meanings in the word *value*. One had to do with the attitude of finding something worthwhile (a completed experience), and the other centered on the operation of comparing and judging to discover worth (experience in action). But how are we to decide, when we are in the process of experiencing, whether a given experience or thought is indeed of worth? Dewey's answer was that "the formation of proper standards on any subject depends upon a realization of the contribution which it makes to the immediate significance of experience, upon a direct appreciation." And again: "Contribution to immediate intrinsic values in all their variety and experience is the only criterion for determining the worth of instrumental and derived values in studies."[9]

Dewey was concerned how contemporary philosophy could integrate some system of values without regressing to the antiquated theory of an axiology based on metaphysical absolutes. The obvious answer, as Clark points out, was to be found "in a more thorough exploitation of scientific method." Two problems, however, faced Dewey at this point. First of all, there were some who could not really believe that experience was a dependable architect for standards and norms of life. Such an attitude depends on external values and appeals to the supreme being. A second problem was that some could not divorce themselves from some kind of pleasures, goods, or values irrespective of the method used to produce that enjoyment.[10] The method, of course, for Dewey was all important, and value could not be recognized apart from method. No value is intrinsic in itself. Value, particularly moral value, is whatever enhances satisfactory experience.

ANTHROPOLOGY

Since there is no God, man is dependent upon himself and his own methods to achieve whatever needs achieving in this universe. Man's mind, like everything else that has life, is a part of evolutionary development. In considering the nature of man, Dewey was neither a pessimist nor an optimist, but rather a meliorist (one who believes the world, with man's help, will tend to become better). Of course, this is a strategic point in relation to educational practice; for it makes all the difference in the world whether the student we educate is good, bad, or neutral in his basic moral nature. Dewey would prefer the latter.

Man, therefore, becomes a product of his environment. Dewey would not hesitate for one moment to say: "The mind of savage people is an effect, rather than a cause of their backward institutions. Their social activities are such as to restrict their objects of attention and interest, and hence to limit the stimuli to mental development."[11] A civilization progresses not because it has learned by revelation or even by reason anything about "the good life," but rather because it has learned to control the natural forces of its environment. The lesser that control, the more savage the civilization. The greater the control, the more superior the civilization. Here again is an example of Dewey's "absolute naturalism."

LOGIC

Dewey felt a compulsion to take logic out of the realm of the transcendental and move it into the realm of the experimental. He opposed the dualistic basis for logic that philosophers before him had held. For Dewey, the world was one and did not include an inner world of conception and an outer world of observation. Melvin C. Baker has stated: "Dewey's logic points to the development of thought through the process of experiencing in problem-solving situations encompassing the typical interests of man."[12]

Clark develops his study of Dewey's logic by pointing up a contrast between Dewey and Aristotle. The latter based his logic on an ontological foundation. To this Dewey objected vehemently. Since there is no antecedent knowledge, logic could not have its basis upon being. No principle of logic is absolute. All principles are subject to change. In rejecting Aristotle's subalternation, Dewey also rejected the law of noncontradiction, according to Clark. Clark says further: "Universal flux is the warp and waft of his philosophy. Dewey is a philosopher of change and flux. Nothing can be admitted as stable and eternal. To allow even one eternal fixity, the law of contradiction, would in strongest repugnance to his deepest esthetic nature utterly confuse the fluctuating design of his art."[13]

Rejection of the law of contradiction allows terms to have multiple significance even to an infinite number of meanings. *Zero* might mean zero or one. *Green* might mean sky, and *table* might mean the European Common Market. Dewey based his logic on science rather than his science on logic, and it is that flaw, according to Clark, upon which the entire system crumbles.

In the musical play of Rogers and Hammerstein, "The King and I," the King of Siam contemplates the difficulties of ruling a modern nation. "He complained that when he was a boy, 'what was so was so, what was not was not.' But now that he is a man, he says, 'some things were nearly so, others nearly not.' And in his head were many facts of which he wished he were more certain he was sure!"[14] This illustration used by Lawrence C. Little to describe educational theory in general can be applied with specific force to Dewey's philosophical thought.

In *A Layman's Guide to Educational Theory,* Charles W. Coulter and Richard S. Rimanoczy quote from an article by Boyd appearing in the *New Republic* in 1949: "It is conceded on all hands that John Dewey is our outstanding educational philosopher; his influence on American education has been immense. One reason for this is that his philosophy has not been very clearly understood. If it had been, the enthusiasm for his teaching would doubtless have been tempered more extensively by fear, or at any rate, by misgivings."[15]

One obvious thing about Dewey's philosophy is that he subjected every aspect of philosophical thought to the supremacy of science. Apparently he did not believe Arnold Toynbee's caveat that the great issues of life are those on which science has nothing to say. Dewey may have swept the educational house clean of the demons of ecclesiastical and pedagogical authoritarianism, but evangelicals cannot accept the authority of pupil experience and change that he substituted in place of those other things.

OBJECTIVES OF EDUCATION

Some have accused Dewey of having no aims in education. In a sense that is valid, but in another sense it is not. Whether he ever achieved satisfactory aims may be questioned, but certainly he gave a great deal of consideration to the importance of aim. Aim, for Dewey, "implies an orderly and ordered activity, one in which the order consists in the progressive completing of a process."[16] Aim in education must allow a "foresight of results" and must also allow a participation of the learner in the setting up of desirable aims.

What would Dewey consider as some legitimate objectives of education?

Self-control. In *Experience and Education,* Dewey wrote clearly and simply, "The ideal aim of education is creation of power of self-control."[17] He criticized some progressive educators for trying to achieve self-control merely by removing external control. When the learner understands the significance of his experiences, then he can intelligently control himself within his environment.

Proper recognition of leisure. Dewey was disturbed by the Aristotelian concept of the relationship between leisure and contemplation. He recognized, however, that it came out of dualistic society. In a democracy, Dewey argued, that dualism must be swept away, and education must be made the practice of all people, thereby making leisure "a reward for accepting responsibility for service, rather than a statement of exemption from it."[18]

Social efficiency. We have already seen that Dewey was absolutely steeped in a concept of the relevance of society. Social efficiency, for Dewey, meant the ability of the educated person to join freely in community activities. Such communal activity actually expands the culture of the individual, because culture is really one's capacity for enlarging one's perception of meanings.

Love of learning. One of Dewey's primary arguments with the traditional school system was that knowledge was forced upon children to such an extent that they came to identify school and learning with unpleasantness. Dewey argued that the knowledge is not as important as the satisfaction of the experience in obtaining it.

Continuing experience. Dewey said "The central problem of an education based upon experience is to select the kind of present experiences that live fruitfully and creatively in subsequent experiences."[19] In other words, we must carefully provide experiences that will not only of themselves produce something by way of truth and virtue but will also contain seeds of future experiences that will be likewise productive.

For Dewey, the goal of life was full development of the individual's intellectual, moral, and aesthetic capacities. That was impossible in a vacuum, for man is a social animal and only achieves his individuality and the aspects of that individuality through social relationships.

PROCESS OF LEARNING

It is at this point that Dewey made his most significant contribution to educational philosophy. Here again he begins with the environment as the sum total of conditions surrounding the learner. To that setting he brought such concepts as dependence upon interaction, activity on the part of the pupil, interest in the things that are being learned, discussion between teacher and pupil, the experimental method in seeking truth, the dynamic of the thinking process, and absolute social involvement with other persons who make up the society—either total or in the specific terms of the classroom.

All those things produce a spirit of inquiry, and learning takes place like growth. Such learning must imply change because it must affect the character of the learner. Problem-solving is basic in Dewey's system, and each problem serves as a catalyst to produce thinking. Mayer summarizes well the five steps in Dewey's concept of thinking: "(1) A felt need, (2) analysis of the difficulty, (3) alternative solutions are proposed, (4) experimentation with various solutions until one passes the mental test, (5) action is the final test for the proposed solution which is to be verified in a scientific manner."[20] No competent educator can quarrel with Dewey's explanation of how learning takes place, though some might disagree with the conclusion that that is the *only* way it takes place.

PLACE OF THE PUPIL IN EDUCATION

Because a school is simply a miniature society, democracy must prevail in the classroom just as it does in the state. This implies freedom for the learner, though not an uncontrolled freedom as some have accused Dewey of advocating. Against the passivity and receptivity of traditional education, Dewey advocated an active part to be played by the pupil in his own learning process. Outward freedom in terms of class discipline and more physical activity certainly is of value, but its purpose is really to lead to inner freedom. Dewey was very clear on this point when he said: "Freedom and restriction, the negative side, is to be prized only as a means to a freedom which is power: power to frame purposes, to judge wisely, to evaluate desires by the consequences which will result from acting upon them; power to select and order means to carry those ends into operation."[21]

In reaction to content-centered curriculum, Dewey posited a child-centered curriculum. He argued that the child and the curriculum really are two limits in the same process. We begin with the child and from his experience we develop the learning process, rather than superimposing what we believe is important upon the child's experience. In *The Child and the Curriculum*, Dewey wrote: "It is continuous reconstruction, moving from the child's present experience out into that represented by the organized bodies of truth that we call studies."[22] The five-step process indicated by Mayer above has to do with the method of learning. The important emphasis here is that it begins with the pupil's recognition of a problem within the framework of his own experience.

ROLE OF THE TEACHER IN EDUCATION

For Dewey the teacher exists largely as a framer of the environment in which learning takes place. Some have argued that this is far too small a role for the teacher to play in education, but one must remember that in Dewey's system the framing of the environment is extremely important. Dewey's teacher is a guide who directs the impulses and interests of the child to some specific process. This is in opposition to the concept of the teacher as one who indoctrinates the pupil with a predetermined body of truth.

What of the authority of the teacher? In Dewey's ideal school the control of the class would result not from the external pressures of a person in charge but from the general interest and involvement of the pupils in their learning experience. The good teacher, he would say, "reduces to a minimum the occasions in which he or she has to exercise authority in a personal way. When it is necessary, in the second place, to speak and act firmly, it is done in behalf of the interest of the group not as an exhibition of personal power."[23]

The training and maturity that should be characteristic of a teacher are of no value in a democratic classroom unless they can be utilized to provide conditions that are conducive to the community activity. The organization of learning experiences itself provides the control in the classroom. Because education takes place through social interaction, the teacher, as the most mature member of the social group called the class, has the responsibility for directing the intercommunications of that social group. The teacher is not outside the group but a part of it and functions in the role of a group leader, according to the concepts of emergent leadership that are currently in vogue.

NATURE OF THE CURRICULUM

Curriculum revolves around the child. In "My Pedagogic Creed," Dewey was very explicit about the subject matter of education. He opposed an introduction of the child to special studies such as reading, writing, geography, and mathematics that may be out of relationship with his social experience at any given age. Therefore, for Dewey, "the true center of correlation on the school subjects is not science, nor literature, nor history, nor geography, but the child's own social activities."[24] Of course, Dewey rejected any concept of core curriculum and any succession of studies to form a set curriculum. The progress of curriculum for him was not in the succession of studies but in the development of experience.

Method and content are really inseparable in Dewey's educational system because method is merely "a statement of the way the subject matter of an experience develops most effectively and fruitfully." Also, because there is no real separation between nature and humanity, a study of nature is in itself the educational experience of human progress and well-being. History, geography, science, literature, and vocational education all have a part in Dewey's curriculum just as long as the educator does not view any one of them or any combination of them as absolutely essential or primary to the educational process. Hence it is never the subject per se that is educative, but rather the stage of growth, which is the experience of the learner when he comes into relationship with the subject.

Because there is nothing absolute or eternal, does Dewey's system put any kind of emphasis on the learning of the past? It does, because his conclusion was that the present cannot be cut off from the past. However, there is no real innate value in the past, but rather in the information it can provide for understanding the present. As experience expands in the future it also enlarges to take in the past.

How much of Dewey's educational philosophy can the evangelical educator conscientiously adopt? That there are theological perversions in Dewey, no Christian can deny. That the excesses of progressivism were made flagrant by some of Dewey's disciples is also another generally known fact. That Dewey's influence has extended itself throughout all of American education, even though progressivism as a movement died some years ago, must be recognized by anyone who is cognizant of the total scene today. For example, Dewey is alive again in Jerome Bruner—in the latter's emphasis on learning by doing, rejection of competition and grading, and encouragement of creative thinking.

Is it legitimate to separate Dewey's educational theory from his philosophy? In philosophy Dewey was an avowed naturalist who for all practical purposes classified man with the animals. He rejected absolute truth and values, and he argued that such things as virtue can be discovered only through scientific experimentation. He had an inadequate view of metaphysics and allowed for no supernaturalism in the universe. His concept of the nature of man was opposed to the biblical doctrine of original sin. All of the above are totally alien to biblical Christianity; and as a philosophy, Dewey's work can never be acceptable to evangelical educators.

It is our contention, however, that the very processes of education described and carried out by Dewey are the processes that are effectively being used today, not only in secular education but in Christian education as well. Group dynamics, creative thinking, controlled environment, activity of the pupil, motivation through interest, and social relevance are proclaimed in every pedagogical textbook of any worth published in the last twenty-five years. The intelligent approach to Dewey then, it would seem, would have to be one that excludes his godless philosophy and adapts his practical methodology. Clark concludes that Dewey's philosophy, particularly in logic, is nonsense, and perhaps it is that very inconsistency of logic that allows us to utilize Dewey's gift to education without imbibing his philosophy; in other words to be *progressive* without being *progressivists*.

The weaknesses in Dewey have been pointed out, but perhaps a brief review is appropriate in closing. Instrumentalism as a philosophy leads to a strengthening of secularism, a worship of science, a belief in the inherent goodness of man, the rejection of absolutes and fixed truth, no genuine goals for education outside of the individual and his society, and rather sinister political implications, as Clark has pointed out.[25] On the other hand, the values of Dewey's instrumentalism as a pedagogical methodology are its emphasis on relevance, a practical and expansive view of curriculum, pupil activity and participation in the learning process, problem-solving techniques, interest and dialogue in the learning process, an attempt at emphasis on democracy in education, concern for the child as an individual, and an emphasis on creativity.

The inherent tendency of progressivism is to go too far, and it is that very danger that evangelicals must avoid in an adaptation of Dewey. For example, a relaxation of authoritarian attitudes in the classroom certainly is important, but that dare not restrict us from communicating the absolute authority of God, which we know to be truth. Freedom of the pupil is also a desirable aspect of methodology in education, but we dare not let the pupil think of himself as not under subjection to the laws of man as well as the laws of God. If the excesses can be avoided, Christian eduation can make valid use of Dewey's principles in the learning process. We have eternal truths that are unchangeable, but they must be related to existential conditions, which are constantly changing. We have an authoritative revelation according to which we must live, but it must be communicated in terms of the life the pupil is living in the twentieth century.

Should John Dewey be included in an overview of Christian thought in education? We have already answered that question in general, but perhaps we can draw more support for our answer from Dewey's "anchorman" position in *A History of Religious Educators*. The very last paragraph of that volume reminds us, "Dewey has been called the first original American philosopher, a pragmatist and instrumentalist who so reflected the new, growing American spirit that contemporary observers have difficulty determining if he shaped American education more than America shaped him."[26]

One can certainly question the inclusion of John Dewey in a book entitled *A History of Religious Educators*. The same reservations can be applied to the large amount of space given to the premier pragmatist in this volume. Nevertheless, every religious educator in the twentieth century (including evangelical Christians) has, to a greater or lesser degree, felt the influence of John Dewey. His larger-than-life presence cannot be ignored.

GEORGE ALBERT COE AND PERSONALISM

Wayne Rood tells the story of a meeting that took place in Chicago the year before Dewey left for Teachers' College, Columbia University. The purpose of the gathering was the formation of a new professional association, presumably to enrich secular education. At least that is what one segment of the group hoped, and their leader was the popular professor of education at the University of Chicago, John Dewey.

Members of another wing, however, were concerned about the development of religious education, particularly an attempt to link theology and science within the strongly emerging liberal patterns at the turn of the century. Said Rood, "Their spokesman was a youngish professor of the philosophy of religion at North-western University named George Coe. His address, 'Salvation by Education,' stated the position that won the conference. It became the Religious Education Association, and John Dewey dropped out."[27]

How important was George Albert Coe (1862-1951) to the development of Christian education in America? According to Kendig Brubaker Cully, Coe stands as a twentieth-century bookend to Clement of Alexandria — on the other side of the shelf!

> The reason for ending the anthology with George Albert Coe is that he was, in a sense, the zenith of one type of Christian education orientation in the modern period, an architect of the liberal religious education movement, certainly in the United States of America. Since his major writings of the nineteen twenties and thirties, the climate has undergone another remarkable change. The influence of the ecumenical movement, the newer Biblical theology, the insights of depth psychology, not to mention the soberer feeling tone of a world that has suffered through two wars and still does not see the emergence of anything like the order Herbert Spencer and his descendants fondly anticipated — these facts have produced different dimensions of concern with which Christian theorists and practitioners recently have been coming to grips. For that reason we have appended at the end of this work a list of books illustrative of trends and developments since Coe. He himself, during his lifetime, saw the changing intellectual and theological climate and publicly lamented all forms of neo-orthodoxy that seemed to him to be a reversion to past and inferior goals. Already we can see Coe in retrospect: that is the reason he seemed to be the logical "giant" with whom to conclude our readings.[28]

Let us not take lightly what Cully is reminding us of. The liberal ship captained by Coe was sailing on smooth seas in the first decade of this century, but its sociocultural approach to religious education was doomed from the start. First of all, it had *no source of authority,* a totally impossible position for any educational philosophy. Second, *two world wars, an economic depression,* and an *obvious deterioration in the moral qualities of the human race* left the ship foundering by the middle of the twentieth century, a date that marks the approximate ending point of our chapter.

It would not be out of line for the student to think of this era as beginning with that Chicago confrontation in 1903 and ending after the Second World War, though Cully suggests that 1940 is really the pivotal date at which the old liberalism lost its punch. He pinpoints that year because of the appearance of Harrison S. Elliott's *Can Religious Education Be Christian?*[29] Coe never did give up the ship and went down with it in 1951, still complaining about the new neo-orthodox influence on theology.

What exactly did Coe teach as representative of the liberal school of religious education during the first half of the twentieth century? Like Dewey, his viewpoints were grounded solidly in a commitment to Darwin's evolution. He was indeed the new scientific educator who, having rejected revelationism, was willing to follow empiricism wherever it led. Various words have been used to describe Coe's philosophy (liberalism, socioculturism, religious pragmatism), but perhaps none was more widely used than *reconstruction*. Coe himself said,

> Of course we cannot reconstruct anything unless we are acquainted with it; we cannot take a creative part in the moral order without intelligence as to its present and its past. But the focal point of true education is not acquaintance with the past, it is the building forth of a future different from the present and from the past. Moreover, creative education implies that the nature and the degree of this difference are to be determined within and by means of the educative process; they cannot be dictated or imposed; they cannot be discovered by exegesis of any historical document.[30]

Cully refers to this as "presentism," yet another term describing the philosophy of Coe. In *Faith and Nature*, H. Shelton Smith lists what he calls "historic tendencies of liberalism" and indicates that they found their most classic expression in the writings of George Albert Coe: divine immanence; the idea of growth—growth of religion in the individual and in the race, as well as growth as a mode of achieving individual and social change; the essential goodness of man; the historical Jesus.[31]

It is obvious from reading any of Coe's works that secular theory such as that espoused by Dewey, rather than biblical, theological, or ecclesiastical commitments, form the basis for his educational philosophy. Burgess says it clearly.

> When he determined to think through the problems of religious education anew under the presuppositions of modern science, Coe accepted the responsibility that traditional theologically derived aims and teaching practices would be found useless. He

proposed, eventually, that the traditional aim of individual salvation would have to be replaced by the broader aim of social reconstruction, and that transmissively intentioned teaching practices would have to be abandoned for vital participation in social interaction. Coe's perception of religious education, then, is antithetical to the traditional theological position that the teacher as an instrument of the church transmits Christianity to the student. He contends that the teacher and student should involve themselves together in the venture of re-creating Christianity itself. Hence, his widely quoted (and misquoted) statement: "Religion changes in the act of teaching it." Within a re-created Christianity (conceptualized by Coe as a democracy of God), the loyalty of the Christian would not be to one person (even to Jesus); rather, his loyalty would be to society, to persons.[32]

In terms of educational theory, the liberals emphasized such things as social justice through the reconstruction of the forms of social organization; salvation by gradual growth, knowledge, and self-control; a free teaching methodology totally opposed to any kind of indoctrination or fenced in by doctrinal authorities and attitudes; the treatment of religion as a vital and healthy result of a child's own creative thought, feeling, and experience; and a constant Dewey-like insistence on the continuous reconstruction of experience.

By mid-century a foundering liberalism split into the naturalistic liberalism of Sophia Lyon Fahs, which was first cousin to unitarianism; the popular liberalism of Harry C. Munro; and the neoliberalism of L. Harold DeWolf.

Perhaps we can end this brief vignette of George Albert Coe by noting his views on the Bible. If the authority and inerrancy of Scripture is the central core of the curriculum and the guiding star of epistemology for evangelical educators (and it is), then all educators in history can be analyzed with respect to their views on Scripture. Evangelical educators argue that experience is judged by the Bible and commended or condemned, therefore, with that authority. Coe argued the reverse, namely that religious experience created theology.

Rood identifies precisely Coe's rejection of orthodox views of theology.

Though his theology is technically implicit, Coe is explicit enough about it. Theology is implicit for Coe because it is projected from the religious experience of man. It is not speculative because it arises directly from data. It is not systematic because it does not deal with the spectrum of classical Christian doctrines. It is not orthodox because Coe makes no effort to correlate his assertions with tradition. It is explicit, however, because Coe states clearly that theological implications of his psychology of religion specifically denies any effort to construct a theological system, and makes no apology for the unorthodox nature of his theological conclusions.[33]

What, then, is Christian education? That precise question forms the title of one of Coe's books published in 1919. His answer: "It is the systematic, critical examination and reconstruction of relations between persons, guided by Jesus' assumption that persons are of infinite worth, and by the hypothesis of the existence of God, the Great Valuer of Persons."[34]

MARIA MONTESSORI AND ESSENTIALISM

The importance of the brilliant Italian educator Maria Montessori (1870-1952) to our chapter is primarily her influence on that giant American peer, the prince of the pragmatists, John Dewey. Like Froebel before her, Montessori stressed the natural goodness of children and sought freedom as a basic goal of education. Children were to proceed in learning at their own rate, and force should be avoided. Anyone who has visited a Montessori school recognizes that she was almost a century ahead of her time. She talked about the period of *absorption* from birth to three, *construction* from three to six, and *stability* from six to twelve. Then adolescence follows as a kind of second childhood, a new period of tremendous physiological as well as mental change. The key to the system at all ages is freedom from inhibition or the substitution of adult will and way.

> Freed to respond to a supporting environment in their own ways, the children demonstrated "the interior laws of the formation of man." They are love of the environment (exhibited in the desire for natural order), a love of work (not playing, but an intense kind of task-accomplishment), spontaneous concentration (the needs of the species acting through the individual), love of silence (though many children are working near each other), sublimation of the possessive attitude (not "to have" but "to use"), power to act from choice (not mere curiosity), obedience (a sense of mutual aid rather than of competition), self-discipline (always the fruit of liberty) and joy (a sheer satisfaction produced by obedience to the laws of one's own nature).[35]

Let us not for a minute think of Maria Montessori as a secular educator. Committed to her native Catholicism, she often used biblical language to describe relationships between children and their world, and regularly suggested that teachers see their children as Jesus saw them. In 1917, she wrote, "I believe that this method of education is the instrument God placed in my hands—for His ends."

It is virtually impossible to categorize Montessori in any of the traditional patterns. Obviously, she was influenced by the same Europeans who influenced Dewey, and she in turn may have had an impact on Dewey's thought. (But Dewey was not pleased to admit that possibility. He was critical of Montessori in *Democracy and Education*, pages 153-54. Dewey's eloquent disciple, William H. Kilpatrick, contributed heavily to the demise of Montessorianism with his *The Montessori System Examined* [1914; reprint ed., New York: New York Times, Arno, 1971].) She definitely stands as a unique way-station along the road of religious education in the first half of the twentieth century.

BIBLE SCHOOLS AND FUNDAMENTALISM

On the opposite theological spectrum from Dewey's pragmatism and Coe's personalism but also during the first half of the twentieth century there was developing a unique system of higher education called "the Bible school movement." Now a reasonably sophisticated branch within Christian higher education, Bible colleges represent a significant percentage of the number of evangelical institutions of higher education in America. They are organized and unified in a professional accrediting association known as the American Association of Bible Colleges, fully recognized by the Council on Postsecondary Accreditation, US Office of Education. They employ some of the finest faculty (not only in Bible, theology, and related subjects, but also in the arts and sciences) within the total evangelical church. But all this came out of a humble beginning in the late nineteenth century.

One cannot resist emphasizing the link between the Moravian church, with its pietistic tendencies, and the contemporary Bible college movement. The mission emphasis and necessity of trained workers, which so occupied the thinking of the Pietists, led to the founding of schools not at all unlike the early American Bible institute. One such institute was the Gossmer Mission, founded by Johannes Gossmer in 1842, followed three decades later by the East London Institute for Home and Foreign Missions, founded by H. Grathan Gunness.

The same year that the East London Institute was founded, T. DeWitt Talmadge organized a lay college as a part of the Presbyterian Tabernacle in Brooklyn, New York. Ten years later the Christian and Missionary Alliance organized the first Bible school still in existence. It was the conception of A. B. Simpson, of whom Eavey writes,

> He started the first Bible school in America in 1882 on the rear platform of an old theater in New York City. Two teachers taught twelve students, using for equipment rough benches and crude tables. Christians showed marked interest in the school and, money having been contributed, plans were made for formal organization. About one year after the beginning, the Missionary Training College was opened, with forty students enrolled in day classes and a large number in evening classes. Thirty completed the first year's work, and soon five of the graduates were on their way to Africa as missionaries.[36]

Almost all Bible college educators recognize Nyack Missionary College, as it later became known (now Nyack College), as the first school founded, while at the same time attributing to Moody Bible Institute (1886) the greatest influence in the movement. That school opened classes in 1889, the same year in which Gordon College began as a missionary training institute geared to sending workers to Africa. Moody was first known as the Chicago Evangelization Society, but adopted the name Moody Bible Institute in 1900, one year after its founder, D.L. Moody, died.

Of course, the existence of schools for the training of Christian workers, was not a new concept on the American scene, merely one that had been forgotten for over two and a half centuries. One could argue that Harvard College was the first Bible college founded in America and then go on to point out the Anglican efforts to train ministers at William and Mary (1693), Congregational commitment to Yale (1701), Presbyterian efforts at Princeton (1746), and on through the denominational efforts to develop institutions of higher learning that would genuinely educate workers for the church's multiple ministries.

But public education ruled in the late nineteenth century, and liberalism was in the religious saddle. Seminary education was all but dead theologically and something had to be done if Bible-believing, Bible-teaching pastors, missionaries, and educators were going to be produced. Gene Getz reminds us,

> Perhaps only a dozen evangelical liberal arts colleges existed when Moody Bible Institute was founded. Although approximately 60 to 70 Protestant seminaries were in operation, these schools were preparing young men primarily for pastoral work. Many needs for other types of full-time Christian vocations were becoming apparent and even the supply of seminary graduates was falling far short of the number of men needed to fill pulpits throughout the land.[37]

Thus far we have said nothing about the significant impact of Christian liberal arts colleges on the American evangelical educational scene. That development is reserved for Chapter 18, though of course many of the colleges were founded during the first half of the twentieth century. Most were not, however, a part of the fundamentalistic, evangelistic, missionary movement that gave birth to the Bible institute-college thrust contrasted in this chapter with the work of Dewey and Coe.

The absolute importance of Christian higher education to the church of Jesus Christ in the late twentieth-century world cannot be overemphasized. The church desperately needs the Christian college, though too often it forgets that need amidst its other problems and pressures.

NOTES

1. Edward J. Power, *Evolution of Educational Doctrine: Major Educational Theorists of the Western World* (New York: Appleton-Century-Crofts, 1969), p. 341.
2. J. Donald Butler, *Four Philosophies and Their Practices in Education and Religion,* 3d ed. (New York: Harper & Row, 1968), p. 373.
3. Cyril D. Garrett, "Democracy—the Religion of Dewey's Pragmatism," *Gordon Review* (Fall 1959): 105-13.
4. John Dewey, *Democracy and Education* (New York: Macmillan, 1916), p. 381.
5. Ibid., p. 267.
6. Arthur W. Munk, *A Synoptic Philosophy of Education* (Nashville: Abingdon, 1965), p. 86.
7. Gordon H. Clark, *Dewey* (Philadelphia: Presbyterian and Reformed, 1960), p. 25.
8. Dewey, p. 274.
9. Ibid., p. 292.
10. Clark, p. 19.
11. Dewey, pp. 43-44.
12. Melvin C. Baker, *Foundations of John Dewey's Educational Theory* (Chicago: Aldine Publ., 1966), p. 44.
13. Clark, p. 67.
14. Lawrence C. Little, *Foundations for a Philosophy of Christian Education* (Nashville: Abingdon, 1962), p. 19.
15. Charles W. Coulter and Richard S. Rimanoczy, *A Layman's Guide to Educational Theory* (New York: Van Nostrand, 1955), p. 148.
16. Dewey, p. 19.

17. John Dewey, *Experience and Education* (New York: Macmillan, 1958), p. 75.
18. Dewey, *Democracy and Education*, p. 305.
19. Dewey, *Experience and Education*, pp. 16-17.
20. Frederick Mayer, *A History of Educational Thought*, 2d ed. (Columbus, Ohio: Merrill, 1966), p. 355.
21. Dewey, *Experience and Education*, p. 74.
22. Martin S. Dworkin, Introduction and Notes to *Dewey on Education* (New York: Columbia U., 1957), p. 97.
23. Dewey, *Experience and Education*, p. 59.
24. Dworkin, p. 25.
25. Clark, p. 31.
26. David H. Roper, "John Dewey," in Elmer L. Towns, ed., *A History of Religious Educators* (Grand Rapids: Baker, 1975), p. 326.
27. Wayne R. Rood, *Understanding Christian Education* (Nashville: Abingdon, 1970), p. 181.
28. Kendig B. Cully, ed., *Basic Writings in Christian Education* (Philadelphia: Westminster, 1960), p. 11.
29. Kendig B. Cully, *The Search for a Christian Education, Since 1940* (Philadelphia: Westminster, 1965), p. 17.
30. Cited in K.B. Cully, ed., *Basic Writings*, p. 337.
31. H. Shelton Smith, *Faith and Nature* (New York: Scribner's, 1941), pp. vii-viii.
32. Harold W. Burgess, *An Invitation to Religious Education* (Mishawaka, Ind.: Relig. Educ. Press, 1975), pp. 64-65.
33. Rood, p. 200.
34. George A. Coe, *What Is Christian Education?* (New York: Scribner's, 1919), p. 296.
35. Rood, pp. 275-76.
36. C.B. Eavey, *History of Christian Education* (Chicago: Moody, 1964), pp. 338-39.
37. Gene A. Getz, *The Story of Moody Bible Institute* (Chicago: Moody, 1969), p. 23.

16

Existentialism and Catholicism

Perhaps it was the holocaust, or the millions of wasted lives, or the realignment of national geography on the map of Europe, but for some reason, since World War II, the world turned once again to an interest in history. The ancient concept of history was a view of philosophy-teaching-by-experience. The French statesman, Jean Jaures, said that we must "take from the altars of the past the fire—not the ashes."

Yet one wonders in this last quarter of the twentieth century whether or not we have really learned the lessons of the past. The twenty-five years we study in this chapter (approximately 1950-1975) represent a less than laudable movement from carnage to chaos. Yet that is not the fault of history, nor of the philosophy of which it is made. Mature thinking is always aided by an analysis of the mistakes of those who have gone before. A sense of history also assists in developing the desirable quality of open-mindedness. The serious student of the past is less likely than others to believe that his opinion is *altogether* right or that any situation is *totally* hopeless.

But history is most pertinent when it has been experienced. The authors of this text as well as most of the teachers who will use it have lived through much of the era we designate "postwar." And the phenomenal change of the period calls for scrutiny of as many of the components as one can mentally grasp. Yet a study of this era is like opening the back panel of a giant computer; being able to see all the parts, but standing totally in awe of the complexity of their arrangement. Kendig Brubaker Cully writes, "Thus, the *kind* of history to which many contemporary Biblical scholars and technical theologians have been drawn is a history that pulsates with vitality, a living history that does not consist merely of lifeless, impersonal data, but a dynamic reality in which the present generation, including the historian himself can actually participate."[1]

He goes on to emphasize that "Protestants especially need to be reminded of the need for historical perspective, since we so often allege freedom of interpretation to be the most essential Christian prerogative."[2]

In an American society hopelessly preoccupied with change, theology has not fared well. But there has been a revival of interest in Christian education, a new dynamic that has gripped the process of nurture in home and church, especially in the past decade. But we were slow in getting there, and it is the purpose of the following pages to describe something of the agony that brought us from pre-World War II confusion in evangelical theology to a relative unity in the 1980s.

We have already suggested that if one word could describe the third quarter of the twentieth century it would be *change. Technical change* has created a computerized age to such a degree that one writer speaks of man as the reproductive organs of his computers. Technology makes behavioral control and manipulation not only possible, but a day-by-day actuality.

Political change is a factor of constant dynamism. The national elections of 1980 stunned many seasoned political observers, indicating the possible new polarization of Americans into essentially conservative or liberal positions.

Cultural change has created sociologists like Herbert Marcuse, who espouses a position perhaps best called Freudian Marxism. Because no one can adjust the economy, Marcuse suggests that people must be adjusted to match the changing economy. Countercultural movements come and go—some helpful to the cause of the gospel, some in bitter opposition, but all part of the countercultural montage.

We are most concerned in this chapter with the kind of *religious change* that affects education. We shall see immediately that existential relativism has ascended the throne and announced that there are no ethical, metaphysical, axiological, or epistemological absolutes. We are forced, therefore, to a situational existence.

Against such a backdrop the Christian educator affirms Jesus Christ as Prophet, Priest, and King. The Word of the Lord is absolute truth, and perhaps just in time we escaped a shallow commitment to Christology, which sacrificed the Bible on its human altars. The cross is still the centerpoint of human history. There the Great High Priest made the supreme sacrifice so that we with Him may be crucified servants.

But in the chaos that surrounds us, we also call for a new

emphasis on Christ as King. The Creator of the universe, the Sustainer of its systems, is also the coming Sovereign with eternal power. Against the anarchy of our day we affirm the Spirit of God as the author of order and peace. A commitment to biblical theology on the part of the true Christian educator will be absolutely inescapable, and it is that commitment we affirm before we work our way through the third twenty-five years of this century. Our commitment helps us to see with thanksgiving the hope of the church as it awaits the final apocalypse.

EXISTENTIALISM

If Hegel was right when he said "the Isle of Minerva spreads its wings only with the falling of the dusk," then it is time for a resurgence of philosophy. Back in the Middle Ages the questions of philosophy were determined by theology—today they are determined by science. As a discipline, philosophy is in shambles with the existentialists fighting the logical positivists. A total surrender to relativism has sapped the strength of any historic system.

Existentialism is a patchwork quilt with its worn pieces showing such things as the transcendence of existence, the love of contradiction, the absurdity of life, extreme individualism, lack of concern for the past or the future, and an occasional patch of rank nihilism. Walter Kaufman says, "Most of the living 'existentialists' have repudiated this label, and a bewildered outsider might well conclude that the only thing they have in common is a marked aversion for each other."[3] Existentialism reflects the breakdown of the classical idea of rational man in an orderly universe, and also the break-up of orthodox religious faith. The era of world wars and nuclear weapons, of science and psychology, has driven many minds into doubt and often despair from which they reach out to ask that haunting question, "Why is there anything at all rather than nothing?"[4]

J.M. Spier gives perhaps the best one-sentence definition of existentialism we have ever seen: [the] "Existentialists' philosophy is an irrationalistic, humanistic philosophy of crisis, in which uprooted modern man seeks to find certainty in his own Existence, which he has elevated to an idol."[5]

Many believe (and perhaps properly so) that existentialism is more a mood than a philosophy since it is not reducible to any set of tenets and refuses systemization. On the one hand, it realizes the futility of explaining the universe rationally, but refuses to look beyond itself for a supernatural explanation. It is therefore forced to the conclusion of irrationality. We rejoice that existentialism concerns itself with the questions of ontology, but shake our heads in disappointment when we see its conclusions bogging down in pessimism, despair, anxiety, and the ultimate absurdity — the omnipresence of death. Our pedagogical countenance brightens once again when we sense an emphasis on the personal relationship between teacher and student, only to be crushed again when we see that such freedom leads to radical subjectivism.

NEO-ORTHODOXY CHANGES CLOTHES

Somewhere between Soren Kierkegaard and Karl Barth on the one hand and Rudolf Bultmann on the other existentialism tricked us into the old shell game, and we are still looking for the pea. Though we still hear Christian college and seminary students use the term, we agree with Roger Shinn that the word *neo-orthodoxy* is meaningless in our day except "as a description of history of the recent past."[6] Kierkegaard, the great Danish philosopher, spoke of the "leap of faith"—trusting even to the extent that the intellect sometimes finds the objects of its trust absurd. Martin Heidegger followed, but the theology of neo-orthodoxy was really formed by Karl Barth at Basel.

Barth emphasized a strong reaction against the insipid liberalism of the first half of the twentieth century and issued a rousing call for a renewed emphasis on biblical revelation, the transcendence of God, an awareness of sin, a knowledge of the heavenly Father through Jesus Christ, and a concern for eschatology. All this sounds very evangelical, but it was not. Barth was couching the ideas of critical scholars in the terminology of fundamentalists to arrive at a compromise which was certainly to the right of the old liberalism, but did not return the church to biblical Christianity. Paul K. Jewett identifies the problem when he writes,

> To sum up, the neo-orthodox have reacted against the liberal doctrine of imminence and sought to solve the problem of authority and religion by restoring to theology its proper foundation, namely, revelation, without becoming involved in a view of the Bible which would implicate one in what appears to them to be a hopeless scientific obscurantism.[7]

One shell is the theological neo-orthodoxy of Barth, Emil

Brunner, and Paul Tillich. But if the pea was ever there, it has been removed.

SECULAR EXISTENTIALISM

Here is our second shell—the eloquent literary delineation of existentialism from the pens of Jean Paul Sartre, Albert Camus, Franz Kafka, and Samuel Beckett. The absurd becomes also the inhuman, the logical result of the consciousness of inevitable death in the absence of values.

Yet modern educators clasp such a view to their pedagogical bosoms because too often they see only the positive contributions of existentialism and not its ultimate consequences. Otto F. Bollnow writes,

> Until now, we have been concerned with investigating the existential events, or, more generally speaking, the unstable processes as they occur in the life of the person to be educated. In this connection, we have suggested that the proper behavior of the educator, whose function it is to consider these events, is to accept them with understanding when they arise, and even to induce them, if possible, within very small limits. There is, however, another sphere in which the existential factor in education is important, in the light of the educator himself. Crises arise in his own life that are due to the particular exposed position of his existence as a result of the unreserved engagement of his person that he is challenged to show. The responsible acceptance of the risk, coinciding with the possibility of failure, characterizes the unavoidable existential moment in every educator's life.[8]

It is not possible to eliminate politics, society, or culture—those things that negatively dominate the education of man (in the view of the existentialist), but one can come to grips with the tragedy that follows. To live in a world with other men means to admit the necessity of forces that would treat men as objects rather than as individuals. This, according to the existentialist, is precisely what threatens education today. Unfortunately, recognizing the problem does not solve it.

Secular existentialism in education stands for an intense, and in some cases even an extreme, individualism. It rejects the current preference for group methods on the grounds that they diminish individual responsibility and encourage conformity. Neither knowledge nor mental discipline are ends in themselves, but rather means to the fulfillment of freedom. What traditional educators call "objective knowledge" is never in itself decisive but must be used by the student to meet his own individual needs and purposes.

Obviously this presupposes the relativity of all truth and knowledge. In secular existential education the student must learn to create his own standards because right and wrong, beauty and ugliness exist only within the individual. Cinderella is only beautiful because the prince loves her—he does not love her because she's beautiful. Furthermore, the student must also be acquainted with the inevitability of suffering and the finality of death, not in the morbid sense of the novelists (who really understand the ultimate implications of the philosophy), but rather in order to understand that freedom in this life, with all its potential, is an end in itself.

RELIGIOUS EXISTENTIALISM

Will we find the pea in the third shell? Certainly religious existentialism is to be preferred to secular existentialism, but it still comes unglued at the crucial point of bibliology, because it views revelation as existential rather than rational, informative, or propositional.

> When Emil Brunner, for instance, says that the hallmark of inconsistency clings to all true pronouncements of faith, he means that religious knowledge is existential, not rational, and that as such it is unsatisfactory from the viewpoint of theoretical reason. Theological statements are not derived from the information an infallible Scripture provides; they are distilled from the existential encounters with God to which a fallible Bible points. They are not concerned with "It-truth"—the sort that scientists and traditional philosophers want;—in fact, they offend the rationalist in that they are imminently satisfying as expression of "Thou-truth"—authentic personal involvement.[9]

When we follow the trail of religious existentialism into religious education, we encounter a multitude of prominent names. A special festschrift edition of *Religious Education* released in the fall of 1978 insisted on the inclusion of William Rainey Harper, Henry F. Cope, George Albert Coe, Harrison Elliott, Sophia Lyon Fahs, and numerous others. These are called the "pioneers of religious education in the twentieth century" and doubtless deserve such recognition. But our space is limited, this is not a festschrift effort, and we must narrow to four representatives of religious existentialism, though we have obviously spoken to several of the other "pioneers" in other sections of this book. We anticipate criticism not for the inclusion of the four names that follow but for the exclusion of other "giants." The reader is referred again to the expanded introduction, which identifies our criteria of selection.[10]

James D. Smart. James D. Smart is well known in Christian education circles for his excellent book *The Teaching Ministry of the Church.* He writes from a Presbyterian position, arguing in Barthian form that recovery of theology is crucial to the practical departments in the life of the church (a theme that many of us in the evangelical camp have defended, but with different definitions). Smart is relatively conservative, and his 1954 book shook the liberal establishment considerably, scarcely four years into the period we are analyzing in this chapter. He summarizes the rationale for Christian education in a terse paragraph early in the book.

> Christian education exists because the life that came into the world in Jesus Christ demands a human channel of communication that it may reach an ever-widening circle of men, women, and children, and become their life. The aim of Christian teaching is to widen and deepen that human channel, to help forward the growth and enrichment of the human fellowship, through which Jesus Christ moves ever afresh into the life of the world to redeem mankind. The program, therefore, must be such that it will lead people from their earliest to their latest years, ever more fully and in the most definite way into the faith and life of the church of Jesus Christ.[11]

The student wishing to pursue further works of Smart should certainly read *Teaching Ministry* and follow that with Sara Little's analysis[12] and several helpful pages in Cully's *The Search for a Christian Education, Since 1940.*

Iris V. Cully. Best known for the *Dynamics of Christian Education,*[13] Iris V. Cully has long served the ecumenical movement in religious education lecturing at Garrett Seminary, Northwestern University, Lutheran School of Theology in Chicago, Pacific School of Religion, Union Theological Seminary, and most recently at Lexington Theological Seminary in Kentucky. A committed ecclesiastical educator, she finds the apex of the movement in the ecumenical activities of the National Council of Churches of Christ and the Religious Education Association. She speaks about "life-centered" education, but does not accept the meaning of that term as it is used in Dewey's *Pragmatism,* where it emphasizes student experience. Cully argues that "Existence

comprises a totality—not the self by itself but the self in relationship to others, things, the universe, and history."[14] Theologically, Cully identifies most closely with process theology represented in the United States by John Cobb, Shubert Ogden, and
Gregory Baum.

D. *Campbell Wyckoff.* Wyckoff, the international editor of
Religious Education, recently celebrated his twenty-fifth year as
Thomas W. Synott Professor of Christian Education at Princeton
Theological Seminary. Along with Randolph C. Miller, Sara
Little, John Westerhoff, and others, he represents the leader-
ship core in the Religious Education Association for the past
quarter century. Though Wyckoff rejects Little's analysis of his
position, her summarization of names and viewpoints is helpful.

> The rather wide survey of writings in the field of Christian edu-
> cation indicates, as might be expected, that some writers, for all
> practical purposes, ignore both the fact and the doctrine of revela-
> tion. Others increasingly reflect a concen for and a use of the
> doctrine of revelation as more recently explicated, although no
> other persons have given such comprehensive consideration to the
> subject as Smart, Miller, and Sherrill. Some can be rather closely
> identified with the positions already described—Norman
> Langford and Elmer Homrighausen with Smart; Reuel Howe, a
> major representative of the "theology of relationships," with Mil-
> ler; Charles Johnson with Sherrill.
>
> Still other persons, like Mary Alice Jones and Howard Grimes,
> show themselves to be more in the tradition of Miller and Sherrill
> than of Smart. Two other persons at first impression seem to begin
> at a point closer to Smart, but actually this is not the case, and the
> positions they work out are independent, although reflecting the
> theological concerns of the time. Campbell Wyckoff, who sees
> "the Gospel of God's redeeming activity in Jesus Christ" as the
> guiding principle for the building of a theory of Christian
> education, is particularly concerned to relate educational theory
> to theology. Iris Cully, concerned to communicate the good news
> of Jesus Christ in such a dynamic way that it will come alive
> continually, recognizes revelation to be confrontation, but neither
> she nor Wyckoff builds theory primarily from the point of view of
> revelation.[15]

Wyckoff affirms Samuel Hamilton's definition of religious
education as

> The guided process of helping growing persons to achieve at each
> stage of their growth such habits, skills, attitudes, appreciations,
> knowledges, ideas, ideals, and intentions as will enable them at

each stage to achieve an ever more integrated personality, competent, and satisfying living in their social environment, and increasing cooperativeness with God and man in the reconstruction of society into a fellowship of persons.[16]

In actuality, Wyckoff does not consider himself an existentialist except "in my use of Kierkegaard's idea of the appropriation of revelation as the essential dynamic in Christian education, and in my use of some existentialist concepts dealing with the dynamics of learning."[17] He is distinctly Christian and, in our opinion, increasingly conservative in his theological approach to education. Like Miller, he insists on the theological nature of the discipline of Christian education: "My norms are theological, taking theology to be both the process and results of considered and faithful reflection and the meaning of revelation and taking the Bible to be God's definitive revelatory Word in written form."[18]

Is this a commitment to propositional revelation and inerrancy? Not quite. Has Wyckoff's position changed since he wrote *Task?* Probably, but his articles in *Religious Education* have been essentially historical, and we have no recent work by which to make a judgment. At this point, therefore, he remains the conservative within the ranks of the religious existential educators.

The reader surely has become aware that the separation point, the cutting edge of the issue, is the doctrine of Scripture. This is the enigma of existential religious education: its very strength in opposition to liberalism, namely an appeal to the Bible, becomes its very weakness, a failure to go far enough in accepting the Bible's own assessment of itself.

> Following the advent of the existential methodology there arose the neo-orthodox existential theology, which says that the Bible in the area of reason has mistakes but nonetheless can provide a religious experience in the area of non-reason. Neo-orthodox theologians do not see the Bible as giving truth which can be stated in contentful propositions, especially regarding the cosmos and history, that is, as making statements which are open to any verification. And for many of them, the Bible does not give moral absolutes either. For these theologians, it is not faith in something; it is faith in faith.[19]

George F. Kneller. George F. Kneller is best known for his *Existentialism and Education* published in 1958. In his article on existentialism, published in the *Westminster Dictionary of Christian Education*, Kneller argues that "the Christian educator . . . will have to strike a balance between the existentialist's hostility to doctrinal systems and the claims of a more orthodox theology."[20] Kneller sees existentialism as a serious world and life view searching for meaning in the depths of life that has reduced twentieth-century individuals to "mass men."

Here again is an almost secular emphasis on individuality, though in the brief quote above Kneller rejects secular existentialism just as he rejects conservative, orthodox theology. According to Kneller, when one has an experience with something, "thingness" departs and "personality" emerges. The reality of the thing or person was made certain by the experiential contact. Education is a creative attempt to solve the differences between the individual and society; to retain the freedom of the individual without succumbing to license that could harm society.

Cully picks up on Kneller's statement and writes a fascinating paragraph that rather summarizes the position of the religious existentialist: "Whether there is any inevitable hostility between doctrinal systems and the existentialist position is debatable. Surely the existentialist would avoid all semblance of finality with regard to any statement *about* theological presuppositions, but he would take seriously the demands *of* such doctrines for actual living."[21]

One could wish that these brilliant educators who have contributed so much to the methodology of Christian education could have walked all the way back to the Reformation when they turned their backs on the cold, dead liberalism of the first half of the century. But there is little evidence that such is the case. All the writers named above and many of the members of the Religious Education Association and the Association of Professors and Researchers of Religious Education continue to hold a view that can be properly categorized only as existential religious education. The student who pays attention to the footnotes will quickly detect that if he wants to read this viewpoint, there is plenty of material available.

ROMAN CATHOLICISM

Classic Roman Catholic education as carried out in the first half of the twentieth century is best described by John D. Redden in *A Catholic Philosophy of Education* (Encino, Calif.: Glencoe Publ., 1956). The basic principles of the philosophy emphasize that God is the highest good; man is not depraved, only deprived; baptism cleanses from original sin; and the church is the "synthesizer" of reason and revelation. The Thomistic strain was still running strong in the middle of the Second World War.

Roman Catholic philosophy basically sees the Person of Christ playing a two-fold role in education. One is the Thomas a'Kempis thrust toward the "Imitation of Christ" by Christians. This carries over into education with the modeling role of both parents and teachers. The other emphasis in which the Person of Christ touches education is the sacrificial and expiatory relevance of the atonement in the educational process. Before the postwar "revolt," Roman Catholic education was still tracing its history through Thomas Aquinas to Aristotle and Plato.

Catholicism, of course, holds to absolute truth. It is willing to recognize new research, but the fundamental principles are never to be rejected. The church has a primary role in education (Matthew 28:19-20), and the basis of that role is truth revealed in the commands of Christ. Philosophically the church has to be involved in education at every level so that no error occurs along the way, lest the final good in God not be realized by the student.

Evangelicals look at historic Roman Catholic educational philosophy with a deserved respect. The church has recognized the necessity of permeating all of curriculum and life with what it believes to be absolute truth. Furthermore, in authoritative books such as the work of Redden and Mary P. Ryan, it has carefully delineated its philosophy down through the years.

The weaknesses in Roman Catholic education stem from the weaknesses in its theology, precisely the malady that appears in every educational system that fails to take a totally serious view of the authority of Scripture, The Thomistic influence provides an inadequate doctrine of original sin, with its diminishing of grace and maximizing of human effort in salvation. Evangelicals would also want to reverse the roles of church and home, arguing that the latter has the priority rather than the former as in the Catholic tradition.

But we must ask whether Redden and Ryan are still recognized in the Roman church and its educational system. Perhaps the answer is that although still recognized as historically authoritative, the emphasis of Redden and Ryan has been replaced by such works as Neil McCluskey's *Catholic Viewpoint on Education* (Garden City, N.Y.: Hanover House, 1959) and Mary P. Ryan's *Are Parochial Schools the Answer?* (New York: Holt, Rinehart, and Winston, 1964). McCluskey basically defends the public school system while trying to retain traditional elements of parochial education. He argues, for example, that public education is really moral education because education is a moral task, a position with very strong Aristotelian overtones.

Of unusual significance in Catholic education is Jacques Maritain. His *Education at the Crossroads* (New Haven, Conn.: Yale U., 1943) was published just one year after the original Redden and Ryan book and well before either McCluskey or Ryan, but he remains a crucial philosopher among Catholic religious educators. Actually Maritain calls himself an existentialist and could very well be the Catholic answer to Shelton Smith or James Smart. In Maritain's view, man is progressing toward some state of happiness, and education provides a corrective for the perversions of the universe such as totalitarianism and war. The educational process helps man move toward the absolute value, and therefore man himself becomes the personification of absolute good. For Aristotle, the lower good was matter and the higher, form; for Maritain the lower good is the individual, the higher is the person.

He argues that in the final analysis there are only two views of man. One is the scientific view, which can only record data about man in a strictly natural way, and the other is the philosophical-religious view, which recognizes man as an animal whose main characteristic is intellect. The individual person possesses absolute dignity in proportion as it relates to God. Learner's intuition is important as the student is allowed to move in spontaneous interest. Education must provide a person with wisdom in order to equip him with ordered knowledge and to enable him to advance toward that evolving dimension in which he finds himself.

Kendig Brubaker Cully sees Jacques Maritain as the genuine Renaissance man and says, "One speaks of him in the same breath with contemporaries such as the late Albert Einstein, or Albert Schweitzer, Martin Buber, and Karl Barth—persons of gargantuan intellectual attainment and universal sympathies. With Etienne Gilson, Maritain is generally regarded as one of the two foremost Thomistic philosophers of this century."[22] Cully also points out how Maritain wants to end "the cleavage between religious inspiration and secular activity in man."

> The present crisis in morality, he thinks, can only be met by the training of children "in proper conduct, law observance, and politeness," and that these must be based on true "internal formation," though he does not spell out how this is to be accomplished, save to suggest that brotherly love needs to be incul-

cated in families. Always, he is concerned to address the principle to the concrete situation. This is Maritain's "Existentialist Thomism."[23]

The encyclical letter of Pope Pius XI issued in 1929, the impact of the Second Vatican Council, and the work of Johannes Hofinger are also important. But let us leapfrog over all of those to a 1975 book written by Harold William Burgess.[24] In Burgess's index one finds many of the names of import in the Protestant camp—Coe, Cully, Howe, Little, Miller, Sherrill, Smart, Smith, and Wyckoff. We even see evangelicals like Gaebelein, and LeBar. But Redden and Ryan? No. Jacques Maritain? No. Neil McCluskey? No. For Harold William Burgess, Director of Religious Affairs at Bethel College in Mishawaka, Indiana, there is just one contemporary Catholic Christian educator—James Michael Lee. He sees Lee as the father of the "social-science approach to theorizing about religious instruction," and describes Lee's scope in the following paragraph:

> James Michael Lee agrees with the majority of Christian religious educational thinkers who hold that the ultimate aim of religious instruction is that *every student should live a life characterized by love and service to both God and man in this present world and attain happiness with God in the world to come.* He contends, though, that this generally accepted aim is so broad in scope as to offer little practical assistance in the actual teaching of religion. Lee argues that it is the *primary proximate aim* of religious instruction which exerts a determinative influence upon the selection of religious instructional practices. In several places in his writings Lee describes what he believes are the three major positions relative to the primary proximate aim of religious instruction, namely the intellectualist position, the moralist position, and the integralist position.[25]

The layout immediately tips off the reader that Lee will choose the third, which he describes as "the fusion in one's personal experience of Christianly *understanding, action, and love* co-equally."[26] The true integralist sees the purpose of Christian education as enabling the person to engage in Christian living. There is a close tie-in in Lee's work with psychologism, which we shall discuss later, though he denies that his use of "behavioral modification" carries the same impact one would attribute to that process in the work of B.F. Skinner.

Though we are of the opinion that Lee, along with the religious existentialists, has jettisoned a serious commitment to

Scripture, there are some interesting findings in his heavily and thoroughly documented volumes published by Religious Education Press. Burgess summarizes them.

> In the extensive body of research literature surveyed by Lee, the weight of evidence suggests that *early family life* constitutes the single most powerful, pervasive, and enduring variable which affects substantially all aspects of an individual's learning of attitudes and values. . . .
>
> A second key finding identified by Lee is that the directness, immediacy, quality, and texture of an individual's *experience* have much to do with the richness, impact, and lasting quality of his learning. . . .
>
> A third example of the findings discovered by Lee from his investigation of the empirical research on learning is that the *environment* in which an individual develops exerts such a powerful influence that the extent of his learning is actually dependent upon the environment's composition and structure. . . .
>
> A fourth finding on which Lee reports is that the total group of *attitudes* held by an individual both shapes and conditions what he will and will not learn. . . .
>
> A final example of these findings on learning is that both moral and religious development are deeply linked with the whole process of human learning and development.[27]

But Burgess notwithstanding, there are other names of consequence in Catholic education today—Mary Boys, Bernard Marthaler, Gabriel Moran, Thomas Groome, and Johannes Hofinger, to name a few. (Thomas Groome has chosen the title *Christan Religious Education* for his truly significant volume. D. Campbell Wyckoff calls it the "only comparable book in the field" to George Albert Coe's *A Social Theory of Religious Education* [1917]. Groome might well emerge as the most outstanding Roman Catholic theoretician of the 1980s.)

Mary Boys. Mary Boys is the assistant professor of theology and religious education at Boston College and the author of *Biblical Interpretation in Religious Education*, a treatment of the salvation history emphasis in religious education. Boys is deeply concerned with the application of biblical criticism to the process of church education in a positive sense. In a *Religious Education* article she perceptively guides the reader through the history of biblical criticism and the development of patterns of interpretation. Boys concludes, "Biblical scholarship needs to move into a post-critical era, that is, into a period in which attention is given to the integration of its findings into the life of churches and synagogues. This integration requires collaboration with religious educators, who are entrusted with the responsibility of mediating academic and pastoral concerns."[28] These concepts are of course much more highly developed in the book mentioned above.

Boys is greatly indebted to Dwayne Huebner, a debt that is reflected in *Biblical Interpretation in Religious Education* and in another journal article published in late 1980. In dealing with the Catholic curriculum of the 1980s Boys insists that the church's approach must be to "suffuse the curriculum." She links Langdon Gilkey's "five uniquely Catholic characteristics" with Richard McBrien's significant work *Catholicism* (Minneapolis: Winston, 1980).

> To summarize briefly, McBrien identifies *Christian realism* as the philosophical focus of catholicism: it sees the world as mediated by meaning and thus rejects empiricism, idealism, biblicism, moralism, dogmatism, and legalism. Theologically, there are three foci: the principles of *sacramentality* (God is present and operative in and through the visible, concrete, created order), *mediation* (God uses signs and instruments to communicate grace), and *communion* (our way to God and God's to us is mediated through community).[29]

Quite a step from Redden and Ryan and even from Maritain, contemporary Roman Catholic education has obviously jettisoned much of its commitment to absolute truth, but at the same time it shows a positive reassessment of practical pedagogy.

Bernard Marthaler. As a professor and chairman of the Department of Religion and Religious Education at the Catholic University of America, Bernard Marthaler exercises enormous influence in defining and spreading the contemporary catechetical movement in Roman Catholicism. Originating in Germany, the "kerygmatic movement" among Roman Catholics has been popularized through the lectures of Johannes Hofinger, whom we have mentioned earlier. Vatican II defines catechesis as a form of the ministry of the Word, and during the 1970s movement grew significantly. In 1977 the National Conference of Catholic Bishops finished an American directory titled *Sharing the Light of Faith*, a five-year effort. Of this crucial year and work Marthaler writes,

If *Sharing the Light of Faith* climaxes the chapter in the history of American catechetics recounted in these pages, the 1977 Senate of Bishops marks the beginning of another. Its theme, "Catechesis in our Time," followed logically on, "Evangelization in the Modern World," the topic of the 1974 Senate. The working papers prepared for the Senate reiterated the fundamental principles of the catechetical movement, emphasizing that catechesis is an aspect of the ministry of the Word and the task of the entire Christian community, not simply the responsibility of a few."[30]

Gabriel Moran. In 1970 Herder and Herder published Gabriel Moran's *Design for Religion: Toward Ecumenical Education.* Wyckoff describes the book as

Incisive thinking on theology and education, leading to the conclusion that traditional religious education has actually lacked the essential religious quality and that henceforth it must be set firmly in an ecumenical framework, that is, with a concern for all that is human. The curriculum is redesigned in light of this principle, particularly with the parochial school and adult education in mind.[31]

Moran, professor of religious education at New York University, is a totally committed ecumenist. Going well beyond his writing of 1970 he suggested seven years later,

The term "Christian Education" should be retired. One could devise some logically defensable meaning for the words but that would be of little help. Obviously, the term is a block to dialogue with Jews. What is less apparent is that "Christian Education" is a protestant possession which effectively excludes Catholics. The term reflects the use of the word Christian that is 350 years old in the U.S. territory; it is at least a century out of date. One could work to bring Catholics inside "Christian Education" but this development is both unlikely and unnecessary.[32]

Perhaps Moran is a Catholic pragmatist with special interests in adult education as well as ecumenism. His more recent book is *Education Toward Adulthood,* and he continues to be a significant though radical voice on the scene of Roman Catholic education.

Existentialism and Catholicism are hardly coordinated movements in terms of history and representation. Yet they demonstrate a common deficiency in their reluctance to commit themselves and their discipline to a genuinely orthodox view of Scripture. Their Christian education is not the same as the Christian education of the evangelical.

NOTES

1. Kendig B. Cully, *The Search for a Christian Education, Since 1940* (Philadelphia: Westminster, 1965), p. 171.
2. Ibid., p. 172.
3. Walter Kaufman, *Existentialism from Dostoevsky to Sartre* (New York: Meridian, 1963), p. 11.
4. William Barret, "The Inner Life—What Is Existentialism?" *Newsweek*, 2 March 1964, p. 85.
5. J.M. Spier, *Christianity and Existentialism* (Philadelphia: Presbyterian and Reformed, 1953), p. 135.
6. Roger L. Shinn, "Neo-orthodoxy," in Kendig B. Cully, ed., *The Westminster Dictionary of Christian Education* (Philadelphia: Westminster, 1963), p. 461.
7. Paul K. Jewett, "Neo-orthodoxy," in Everett F. Harrison, ed., *Baker's Dictionary of Theology* (Grand Rapids: Baker, 1960), p. 376.
8. Otto F. Bollnow, "Risk and Failure in Education," in John Paul Strain, ed., *Modern Philosophies of Education* (New York: Random House, 1971), p. 521.
9. Arthur F. Homes, "Existential and Rational," *Gordon Review* 8, no. 2-3 (Winter 1964-65): 66.
10. Boardman W. Kathan, ed., "Pioneers of Religious Education in the Twentieth Century," *Religious Education*, special ed. (September-October 1978).
11. James D. Smart, *The Teaching Ministry of the Church* (Philadelphia: Westminster, 1954), p. 108.
12. Sara Little, *The Role of the Bible in Contemporary Christian Education* (Richmond, Va.: John Knox, 1961).
13. Iris V. Cully, *The Dynamics of Christian Education* (Philadelphia: Westminster, 1958).
14. Ibid., p. 119.
15. Little, pp. 88-89.
16. D. Campbell Wyckoff, *The Task of Christian Education* (Philadelphia: Westminster, 1955), p. 18.
17. Wyckoff, personal correspondence, 2 March 1981.
18. Ibid.
19. Francis A. Schaeffer, *How Should We Then Live?* (Old Tappan, N.J.: Revell, 1976), p. 176.
20. George F. Kneller, "Existentialism," in K.B. Cully, ed., *Westminster Dictionary*, p. 247.
21. K.B. Cully, *Search for a Christian Education*, p. 82.
22. Ibid., p. 125.
23. Ibid.
24. Harold W. Burgess, *An Invitation to Religious Education* (Mishawaka, Ind.: Relig. Educ. Press, 1975), pp. 130-31.
25. Ibid., p. 131.
26. Ibid.
27. Ibid., pp. 152, 154.
28. Mary C. Boys, "Religious Education and Contemporary Biblical Scholarship," *Religious Education* 74, no. 1(March-April 1979): 196-97.
29. Mary C. Boys, "Curriculum Thinking from a Catholic Perspective," *Religious Education* 75, no. 5 (September-October 1980): 526.
30. Berard L. Marthaler, "The Modern Catechetical Movement in Roman Catholicism," *Religious Education*, special ed., (September-October 1978): 5-19.
31. D. Campbell Wyckoff, "Curriculum Theory and Practice," in Marvin J. Taylor, ed., *Foundation for Christian Education in an Era of Change* (Nashville: Abingdon, 1976), p. 136.
32. Gabriel Moran, "Religious Education Toward America," *Religious Education* 72, no. 5 (September-October 1977):481.

17

Psychologism and Evangelicalism

Riding side by side for the last three and a half decades with existentialism and Catholicism have been two other important movements closely related to religious education. The one we have called "psychologism" for reasons that shall be explained shortly. The other picks up the term commonly used throughout this volume to describe the viewpoint of historic orthodox Christianity — "evangelicalism."

We do not suggest that evangelicals were not active in Christian education before 1945. Obviously, the emphasis on Christian educators down through the ages belies any such conclusion. But there has been a new wave, a whole new field arise within the framework of Christian higher education in recent years. Colleges and seminaries that never before offered a course in Christian education now require a minimum number of hours for graduation. Churches are hiring "Ministers of Education," and the Christian school movement was the most phenomenal educational development of the 1970s.

It is therefore with a sense of excitement that we turn to the secular domain to analyze the contributions of the researching and writing psychologists and then turn inward to look at ourselves and the contributions of outstanding evangelical leaders of recent years.

PSYCHOLOGISM

According to *Webster's New Collegiate Dictionary* (1973 edition) psychologism is "a theory that applies psychological conceptions to the interpretation of historical events or logical thought." In both religious and secular domains, psychology has been inseparable from education for most of the twentieth century. The first experimental psychology laboratory was established by Wilhelm Wundt in Leipzig in 1879. Less than three decades later, Edward Lee Thorndike published his monumental three-volume *Educational Psychology*. Were we treating psychology itself at this point, we would want to examine the structuralism of Wundt, the functionalism of William James and John Dewey, the behaviorism of Ivan Pavlov, John B. Watson, and B. F. Skinner; the Gestalt mechanism of Wolfgang Kohler and Leo Wertheimer; and the psychoanalysis of Sigmund Freud. We must, however, always keep the central theme of our book before us and therefore, under the broad umbrella of psychologism, speak only of the views of four men and how their work has had influence on the history of Christian education in the past thirty years.

B. F. SKINNER

The work of B. F. Skinner basically comes out of the environmentalism of John Watson, although Skinner developed a much more sophisticated accounting for genetic factors and neurological findings. Nevertheless, the claims regarding the power of environment to determine the shape of adult personality are similar. James E. Loder strikes at its central weakness when he writes, "Environmentalism makes the same mistake as predeterminism, but from the outside in rather than from the inside out. It fails to take account of human uniqueness, assuming that persons can be shaped in all registers of behavior by the same techniques that shape laboratory rats and pigeons."[1]

Skinner works on the basic assumption that there is order in nature, including human nature. It is the function of science to discover that order, and when science takes a realistic outlook on its task, it finds itself concerned only with the discovery of pre-existent laws that govern the world about us. Furthermore, one should not assume that human behavior has any particular or peculiar properties that require a unique method or a special kind of knowledge. The assumption of Skinner's psychology is the implication of a strictly naturalistic determinism; behavior is caused, and the behavior that appears is the only kind that could have appeared.

Behaviorism has sometimes been called "the psychology of an empty organism" because Skinner is convinced that looking inside an organism for an explanation of behavior tends to obscure the external variables that are really available for empirical investigation.

Is there anything in Skinnerian psychology of benefit to the evangelical educator? We pose an immediate affirmative. The whole operant conditioning approach has emphasized the significant principle of reinforcement and has issued a strong call for a specific behaviorally oriented objectification of the learning task. But students of educational theory should remember that no philosophy or psychology is right simply because it works — that is the position of pragmatism. In general, Skinner's underlying philosophy is to be rejected on at least four very specific counts:

1. It recognizes no inner qualities of man such as conscience, sin, spirit, and so forth, which are clearly described in Scripture.
2. It views man only as an animal, hence sees all his behavior as externally conditioned rather than motivated by internal qualities of sin or righteousness.
3. It recognizes only experiential knowledge and therefore denies "purposeful" behavior.
4. It is dependent upon a Darwinian view of evolution, which makes man of little or no difference from the animal kingdom.

In his reaction to Skinnerian behavioristic psychology, Francis Schaeffer posits an evangelical view.

> The Christian position is *not* that there is no element of conditioning in human life, but rather that by no means does conditioning explain what people are in their totality. To a determinist, however, if one removed all the bundle of conditioning in man, there would be no man *as* man. Christianity rejects this. It insists that each individual person exists as a being created in the image of God, and that therefore each person is an ongoing entity with dignity. To proud, humanist man, who demands to be autonomist, technology of one kind or another is to be used to get rid of the limitations of nature, *including human* nature, which autonomist man finds insufferably confining. There is here a tension in modern people, especially perhaps among students: Modern people want to be free to shape their own destiny, and yet they think they know they are determined.[2]

LEWIS JOSEPH SHERRILL

In treating what he calls "Psychologically-oriented Nurture," Kendig Brubaker Cully offers the work of two theorists — Reuel Howe and Lewis J. Sherrill. Of these two, we believe the latter has been the more influential, and so we select as one of the representatives of religious psychologism the former Dean of Louisville Presbyterian Theological Seminary.

Sherrill rejected the experimentalists and the developmentalists and turned instead to psychoanalysis for his insights into the religious nature of man. In his two most important books, *The Struggle of the Soul* (1953) and *The Gift of Power* (1955), we see Sherrill groping for a solid and consistent theory of human nature upon which to base his view of pastoral nurture. He talks about "depth theology" much in the way psychologists speak of "depth psychology," another hint of the psychoanalytical concern for the self. Both human self and divine self keep their identities in the "dialogue," to borrow one of Howe's favorite words. As Cully describes it,

> The process itself takes place in the twofold relation between man and God which he (Sherrill) calls "confrontation" and "encounter." It is "confrontation" from God's side. That is, God takes the initiative. "To speak thus of 'confrontation' means that God as infinite Personal Being faces man as a finite personal being. . . . To speak of revelation as God's *Self*-disclosure implies that *what* is revealed in the encounter between man and God is not information *about* God, but God *Himself* as Personal Being. The reports of revelation may have to be cast in terms that contain information or that attempt to describe what was perceived in the encounter. . . . Revelation is Revelation to *human beings*.[3]

The student can see immediately that Lewis J. Sherrill was well within the existential camp, but he placed his emphasis on psychology for insight rather than on some Barthian view of biblical revelation. For Sherrill, Christian education is an attempt by members of the church to participate in and in some way direct changes which take place in persons as they relate to God, to the church, to other people, to the physical world, and to themselves.

RANDOLPH CRUMP MILLER

The Clue to Christian Education (1950) by Randolph Crump Miller was essentially a response to Shelton Smith's *Faith and Nurture*. In it Miller tried to develop a reconstructive theology that met the psychological demand for relationship as that demand was emerging in postwar thought. What is the "clue?"

> *The Clue to Christian Education* is the rediscovery of a relevant theology which will bridge the gap between content and method, providing the background and perspective of Christian truth by which the best methods and content will be used as tools to bring the learners into a right relationship with the living God who is revealed to us in Jesus Christ, using the guidance of parents and

the fellowship of life in the Church as the environment in which Christian nurture will take place.[4]

Doubtless some will argue that Miller should not be a part of "psychologism," for his commitment to theology was far superior than others whose names appear in this section. Nevertheless, his theology was so existentially related to the nature of man that *relationship* rather than *revelation* became the key idea. Sara Little admits that "when Miller spoke of the 'clue,' he was not referring to a 'correct' theology formulated as doctrine to be transmitted through education. For him, theology had to do with the 'truth about God in relation to man.' Truth lay in the experienced reality of the relationship—theology, in the interpretation of that reality, informed by the biblical witness."[5]

No wonder the theology to which Miller called us in 1950 was still deficient in 1980 at the publication of his most recent book, *The Theory of Christian Education Practice.* It was not biblical theology to begin with and was therefore subject to all the nuances of existential perversion that buffeted it during the years of psychologism's control over education. But Miller deserves better than just a listing with Skinner—he is, by all measurements, a giant among religious educators in the twentieth century. Furthermore, though he never extricates himself from the neo-orthodox—existentialist—process theology web, forty-five years of study in the field dare not be treated lightly. Let us take a closer look at *The Theory.*

Miller subtitles the book, "How Theology Affects Christian Education." Many of the chapters are journal articles that appeared during the 1970s, and even as early as 1945, so the distinctive flow of the book is not as smooth as it might be. But there is no mistaking Miller's message for Christian educators—he intends an application of process theology to the teaching of the Bible in Christian education settings and, on his way to a description of the *Practice*, proceeds to deny verbal inspiration (p. 15), the historicity of creation (p. 25), the sovereignty of God (p. 27), the total omnipotence of God (p. 28), the perfection of God (p. 34), and the doctrine of election (p. 39) among other theological viewpoints.

He links himself closely with liberation theology and openly admits that "process thinking is only beginning to work out a full Christology."[6]

Miller is most kind to naturalism and speaks often of natural theology, although apparently he is hesitant to use the term "natural revelation." Obviously he is an empiricist and not a revelationist in the development of a theology of Christian education.

Evangelical educators are always accused of misunderstanding existentialists and liberals, but Miller must be brought to task for his chapter on "varieties of biblical authority." He offers a five category break-down:

> We will look at the Eastern Orthodox who place Scripture and tradition on the same level, the Roman Catholics who hold tradition to be superior to the Scriptures, the fundamentalists who assert the verbal infallibility of the Bible, the left-wing groups who believe reason to be superior to any historical revelation, and the classical Protestant as represented by Anglicans or Episcopalians who accept a soft view of the authority of Scripture and treat tradition with great respect.[7]

His treatment of the fundamentalist is questionable though the chapter originally appeared in 1952 — and one certainly has a right to expect some updating for a 1980 publication. The only authority cited is J. Gresham Machen; no writing evangelical educators of the twentieth century are referred to in any form; the impact of the *New International Version* is ignored because "fundamentalists" clearly prefer the King James Version; and "the biblical literalism of the fundamentalists may be seen as colored by theological presuppositions." The ultimate condemnation is that "the extreme literalism of the fundamentalists has placed them outside the main stream of ecumenical christianity . . . the sectarian groups which are officially fundamentalist do not seek the ecumenical fellowship on either the local or international level and often they stand in opposition to the work of the ecumenical bodies."[8]

Of course there are Christians of the kind that Miller describes in those few brief paragraphs. But they have made virtually no contribution to the field of Christian education in the last fifty years, and he appears totally ignorant of mainstream evangelicalism, its institutions, its literature, and its leaders.

The psychologism of Miller interacts with his commitment to theology at the point of practice. Chapter 14 entitled "Religion is Any Subject" picks up this theme as it talks about basic needs and key questions. The chapter on worship and education is very good and, although ten years out of date, the chapter "The Discipline of Theology and the University and the Divinity School" is interesting. In short, Miller is attempting to jump without pause from Barth's existentialism to modern process theology. His lodestar is Richard Niebuhr's theology and the captain of his craft, Alfred North Whitehead's philosophy. One final quote is necessary.

> The crucial point for Christian education is the experiential or existential one: no education is religious unless it is *God-centered*. We teach within the framework of relationships between humanity and God and between persons and persons. Of course, this forces us back to the theological question: to what reality does the word God point? The techniques will pretty much take care of themselves once we grasp the fundamental theological significance of what we're doing.[9]

LAWRENCE KOHLBERG

A contemporary psychologist whose popularity is definitely on the rise is Lawrence Kohlberg of Harvard, who claims that moral development—like intellectual development—is a natural process that teachers can nurture in children. Kohlberg claims that morality can be taught without indoctrination in any particular value system, and insists he is not teaching values and has no intention to inculcate a particular philosophy of right and wrong.

In many ways he follows the thinking of Jean Piaget, a Swiss child psychologist who believed that the ability to reason about moral problems develops by stages, much in the way a child learns to crawl before he walks.

Kohlberg talks about six different stages and three levels of moral development:

> *Stage one:* Obedience and punishment
> *Stage two:* Back scratching
> *Stage three:* Conformity
> *Stage four:* Law and order
> *Stage five:* Social contract
> *Stage six:* Universal principles.

There is certainly something to be said for a process of developing moral reasoning rather than moralizing on the basis of inherited value judgments. Nevertheless, it would seem that Kohlberg's theories cover only part of the process of moral development, and that the various systems being used by those attempting to implement his theories simply cannot control all the variables. Furthermore, it is very easy to stereotype students as "Stage two children" or "Stage four children" much in the way the so-called Four Temperaments have been misused in Christian education.

In our opinion, Kohlberg has made a contribution, but one which neglects the crucial biblical roles of the Holy Spirit's power to change human will and the significance of fundamental convictions on the part of the Christian child or teenager to play a really significant role in moral development. Certainly, Kohlberg's concept that culture and religion are relatively unimportant as the mind develops a capacity to moral judgments is not in line with evangelical theology. Lawrence O. Richards refers to Kohlberg's work as "devastating" and says,

> Clearly, if we accept the findings of Piaget and Kohlberg . . . our entire approach to Christian Education—and particularly to the use of the Bible in Christian Education—will shift dramatically. Rather than be concerned about the communication of Bible truths, we may be concerned only about environmental conditions which stimulate internal development. And, because such internal development *is* sequential and progressive across childhood and into adulthood, we probably will have to agree with Goldman that teaching in the Bible to children is really not terribly important after all.[10]

Students of Christian education and its relationship to psychology will find an excellent bibliography of the works of Piaget and Kohlberg in Richards's book.

Is it our conclusion that evangelical educators should totally reject psychology? Absolutely not! The issue again is integration, the ability to be sufficiently eclectic while holding on to a solidly biblical theology, to apply whatever findings of psychologists—secular or religious—that may legitimately demonstrate positive correlation with biblical truths. A good bit of effort has been done in this area by Christian leaders who work in clinical psychology and counseling, but there is still plenty of room for those who want to make a contribution to educational psychology.

EVANGELICALISM

The crucial issues of philosophy, including philosophy of education, force a consideration of theology. The two have always been related, although scholars have not always agreed on which gives birth to which. But it is immediately obvious, even to the beginning student, that the central issues of philosophy (metaphysics, epistemology, anthropology, axiology) are also the central issues in theology.

Although it is terribly oversimplified to state it this way, the forces of God and the forces of Satan have been identified philosophically through the years by assigning the former to revelationism and the latter to rationalism. New Testament faith has always involved an understanding of reality, a commitment to propositional revelation, and the verifiability of certain observable facts. Calvin argued that faith brought forth both theological and philosophical insights.

Furthermore, the truly Christian philosopher rejects the prevailing system of his day, whether it is idealism, realism, naturalism, logical positivism, pragmatism, or existentialism. He has generally found himself in a "Paul-in-the-marketplace" situation as a *spermalogos* — one picking up the seeds of truth from various systems and forming a "system" that displeases proponents of any worldly pattern because its primary concern is to be biblical.

More than twenty years ago, J. Oliver Buswell, Jr., claimed that a Christian system of philosophy could be traced on a line extended "from Moses through the biblical writers and on through Augustine, Thomas, Luther, Calvin, Butler, Kuyper, and Warfield."[11] He went on to suggest Christian answers to three basic philosophical questions: What is the nature of being? What is the nature of knowing? and What is the nature of good and evil? Of these, the second is most closely related to education (though none can be totally out of reach for very long) and therefore Buswell's brief answer is reproduced here.

> We hold that the mind of man, created in the image of God, is endowed with thought-forms and capacities which can receive and correlate truth about reality.
>
> I wish there were space for a study of the constant appeal to inductive factual evidence of the Bible, space to point out the remarkable biblical pictures of God accommodating his message to our natural processes, space to discuss the Holy Spirit as teacher and illuminator, space to present the Christian view of the axioms of logic as derived from the character of "God who cannot lie."
>
> We hold that faith is never to be contrasted, but rather correlated, with the acceptance of reasonable evidence. It is significant that in a culture in which the Christian theory of knowledge has been a strong molding influence, freedom of thought and expression has reached its highest point in history.[12]

Whereas existentialism and psychologism are relatively new thought patterns on the historical scene, evangelicalism goes back at least to the New Testament, and if we borrow Buswell's viewpoint, back to Moses. We deal here, however, with those evangelicals who have made a contribution since World War II and in doing so, select four names of Christian education leaders who have *by their writings* had an impact on evangelical Christian education during this period.

FRANK E. GAEBELEIN

In dealing with what he calls "fundamentalism and neo-evangelicalism" Cully refers to the formation of the National Association of Evangelicals in 1943, mentions briefly the contributions of Carl F. H. Henry, founder of *Christianity Today,* and then centers on two representatives of the movement, one of whom is Frank E. Gaebelein, the retired headmaster of Stony Brook School in Long Island, New York, and former associate editor of *Christianity Today.* Gaebelein was also chairman of the committee to draw up a comprehensive statement on the philosophy and practice of Christian education from the viewpoint of the National Association of Evangelicals. That statement, originally published in 1951 under the title *Christian Education in a Democracy,* was supplemented later by Gaebelein's treatment of the integration of faith and learning—*The Pattern of God's Truth*—still a required classic for every beginning student of a Christian philosophy of education.

The concept of integration has to do with making a whole by bringing parts together. Gaebelein argues that learning unrelated to life is as good as faith without works, and that though natural truth may be of a different order than revealed truth, it is thereby nonetheless God's truth. Gaebelein adopts certain foundational truths of Christian learning: the existence of the triune God; the Fall of man; the redemptive sovereignty of God; the incarnation of Christ; the church as the Christian community; and the consummation of history at Christ's coming. Christian educators who really seek integration must recognize Christ as the measure and unifying force of all things and must completely commit themselves to the Bible as the primary sourcebook of truth.

Gaebelein states the historic Christian position when he says that no man ever makes up truth because it is always around us. What happens is that we experience it formally or informally and then, because of our understanding of special revelation, we are able to ascertain precisely how that truth fits into life. The prepared mind of the Christian student is fertile ground for both formal experiencing of truth (study or research) and informal experiencing of truth ("inspiration" or spontaneous awareness). One is hard pressed to single out a sentence or paragraph in *The Pattern* that serves as representative of Gaebelein's thinking. The following certainly is one of many keys to the book:

> On the one hand, God's truth is external to Christian education in that it is not dependent upon what education is or does. On the other hand, there is, as integration proceeds, a merging of the internal into the external, thus the internal, though always subordinate to the external, joins in living union with the external, which remains transcendently beyond it. This is the heart of integration and the crux of the matter.[13]

Incidentally, although much is made of the two Frank Gaebelein volumes already identified, too few students of an evangelical philosophy of education have been introduced to *A Varied Harvest* (Grand Rapids: Eerdmans, 1967) and his four-part series in *Grace Journal* "Toward a Christian Philosophy of Education," 3, no. 3 (Fall 1962) both of which expand and supplement his work in *The Pattern.*

Of course, the concept of integration is totally opposed to the thinking of the existential religious educators, and Cully allows Howard Grimes to raise their objections.

> He feels that Gaebelein takes a dangerous stand in equating the written word of the Bible with God's truth, for this "is to ignore biblical scholarship of the nineteenth century as well as current biblical theology." Grimes feels, too, that Gaebelein's rationalistic structure for the supporting of Biblical truth misses the meaning of faith as contrasted to reason. "He almost says—but not quite—that the biblical faith gives a context and a basis for the work of human reason, but in the final analysis he seems to be shoring up the biblical faith by a rational structure. He is willing to admit that the world is more than six thousand years old, but not that biblical science is wrong.[14]

LOIS E. LEBAR

The retired professor of Christian education at Wheaton College, Lois E. LeBar, has written several books, but the one that qualifies her for a position as spokesperson for evangelical educational philosophy in the twentieth century is her 1958 volume entitled *Education that is Christian.* It is an eloquent call for creative use of the Bible throughout the entire system of Christian education with a strong plea to build on the work of John Amos Comenius. Methodologically, LeBar rejects traditional Herbartianism for a Comenian approach to the teaching-learning process.

> We evangelicals concur wholeheartedly on the *place* of the Bible in teaching, but we have given little thought to the *use* of the Bible. We have staunchly defended the verbal inspiration of the Scriptures and the infallibility of their authority against those who would judge the Word of God rather than letting it judge them. We hold that God has revealed Himself objectively in the propositions of Scripture, as well as in its history and narratives and poetry. Our subjective experience of Christ stems from the doctrines of the Word. We hold that "faith cometh by hearing, and hearing by the Word of God" (Romans 10:17).[15]

GENE A. GETZ

The 1970s have produced a plethora of renewal literature with respect to church ministry and particularly the nurturing task of local congregations. Much of that literature is very shallow with little handling of the biblical text and a heavy emphasis on "how we did it," or a heavily psychologized treatment of the way persons' needs are met in small groups. By making irresponsible statements about the church and its various educational ministries, some of it is actually destructive in the specific author's attempt either to capture attention, sell books, or both.

Out of that literature there has emerged at least one volume, however, that is thoroughly biblical, well thought-out, and has stood well above its competitors in the renewal sector of evangelicalism during the decade of the '70s—*Sharpening the Focus of the Church* by Gene A. Getz, founder and pastor of Fellowship Bible Church, Dallas, Texas, who also teaches part-time at Dallas Theological Seminary. Getz views the church's task in four dimensions: the lens of Scripture, the lens of history, the lens of culture, and a fourth section entitled "Developing a Contemporary Strategy."[16]

The strength of the book rests in its development of the New Testament patterns of church organization and edification. The author's handling of "the lens of Scripture" makes up almost two-thirds of the book. The central theme of Getz's treatment is *discipleship*. He identifies his direction at the outset: "The church, therefore, exists to carry out two functions—evangelism (to make disciples) and edification (to teach them). These two functions, in turn, answer two questions. First, why does the church exist in the world? And second, why does the church exist as a gathered community?"[17]

LAWRENCE O. RICHARDS

The creative director of Alive Ministries in Lansing, Michgan, Lawrence O. Richards, is a prolific writer whose works have had significant impact on evangelical Christian education in the last half of the twentieth century. But again, one single volume establishes his role in our treatment of the philosophic flow, namely, *A Theology of Christian Education* published in 1975 by Zondervan. Richards is a committed renewal educator who first startled the evangelical establishment with *A New Face for the Church* (Grand Rapids: Zondervan, 1970). Although it was not Richards's first book, *New Face* catapulted him into the forefront of renewal writers, a position he held with consistency throughout the decade.

As is unfortunately typical of too many evangelicals, *Theology* received a considerably less enthusiastic reception than *New Face*. The former is by far a superior book. One gets the impression that in the earlier volume Richards just wanted to hit the mule with the two-by-four, but in *Theology* (now that he has our attention) he wished to say something of more importance.

> For Richards, Christian education means "nurturing the development of God's life within believers." It is for this task that the Body is designed. Hence "our educational ministry must focus on adults . . . and on discipleship." No longer can Christian education be confined primarily to the classroom; it must be seen to involve "all the activities and transactions that take place within the Body of Christ." Richards explores in depth how these concepts can affect the approach to childhood education and to evangelism.[18]

It is ironic that the strength of Richards's *Theology* is also its weakness. He is always the practical theorist, and therefore, in his great concern that readers discuss and debate the ideas of the book, he gives over large sections to case histories, discussion questions, and other formats for handling the book as a text. Although very valuable, these pages must be deleted from a serious theology that would seek to stand up to the scholarly work of the existentialists, whose books we have already discussed.

Theology is an important book, and it is hoped that all serious students of Christian education will study it carefully along with the works of Gaebelein, LeBar, and Getz. Though each writer is different in his approach to the development of a distinctly evangelical philosophy, they all share in the common foundation of serious commitment to inspiration and authority of Scripture, *a commitment that must characterize all evangelical educational philosophy worthy of the label.* That foundation was affirmed in print when the National Association of Evangelicals adopted a doctrinal statement in 1943 and reaffirmed it in a summit meeting on inerrancy held in Chicago in November 1978. Both statements are sufficiently brief to be included here.

> We believe the Bible to be the inspired, the only infallible, authoritative Word of God. We believe that there is one God, eternally existent in three Persons, Father, Son and Holy Ghost. We believe in the deity of our Lord Jesus Christ, in His virgin birth, in His sinless life, in His miracles, in His vicarious and atoning death through His shed blood, in His bodily resurrection, in His ascension on the right hand of the Father, and in His personal return in power and glory. We believe that for the salvation of lost and sinful man regeneration by the Holy Spirit is absolutely essential. We believe in the present ministry of the Holy Spirit by whose indwelling the Christian is enabled to live a godly life. We believe in the resurrection of both the saved and the lost; they that are saved unto the resurrection of life and they that are lost unto the resurrection of damnation. We believe in the spiritual unity of believers in our Lord Jesus Christ.[19]

> 1. God, who is Himself Truth and speaks truth only, has inspired Holy Scripture in order thereby to reveal Himself to lost mankind through Jesus Christ as Creator and Lord, Redeemer and Judge. Holy Scripture is God's witness to himself.
> 2. Holy Scripture, being God's own Word, written by men prepared and superintended by His Spirit, is of infallible divine authority in all matters upon which it touches: it is to be believed, as God's command, in all that it requires; embraced, as God's pledge, in all that it promises.
> 3. The Holy Spirit, Scripture's divine Author, both authenticates it to us by His inward witness and opens our minds to understand its meaning.
> 4. Being wholly and verbally God-given, Scripture is without error or fault in all its teaching, no less in what it states about God's acts in creation, about the events of world history, and about its own literary origins under God, than in its witness to God's saving grace in individual lives.

5. The authority of Scripture is inescapably impaired if this total divine inerrancy is in any way limited or disregarded, or made relative to a view of truth contrary to the Bible's own; and such lapses bring serious loss to both the individual and the Church.[20]

NOTES

1. James E. Loder, "Developmental Foundations for Christian Education," in Marvin J. Taylor, ed., *Foundations for a Christian Education in an Era of Change* (Nashville: Abingdon, 1976), p. 55.
2. Francis A. Schaeffer, *How Should We Then Live?* (Old Tappan, N.J.: Revell, 1976), p. 229.
3. Kendig B. Cully, *The Search for a Christian Education, Since 1940* (Philadelphia: Westminster, 1945), pp. 55-56.
4. Randolph Crump Miller, *The Clue to Christian Education* (New York: Scribner's, 1950), p. 15.
5. Sara Little, "Theology and Religious Education," in Taylor, p. 30.
6. Randolph Crump Miller, *The Theory of Christian Education Practice* (Birmingham, Ala.: Relig. Educ. Press, 1980), p. 43.
7. Ibid., p. 76.
8. Ibid., p. 87.
9. Ibid., p. 160.
10. Lawrence O. Richards, *A Theology of Christian Education* (Grand Rapids: Zondervan, 1975), p. 170.
11. J. Oliver Buswell, Jr., "Why We Need a Christian Philosophy," *Eternity*, November 1961, p. 35.
12. Ibid.
13. Frank E. Gaebelein, *The Pattern of God's Truth* (Chicago: Moody, 1968), pp. 8-9.
14. Cited in K. B. Cully, *Search for a Christian Education*, p. 109.
15. Lois E. LeBar, *Education That Is Christian*, rev. ed. (Westwood, N.J.: Revell, 1980), pp. 122-23.
16. Kenneth O. Gangel, "Biblical Renewal," *Christianity Today*, February 14, 1975, p. 45. (This is a review of *Sharpening the Focus*.)
17. Gene A. Getz, *Sharpening the Focus of the Church* (Chicago: Moody, 1974), p. 22.
18. Edith Bender, "The Need for New Approaches," *Christianity Today*, August 6, 1976, p. 30. (This is a review of *Theology of Christian Education*.)
19. Carl F. H. Henry, "National Association of Evangelicals," in Kendig B. Cully, ed., *Westminster Dictionary of Christian Education* (Philadelphia: Westminster, 1963), p. 445.
20. "The Chicago Statement on Biblical Inerrancy," *ICBI Update*, December 1978, no. 2, p. 4.

18

Evangelical Education in the Last Quarter of the Twentieth Century

On August 28 in the year A.D. 476, Emperor Romulus Augustulus abandoned the throne of the Roman Empire to Odoacer, a leader of the Germanic tribes. Romulus became the last emperor of the West when the fall of Rome occurred fifteen hundred years before the bicentennial of the United States. Yet historians and theologians are insistent in making comparisons of these two Western cultures, so distant in time and geography, but so similar in cultural practice. Arnold J. Toynbee, for example, in his monumental *A Study of History* charted the similar "cycles of triumph, disintegration and collapse. Like the empire of Augustus and Tiberius, imperial America could end in 'a schism in the soul'."[1] Edith Hamilton, one of the most eminent classical scholars of this century observed: "It is worth our while to perceive that the final reason for Rome's defeat was the failure of mind and spirit to rise to a new and great opportunity, to meet the challenge of new and great events."[2]

Theologian Howard Snyder puts it a different way:

> Rather than coming of age, our world has, it seems to me, come full circle, returning in several key respects to the spirit of the first-century Roman world. Therefore this age to which we have come may be *the best possible one for the effective proclamation of the biblical Gospel.*
>
> Recently E. M. Blaiklock observed, "Of all the centuries, the twentieth is most like the first: city-ridden, marred by tyranny, decadent, and wracked by those crises that man's abuse of man and of his native earth engenders" (*Christianity Today*, May 7, 1971, p. 6). This parallel between today and the new first century has also been suggested by (no less!) futurologists Herman Kahn and Anthony J. Wiener of the Hudson Institute. In their 1967 book *The Year 2000* they note that "there are some parallels between Roman times and ours" and suggest, "Some of the prospects for the year 2000, are in effect, a return to a sort of a new Augustinian

age" (p. 189). Discussing current culture, they say that "something very much like our multi-fold trend occurred in Hellenistic Greece, the late Roman Republic, and the early Roman Empire."[3]

Meanwhile, much to the embarrassment of the Malthusians, the nightmare of overpopulation so desperately feared just seven or eight years ago is giving way to a considerably more positive analysis of the future—at least as far as the population is concerned. In 1971 *Time* magazine could report, "If the progression continues, it is widely and formally predicted by the spiritual heirs of Thomas Malthus, there will be 7 billion people standing in line for food rations in the year 2000. By 2050 perhaps, 30 billion will be fighting like animals for a share of the once green earth."[4]

In the early 1970s former Secretary of the Interior Stuart Udall was actually suggesting that we cut the population in half! That was before the Hudson Institute people began to suggest that technology will solve all our problems; now the cornucopian futurists attack with a more positive view, throwing all of us into confusion regarding what we should expect next.

THINKING AHEAD

Along with the nation's other institutions, the church at the end of the twentieth century is caught in a revolution of moral, ethical, economic, political, and demographic turmoil. About 75 percent of the American people think "religion is losing its influence." Only 50 percent of Roman Catholics attend church during an average week, and only about 37 percent of Protestants do so. Just a few years ago in the preface to his *The Religions of America: Faith and Ferment in a Time of Crisis*, Leo Rosten wrote,

> It is not hyperbole to say that we are witnessing a remarkable erosion of consensus within the citadel of belief. What prophet, what theologian, what historian or scholar could have predicted the militant participation of clergymen in civil rights marches, the presence at Catholic altars of Protestant and Jewish clergymen during marriage ceremonies, the "God is dead" debate, the open campaign of homosexuals against anathamatization, the mounting skepticism about the validity or effectiveness of church teachings, the growth of "charismatic" groups and interfaith communes, the phenomena of "jazz masses" and rock-and-roll music in cathedrals? We are in the eye of a storm. The velocity and power of that storm should surprise the most sophisticated observers.[5]

EVANGELICAL RENAISSANCE?

Just one year after Rosten's words were published an unknown Georgian by the name of Jimmy Carter won the presidency of the United States, and people began talking about an evangelical revival. For the rest of the decade the media were infatuated with how many evanglical noses they could count and how the nation was turning again to a conservative mood in politics and religion. By the summer of 1979, however Erling Jorstad was not so sure. In *Religion and Life* he wrote about "the born again resurgence," noting that evangelical leaders today talk more of internal conflict than of unity among their people. He complained that any kind of evangelical revival certainly is not making much headway at the local level: "We hear little about those who would visit prisoners or the elderly, be in prayer for terminally ill patients, stand in vigil with families of alcoholics, work with the handicapped and the oppressed and the ugly. Instead the media give us the born again beauty pageant winners, testimonies of winning professional athletes, indeed a picture of wholesome Anglo-Saxons talking openly about being born again."[6]

FAITH AND FUTURISM

As one studies the work of the futurists he senses a mixture of caution and confusion, an awareness that the only constancy in this last quarter of the twentieth century is change. Already popular magazines are referring to young adults in the decade of the 1980s as "the procrastinating generation"; for fear of the future they give evidence of putting off decisions that their parents and grandparents had made before the age of 25.

The future has perhaps never been more difficult to predict, but there have never been more who are willing to try prediction. Of course the prophets have always been with us and sometimes they have come from the most unlikely quarters. In 1918 Lenin foresaw an inevitable conflict between the United States and Japan over control of the Pacific. In 1924 General Billy Mitchell predicted the potential of air power and its accompanying warfare, actually identifying how the Japanese would begin conflict some morning with an attack on Pearl Harbor. In 1937 Charles DeGaulle announced almost exactly how long the approaching Second World War would last, who would win, and what kind of peace would follow.

This chapter is not offered as either prophecy or futurism. Nor do the authors accept the view that *all* is subject to Alvin Toffler's theory of rapid change, which constantly throws society into future shock, overcome by "the third wave." It is precisely its link with the ongoing solidarity of orthodox theology that gives evangelical education a foothold in these turbulent times. Eschatology provides the backdrop—our understanding of God's sovereign control over His universe is the stage. And on that stage we let the futurists dance while we watch, hoping from their dance to learn something that will enable us better to choreograph the ministry of the church as we rush hard toward the year 2000.

Futurists project coming trends on the basis of available current data, suggesting several scenarios that might occur. Perhaps that is what we are doing in this final chapter. Several of the postwar issues have crystallized into "movements" or ongoing concerns for evangelical Christian education. It is within the framework of these scenarios that the reader will live and learn for the remainder of the century.

FAMILY LIFE EDUCATION

In a survey conducted by Lawrence O. Richards in the late 1970s, 5,000 ministers, randomly selected by computer, responded to a confidential poll asking about "the greatest needs in strengthening the life and program of your church." More than 83 percent ranked "developing the home as the center of Christian nurture" as a number one or number two priority, thereby giving it a solid second place behind "getting my lay people involved as ministering men and women."[7] Many of us have been saying for years that the church has stumbled badly in allowing Christian families to delegate their God-given tasks to surrogate institutions such as schools, para-church organizations, and the church itself.

Hundreds of books have been published in the last fifteen years on the subject of family life, perhaps most of them written by Christian authors. Yet the secularization of society continues to erode the sanctity of the family as the primary institution established by God. Ted Ward calls the church to a new commitment, a prophetic voice, and a sense of history: "Secular society sees the family as having been pragmatically useful in the past but expendable in the present. New forms and substitutes are being sought. Can we share this view?"[8]

The question is rhetorical. We are surrounded by the chaos of a changing culture with its permissiveness in such aberrations as abortion, homosexuality, deviant marital forms, and exploitative sexism. Few families can stand up to the constant barrage of barbarianism that hangs like a smog over every major American city and is piped from them to almost every corner of the continent. The church must respond to a continuing, indeed *increasing* need for solid education in family life. It is a small wonder that the pastors in Richards's survey are calling for help. A fascinating book by Peter Marshall and David Manuel entitled *The Light and the Glory* pinpoints the behavior of the early American family with respect to discipline, contrasting it with contemporary attitudes: "And here is the greatest difference between the Puritans and most present-day American parents. For we are not willing to risk losing the "love" in our relationship with our children by persevering with them in matters of discipline. The biggest single cause of the breakdown of the American family is that so much of what we could call *love* the Puritans would have another name for: *idolatry*."[9]

Ted Ward is right. We need a new sense of history if we are to redeem the families of which we are and will be a part in these last few decades of the century.

> The crisis in the family has implications that extend far beyond the walls of the home. "No society has ever survived after its family life deteriorated," warns Dr. Paul Popenoe, founder of the American Institute of Family Relations. Harvard Professor Emeritus Karle Zimmerman has stated the most pessimistic view: "The extinction of faith in the familistic system is identical with the movements in Greece during the century following the Peloponnesian Wars, and in Rome from about A.D. 150. In each case the change in the faith and belief in family systems was associated with rapid adoption of negative reproduction rates and with enormous crises in the very civilizations themselves."[10]

CHURCH EDUCATION

Since one of the authors has treated church education in a recently released book, we focus here on the church's response to the montage of societal problems rather than on specific trends in Christian education at the local church level.[11] Sufficient to this chapter is the issue of how the church can have an effective ministry in a world gone out of control.

For example, the Princeton Religious Research Center publishes an interesting pamphlet entitled *Emerging Trends*. The

May 1979 issue discussed the "electric church" and said that 28 percent of "unchurched people" listened to or watched radio and television programs produced by some religious organization during the 30 days prior to the survey. During the same time period, six in ten unchurched Americans were *not* exposed to religious broadcasting. One of the issues, therefore, is the evidence that media religion might possibly lead people away from involvement in a local assembly, though other surveys appear to offer contradictory arguments.

THEOLOGICAL IGNORANCE

Of continuing concern to the church must be the lack of biblical understanding so rampant in contemporary North American culture. Again, the findings of the Princeton Religion Research Center:

> Few trends in religion so threaten to undermine organized religion in the 1980s as does the sorry state of biblical knowledge in our nation and the shocking lack of knowledge about the basis of our Judao-Christian heritage.
>
> A recent Gallup Youth Survey shows that only three teens in ten — most of whom stated their religious preference as Christian — are correctly able to answer three simple and basic questions drawn from the New Testament that are keystones of the Christian heritage. Even among teens who attend church regularly (about half of those polled by the Gallup Youth Survey) only 43% answered all three questions correctly. One teen-ager in five (19%) was unable to come up with the right answer to *any* of the questions.[12]

SECULARIZATION

What role will the church be playing in an increasingly secularized world over the next two, three, or even five decades? One sociologist of religion, Robert Bellah of the University of California, has outlined three scenarios that he labels "liberal, traditional authoritarian, and revolutionary."

In the *liberal scenario,* Bellah envisions society continuing in strong industrial development and material progress with capitalism remaining the dominant economic form. As secularization progresses virtually unimpeded, religion exerts correspondingly less influence in the social realm. Its replacement, according to Bellah, would be "scientism—the idolization of technical reason."

The *traditional authoritarianism scenario* leads Bellah and his readers to consider the implications of a global catastrophe. In the post-catastrophic world, authoritarian regimentation could very well be necessary, giving way to an absolutist kind of political and religious ideology. Bellah sees "right-wing Protestant fundamentalism" as best equipped to fill that role.

> Support for this outlook comes from the fact that, as mainline Protestantism has faltered, conservative Christian organizations have been booming. Russell Chandler, Religion Editor for the *Los Angeles Times,* observes that ultraconservative denominations are now the most influential religious bodies in America. Chandler notes that "religious broadcasting exceeded $500 million in 1977," that religious publishing, which topped this mark, grew "much faster than secular publishing," and that "the lion's share of these sums was produced by evangelical groups."[13]

The *revolutionary scenario* is one Bellah does not consider very likely because it would require a total structural change in society. Replacing the present secularism with its concomitant quest for wealth and power would be a new self-awareness and a concern for developing the full human potential. We agree with Bellah—given the state of sin in the world today—that that kind of revolution is highly unlikely. But let us look further at secularization.

In what some have called "a post-Christian era," Western culture demonstrates its secularization in numerous ways. Certainly, one is the dominance of *materialism*. We dare not equate materialism and affluence, because it is quite possible to be affluent without being materialistic. Materialism is an attitude—an infatuation with the "things" that one owns or uses. Usually those "things" are purchased with money. Consequently, affluence and materialism tend to run hand in hand. The United States is hardly the only victim of a materialism brought on by affluence (consider Japan, Canada, Germany, and the oil exporting nations), but American society is the one in which both affluence and materialism seem to be the most aggressive.

Then there is the secularization shown in *morality*. As absolutes give way to the creeping paralysis of relativism, standards of ethics, values, and morality all decline. To be sure, there is a strange and frightening infatuation with Near Eastern religions and the occult, but they neither take the place of traditional Christian theism nor hinder the progress of secularization.

There is also a secularization of *mentality*. Perhaps a clear-cut example is easily seen in any bookstore or airport newsstand. The titles selling toward the end of the twentieth century favor the pop-psychology of self-improvement (*Looking Out for Number One, Winning by Intimidation,* etc.). So ultimately, the process of secularization is not just believing or not believing the Bible, attending or not attending church,—but rather a whole mind-set of selfish humanism that leaves God out of the picture.

Then the student of educational philosophy must consider the secularization of *theology*. Perhaps it started with Paul Tillich in the first half of the century. Some have identified Tillich as the last of the neo-orthodox theologians and the first of the existential theologians! Tillich called it his "method of correlation" but the end result was an accommodation of biblical revelation to Hegelian idealism and modern existentialism.

Then came Harvey Cox's *The Secular City,* a bestseller translated into eleven languages. According to Cox, religion and metaphysics are "disappearing forever, and that means we can now let go and immerse ourselves in the new world of the secular city." In 1966 the death of God theologians appeared on the scene in the form of Thomas J. J. Altizer's *Radical Theology and the Death of God.* This was followed by Joseph Fletcher and *Situation Ethics.* By 1970 secular sociologists had analyzed the church until it was afraid to assert itself in any way.

CHURCH-IN-THE-WORLD

Within the past decade things have turned around almost completely. The church, although not vibrant and healthy in all quarters, is at least alive and functioning. In some instances, it is downright healthy. But it is only healthy where theology has resisted the trend of secularization and committed itself to biblical revelation and the biblical task of the church. Perhaps Ted Ward is right when he talks about a "ghetto mentality" and suggests that it might take a new wave of persecution to drive us to a biblical ministry.

> As the church comes more directly in confrontation with secular society, the conditions for persecution will have been met; then it will be only a matter of time and a question of intensity, and the church will once again come under sustained and systematic persecution. The community of God's family may be invited, encouraged, or even compelled to keep to itself. The church will then be the ghetto of godly influence—isolated, its effect as salt and light neutralized."[14]

So the ecclesiastical future is frightening, yet promising. One can hardly be optimistic about the scenario of the world, but he must be optimistic about the power of the Father who presides over our meager earthly meanderings.

THE CHRISTIAN SCHOOL MOVEMENT

It is virtually impossible to keep up with the statistics as the Christian school movement continues to explode on the educational landscape. One organization alone, the Association of Christian Schools, International, claims a membership of over 1,500 schools enrolling more than 300,000 students in the United States and Canada. In 1980-'81 more than 15,000 teachers attended ACSI conventions. But by the time this book is published, those figures will be well out of date, in every case replaced by larger numbers.

The international scene is also growing at unprecedented dimensions with Christian schools in Manila enrolling 5,000, another 5,000 in Calcutta, and 6,000 in Seoul. Robert S. McBirnie suggests several reasons for this phenomenal growth.

> Education is a vital part of the culture of America. Secular education, better known as mass education, is the largest segment of the educational process and must therefore bear a proportionate responsibility for the society trained to serve individuals and perpetuate the nation.
>
> The proof that secular education is in trouble is supported by the many voices of alarm now being heard from nearly every discipline of learning. Standards of education are slipping; factual evidence of rising crime in American secondary schools is irrefutable; a marked decline of confidence in the ethicacy of secular education is evident; increasing frustration and uncertainty is widespread; and the rise of a vibrant, fast-growing Protestant school movement is the final verdict that an important segment of America is withdrawing from the secular educational system.[15]

McBirnie's argument is not overstated. The secular humanism of American public education is in even greater trouble now than when his paragraphs were written. Over the past 15 years per pupil expenditures in public education have tripled—from $559.00 to approximately, $1,800.00. Even the "back to basics" emphasis of many hard-pressed principals around the nation cannot combat the obvious incipient functional illiteracy and the danger of public school crime. So the beat goes on with *a new Christian school being started in the United States every seven hours* and some educational experts predicting that by 1990 51 percent of all American high school graduates will graduate from private religious schools.

MONOPOLY OR OPTION?

There are those who still argue for the voucher system whereby parents can choose any school they wish, and schools are free to set their own curricula, choose facilities, and govern themselves without harassment by local, state, and federal bureaucracies. Such suggestions are hardly just the ravings of reactionary politicians. Law professor John Coons, on the faculty of the University of California at Berkeley, strongly favors "education by choice."

> Perhaps the biggest winners in the new system would be teachers. Families favor schools that concentrate resources on teaching, not administration. Teachers would at last be in a solid economic position to start their own schools, and financial institutions would have reason to back them. We could do worse than return to the small school operated by the faculty responsible to its clients. Choice is the chief hope in the 1980s for a Renaissance in education.[16]

To be sure, not all the fledgling Christian schools are large and not all of them are of satisfactory quality. But the movement is giving serious attention to a developing philosophy as seminars are conducted and literature is disseminated that will assist administrators, teachers, boards, and parents in steering a proper philosophical course. Of importance in all this is that three-fourths of all Christian schools today are "parochial" or church-related, a drastic change from the early postwar days (1950s) of the movement when "parent-society" schools dominated this scene. The church affiliation certainly should assist in providing a biblical orientation, but sometimes it creates organizational and administrative deficiencies, and denominational obscurantism is a constant threat.

OBJECTIVES OF THE CHRISTIAN SCHOOL

An institution's purpose is always part of its philosophy, and philosophy is dependent upon theology. Any theocentric philosophy of education requires that biblical truth permeate the entire academic program and every subject in that program. The Christian school is really an extension of the home and the church (in that order) and therefore partakes in the general goal of making the individual like Christ. Some Christian schools would include evangelism as a part of their overall objective, whereas others would focus on the development of the student who already professes a relationship with Christ. This second overall *biblical objective* is nowhere spelled out more clearly than in Colossians 1:28-29 (NIV): "We proclaim him, admonishing and teaching everyone with all wisdom, so that we may present everyone perfect in Christ. To this end I labor, struggling with all his energy, which so powerfully works in me."

From the biblical objective, one can draw a more general *educational objective* that might sound something like this: "to search for and communicate truth." The contrast with public education here centers in whether the truth is relative, natural, and taught to basically "good minds," or absolute, supernatural, and taught to minds under the effects of original sin.

As educators, we would be among the first to affirm that education has done much to raise the quality of life in America. But as Christian educators, we qualify that statement by insisting that education is not redemptive in and of itself. Even liberal journalist Walter Lippmann once wrote, "We ourselves were so sure that at long last a generation had arisen, keen and eager, to put this disorderly earth to right . . . and fit to do it . . . we meant so well, we tried so hard, and look what we have made of it. We can only muddle into muddle. *What is required is a new kind of man*" (italics added).

Education cannot redeem a society, otherwise the Greeks, the Romans, and the Germans could have demonstrated such a redemption most efficiently. History testifies to the ruin of man and his social institutions without the intervention of the God of creation.

BIBLICAL PRIORITIES

The Scriptures make plain that the child is primarily a ward of the parents. Only in godless societies such as communism and raw paganism do we find the all-powerful state or social unit controlling the family. Yet parental rights carry certain parental responsibilities. Mandatory education is the law of the land, but the place and pattern should be within the dictates of the consciences of parents. We state again that this right to educate children is not a *bestowed* right but a *natural* right. Part of our overall purpose ought to be to involve parents with Christian education for the right reasons and to give them an understanding of the distinctive difference between a Christian school and a secular (public or private) school.

Roy W. Lowrie, the president of the Association of Christian Schools, International, synthesizes the philosophical position of the legitimate Christian school.

> The school is based on a Biblical philosophy of life. Its objectives are biblical, not humanistic. The school exists because of this philosophy and its objectives. Board members must comprehend these to make wise decisions which enable the school to achieve its purposes. A clear vision of the educational goal is needed if it is to be obtained. This requires study, reading, seminars and discussion to sharpen the focus on what the local Christian school is all about.[17]

In 1980 Christian Schools International (not to be confused with the Association of Christian Schools, International)[18] conducted a self-evaluation of member schools intended to reflect on priorities and needs for the future. The following list represents the top ten goal categories (out of a list of thirty) in order of rank.

1. Personal integrity	6. Oral communication
2. Providence	7. Social justice
3. Self-respect	8. Written communication
4. Social respect	9. Social responsibility
5. Stewardship	10. Persistence

The list makes interesting reading when compared with the career orientation and bilingualism now strongly emphasized in contemporary public education. Christian Schools International listed "career awareness" in twenty-seventh place and the learning of a foreign language dead last.

Though many books currently speak to the distinct Christian philosophy of education those schools must hold to, there is one significant volume that must be mastered. Frank Gaebelein spelled out a definitive philosophy of Christian education 30 years ago in his Griffith Thomas Memorial Lectures at Dallas Theological Seminary. Those lectures were later published under the title *The Pattern of God's Truth*. One paragraph hardly serves as reflection of the strategic centrality of this little volume, but it may direct the student to further study.

> Once more, then, we set down the premise: All truth is God's truth. Whereupon we must conclude that Christian education has a holy obligation to stand for and honor the truth wherever it is found. . . . To be sure, revealed truth, as stated in the Word of

God and known through Christ, is of higher importance than natural truth. But the latter is also within the pattern of God's truth.

CHRISTIAN COLLEGES AND SEMINARIES

The history of higher education since the founding of Harvard spans almost 350 years. More than 3,000 colleges dot the map of the fifty states and in the fall of 1981 their collective enrollment exceeded 13,000,000 students. More than fifty percent of all American high school seniors now go to college and that figure is expected to increase through the 1980s. Predictions of declining enrollments and subsequent survival tactics by colleges have been common in higher education for a decade, but each year enrollments increase rather than decrease. The sheer demographics of the population shift, however, dictate that somewhere in the mid-1980s college enrollment in the United States will level off and then slide until sometime in the 1990s when the recent turn-of-the-decade baby boom crowd gets ready for college.

HOW DID THEY START?

There is no question that the earliest colleges in America were Christian institutions. The colonial Anglicans and Calvinists wanted a highly literate and college-trained clergy functioning in their churches and so established their colleges with that goal in mind. John S. Brubacher and Willis Rudy, in their authoritative history entitled *Higher Education in Transition*, clearly state that "the Christian tradition was the foundation stone of the whole intellectual structure which was brought to the New World."[20]

To those early American church leaders the advancement of learning and the service of the church were merely two sides of the same coin. Piety was not to be separated from intellect, and their religious faith was to be taught in a rational and systematic manner not only to clergymen but also to potential professional men in other fields, notably public officials of various kinds. Because there was no separation of church and state in the early colonies, the emphasis and structure of a theocratic government called for theologically sensitive civil servants as well as orthodox ministers.

In the early years educational institutions set the pattern for society and were largely governed by the influence of the churches. However, as secularization gradually spread throughout the growing young nation, it also strengthened its grip on her educational institutions. The size of the country, its heterogenous makeup, and the increasing geographical spread of its population fostered a pluralistic trend in both theology and style of educational institutions.

William Warren Sweet, noted church historian, suggests that the principal dynamic behind the college-founding enthusiasm of American Christians was the spirit of revivalism and missionary thrust. The Great Awakening in the mid-eighteenth century was a major impulse to the development of Christian colleges, but the mortality rate of colleges founded in the eighteenth and nineteenth centuries amounted to nearly eighty percent by the end of the Civil War.

Part of the problem of dying colleges was geographical location as denominations fought to establish themselves in new states by immediately developing an educational institution of some kind. Sometimes a minister and his wife constituted the entire academic staff. One amusing line echoes down from the Illinois frontier in the 1830s: "A settler could hardly encamp on the prairies but a college would spring up beside his wagon."

Of course there was more than just "empire building" in the mind of the frontier church leaders who established those schools. Partly they wanted to preserve the traditional culture and world view of their denominations as represented in the Eastern centers of learning. They also considered knowledge without religion worse than useless. In 1856 the Reverend T. M. Post, in a commencement address at Iowa College, articulated a truth that still stands as a cardinal foundation stone of any respectable Christian college: religion and science belong together because all truth at base is one.

CURRICULUM DISTINCTIVES

Perhaps the distinction of a curriculum in the Christian college can be defined as a threefold pattern. First of all, there is the emphasis on *biblical foundations*. If the fear of the Lord genuinely *is* the beginning of wisdom, then the most important study content of all is study in the Word of God. The assumption of faith that underlies the biblical foundations of curriculum is an awareness of God's revelation. If God has spoken, then the most important thing in all the world is to learn what He has said. All other knowledge is important, but secondary.

Another curriculum distinction of the Christian college is *the integration of all truth,* because all truth is God's truth. The Bible is special revelation, but God also has revealed Himself in other ways. The study of natural science, properly conceived, is a study of God's natural revelation. The ideal pattern, of course, is a wise balance of the study of natural revelation and special revelation based on a fixed standard of truth and morality—an objective order to the universe that can only be grasped by the mind-enlightened heart. C. S. Lewis once described approval and disapproval in the educational process as

> recognitions of objective value or responses to an objective order, . . . therefore emotional states can be in harmony with reason (when we feel liking for what ought to be approved) or out of harmony with reason (when we perceive that liking is due but cannot feel it).
>
> No emotion is, in itself, a judgment: in that sense all emotions and sentiments are alogical but they can be reasonable or unreasonable as they conform to Reason or fail to conform. The heart never takes the place of the head: but it can, and should, obey it.[21]

A third "handle" for looking at the distinctives of the Christian college is its attempt to develop in students what might be called *a Christian world view.* Calvin Seerveld, an articulate evangelical philosopher, tells us that the student should "develop a dynamic religious perspective. A Christian world view, then, is an awareness on the part of the individual that whether he eats or drinks, plays or studies, whatever he does issues from a heart committed to a true and jealous Almighty God revealed in Jesus Christ recognizing God's sovereign control on him, and indeed, over the entire universe."[22]

Perhaps we should not leave this portion of the chapter without at least offering a definition of the Christian college—the same one that already appears in a companion Christian education textbook—"This kind of school is more specifically defined as *a post-secondary institution of learning that takes seriously an evangelical doctrinal statement, classes in Bible and Christian ministry, a distinctively Christian philosophy of education and life, and the quality of spiritual life on campus.*"[23]

KINDS OF INSTITUTIONS

Three different kinds of schools qualify under such a definition (assuming all components are in place). A theological seminary is a graduate school for ministerial training generally offering a variety of masters degrees and possibly one or more doctoral programs. The basic degree of a seminary curriculum is a three-year Master of Divinity that is geared toward the graduate preparation of pastors and other professional church staff. The Christian liberal arts college is an undergraduate institution (though it may have a graduate division) offering a variety of majors in the arts and sciences as well as distinctly career-oriented programs. Some Christian liberal arts colleges have full departments of Bible and offer degrees in biblical and theological studies. Almost all would require of every student some minimal study in Bible and theology.

The Bible college is also undergraduate and degree-granting, but it differs from the Christian liberal arts college in three basic ways: its primary objective is vocational or professional, some form of ministry; its curriculum requires a major in Bible and theology (a composite thirty hours mandatory for member schools of the American Association of Bible Colleges) in addition to other studies in vocational and general education; and its emphasis on practical training requires some form of "Christian service involvement" during the student's college career.

PARA-CHURCH ORGANIZATIONS

Of course Christian schools at the elementary, secondary, and higher levels are para-church organizations as well, but we chose to group them separately in this chapter for more special treatment. The five remaining kinds of para-church organizations dealt with in greater detail in *An Introduction to Biblical Christian Education* include child/youth organizations not under local church sponsorship; child/youth organizations operating under local church sponsorship; mission boards; Christian publishers; and camping organizations. Without going into detail regarding the history and present status of such organizations, it is certainly essential to recognize their enormous contribution to evangelical Christianity, particularly in the twentieth century and, more precisely, in the last quarter of the twentieth century.

> Evangelical parachurch organizations should not be seen as appendages to the church. Although they may operate outside the local church organizational structure, they are not outside the Body of Christ. Certainly they need to work with the local church and provide dynamic vision and implemental skills when at all possible. Indeed, many parachurch organizations increasingly have blended their ministries with local churches. Mutual growth, power, and fellowship have been the result. A relationship of ap-

preciation and respect among organizations and churches is mandatory if the evangelical movement is to maximize its mission.[24]

FACING THE 1980s

The church in a changing age faces challenges that are both frightening and exciting. Sharon Begley tells us that by July 1, 1986 "the population aged 60-64 reaches its peak and declines through the rest of the decade; the black youth population (15-29) also peaks"; that the US economy will surpass five trillion dollars in output, more than double the total in 1979, but 80 percent of the increase is inflation; and that by July 1, 1989 the median age of the US population will reach 32.5.[25]

George Gallup has identified "10 Key Trends in Religion in the United States as the nation enters the 1980s."

1. An intensive spiritual search and a desire for inward and individual spiritual growth.
2. A proliferation of religious groups to answer these spiritual needs—a clear warning to established churches that are sometimes perhaps ill-equipped to deal with religious experience.
3. A blurring of boundaries between various faiths and denominations.
4. The influence of Charismatics and Pentecostals which is being felt across denominational lines.
5. A growing interest in interfaith dialogue.
6. A decline in the growth of most of the largest Protestant denominations and the growth and revitalization of the Evangelical churches, notably the Southern Baptist Church.
7. An increase in secularity: Far fewer today than in earlier years, for example, believe religion can answer all or most of today's problems.
8. An increase in religiosity, described by Martin Marty as "a diffusion of religion into the larger culture."
9. At the same time, basic beliefs remain intact. Even those who are not church members are surprisingly orthodox in their Christian beliefs. The high level of belief in the U.S. is in sharp contrast to the situation in Western Europe, for instance.
10. While basic beliefs remain intact, a growing gap is noted between believing and belonging to a church.[26]

In the stressful technocracy of the 1980s and 1990s Christian education continues to be a strategic imperative for the evangelical church. But it must be an education in touch with rapidly changing human needs while refusing to compromise on its commitment to the authority of Scripture. An awareness of the lessons of history and a clarity of philosophical commitment are essential to the ongoing of Christian educational institutions, formal and informal, for the rest of the century. Perhaps the words of Malcolm Muggeridge can end our chapter on the high note of faith toward which we must strive during these days.

> There is this marvelous Christian alternative: this possibility of relating ourselves, not to an earthly city which can't go on forever but to the City of God; not to earthly hopes or plans or expectations, but to the everlasting truths that were conveyed through the incarnation which has governed 2000 years of Christendom and which (whatever may happen to Christendom) will continue to govern the minds and lives and hearts of those who wish it to. So that is the hope based on faith, not based on knowledge, not based on power, not based on wealth, not based on self-indulgence, but based on the Christian faith as it has come down to us.[27]

NOTES

1. Arnold J. Toynbee, *A Study of History* (New York: Oxford U., 1947).
2. "The Score: Rome 1500, U.S. 200," *Time*, August 23, 1976, p. 59.
3. Howard A. Snyder, "A World Come Full Circle," *Christianity Today*, January 7, 1972, p. 193.
4. "Population Explosion: Is Man Really Doomed?" *Time*, Sept. 13, 1971, p. 58.
5. Leo Rosten, *The Religions of America: Faith and Ferment in a Time of Crisis* (New York: Simon and Schuster, 1975).
6. Erling Jorstad, "The Born Again Resurgence," *Religion in Life*, summer 1979, p. 153-61.
7. Lawrence O. Richards, "The Greatest Needs of My Church," *United Evangelical Action*, summer 1976, pp. 8-9.
8. Ted Ward, "The Church and the Christian Family." Monograph no. 7, *Evangelical Newsletter*, Philadelphia: n.d.
9. Peter Marshall and David Manuel, *The Light and the Glory* (Old Tappan, N.J.: Revell, 1977), p. 178.
10. "The American Family: Future Uncertain," *Time*, December 28, 1970, p. 34.
11. See Chapter 35, in Kenneth O. Gangel, *Building Leaders for Church Education* (Chicago: Moody, 1981).
12. George Gallup, Jr., "Religious Knowledge Seen at Nadir," *Emerging Trends*, May 1981, p. 1.
13. Hugh Myers, "Christianity in the Coming Decades," *The Futurist*, June 1979, pp. 169-70.
14. Ted Ward, "The Church in the Intermediate Future," *Christianity Today*, June 29, 1979, p. 17.
15. Robert S. McBirnie, "Assessing the Inadequacy of the Present System of Education," in Paul A. Kienel, ed., *The Philosophy of Christian School Education* (Whittier, Calif.: ACSI, n.d.), pp. 196-97.
16. John Coons, "The Public-School Monopoly," *Newsweek*, June 9, 1980, p. 21.
17. Roy W. Lowrie, Jr., *Serving God on the Christian School Board* (Whittier, Calif.: Western Assoc. of Christian Schools, 1976), p. 129.

18. It is unfortunate that the two most significant interdenominational Christian school associations have chosen such similar names. Every student of the Christian school movement must be familiar with both however, and full information can be obtained by writing their respective headquarters:

    Association of Christian Schools, International
    P.O. Box 4097, Whittier, Calif. 90607

    Christian Schools International
    865 28th Street, South East
    Grand Rapids, Mich. 49508.

19. Frank E. Gaebelein, *The Pattern of God's Truth* (Chicago: Moody, 1968), pp. 23-24.
20. John S. Brubacher and Willis Rudy, *Higher Education in Transition* (New York: Harper & Row, 1958), p. 6.
21. C. S. Lewis, *The Abolition of Man* (New York: Collier, 1962), pp. 29-30.
22. Calvin Seerveld, "Relating Christianity to the Arts," *Christianity Today*, November 1980, pp. 48-49.
23. Kenneth O. Gangel, "Christian Higher Education and Lifelong Learning," in Werner Graendorf, ed., *Introduction to Biblical Christian Education* (Chicago: Moody, 1981), p. 333.
24. Warren S. Benson, "Parachurch Vocations in Christian Education," in Graendorf, pp. 348-49.
25. Sharon Begley, "A Decade's Datebook," *Newsweek*, November 19, 1979, p. 175.
26. George Gallup, Jr., "10 Key Trends in Religion in U.S.," *Emerging Trends* 2, no. 4 (April 1980).
27. Malcolm Muggeridge, "Faith and the Future," *Destiny*, August 1979, p. 23.

Epilogue

Blaise Pascal once said "The present is never our goal: the past and the present are our means: the future alone is our goal." Inevitably the understanding of the past and the present will mark the historian's attempt to write history. An interpretation of the past and present will reveal one's projection of the future. A philosophy of history is inescapable because we cannot eliminate our own value orientation despite our commitment to total objectivity. Clarence J. Karier, historian of American education, contends that

> Although history is an imaginative creation of the past, it is not a fictional creation. Its validity is derived from both the artifacts of the past and the meanings that it illuminates in the present. History is an art. The historian as an artist is different however from the painter as an artist. While both are ultimately judged by the meaning achieved in the present, the evidence with which the historian works must itself be validated by reason, logic, and empirical analysis. Context, internal consistency, cross referencing, authenticity of documentation are all instrumental tools with which the historian shapes and colors his picture of the past.[1]

On the basis of the limitations stated in the Introduction of this book, certain important educators, ideas, events, and even movements have received little or no mention. Two examples are Vittorino Da Feltre (1378-1446) and William Holmes McGuffey (1800-1873). Da Feltre was a well known Italian educational reformer who transmitted the ideals of classical culture within a Renaissance setting. His "Joy House" was more than a precursor of contemporary creative urban educational enterprises. The educational objective of Da Feltre was the forming of the complete citizen through harmoniously developing the mind, body, and moral character of the student. His single purpose was to educate adolescents to serve God irrespective of their vocational choices. Da Feltre taught the youth of the wealthy and the poor, often supporting the latter himself. His personal involvement with his students and their parents, his use of games in the teaching-learning process, and his skill in creating an enjoyable context for disciplined learning characterized his educational philosophy.

McGuffey compiled graded readers that sold 120 million copies between 1836 and 1920 (others compiled the editions of 1857 and 1879). McGuffey effectively communicated his Scottish Presbyterian world view and value system and left his mark on the American scene. Westerhoff is of the opinion that for the "common folk, McGuffey represents the most important figure in the history of American public education—THE schoolmaster of the nation!"[2] Yet even the celebrated historian Samuel Eliot Morison in his *Oxford History of the American People* cites seven nineteenth-century persons for their contributions to education and neglects to mention McGuffey. Only one paragraph is given to McGuffey in *The Encyclopedia of Education* and two brief citations are given in *Growth of the American Republic*, written by Morison, Henry Steele Commager, and William Edward Leuchtenburg. Although no amount of such superficial analysis proves much, it does give credence to the dilemma faced in attempting a history of Christian education. Choices must be made and an exhaustive treatment is not the province of this volume.

We have attempted to emphasize persons, their ideas, and their influence on society, culture, and particularly the historical development of the ministry of Christian education in the church of Jesus Christ.

We heartily affirm George Marsden's assertion that

> "The Christian . . . must view himself as participating in an ongoing active relationship between God and man in which the revelation of God's acts and will in the past provides continuing norms for creative responses to the present.
>
> While biblical history contributes the most crucial perspective necessary for understanding ourselves and others, the rest of history . . . can help somewhat as well. If we better understand what other men and other cultures have done, we can contribute something toward reinforcing a perspective that will help destroy our self-made, self-centered worlds. With an historical perspective it will become much more difficult to believe that the world really revolves around ourselves or that the values and ideals of our culture and our era are the best there have ever been."[3]

To engage in authentic interaction with contemporary thinking is crucial to our view of reality. "But the dialogue can all too easily degenerate into an acceptance of the premises of contemporary thought. Conventional wisdom is transient, not eternal."[4] We must remember what the last part of 1 Corinthians 1:20 says, "Has not God made foolish the wisdom of the world?"

The only constants in our world are God and Scripture. Immediate needs of our society are constantly in flux. Educationists jump from one trend to another. The drive to be contemporary is unending. A biblically informed philosophy of education will provide stability in the midst of change. A commitment to the biblical view of reality and the role of the church in history will give direction for the future. The Lord of the church is the Lord of history. And it is God who stands in the center of the universe. Not ourselves.

NOTES

1. Clarence J. Karier, "American Educational History: A Perspective," *Educational Forum* 37 (March 1973):273.
2. John H. Westerhoff III, *McGuffey and His Readers: Piety, Morality, and Education in Nineteenth Century America* (Nashville: Abingdon, 1978), p. 13.
3. George M. Marsden and Frank C. Roberts, eds., *A Christian View of History?* (Grand Rapids: Eerdmans, 1975), pp. 32-33.
4. D. W. Bebbington, *Patterns in History: A Christian View* (Downers Grove, Ill.: Inter-Varsity, 1979), p. 182.

Selected Bibliography

Ahlstrom, Sydney E. *A Religious History of the American People*. New Haven, Conn.: Yale U., 1972.

Anderson, Clifford V. "Christian Education in Historical Perspective." In *Introduction to Biblical Christian Education*, edited by Werner C. Graendorf. Chicago: Moody, 1981.

Augustine. *The Teacher*. Translated by Robert P. Russell. Washington, D.C.: Catholic U., 1968.

Bailyn, Bernard. *Education in the Forming of American Society*. Chapel Hill, N.C.: U. of North Carolina, 1960.

Barclay, William. *Educational Ideals in the Ancient World*. Grand Rapids: Baker, 1959.

Bebbington, D. W. *Patterns in History*. Downers Grove, Ill.: Inter-Varsity, 1979.

Benko, Stephen, and O'Rourke, John J. *The Catacombs and the Colosseum: The Roman Empire as the Setting of Primitive Christianity*. Valley Forge, Pa.: Judson, 1971.

Benson, Clarence H. *A Popular History of Christian Education*. Chicago: Moody, 1943.

Benson, Warren S. "A History of the National Association of Christian Schools During the Period of 1947-1972." Ph.D. dissertation, Loyola University (Chicago), 1974.

Boehlke, Robert R. *Theories of Learning in Christian Education*. Philadelphia: Westminster, 1962.

Bolgar, R. R. *The Classical Heritage and Its Beneficiaries from the Carolingian Age to the End of the Renaissance*. New York: Harper & Row, Harper Torchbooks, 1964.

Boys, Mary C. *Biblical Interpretation in Religious Education*. Birmingham, Ala.: Relig. Educ. Press, 1980.

Bromiley, Geoffrey W. *Historical Theology—An Introduction*. Grand Rapids: Eerdmans, 1978.

Brown, Colin, ed. *History, Criticism and Faith*. Downers Grove, Ill.: Inter-Varsity, 1976.

————,ed. *New International Dictionary of New Testament Theology*. 3 vols. Grand Rapids: Zondervan, 1975.

————. *Philosophy and the Christian Faith*. Downers Grove, Ill.: Inter-Varsity, 1969.

Bruce, F. F. *The Spreading Flame*. Grand Rapids: Eerdmans, 1964.

Burgess, Harold William. *An Invitation to Religious Education*. Mishawaka, Ind.: Relig. Educ. Press, 1975.

Bushnell, Horace. *Christian Nurture*. Reprint. Grand Rapids: Baker, 1979.

Butler, J. Donald. *Four Philosophies and Their Practice in Education and Religion*. 3d ed. New York: Harper & Row, 1972.

———. *Religious Education*. New York: Harper & Row, 1962.

Butts, R. Freeman. *The Education of the West*. New York: McGraw-Hill, 1973.

Butts, R. Freeman, and Cremin, Lawrence A. *A History of Education in American Culture*. New York: Holt, Rinehart, and Winston, 1953.

Byrne, H. W. *A Christian Approach to Education*. Milford, Mich.: Mott Media, 1978.

Cairns, Earle E. *Christianity Through the Centuries*. Rev. ed. Grand Rapids: Zondervan, 1981.

Chadwick, Ronald P. *Teaching and Learning*. Old Tappan, N.J.: Revell, 1982.

Chave, Ernest J. *A Functional Approach to Religious Education*. Chicago: U. of Chicago, 1947.

Coe, George Albert. *A Social Theory of Religious Education*. Reprint. New York: New York Times, Arno, 1967.

Collins, Joseph B. ed. *The Catechetical Instruction of St. Thomas Aquinas*. New York: Joseph F. Wagner, 1947.

Comenius, John Amos. *The Great Didactic*. Translated and edited by M. W. Keatinge. New York: Russell, 1967.

———. *John Amos Comenius on Education*. New York: Columbia U., 1967.

Cremin, Lawrence A. *The American Common School*. New York: Columbia U., 1951.

———. *American Education: The Colonial Experience, 1607-1783*. New York: Harper & Row, 1970.

———. *Traditions of American Education*. New York: Harper & Row, 1977.

———. *The Transformation of the School*. New York: Random House, 1961.

Cully, Iris. V. *The Dynamics of Christian Education*. Philadelphia: Westminster, 1958.

Cully, Iris V., and Cully, Kendig B., eds. *Process and Relationship*. Birmingham, Ala.: Relig. Educ. Press, 1978.

Cully, Kendig B. *Basic Writings in Christian Education*. Philadelphia: Westminster, 1960.

———. *The Search for a Christian Education, Since 1940*. Philadelphia: Westminster, 1965.

Curti, Merle. *The Social Ideas of American Educators*. Totowa, N.J.: Littlefield, Adams, 1971.

Daniel, Eleanor; Wade, John W.; and Gresham, Charles. *Introduction to Christian Education*. Cincinnati: Standard, 1980.

DeJong, Norman. *Education in the Truth*. Nutley, N.J.: Craig, 1969.

Dewey, John. *Democracy and Education*. New York: Macmillan, 1916.

———. *Experience and Education*. New York: Macmillan, 1938.

Douglas, J. D., ed. *The New International Dictionary of the Christian Church*. Rev. ed. Grand Rapids: Zondervan, 1978.

Dowley, Tim, ed. *Eerdmans' Handbook to the History of Christianity*. Grand Rapids: Eerdmans, 1977.

Drazin, Nathan. *History of Jewish Education from 515 B.C. to 22 C.E.* New York: Macmillan, 1970.

Dropkin, Stan; Full, Harold; and Schwarcz, Ernest. *Contemporary American Education*. 2d ed. New York: Macmillan, 1970.

Duckett, Eleanor Shipley. *Alcuin, Friend of Charlemagne*. New York: Macmillan, 1951.

Dunkel, Harold B. *Herbart and Education.* New York: Random House, 1969.

Durka, Gloria, and Smith, Joanmarie, eds. *Aesthetic Dimensions of Religious Education.* New York: Paulist, 1979.

Elliot, Harrison S. *Can Religious Education Be Christian?* Reprint. New York: Macmillan, 1953.

Fahs, Sophia L. *Today's Children and Yesterday's Heritage.* Boston: Beacon, 1952.

Ferre, Nels F. S. *A Theology for Christian Education.* Philadelphia: Westminster, 1967.

Fleming, Sandford. *Children and Puritanism.* New York: New York Times, Arno, 1969.

Foh, Susan T. *Women and the Word of God.* Phillipsburg, N.J.: Presbyterian & Reformed, 1980.

Fowler, James W. *Stages of Faith.* New York: Harper & Row, 1981.

Freire, Paulo. *Pedagogy of the Oppressed.* New York: Seabury, 1970.

Fuller, Edmund, ed. *The Christian Era of Education.* New Haven, Conn.: Yale U., 1957.

Gabert, Glen. *In Hoc Signo?: A Brief History of Catholic Parochial Education in America.* Port Washington, N.Y.: Kennikat, 1973.

Gaebelein, Frank E. *Christian Education in a Democracy.* New York: Oxford, 1951.

————. *The Pattern of God's Truth.* Chicago: Moody, 1968.

Gangel, Kenneth O. *Building Leaders for Church Education.* Chicago: Moody, 1981.

Gay, Peter. *The Enlightenment: An Interpretation.* 2 vols. New York: Knopf, 1969.

Geisler, Norman, and Feinberg, Paul D. *Introduction to Philosophy.* Grand Rapids: Baker, 1980.

Getz, Gene A. *Sharpening the Focus of the Church.* Chicago: Moody, 1974.

Goldman, Ronald. *Readiness for Religion: A Basis for Developmental Religious Education.* New York: Seabury, 1968.

————. *Religious Thinking from Childhood to Adolescence.* New York: Seabury, 1968.

Graendorf, Werner C., ed. *Introduction to Biblical Christian Education.* Chicago: Moody, 1981.

Greaves, Richard L. *The Puritan Revolution and Educational Thought: Background for Reform.* New Brunswick, N.J.: Rutgers U., 1969.

Groome, Thomas H. *Christian Religious Education.* New York: Harper & Row, 1980.

Gutek, Gerald L. *A History of the Western Educational Experience.* New York: Random House, 1971.

————. *Pestalozzi and Education.* New York: Random House, 1968.

Gutzke, Manford G. *John Dewey's Thought and Its Implications for Christian Education.* New York: Columbia U., 1956.

Hadas, Moses. *Hellenistic Culture: Fusion and Diffusion.* New York: Columbia U., 1959.

Haskins, C. H. *The Renaissance of the Twelfth Century.* Cleveland: Meridian, 1959.

Herbart, Johann Friedrich. *The Science of Education.* Translated by H. Felkin and E. Felkin. Boston: Heath, 1896.

Hofinger, Johannes. The Art of Teaching Christian Doctrine. 2d ed. Notre Dame, Ind.: U. of Notre Dame, 1962.

Holmes, Arthur F. All Truth Is God's Truth. Grand Rapids: Eerdmans, 1977.

————. The Idea of a Christian College. Grand Rapids: Eerdmans, 1975.

Howie, George. Educational Theory and Practice in St. Augustine. London: Routledge and Kegan Paul, 1969.

Hutchins, Robert M., ed. Great Books of the Western World. 54 vols. Chicago: Encyclopaedia Britannica, 1952.

Hyma, Albert. The Brethren of the Common Life. Grand Rapids: Eerdmans, 1950.

Illich, Ivan. Deschooling Society. New York: Mentor, 1969.

Jarrett, James L., ed., The Educational Theories of the Sophists. New York: Columbia U., 1969.

Kahn, Herman, and Wiener, Anthony J. The Year 2000: A Framework for Speculation on the Next Thirty-Three Years. New York: Macmillan, 1967.

Karier, Clarence J. Man, Society and Education: A History of American Educational Ideas. Glenview, Ill.: Scott, Foresman, 1967.

Kathan, Boardman W. "Pioneers of Religious Education in the Twentieth Century." Religious Education. Special ed. September-October, 1978.

Kennedy, William Bean. "Christian Education Through History." In An Introduction to Christian Education, edited by Marvin J. Taylor. Nashville: Abingdon, 1966.

————. The Shaping of Protestant Education: An Interpretation of the Sunday School and the Development of Protestant Educational Strategy in the United States, 1789-1860. New York: Association, 1966.

Kevan, Eugene. Augustine the Educator: A Study in the Fundamentals of Christian Formation. Westminster, Md.: Newman, 1964.

Kienel, Paul A., ed. The Philosophy of Christian School Education. Whittier, Calif.: Association of Christian Schools International, n.d.

Kinloch, T. F. Pioneers of Religious Education. Freeport, N.Y.: Books for Libraries, 1969.

Kittel, Gerhard, ed. Theological Dictionary of the New Testament. Edited and translated by Geoffrey W. Bromiley. 10 vols. Grand Rapids: Eerdmans, 1967.

Kneller, George F. Introduction to the Philosophy of Education. 2d ed. New York: Wiley, 1971.

Kohlberg, Lawrence. The Philosophy of Moral Development. Vol. 1. New York: Harper & Row, 1981.

Kramer, Samuel Noah. The Sumerians: Their History, Culture, and Character. Chicago: U. of Chicago, 1963.

Latourette, Kenneth Scott. A History of Christianity. New York: Harper, 1953.

Laurie, S.S. Historical Survey of Pre-Christian Education. St. Clair Shores, Mich.: Scholarly Press, 1970.

LeBar, Lois E. Education That Is Christian. Rev. ed. Old Tappan, N.J.: Revell, 1981.

Lee, James Michael. The Flow of Religious Instruction. Dayton, Ohio: Pflaum, 1973.

————. The Shape of Religious Instruction. Dayton, Ohio: Pflaum, 1971.

Leff, Gordon. Paris and Oxford Universities in the Thirteenth and Fourteenth Centuries. New York: Wiley, 1968.

Little, Sara. The Role of the Bible in Contemporary Christian Education. Richmond: John Knox, 1961.

Lockerbie, D. Bruce. *The Way They Should Go.* New York: Oxford, 1972.

Loder, James L. *The Transforming Moment.* New York: Harper & Row, 1981.

Lovelace, Richard F. *Dynamics of Spiritual Life.* Downers Grove, Ill.: Inter-Varsity, 1979.

Lynn, Robert W. "A Historical Perspective on the Futures of American Religious Education." In *Foundations for Christian Education in an Era of Change,* edited by Marvin J. Taylor. Nashville: Abingdon, 1976.

Lynn, Robert W., and Wright, Elliott. *The Big Little School.* 2d ed. Birmingham, Ala.: Relig. Educ. Press, 1980.

Marrou, H. I. *A History of Education in Antiquity.* New York: Sheed and Ward, 1956.

Marsden, George M. *Fundamentalism and American Culture.* New York: Oxford, 1981.

Marsden, George M., and Roberts, Frank. *A Christian View of History?* Grand Rapids: Eerdmans, 1975.

Marty, Martin E. *By Way of Response.* Nashville: Abingdon, 1981.

Mayer, Frederick. *A History of Educational Thought.* 2d ed. Columbus, Ohio: Merrill, 1966.

Mayers, Marvin K.; Richards, Lawrence O.; and Webber, Robert. *Reshaping Evangelical Higher Education.* Grand Rapids: Zondervan, 1972.

McBrien, Richard P. *Catholicism.* Minneapolis: Winston, 1980.

Miller, Randolph Crump. *The Clue to Christian Education.* New York: Scribner's, 1950.

————. *Education for Christian Living.* 2d ed. Englewood Cliffs, N.J.: Prentice-Hall, 1963.

————. *The Theory of Christian Education Practice.* Birmingham, Ala.: Relig. Educ. Press, 1980.

Montgomery, John Warwick. *History and Christianity.* Downers Grove, Ill.: Inter-Varsity, 1964.

————. *The Shape of the Past: A Christian Response to Secular Philosophies of History.* Minneapolis: Bethany Fellowhip, 1975.

Moran, Gabriel. "Religious Education: Past, Present and Future." *Religious Education* 66 (September-October 1971): 337.

Morison, Samuel Eliot. *Harvard College in the Seventeenth Century.* 2 vols. Cambridge, Mass.: Harvard U., 1936.

Murch, James DeForest. *Christian Education and the Local Church.* Cincinnati: Standard, 1943.

Neill, Stephen Charles, and Weber, Hans-Rudi, eds. *The Layman in Christian History.* Philadelphia: Westminster, 1963.

Nelson, C. Ellis. *Where Faith Begins.* Richmond: John Knox, 1971.

O'Hare, Padraic, ed. *Foundations of Religious Education.* New York: Paulist, 1978.

Peatling, John H. *Religious Education in a Psychological Key.* Birmingham, Ala.: Relig. Educ. Press, 1980.

Perkinson, Henry J. *The Imperfect Panacea: American Faith in Education, 1865-1965.* New York: Random House, 1968.

Piaget, Jean, and Inhelder, Barbel. *The Psychology of the Child.* New York: Basic Books, 1969.

Piveteau, Didier-Jacques, and Dillon, J. T. *Resurgence of Religious Instruction.* Notre Dame, Ind.: Relig. Educ. Press, 1978.

Reischauer, Edwin O., and Fairbank, John K. *A History of East Asian Civiliza-tion.* Boston: Houghton Mifflin, 1965.

Richards, Lawrence O. *A Theology of Christian Education.* Grand Rapids: Zon-dervan, 1975.

———. *A Theology of Church Leadership.* Grand Rapids: Zondervan, 1980.

Rood, Wayne R. *Understanding Christian Education.* Nashville: Abingdon, 1970.

Rousseau, Jean-Jacques. *Emile: Selections.* Translated and edited by William Boyd. Classics in Education, no. 10. New York: Columbia U., 1963.

Rushdoony, Rousas J. *The Messianic Character of American Education.* Nutley, N.J.: Craig, 1972.

Sanner, A. Elwood, and Harper, A. F., eds. *Exploring Christian Education.* Grand Rapids: Baker, 1978.

Schaeffer, Francis A. *How Should We Then Live?* Old Tappan, N.J.: Revell, 1976.

Sell, Charles M. *Family Ministry.* Grand Rapids: Zondervan, 1981.

Sherrill, Lewis Joseph. "A Historical Study of the Religious Education Move-ment." In *Orientation in Religious Education,* edited by Philip Henry Lotz. New York: Abingdon, 1950.

———. *The Rise of Christian Education.* Philadelphia: Macmillan, 1944.

Sisemore, John T., ed. *The Ministry of Religious Education.* Nashville: Broad-man, 1978.

Skinner, B. F. *Beyond Freedom and Dignity.* New York: Knopf, 1972.

Smart, James D. *The Teaching Ministry of the Church.* Philadelphia: Westmin-ster, 1954.

Smith, H. Shelton. *Faith and Nurture.* New York: Scribner's, 1941.

Stewart, Donald Gordon. "History of Christian Education." In *The Westminster Dictionary of Christian Education,* edited by Kendig B. Cully. Philadelphia: Westminster, 1963.

Stewart, George, Jr. *A History of Religious Education in Connecticut.* New York: New York Times, Arno, 1969.

Stumpf, Samuel Enoch. *Socrates to Sartre: A History of Philosophy.* 3d ed. New York: McGraw-Hill, 1982.

Swanstrom, Roy A. *History in the Making: An Introduction to the Study of the Past.* Downers Grove, Ill.: Inter-Varsity, 1978.

Taylor, H. O. *The Mediaeval Mind.* 4th ed. Cambridge, Mass.: Harvard U., 1949.

Taylor, Marvin J. *Foundations for Christian Education in an Era of Change.* Nashville: Abingdon, 1976.

———. "A Historical Introduction to Religious Education." In *Religious Educa-tion: A Comprehensive Survey,* edited by Marvin J. Taylor. New York: Abingdon, 1960.

Thompson, Norma H., ed. *Religious Education and Theology.* Birmingham, Ala.: Relig. Educ. Press, 1982.

Towns, Elmer L., ed. *A History of Religious Educators.* Grand Rapids: Baker, 1975.

Trumbull, H. Clay. *The Sunday School: Its Origin, Mission, Methods, and Aux-iliaries.* Philadelphia: John D. Wattles, 1893.

Ulich, Robert. *A History of Religious Education.* New York: New York U., 1968.

Westerhoff, John H., III. *McGuffey and His Readers: Piety, Morality, and Educa-tion in Nineteenth Century America.* Nashville: Abingdon, 1978.

———, ed. *Who Are We? The Quest for A Religious Education.* Birmingham, Ala.: Relig. Educ. Press, 1979.

————. *Will Our Children Have Faith?* New York: Seabury, 1976.

Whitehead, Alfred. N. *The Aims of Education and Other Essays.* London: Ernest Benn, 1962.

Wilds, Elmer H., and Lottich, Kenneth Lee, *The Foundations of Modern Education.* New York: Holt, Rinehart, and Winston, 1970.

Willis, Wesley R. *Two Hundred Years—And Still Counting.* Wheaton, Ill.: Scripture Press, Victor, 1979.

Wilson, J. Donald; Stamp, Robert M.; and Audet, Louis-Philippe, eds. *Canadian Education: A History.* Scarborough, Ont.: Prentice-Hall, 1970.

Wilson, John A. *The Culture of Ancient Egypt.* Chicago: U. of Chicago, 1961.

Witmer, S. A. *Education with Dimension: The Bible College Story.* Wheaton, Ill.: Accrediting Association of Bible Colleges, 1962.

Woodbridge, John D.; Noll, Mark A.; and Hatch, Nathan O. *The Gospel in America.* Grand Rapids: Zondervan, 1979.

Woodward, William Harrison. *Desiderius Erasmus Concerning the Aim and Methods of Education.* New York: Columbia U., 1964.

Worley, Robert C. *Preaching and Teaching in the Earliest Church.* Philadelphia: Westminster, 1967.

Wyckoff, D. Campbell. *Theory and Design of Christian Education Curriculum.* Philadelphia: Westminster, 1961.

————. *The Task of Christian Education.* Philadelphia: Westminster, 1965.

Index of Subjects

Absolute naturalism, 297
Absolute truth, 323, 327
Academies, in Middle Colonies, 243-46
Adult education, 328
Albingenses, 171
American Association of Bible colleges, 309, 362
American Institute of Family Relations, 351
American Missionary Fellowship, 285, 286
American Missionary Society, 283
American Sunday School Union. See American Missionary Fellowship
Amish, 148
Anabaptists, 144, 148-49, 181
Anglicans, 147, 241, 242, 243, 246, 248-50
  and education in America, 252
Anthropology, 339
  and Dewey, 296-97
Apocrypha, 21
Apostles, 78
Apperception, 207-9
Apprenticeship, 243, 250-52
  in New England, 232
  in Southern colonies, 249
Approach to education
  by Pestalozzi, 199
  by Spencer, 217
Arianism, 83, 93, 99
Aristotelian education system, 46-48
Arminianism, 258-59
Association of Christian Schools, International, 355, 358

Association of Professors and Researchers of Religious Education, 322
Associationism, 206
Athens, education in, 33, 34, 39
Authority of Scripture, 344
Axiology, 295, 339

Baptists, 148
Behaviorism, 292
  and Skinner, 332
Bible colleges, 362
Bible school movement, 309-11
Biblical teaching as part of education, 219
Bohemian Brethren, 171-72
Brethren, 148, 181
Brethren of the Common Life, 125-26, 128, 131

Calvinism, 145, 229, 231
Calvinists, 164
Catechetical schools, 90-91
Catechumenal schools, 88-90
Cathedral school in Middle Ages, 108-9
Catholic church. See Roman Catholic Church
Catholicism. See Existentialism
Chicago Evangelization Society, 310
Child development
  according to Pestalozzi, 201
  according to Quintilian, 59-60
  according to Rousseau, 194-95
  role of play in, 214
Chivalric training in Middle Ages, 107
Christian and Missionary Alliance, 310

Index of Persons

Index of Scripture